The Empire Strikes Out

The Empire Strikes Out:
Kurd Lasswitz, Hans Dominik, and the Development of German Science Fiction

William B. Fischer

Bowling Green State University Popular Press
Bowling Green, Ohio 43403

Contents

Preface

FOR SOME DECADES now science fiction has enjoyed a certain prominence, even notoriety, in the cultural life of the entire industrialized world. There is little agreement about what "science fiction" means, and still less reluctance to apply the term or its common abbreviations "sci-fi" or "SF." Producers of SF, as well as critics, publishers, advertising agents and the general public, are quick to disregard distinctions of quality, artistic medium, genre, channel of distribution, and audience. Thus there are not only SF magazines and books, but also films, television programs, plays, works of graphic art, and even lyric poems. The mass-entertainment and consumer-goods industries offer many commercialized "spin-offs" of SF, among them toys, games, futuristic household gadgets, and entire environmental experiences like Disney's "Tomorrowland." Whatever it is, whatever form it assumes, SF is an integral part—both a reflection and a cause—of a modern consciousness very much occupied with science, technology and "future shock."

But SF, as the name suggests, is first and foremost a form of prose fiction, one characterized by a decidedly popular background and appeal. Perhaps no other single kind of literature has gained such currency among so large and varied a body of readers. Millions of people devote a major portion of their discretionary reading time to SF. Seldom also has any kind of modern literature inspired such intensive ancillary activity among a fairly sizable community of serious enthusiasts. SF clubs meet regularly in numerous cities, and the periodic local, national and international SF conventions attract thousands of participants. Multitudes of amateur journals or "fanzines"—some of impressive format and long history, most primitive and ephemeral—publish original SF, criticism and personalia. A coterie of zealous "fans" which flourished in America from the late Twenties until at least the Fifties went so far as to maintain that "Fandom is a way of life."[1] Their successors are today's "sci-fi" enthusiasts, nostalgia buffs and *Star Trek* aficionados ("Trekkies"). Since the boundary between avocational enthusiasm and neurotic obsession can be vague, it is not surprising

1

that at least one observer claims to have detected symptoms of psychological addiction to SF.[2]

Recently SF has become intellectually and artistically respectable. SF authors write for major fiction and non-fiction publications, express their opinions about the future on serious radio and television programs, and appear as featured commentators during media coverage of space-shots. Universities, motivated by either genuine if belated scholarly interest or timely cupidity, offer courses about SF, maintain SF collections, sponsor journals of SF criticism, publish books about SF, and engage SF writers as authors and critics in residence. In 1970 Leslie Fiedler described SF as one of the great forms of modern popular expression, along with pornography and Western fiction. Almost rapturously he predicted that it will determine the shape of future literature.[3] Writing five years later, Robert Scholes offers an assessment of SF and its importance for literary criticism which is less spectacular but more accurate and far more profound. He carefully examines the nature and quality of individual works, analyzes the relation of SF to other literature, and evaluates its artistic functions in the modern world.[4]

Both the popularization and the intellectualization of SF have often annoyed the veteran community which has steadily and quietly cultivated SF during the past half-century or more. Long-time devotees deplore the supposed trivialization of scientific content in recent works, the confusion of SF with pseudo-scientific fantasy and adventure fiction, and the mercenary publication of all sorts of hack literature under the fashionable label of SF. Many "indigenous" authors and critics, as they might be called, have also taken the academic critics to task for their belated recognition of SF, their pedantry, their ignorance of science and technology, their often poorly-concealed hostility to popular literature, and their tacit assumption that the critical analysis of SF requires little or no adaptation of interpretative methods. Such reproaches are not always unjustified. Nevertheless, both mass popularity and scholarly attention have brought delayed but welcome reward and recognition to a form of literature which has always inspired great loyalty among its followers but has previously offered little in the way of remuneration or literary prestige.

The systematic study of SF is a notably recent and still controversial enterprise, and it has changed greatly since I began my own formal research. Much of the increased sophistication found in modern SF criticism stems from a partial rapprochement between the "indigenous" SF community and the academic world. In an essay on SF C.S. Lewis once remarked, "It is very dangerous to write about a kind [of literature] you hate," for "those who hate the thing they are trying to explain are not perhaps those most likely to explain it."[5] But Lewis, who was a professor of English at Oxford as well as a writer and critic of SF, also understood the value of scholarly knowledge and precision. The present book belongs to what, with some disregard for chronological exactitude, might be called the third generation of SF criticism, which is composed largely of works written by academically trained students of literature who nevertheless grew up with SF, or who at least seek to approach it without the preconceptions of a questionable cultural elitism. Such studies, which have become ever more common since the early Sixties, attempt to unite the virtues or at least the ideal qualities of the two previous generations or types of SF criticism, namely the intimate specialized knowledge and empathy valued by the "indigenous" student of SF, and the close textual scrutiny, systematic methodology and broad literary background prized by the academic critic.

Although this study is one of the first full-length discussions of German SF, it does not lack predecessors in other SF criticism or models in other areas of literary interpretation. Wherever appropriate I have acknowledged the contributions of other critics. Here I would like also to mention several other intellectual obligations, as well as some personal debts. My original interest in SF I owe to the Josephine County Library, Grants Pass, Oregon, and to an avocational fascination with astronomy, technology and the history of science which was fostered by many unselfish elders. Whatever critical ability I have, I credit in large measure to my teachers at Yale University, especially Peter Demetz, who has opened up for me and others so many broad vistas of literary interpretation and closed off perhaps even more blind alleys of prosaic exposition. Dr. Franz Rottensteiner of Vienna, one of the leading European SF critics, has given me valuable advice and has also furnished me with several important primary texts. A Fellowship for College Teachers, awarded by the National Endowment for the Humanities (may it survive and thrive anew!), enabled me to interview several modern German writers of SF and to familiarize myself with the most recent scholarship shortly before the final chapters and bibliography went to press. To Ray B. Browne and Pat Browne of the Popular Press I express my appreciation for their willingness to undertake publication of a study whose subject belongs under the three quite heterogeneous rubrics of SF, popular culture, and German literature. Lastly I wish to thank my family, friends and colleagues for their interest and encouragement. My wife, Dee Lane, I say with some pride, neither typed nor proofread a single page of this book. Her contribution was of a different and far greater kind.

Note on documentation and translation

Full bibliographical references are not provided for works of American or European SF about which information is readily available in standard specialized reference works. Where two dates are given after a fiction title, the first is that of original magazine appearance, the second that of first book publication. When citing texts that have appeared in numerous editions I have sometimes found it advisable to furnish chapter numbers.

In quoting from secondary works I have sparingly altered punctuation, capitalization and grammatical forms to fit context. All primary texts are quoted in their original form, except for the substitution of *ss* for the German symbol β and for inconsequential changes of case or capitalization in single words or phrases.

All translations are my own unless noted otherwise.

Introduction

THE SUBJECT of the following study is German SF of the period 1871-1945. Since SF critics, Germanists and students of popular culture all too commonly lack common ground, Chapter I presents a descriptive and theoretical analysis of SF, parts of which—but not always the same parts of course—will be considered painfully obvious by one reader or the other. But for the same reason neither German SF itself, nor even the introductory theoretical discussion, can be understood adequately without some familiarity with the broader history of both SF and its criticism. Some more specific reference must also be made to the development and present state of German criticism of SF and—something quite different— the criticism of German SF.

The "normative" tradition of the genre is Anglo-American SF. It is this young and colorful literature which has given SF its name, has produced most of its writers and texts, and has most strongly affected the development of SF criticism. The term "science fiction" itself, which has now entered many languages unchanged or in close translation, was coined in America in 1929 and quickly gained currency.[1] Originally the appellation was used to designate a kind of recent prose fiction which had to do in some way with imaginary science and technology. Earlier such fiction had appeared with no distinguishing label or else under a variety of names, such as "utopia," "imaginary voyage," "scientific romance," and "scientific fantasy," or as "off-trail," "different," "impossible," or "pseudo-scientific" fiction. Many authors, some of them writing in languages other than English, contributed to the early development of modern Anglo-American SF. Among the most important direct forebears or early practitioners of modern SF were Jules Verne (1828-1905) and H.G. Wells (1866-1945), of course, and such lesser-known writers as George Allan England (1877-1936), A. Merritt (1884-1943), Ray Cummings (1887-1957), H. Rider Haggard (1856-1925), Edgar Rice Burroughs (1875-1950) and Murray Leinster (pseud. of William Fitzgerald Jenkins, 1896-1975). The variegated pedigree of SF also includes a large number of conceptual and stylistic ancestors or cousins of greater or lesser significance and varying degrees of kinship, for example the utopia, adventure, horror and detective fiction, the popularized myth, juvenile literature about technology, and even non-fiction scientific prose— to name only some.

In the twentieth century the United States became the main geographical center of SF. English, of course, was the language of publication, if sometimes not that of original composition. Historians of SF frequently consider 1926 to be the birthyear of modern SF, for it was then that Hugo Gernsback (1884-1967) founded the pulp fiction periodical *Amazing Stories,* the first magazine devoted expressly and completely to SF.

Gernsback, an engineer, scientific journalist, and editor of technical magazines, emigrated to the United States from Luxembourg in 1904. His early SF novel *Ralph 124C 41+: A Romance of the Year 2660,* rich in exciting, carefully described imaginary technology but crude in its literary aspects, was first published serially in Gernsback's own journal *Modern Electrics* in 1911.

During the decade after 1926 the specialized SF magazine flourished and became the center of the first of several SF "booms." *Amazing* was quickly joined by other magazines. Readers, most of whom were apparently young, male, and interested more in spectacular science than literary refinement, soon numbered in the hundreds of thousands. Dozens of new writers entered the field, augmenting the much smaller group of older writers who had previously published their SF in other media and had then made the transition to the specialized "pulps." The SF magazines published short stories and short serial novels or "novelettes," as well as editorials, readers' letters, occasional non-fiction scientific articles, and reprints of older SF.

The ten or twelve years after 1926 are commonly and often nostalgically termed the period of "space opera" or "gosh-wow!" SF, as fans called the adventurous tales written by E.E. "Doc" Smith (1890-1965) and others. Heroic deeds and exciting, if not always strictly accurate science and technology were the stuff of early pulp SF. Frequently the entire Universe furnished the scenic backdrop for the "space operas," whose grandiose and episodic plots might span centuries or even eons. The magazine covers were temptingly sensationalistic, but the stories themselves were far more chaste than was implied by the ubiquitous thinly-clad Martian princesses threatened by the "Bug-Eyed Monsters" in the illustrations. Ads for correspondence schools and rupture trusses obtruded rather incongruously, but were necessary to help turn a profit. The magazines, usually owned by large publishing houses which issued a variety of popular periodicals, sought to appeal to the mass reader by keeping prices down. Budgets were slim, and the writers were paid at rates which were low even for authors of pulp literature.

Toward the end of the Thirties there began to appear in the specialized magazines a kind of SF which was far maturer in content and style than "space opera." The SF of the so-called "Golden Age" was created by such authors as Robert A. Heinlein, Isaac Asimov, Arthur C. Clarke, Theodore Sturgeon, A.E. van Vogt, Lester Del Rey, Fritz Leiber, Cyril Kornbluth, Henry Kuttner, Judith Merril, Frederik Pohl, Clifford Simak, Eric Frank Russell, Damon Knight, Jack Williamson, and Ray Bradbury. While the writers of the "Golden Age" were a diverse lot, some recurring characteristics can be discerned. Most were quite young when the "Golden Age" began; Heinlein, for example, was born in 1907, Clarke in 1917, and Asimov in 1920. Most, too, were Americans, although a few important writers, like Clarke and Russell, were British. Many had been educated in science and technology, and of necessity they maintained a working familiarity with contemporary research and development. While they did not lack creative gifts or basic literary skills, few had any formal training in literature or any close contact with the highbrow literary Establishment. Like many American writers, they learned their trade in the school of mass fiction. The newer SF owed much of its thematic sophistication, and not a little of its literary quality, to the inspiring scientific ideas and editorial abilities of the magazine editors, particularly John W. Campbell, Jr. (1910-1971), who from 1937 until his death was editor of *Astounding Science Fiction* (now *Analog),* the greatest of the SF pulps.

During the "Golden Age" some English-language SF of comparable conceptual maturity and perhaps even greater literary quality appeared elsewhere, mostly in Britain. Of such SF, which consists typically of larger works rather than short stories, *Brave New World* (1932) by Aldous Huxley (1894-1963) and *1984* (1949) by George Orwell (1903-50) are best known to the general readership. The novels of C.S. Lewis (1898-1963) and of Olaf Stapledon (1886-1950), professor of philosophy at Liverpool University, also enjoy a considerable reputation among some readers of SF. Seldom, however, was the still disreputable label "SF" then applied to such fiction, except within the SF community.

The "Golden Age" of Anglo-American SF lasted from the late Thirties until perhaps the middle or late Fifties. Writers, editors, critics, and readers, among them especially the active "fans," formed a cohesive community. It was in fact not unusual for a "fan" to become a writer or editor, even while still quite young. The SF community was acutely and insistently conscious of its own identity and that of SF. It maintained a notable distance between itself and the world of what it called "mainstream" literature. The term was applied sometimes with contempt, sometimes with envy, but in any case with little regard to traditional distinctions of form, content, or quality. "Mainstream" authors and critics, for their part, seldom acknowledged SF as a potentially serious art-form or object of critical study. Consequently, SF criticism was mainly the product of the "indigenous" SF community.

Since the late Forties the isolation of SF from other literature has steadily lessened. Scientific, economic, and aesthetic factors have all contributed to the mutual rapprochement. The general reading public, its interest and credence encouraged by the atomic bomb and Sputnik, discovered SF. At the same time, writers of SF sought to enter the more lucrative markets served by "mainstream" magazine and book publication, the cinema, and television. The result was the first of a series of postwar SF "booms." The so-called "New Wave" or "inner space" SF of the mid-Sixties and later represents a programmatic attempt to liberalize the aesthetic and thematic conventions of "classical" SF and to adapt avant-garde stylistic techniques and subjects to SF. Both "New Wave" authors and older writers like Heinlein have become more explicit in their treatment of sexuality and ideology. They have also explored new scientific themes, particularly those having to do with psychology, biology, and cybernetics. A tendency toward romance and the occult—in not only my own view an unfortunate one—has also emerged, or rather re-emerged. Best known among the younger writers of SF are Frank Herbert, Samuel Delany, Ursula K. LeGuin, John Brunner, Roger Zelazny, J.G. Ballard, Robert Silverberg, James Blish, Philip K. Dick, Thomas M. Disch, Michael Moorcock, Harry Harrison, Harlan Ellison, Philip José Farmer, and Walter M. Miller, Jr. Other writers, like Kurt Vonnegut and Ray Bradbury, whose names are even more familiar to the general public, constantly cross and recross the boundaries between SF, fantasy fiction, and "mainstream" literature. Whether the rapprochement between SF and "mainstream" literature will continue remains to be seen; it appears certain, however, that SF will survive as a fairly distinct kind of literature.

The boundaries of the term "science fiction" have gradually been extended—not without vigorous debate—to encompass literature written before recent times and in languages other than English. Generic liberalization has no doubt been encouraged by the fiction of Jules Verne, whom the "indigenous" SF community has of course long regarded as a "native" writer of SF. Many older works, especially some which earlier were customarily categorized as utopias or imaginary voyages, are now often also classified, rightly or wrongly, as SF. Presently SF is written throughout the industrialized world. Eastern European SF, particularly Soviet SF and the works of the Polish author Stanisław Lem (b. 1921), has lately received a good deal of attention and approval from readers and critics.

German SF, however, has attracted little notice from either the critics or, outside the German linguistic area, the readers of SF. The neglect is puzzling, for it might well be suspected that Germany, with its history of notable literary and scientific achievements, would have produced at least some SF worthy of note. Yet German SF indeed offers a most interesting and instructive contribution to the history and criticism of SF. Although there is undoubtedly more Anglo-American and, perhaps, more Eastern European SF than German SF, I have in fact found it advisable to limit the present study primarily to just two writers, Kurd Lasswitz (1848-1910) and Hans Dominik (1872-1945). The two, however, suggest much of the variety of German SF and the conditions which helped to produce it. Lasswitz, a theoretical scientist, educator, and political liberal, wrote almost a score of early SF short stories and novellas. His lengthy novel *Auf zwei Planeten* (1897) does not suffer in comparison to the contemporaneous novels of H.G. Wells. But Lasswitz' appeal was limited, and his works left little mark on German literary history or the development of German SF. Dominik, an engineer and technical journalist, stands at the other extreme from Lasswitz in literary sophistication, popularity, and ideology. Even during his own lifetime the aggregate hardcover circulation of his sixteen SF novels exceeded two million copies. The history of German SF includes, in addition, a modest handful of other early writers who devoted some or all of their literary efforts to SF, perhaps hundreds of little-known or as yet even undiscovered works of utopian and technological fiction, a number of experiments in the genre by distinguished "mainstream" writers, several mass-circulation pulp novel series, and a few important modern practitioners of SF, most notable among them Herbert W. Franke (b. 1927) and Wolfgang Jeschke (b. 1936).

Much material has remained virtually untouched. Reliable bibliographical information is extremely scarce, and it is likely that more than a few works have simply not been identified yet as German SF. Many texts are virtually inaccessible or, quite possibly, are even no longer in existence. Definitive editions or even trustworthy reprints are, to understate, extremely rare. Historical and critical interpretations are meager, as are biographical data. Clearly the prospective historian and critic of German SF faces formidable but also fascinating problems.

It is somewhat surprising that non-German critics have generally neglected German SF, although it cannot be said that any field or facet of SF has been overworked. Far more startling, however, is the state of SF criticism in German-speaking countries. Postwar German readers, both the mass consumers and the serious critics, have evidenced considerable enthusiasm for almost all SF— except their own. Certainly Dominik's novels have maintained some of their popularity, at least among the mass readership. But only recently has native German SF, for example the *Perry Rhodan* pulp novel series, offered serious competition to imported SF, and several of the writers who produce the series have found it advisable to adopt American-sounding pennames.

German critics of SF, of whom there are a goodly number, have devoted equally little attention to German SF. Major studies of SF by Martin Schwonke and Hans-Jürgen Krysmanski appeared almost as early as the first important works by historians and critics writing in English.[2] Yet neither Schwonke nor Krysmanski gives Lasswitz or Dominik more than peripheral mention. Recent German-language criticism of SF is among the best anywhere, and is quite provocative in the variety of its sociological, ideological and literary approaches. Worthy of particular note are the studies of Jörg Hienger, Vera Graaf, and Dieter Wessels, the illustrated monograph by Franz Rottensteiner, the collections of essays edited by Eike Barmeyer and Karl Ermert, and the eclectic analysis undertaken jointly by Suerbaum, Broich and Borgmeier.[3] Several German-language periodicals, such as *Science-Fiction Times* (Bremerhaven, edited by Hans-Joachim Alpers) and *Quarber Merkur* (Quarb/Vienna, edited by Franz Rottensteiner), also offer critical interpretations of high quality. Yet the discussion of German SF, especially its aesthetic aspects, constitutes only a lesser part of such studies and publications.

The relative neglect of German SF in Germany and elsewhere can be ascribed to several causes. Both German science and German SF were thoroughly disrupted and isolated from the international SF community by the policies of the National Socialist regime and the events of World War II. The Hitler goverment, for example, pre-empted and classified the open rocket experimentation being conducted by civilians in Germany. The consequences for SF were not inconsiderable. The Nazis also suppressed, among other texts, Lasswitz' *Auf zwei Planeten*, which was the greatest work of German SF and a major inspiration for the German rocket experimenters. In my concluding chapter I will discuss the effects of these circumstances on the subsequent development of German SF itself. Important here is the fact that the unwarranted obscurity of major texts like *Auf zwei Planeten*, and the concomitant domination of German SF by works of lesser literary quality and sometimes dubious ideological content, have made German SF widely disreputable in Germany and generally unknown abroad.

Not unrelated to larger historical conditions are certain patterns in the development of SF and SF criticism outside Germany, especially in America and Britain. The language barrier has impeded whatever impact German SF might have had abroad. Equally detrimental, if more understandable, has been the tendency of non-German critics, particularly those belonging to the "indigenous" SF community, to concentrate most of their attention on the "normative"—and readily accessible—tradition of Anglo-American SF, a practice which has been emulated by German-speaking critics.

The general neglect of German SF, and foreign SF as well, among German-speaking literary critics can also be traced to certain tendencies in German literary criticism as it has developed over the past two centuries. While the crude but short-lived literary policies of National Socialism were in themselves inimical enough to the development of German SF and SF criticism, the study of SF in Germany has also been obstructed over a longer period of time by the persistent ideological conservatism and the aesthetic and social elitism of German cultural and intellectual life. Recent students of popular literature, receptional history and aesthetics, and the ideological aspects of literature have attempted to correct previous imbalances which hindered the study of mass culture and of literature about such supposedly unartistic matters as science and technology. SF is frequently a subject of discussion in the works of both the best and the worst of such critics.

It is unfortunate, I think, that the examination of German SF is still almost automatically considered a branch of the study of popular culture and *Trivialliteratur*. Sometimes, too, the ideological reaction against earlier modes of interpretation has been excessive. A number of critics, most conspicuous among them Michael Pehlke and Norbert Lingfeld, have subordinated the interpretation of SF to a radical leftist attack on Western ideology and the West German cultural and political system.[4] Such critics, whatever the merits of their ideological convictions, are often too preoccupied with polemics against the evils of imported American culture, late-bourgeois capitalism, and the reactionary nature of West German society to have much time either for literary interpretation in general or for German SF in particular, except perhaps its most disreputable examples. Thus, in a perverse way, some ostensibly progressive German critics of SF perpetuate the cultural snobbism of their reactionary adversaries.

A far greater competence in sociological, ideological and, sometimes, aesthetic analysis is exhibited in the monograph *Science Fiction in Deutschland* by Manfred Nagl, and in a number of essays in the anthology *Die triviale Phantasie* edited by Jörg Weigand.[5] As Nagl's title subtly indicates, however, the focus of his attention is the broader topic of SF in Germany rather than German SF specifically. Among other major German-speaking critics, Franz Rottensteiner of Austria, who is well known in the international SF community, has examined some historical and aesthetic aspects of German SF. Although Rottensteiner's main interests are still Anglo-American and Eastern European SF, he has written excellent articles on Lasswitz. His work, and that of several others of the few critics who have dealt extensively with German SF, will be discussed in detail later.

The present state of German SF research and criticism precludes a comprehensive and definitive history and critical interpretation of German SF. My study is therefore intended as an initial contribution to the field. If I have felt it necessary to confine most of my attention to Kurd Lasswitz and Hans Dominik, in discussing the two writers—whom I consider in any case to be the two most important figures in the history of German SF—I have adopted a broad approach which draws on many methods of interpretation and sources of information. My procedure was determined by the exigencies of the material available, by an overall assessment of the basic characteristics of German SF and its relation to other SF, and by methodological convictions of a more general nature.

The study of SF shows very clearly, I think, how necessary it is that one take into account extrinsic or "non-literary" factors, such as scientific and technological background, political and social conditions, media of publication, and the characteristics of the reading public. Nevertheless, the text must still be examined as a work of literature. I hope to have offered valid textual explications of the works of Lasswitz and Dominik, considered as SF and, where the distinction is appropriate, as literature in general—although I think that "good" SF must also be "good" literature. Still another part of my effort has been directed toward evaluating the extent to which German SF can be considered a cohesive genre or literary tradition. In examining the question I have been quite wary of indulging in a quest for manifestations of the *Zeitgeist* or a search for neat concatenations of literary "influences" which somehow generate a genre. It is even possible, as I will suggest in my final chapter, that German SF, in distinct contrast to the "normative" tradition of modern Anglo-American SF and to many other literary traditions as well, provides a classic example of a body of texts which, at least until recently, owes its synchronic and diachronic unity less to a sense of shared literary heritage than to a common extra-literary element, science and technology. I do not regard that conclusion as a violation of the "autonomy" of literature, but rather as a reaffirmation of its social relevance and enduring cultural vitality.

Chapter I

Imaginary Worlds, Imaginary Science: A Descriptive and Theoretical Analysis of Science Fiction

DEFINITIONS OF SF are legion, but none has gained more than a limited acceptance among the extremely diverse company of SF critics.[1] The disagreement is scarcely surprising. SF has evolved in many countries and at many times. It has appeared in a wide range of forms of publication and has been associated with numerous other kinds of literature. Moreover, SF is a living literature which is constantly changing, often in ways which puzzle or even irritate critics and established writers. But literary taxonomy is not the only subject of disputation. No one has yet determined whether SF should be defined and evaluated according to its worst, its most typical, or—like many other forms of literature—its best examples. There is little accord even about the initial premises on which a definition of SF should be founded. Although not a few critics attempt to discern in SF some sort of characteristic literary style,[2] many contend that SF is best distinguished from other literature by its method of imagination and its special content, both of which they usually relate in some way to science.[3] Still others—interdisciplinarians and students of mass culture—base their analyses of SF on ideological presuppositions, sociological principles, or theories of myth and archetypes.[4] At least one serious but exasperated critic has suggested that SF is anything any author, editor or—one might add—reader chooses to call SF.[5]

The lack of a single universally accepted definition does not preclude useful criticism, especially the explication of individual texts. But a systematic interpretation of SF as a whole is impossible without some kind of formal definition, one which would describe the underlying intentionality of SF and the way it is objectified in the text.[6] The following definition of SF will be the basis for the present study:

Science fiction is a modern form of literature characterized by the methodical conception and description of an imaginary world which is manifestly different from our own "real" world. The description of the imaginary world may refer to its landscape, as well as to the beings who inhabit it, including their individual actions, social organization, history, and culture. By using various stylistic devices which may be derived from many kinds of literature, the author seeks to convince the willing but exacting reader of both the fictive reality and the intellectual plausibility of the imaginary world.

Science and technology always play an essential and evident part in the conception of the imaginary world and in its presentation in and through the text. Science provides the special distinguishing content of SF, affects the writer's method of imagination, furnishes themes and motifs, influences form and language, and serves as the basis of an aesthetic principle of SF according to which value judgments are made.

The intended result of SF is both edification and pleasure, in the widest sense: intellectual exercise, new insight, and sheer enjoyment of fiction.

Works which may conveniently and reasonably be categorized as SF will of course vary in the degree to which they satisfy this definition, either in their entirety or in some of their parts.

SF is, first of all, a *modern* form of literature. The temporal criterion cannot be applied with absolute precision, but it is nonetheless meaningful. Although there are legitimate links between SF and older kinds of literature, genuine SF could neither be created nor understood before science and technology had become significant parts of human experience and consciousness. To locate the essential beginnings of such developments very much before the Renaissance or even the Industrial Revolution vitiates the meanings of both "science" and "science fiction." In any case, almost all SF has been produced within the last century, the greater part of it within the last fifty years.

Much more problematic are distinctions which have to do with the content, literary style, and philosophical foundations of SF. At one time or another writers, editors, publishers, readers and critics have associated SF with utopian thought and literature, the imaginary voyage, fantasy and "weird" fiction, prophecy, futurology, popularized science, and fiction about modern science and the industrial society. Yet SF must be something other than an agglomeration of *The Lord of the Rings*, H.P. Lovecraft's *The Call of Cthulhu, Gulliver's Travels,* Lucian's *True History,* More's *Utopia,* the prophecies in Nostradamus' *Centuries,* the reports of the Club of Rome, Maeterlinck's *Life of the Bee,* Sinclair Lewis' *Arrowsmith*, and *The Jungle* by Upton Sinclair.

Many of the confusions outlined here can be resolved—with allowance for marginal cases, of course—by reference to certain individual features which are apparently essential to SF but not to other types of expression. Thus neither fantasy fiction, the utopia, nor satire, for example, necessarily includes reference to science and technology, as does SF. Similarly, while both SF and literature about modern theoretical science or industrial society refer to science and technology, SF is not limited to the description of existing science and technology. Still other distinctions concern larger differences. Unlike prophecy, futurology, scientific exposition, or even some utopian writing, SF always involves an element of artistic fiction. The reader who mistakes a work of SF for an outright prediction or for a scientific or historical discourse has failed to grasp the author's purpose.

The problem of generic distinction is best approached by a discussion of the location of SF within the larger category of fiction itself. Writers and critics, especially those who belong to the older "indigenous" SF community, often insist quite vehemently on the difference between SF and what they have long called "mainstream" fiction. The latter category is taken to include all literature which is not SF, regardless of content, stylistic affinities, aesthetic quality, or popularity. In my opinion the sweeping distinction between "mainstream" fiction and SF is essentially correct and in fact coincides with the basic intentionality of the genre. It expresses an awareness that SF differs from other literature in the way in which, at least ideally, the fiction and the world it represents are created by the writer and perceived by the reader.

The essential distinction between SF and other literature involves the "imaginary world" of SF and its relation to our own "real" world. Of central importance in the generic classification and theoretical analysis of SF are two ancient notions which are still fundamental to all aesthetic discussion: "imagination" and "imitation" or "mimesis." But the two ideas and terms have special meanings for SF. Every work of fiction is of course "imaginative" or "inventive" in one sense, for at least some of the objects, people and even entire environments which the author describes are his own creations. Much of modern literature, however, is dominated by the conceptual presuppositions and stylistic conventions of "realism," and even much non-realistic literature can be viewed as a conscious rebellion against the strictures of realism. By convention— generally tacit—the worlds of most modern "mainstream" fiction are offered to the reader as "real," and the reader, usually with little question, accepts them as such. He has indeed good reason to assume—or at least pretend to assume—that the settings, objects and characters represented in the fiction exist or have once existed outside the text, and that the narrated events have taken place, or might well have taken place, in the "real" world. After all, almost all modern "mainstream" fiction is "of course" set on Earth in the past or present, and its characters are always terrestrial life-forms, most usually human beings. The reader of "mainstream" fiction, therefore, can bolster his inclination to believe in the "reality" of the fictional world by his supposed ability to refer to history and to his own contemporary world, in which there can be found persons, objects or events very much like those described in the fiction. The author of realistic fiction, obviously, will seek to reinforce in the reader a sense of verifiability or "sharable experience," as Peter Demetz calls it.[7]

The fundamental presuppositions of SF strain or sometimes even contradict the assumption, usually but not always tacit, that the world presented in the fiction could be verified by reference to sharable experience of the "real" world. Indeed, one of the chief distinguishing characteristics of SF is the manifest difference between the real and imaginary worlds in their most basic features. SF texts, as Robert Scholes puts it, "insist on some radical discontinuity between the worlds they present to us and the world of our experience."[8] The extent of the "radical discontinuity" is evident in the way SF introduces alterations in such fundamental categories of human experience and psychological intuition as time, place and sense of identity. Almost all SF is set in the future, very often on other planets or in space itself. Some or all of the characters may be alien beings or even machines, and almost always there is emphatic reference to scientific theories and technological devices which are not part of our world. Sometimes the imaginary world differs from the "real" contemporary world even in its fundamental physical laws. The fictional world of a work of SF is intended and perceived as a truly different world, not just as an "imaginative" version of our own. It consists of places, times and beings of which neither the reader nor the writer has had, can have had, or—at least when the fiction is created—can have any direct experience.[9]

Yet even though SF describes worlds which simply cannot represent "real" worlds, the writer still aims to inspire in the reader an immediate sense of "reality," a conviction of verifiability through sharable experience. The ultimate effect of SF, however, is neither a sense of disillusionment or deception, nor a blithe dismissal of the fiction as a mere fantasy or fairy tale. For, besides offering fictions which can temporarily be accepted as real and enjoyed like those of other literature, SF seeks to win from the reader the acknowledgment that the imaginary world is *plausible*, in an intellectual, logical, or even "scientific" sense which is not independent of, or inconsistent with, the reader's subjective impression of reality. The fundamental intentionality of SF is reflected in the interaction among the aims of the author, the responses of the reader, and the text as a set of generic "signals" which has evolved to facilitate communication between writer and reader.

Creating the Imaginary World:
Imagination and the Function of Science

SF is about science, or it would not be SF. But "science" has many meanings in modern parlance and in SF. Not only does the word refer to both theoretical science and technology; it also describes a way of intuiting and structuring the world. SF always reflects the belief that science, especially in the modern age and in the future, is a major determinant of historical processes, social forms, and individual consciousness. It would not be excessive to suggest that in SF science is virtually equivalent to an ideology, in the sense of a conviction that a single mode of perception and thought provides ultimate categories of knowledge, standards of truth, and explanations for history, society and human experience.[10] The "ideology" of science in SF, however, is not simply a complacent faith in a philosophy of history or in the workings of some transcendental spirit. Despite popular misconceptions, the writers of SF are not necessarily or invariably optimists or fervent technocrats whose belief in the importance of science and technology precludes the ability to perceive the dangers which can result from the misuse of theoretical or applied science.

Equally essential to SF is the concept of meaningful, systematic, and thus potentially predictable historical change. The notion of such change, in SF and in much other modern thought as well, is closely associated with the products and the very methods of science. Isaac Asimov and other writers of SF are scarcely alone in their suggestion that the explosive growth of science and technology in the last five hundred years may well have brought about real change.[11] Certainly science has at least helped to foster the characteristically modern conviction that the passage of time involves something other than the mere ebb and flow of events and the inconsequential mutability of human existence. Perhaps the development of analytic geometry and the calculus encouraged the quantification of historical change, and even its abstraction to the form of curves of progress or decline plotted against perpendicular axes of time and change. More recently, Darwin's theory of evolution has also reinforced the notion of continuous, systematic, quantifiable change. Whatever the case, it is impossible to accomplish or even attempt the creation of consistent and plausible future or alternative worlds without a concept of meaningful secular change which can be analyzed in what is considered to be a scientific manner.

The importance of science and the concept of systematic change are not mere dogmas which SF enunciates within some perfunctory fictional framework. They affect the way in which, at least ideally, the author conceives and presents the imaginary world and in which the reader, again ideally, responds to it. SF is—or at least aims to be—the product of impartial, restrained, systematic, and thus "scientific" speculation about history, society, individual human existence, and even science itself. This formulation of the fundamental intentionality of SF is implied in the very term "science fiction" and in many other expressions which have been devised to describe SF, such as "structural fabulation" (Scholes), "strictly disciplined" or "controlled imagination" (Olaf Stapledon), and "restrained" or "bridled fantasy" (Lasswitz).[12] In their disquisitions on the theoretical principles and practical techniques of SF, many critics and, even more significantly, many writers of SF constantly assert that the imaginary world, however "fantastic" it may seem to the author when he sets out to envision it, or to the reader when he first confronts the text, must be constructed according to logical principles, and the reader must be able to perceive its systematic, rational, "scientific" nature.

The sharp remarks that Wells and Verne directed at each other's SF[13] show that writers and critics have long attempted to analyze the distinctive nature of imagination in SF and to refine the standards which determine what is and what is not "scientific" in it. Many striking preferences for certain patterns of "scientific" reasoning have emerged. Frequently, theoretical and practical discussions of SF are founded on the concept of "extrapolation," a term which refers both to a certain process of imagination and to its products.[14] The point of departure for "extrapolation" is the author's systematically formulated notion of his own world, based on his assessment of its most significant and interesting features. Like an experimental scientist—the comparison is not unconsidered and will be discussed at length shortly—the writer of SF first attempts to quantify available information from the past and present. He then isolates and projects trends, introduces variables, and observes changes. The results of the process of extrapolation, when it is pursued resolutely, constitute a new and imaginary world significantly different from our own.

Despite its emphasis on rational, "scientific" speculation, extrapolation is not an iron-bound method which produces monotonously identical worlds. Not even non-fiction futurology claims such precision. If extrapolation seems to offer a "cookbook" for the concoction of SF, the process in fact produces countless recipes and allows the chef much latitude. The imaginary world may differ radically from our own in spatial or temporal location, or indeed both. New forms of life may be introduced, and even the physical laws which govern Nature in the imaginary world may not resemble those we know. The end-products of extrapolation may be appetizing, bland, or—often enough—fiery or even repulsive, for the author of SF is capable of imagining worlds which are far better than our own, quite similar to it, or bleakly catastrophic. Generally, however, writers of SF prefer to create imaginary worlds markedly unlike our own, for they are convinced that change is often underestimated and that the immensity of space and time revealed by modern science provides room for an unexpectedly great diversity of environments and life-forms. They are also aware that a strikingly different imaginary world, if it can be made plausible, will quickly and powerfully attract the reader's attention.[15]

Writers (and readers) of SF pay particular heed to the conception and presentation of imaginary science and technology. Some SF focuses on a single "gadget," theory, or technological project. In longer works, especially, the writer seeks to describe a world filled with many imaginary devices and new ideas. He may choose to concentrate on the careful description of imaginary science and technology, or he may seek to explore in depth the social, philosophical or even theological consequences of some imaginary theory or device. He may even imagine a world whose inhabitants, through some disaster caused or explained by science, have regressed to a prescientific or pretechnological state. Science may be seen through the eyes of ordinary human beings; but often the figure of the scientist or technologist, or even some alien but still "human" being, provides the human perspective, which is never absent from SF.

In employing extrapolation to fabricate imaginary

technological devices or abstract scientific concepts, the author of SF enjoys great latitude in some ways, but in others his freedom is quite circumscribed. Any notion which does not explicitly violate the established facts of *present* science may be entertained.[16] The author may go so far as to challenge basic scientific ideas, such as the theory of relativity, for a scientific theory is always subject to modification or even refutation in accord with new experimental evidence or new and better methods of interpreting data already available. The rapid development of theoretical and applied science in recent centuries has done much to encourage writers of SF to treat science and technology in a boldly speculative manner. But the license to speculate is balanced by another requirement often expressed by writers, critics and readers: the author must firmly substantiate his imaginary science with copious evidence—some of it perhaps itself imaginary—and with rhetorical devices which reinforce the senses of reality and plausibility. Such strictures do not admit of absolute direct application in practice, of course, for what is permitted the author is determined by his subsequent success in gaining the credence of the demanding reader.

The principle of extrapolation is applied with comparable enthusiasm to patterns of historical progression and social structure. Much SF recounts the subsequent fate of terrestrial humanity on Earth or elsewhere, whether in the next few years or the next few billion. But extrapolation of historical trends and mutation of social forms may also be used to create terrestrial worlds located in alternate versions of the past or present, or alien worlds whose origins lie in recent scientific research and in the transferred characteristics of terrestrial life-forms, though not necessarily those of our species.

The patterns which are abstracted from history and present conditions and are then used to create future, alternate or alien history are commonly termed "analogs."[17] SF clearly favors certain analogs and certain periods of history, whether for their romantic associations, their actual historical significance, or their compatibility with its marked preference for colorful characters and exciting plots. Thus the Roman Empire has figured in the creation of many monumental narratives which, like Asimov's *Foundation* trilogy (1942ff., 1951ff.), detail the rise, glory, decline and fall of future "Galactic Empires." Other SF has looked to the Middle Ages for examples of semi-barbaric feudalism and the dedicated preservation of knowledge in times of ignorance. The image is congenial to those many writers who are troubled by the neglect, misunderstanding and outright rejection of science in their own time. The medieval analog is also often encountered in SF where religion is a major theme. Both aspects of the analog are evident in the classic work *A Canticle for Leibowitz* (1955-57; 1960) by Walter M. Miller, Jr. Still other historical and geographical analogs, frequently drawing on the attendant travel literature, echo European colonialism—sometimes approvingly, often not.

American history has provided SF, both American and foreign, some of its most notable or even notorious historical and social analogs. The exploration and colonization of space are often modeled on early voyages of discovery, the settlement of the Atlantic seaboard, the American Revolution, or the opening and passing of the frontier. It would seem that centuries of popular conception and artistic expression have engendered, in both America and Europe, an image or even nascent myth of America particularly congenial to SF. The myth actually appears in two alternate manifestations or displaced formulations. One presupposes America as a pre-technological, virgin frontier untouched by the intrusions of European civilization. The model for the other is America as the land of the future which, again because it is not burdened by the weight of history, quickly surpasses the Old World in science, technology and the modernization of social institutions, thus creating a different and most sophisticated kind of frontier.

The historical and social content of SF—its ideological ingredient—has often incited vehement debate, sometimes to the detriment of careful critical evaluation. Among certain critics SF has a reputation for espousing crude, quasi-fascistic political notions.[18] In its ideology some SF—and 'SF is not unique in this respect—is indeed rabidly reactionary and nationalistic, or often just naive; it might of course be remarked, conversely, that much political writing fails to grasp the significance of science and technology. But despite its emphasis on the analogs of the New World and of American history, SF—even American SF—is not invariably nationalistic, complacently confident, or reactionary. Indeed, the new cosmological perspective ideally present in SF often begets a liberal "one-world" consciousness. The writers of such SF, to the possible annoyance of both jingoists and leftist ideologues, envision the elimination of national boundaries, the creation of unified planetary or even galactic governments, and the obsolescence of contemporary social problems and ideological disputes in the face of larger issues affecting the fate of entire species, worlds, or perhaps the Universe itself. Although such SF is often patterned on the image of American democracy and the somewhat dubious myth of the melting pot, American SF is equally capable of describing future worlds in which America has become morally decadent, imperialistic and dictatorial. SF also tends strongly to advocate the free dissemination of information, or to recognize pragmatically that scientific knowledge is difficult to suppress—ideas which can be unpopular with nationalists.[19]

In still broader ideological terms it might even be argued that the European discovery of the New World and the later history of the frontier have provided SF with its most provocative and, potentially, its most liberal and humanistic theme: the confrontation of terrestrial Mankind with other and perhaps superior forms of life. Frequently the extermination of the American Indian is recapitulated in the treatment of alien life, and the conquering soldier and settler are not always glorified. Often enough it is Western civilization itself, or even the entire human species, which must play the role of the subhuman Redskin or vanishing Noble Savage. The confrontation of terrestrial and extra-terrestrial human beings, like the vision of terrestrial future history by itself, renders contemporary racial and ideological distinctions insignificant. On a deeper level, both themes require a new definition of "humanity."

The use of extrapolation and analogs to create fictional imaginary worlds raises yet another question which reveals much about the fundamental intentionality of SF. It might be suggested that SF, considered from a strictly philosophical or logical perspective, involves a true *aporia* or insoluble dilemma in our response to the text and the imaginary world. The author of a SF text claims that the imaginary world is not merely a disguised image of our own, even if, in some cases, it is obviously the direct historical descendant of our own world. Instead, the imaginary world—or more precisely, the imaginary world to which the words of the text refer—is supposedly an independent construct which functions in accord with its own presuppositions and laws. Yet if pressed the author of SF must concede that he cannot divorce himself from his own world, for he does not create the imaginary world *ex nihilo*.

The manner in which the reader of SF views the divergence between assertion and actuality affects his attitude toward the status of the imaginary world, and thus influences the nature of his immediate subjective response and his later aesthetic judgments.

Quite often, I think, the ontological status of the imaginary world is misjudged, especially by those most hostile and those most partial to SF. The imaginary world is not a mere pretense behind which— either because the writer is a clever satirist or an inept primitive— the features of our own world are to be perceived. Nor is it the fundamental assertion of SF that the imaginary world is, or rather will become, "reality"; SF is not to be confused with prophecy, whether one admires or disdains the latter. Neither attitude properly assesses the role of the writer, and neither takes into account the status of the work of SF as a *literary* text. The imaginary world is not intended to be viewed according to such crude distinctions as that between asserted reality and transparent sham. The writer's and reader's response to the imaginary world is tentative, even skeptical, but it is also sincere.

The evolution of the science-fictional intentionality may well have been influenced by the scientific method, considered as a pattern of empirical investigation, as a paradigm for abstract reasoning, and as a mode of formulating and expressing arguments. The scientific method, at least as it is commonly conceived, consists of a process of observing phenomena, formulating theories, testing and revising such hypotheses against further data, and—a stage sometimes overlooked—presenting the results of the scientific investigation in convincing form. Any theory represents a selected moment in an ongoing sequence of investigation, exposition, and revision or even revolution which occurs within the work of the individual scientist and throughout the development of a science. If "truth" is the goal of science, it is indeed an elusive ideal. One theory replaces another because it is considered "better," but the new theory is not necessarily viewed as an eternally valid solution which can explain all data and encompass all concepts, both extant and eventual, with absolute finality. Moreover the scientist is aware, ideally at least, that no theory can actually be proved, because inductive reasoning is not valid logically. In a sense, however, the objection is moot; for, as Kant, Heisenberg and others have shown, it is not possible to verify a theory by comparing it directly to the noumenal world which, we assume, lies behind appearances. But the scientist and his audience know that, nevertheless, a theory can still be judged according to its practical usefulness, its internal coherence, its consistence with data already available, and its later compatibility with data not previously considered.[20]

The SF text, I would suggest, is meant to be understood in a similar way. Ample support for that contention is furnished by the statements of writers belonging to many diverse traditions of SF, and by the recorded utterances of readers, when such elusive documentation can indeed be found, as it can, for example, in the American pulp magazines of the "Golden Age." SF, then, capitalizes on the modes of thought and argument which govern, or are assumed to govern, actual science. It operates with many of the same instruments of formal logic, inductive reasoning, and—not least of all—rhetorical appeals to the audience. The reader tends, and is encouraged, to adopt the attitude of a fellow scientist who evaluates the ideas of his colleague by subjecting them to criteria of logical validity and compatibility with observable phenomena. The specific stance described here is not at all inconsistent with the role of the reader as a representative of his species, someone who, like readers of much other fiction, looks for evidence which will convince him, as a reasonable and sensitive person, that the imaginary world is in its own way as real and believable as his own.

The imaginary worlds created in SF, then, are intended to be viewed as "realities," like the fictional worlds of realistic literature. But they are also "thought-models," literary equivalents of scientific hypotheses. The writer of SF, like the scientist, records phenomena and proposes theories to explain them. Neither the author of SF nor the scientist, however, claims that his "model," when viewed rationally, directly represents reality or expresses absolute "truth." The reader or addressant of SF is invited to entertain the "thought-model" on a provisional basis. He is asked to enjoy it as fiction, but also to examine it for its internal validity and its compatibility with available data. He may also wish to appreciate it as a logical construct which, like a scientific theory, may indeed exhibit elegance of form and thus evoke an aesthetic response.[21]

The Content of the Imaginary World: Setting, Character, and Plot

> There is no art delivered to mankind that hath not the works of Nature for his principal object.... So doth the astronomer look upon the stars, and, by that he seeth, setteth down what order Nature hath taken therein. So do the geometrician and arithmetician in their diverse sorts of quantities.... Only the poet, disdaining to be tied to any such subjection, lifted up with the vigour of invention, doth grow in effect another nature.... So as he goeth hand in hand with Nature, not enclosed within the narrow warrant of her gifts, but freely ranging only within the zodiac of his own wit.... Her world is brazen, the poets only deliver a golden.
> Sir Philip Sidney, *An Apology for Poetry* (1595)

Neither the scientist nor the writer of SF can simply ask his audience to intuit his ideas and then accept them. In presenting their arguments or thought-models both make use of a generally similar vehicle: language, usually printed prose. Both also adduce evidence to substantiate their arguments. If the entire imaginary world, as the writer of SF envisions it before creating the text, is in some respects like the thought-models conceived by the scientist, then it is through the narration itself that the imaginary world is presented to the reader. Correspondingly, the content of the narration—setting, character and events of the plot—constitutes the evidence or "data" with which the author seeks to demonstrate his argument. Unlike the scientist, however, the writer of SF is free to fabricate much of his "data," although he is subject to certain strictures. He must not, for example, directly contradict the established facts of science. Above all, he must make the content of the narration plausible to the reader, which is ultimately a matter of literary technique.

(i) Setting

The generic presuppositions of SF require that the imaginary world be different from our own, and that the author impress the difference upon the reader. At the same time the reader must be persuaded to accept the imaginary world as a real and plausible environment. Thus the "exploration" of the imaginary world which is conducted in SF has a complex effect on the reader, one involving elements of both alienation and familiarization or "domestication," as H.G. Wells called it.[22] The element of alienation itself is far from simple with regard to its referents and operation. At first the reader is struck by the strangeness of the imaginary world, but the impression gives way to a sense of familiarity. Concomitantly, the successful "domestication" of the reader in the imaginary world temporarily alienates him from the "real" world. He comes to look upon his own spatial and temporal environment with a certain distance or detachment. The subjective alienation corresponds to, and is amplified by, the actual distance—usually both physical and temporal—which separates the two worlds. The inhabitants of the imaginary world themselves may refer to the reader's own world as a spatially and temporally distant world peopled—or at least once inhabited—by strange beings with equally strange ideas and behavior. After the reader ceases reading, his sense of the alien nature of his own world subsides. But he may well retain a sense of relativity and mutability, a new appreciation of the position of his world and himself in the immense expanse of time, space, and the possible forms of individual existence and social organization. The reader may also reflect more dispassionately upon the imaginary world with which he had once been so familiar. More and more he may comprehend how alien the imaginary world actually is.

Both effects, alienation and familiarization, are created simultaneously by the very process of narration. Since the fundamental aim of SF is the evocation of an entire imaginary world, the apt presentation of setting, although it is a major part of all realistic narrative fiction, is crucial. In longer works descriptions of landscape (or "spacescape") may be quite elaborate; in short stories a few details and allusions often must suffice. As might be expected, writers and readers pay particular attention to introductory scenes. The opening paragraphs of Robert A. Heinlein's novel *Red Planet* (1949) illustrate how a subtle but vibrant and effective balance between the senses of alienation and familiarization can be created by the careful mixture of familiar objects, alien objects, and even seemingly alien elements which turn out to be familiar ones viewed from an alien perspective:

> The thin air of Mars was chill but not really cold. It was not yet winter in southern latitudes and the daytime temperature was usually above freezing.
>
> The queer creature standing outside the door of a dome-shaped building was generally manlike in appearance, but no human being ever had a head like that. A thing like a coxcomb jutted out above the skull, the eye lenses were wide and staring, and the front of the face stuck out like a snout. The unearthly appearance was increased by a pattern of black and yellow tiger stripes covering the entire head.
>
> The creature...opened the outer door of the building and stepped inside...A loudspeaker over the inner door shouted in a booming bass, "Well? Who is it? Speak up! Speak up!"
>
> The visitor... grasped its ugly face and pushed and lifted it to the top of its head. Underneath was disclosed the face of an Earth-human boy. [The outer "face" is part of a breathing device necessary on Mars— WBF.]

Detailed and scientifically accurate descriptions of imaginary settings are showpieces of scientific knowledge and literary skill in SF, and the passage quoted here is by no means an exceptionally complex example.

In their scenic descriptions writers of SF tend to favor—at least in third-person narration—uncomplicated syntax and a matter-of-fact tone which do not deter the reader from focusing his attention on the scene itself. Blunt, vivid, even garish scene-painting is preferred, except where it is felt that subtlety and intricacy, despite the risks of delaying the plot or confusing the reader with truly incidental detail, will help gain his credence by suggesting that the imaginary world, if it can be described with such leisurely precision, must be real and the narrator superbly familiar with it. The narrator usually does not speculate extensively about his observations or otherwise encourage doubt about the reality of the setting by drawing attention to his own existence and subjectivity.

The writers of SF, mindful of the need to get the story underway and keep it moving, have evolved a number of conventions which facilitate the concise but detailed exposition of setting, or at least persuade the reader that a wealth of information has been presented. Experienced readers, conversant with genuine scientific speculation and conditioned by their previous reading of SF, are acquainted with many imaginary environments, particularly the planets of the Solar System. For decades readers of SF about Mars, for example, were encouraged to expect or, where narrative time was short, to conjure up for themselves a picture of a cold, dry place, a red desert of sand and rock inhabited, presently or previously, by an ancient race of canal-builders culturally more advanced than our own species, but, because of Mars' weaker gravity and the evolutionary selection of cerebral traits, physically less robust.[23] Many other settings have become more or less conventional in SF, and may be evoked economically by the use of short-hand terms which, like Heinlein's "G-type star" in *Time for the Stars* (1956), are familiar to the experienced reader. Like all artistic conventions, those of SF may be overused and therefore degenerate into stereotypes. Moreover, later scientific research can demonstrate the inaccuracy of SF conventions and thus render them obsolete. The more sophisticated writers are aware of both the benefits and the dangers of such conventions, and they strive to create new variations and adapt to new research. Occasionally they also satirize the use of conventions, as Heinlein seems to do in his allusions to "Marsopolis" and "Venusburg" in the short story "The Green Hills of Earth" (1947).

(ii) Character

Since the imaginary world is almost always inhabited, whether by terrestrial humans or alien beings, the description of imaginary societies, including government, history, cultural achievements and daily life, is also a legitimate part of SF. The writer enjoys considerable latitude in the kind of society which he conceives and the amount of attention he gives to it. If individual characters or scientific ideas are the major focus of interest, the imaginary society is sketched in only briefly. Even so, the author will still construct it carefully, for incongruities can affect the believability of the rest of the imaginary world. Often, however, the imaginary society itself is the chief interest and consequently becomes the subject of elaborate description.

In conceiving imaginary societies and their individual inhabitants the author is free to select patterns from all of human history and from other forms of terrestrial life. But certain familiar historical "analogs" recur frequently. In other SF the imaginary society, whether terrestrial or alien, is patterned on less familiar cultures or on the social organization of other species. H.G. Wells' *War of the Worlds* (1897), for example, is the ancestor of many stories about alien beings who resemble insects or other invertebrates. Sometimes, as in Olaf Stapledon's *Last and First Men* (1930), the author envisions a world in which the successors of *homo sapiens* have evolved into beings radically different from ourselves in physical appearance and social organization. The actual disparity between the imaginary society and that of the reader is less important than the author's ability to inspire the dual effects of alienation and familiarization, which is a matter of conceptual and literary skills.

Students of literary types would consider the stock of terrestrial human characters in SF rather primitive and monotonous. Early SF, particularly, is thickly populated with amazing heroes, dastardly villains, threatened maidens, and powerful, mysterious sages. Such figures were appropriated from myth, the fairy tale, and popular melodrama which, as Northrop Frye argues in his *Anatomy of Criticism*, reflect the basic mode of romance. Mature SF has progressed considerably beyond its roots in popular romance and pulp fiction. Yet until the mid-Sixties and the "New Wave," terrestrial human characters in SF generally remained conventional, and relatively little effort was devoted to the portrayal of psychologically complex or highly unusual terrestrial human characters. Most often, indeed, the protagonist in SF is still male. But at least there is a wide range in age, from adolescence or even infancy to old age—a span which may indeed be great in SF; Heinlein's Lazarus Long, hero of "Methuselah's Children" (1941) and *Time Enough for Love* (1973), is several thousand vigorous years old. Although fairly rare, female protagonists are not totally absent, especially in more recent texts. Women who are quite emanicipated personally and professionally appear frequently in SF, if often in only minor roles. The presence of such figures may be due less to political activism than to the recurrent tendency of SF to generate the features of the imaginary world by inversion of salient characteristics of our own.

In keeping with its special intentionality SF has also evolved a distinctly new type of terrestrial human character, one which is both normal and conventional in many respects but, with regard to our own world, quite abnormal. Many of the terrestrial human characters in SF are instances of the "sub-species" *homo futurus*, as Vera Graaf (1971) calls it. Various writers of SF have invented similar expressions. As beings fully conscious of science and technology they are quite in harmony with their futuristic surroundings. While some—but not as many as might be supposed—are scientists or rocket pilots, many are quite ordinary people who, as inhabitants of their own future worlds, are familiar with science and technology as a matter of course. Indeed they are not nearly as fascinated by imaginary science and technology, or for that matter any of the other "everyday" features of their own worlds, as the reader is, for what to us is imaginary and therefore striking is to them a natural part of their "real" world. While for some critical readers such characters, and others which are often presented favorably in SF, are too rational and too preoccupied with science, the best examples are quite human. The *homo futurus* and similar characters reinforce the reader's sense of plausibility by satisfying the desires for wish-fulfillment and for identification with figures who are, in their own way, as "normal" and yet as exceptionally well-informed about science as the reader may conceive himself to be.

The most striking, even notorious contribution of SF to the stock of literary characters is its repertory of figures which, from the customary perspective and in traditional parlance, might be regarded as non-"human." Such characters, whether alien, terrestrial but quasi-human, or mechanical, are often conceived and portrayed with greater psychological subtlety and "humanity" than ordinary terrestrial human beings, for the examination of imaginary consciousness is a legitimate and important part of the basic intentionality of SF.

The imaginary aliens of SF vary greatly, from anthropoid beings ("humanoids") who closely resemble contemporary terrestrial humans in appearance and intellect, to strange creatures virtually incomprehensible in their cultural superiority, their loathsomeness and hostility, or simply in their unearthly physiology, psychology and social organization. The author's conception of aliens is influenced by available scientific information, the treatment of aliens in other SF, his own ideological predilections, and his assessment of the contributions the alien species may make to the goals of entertainment and edification. Often—whether intentionally or not—an alien figure or race is given the features of some familiar human stereotype. In some SF aliens are viewed with little insight or amiability; often they seem to be crude allegories of national enemies of the moment, whether the hordes of Asia, the militaristic Germans, or the Russian Communists. But the transferral of stereotypical human characteristics to an alien species can add a new dimension to the stereotype, and may serve not only to encourage the reader's sense of plausibility but also to suggest that certain traits, wherever they are encountered, are touchstones of what is human. An honest and at times anguished investigation of the notion that Man might not be the crown of creation after all is not rare in SF about aliens. If the idea is not original as a philosophical or theological theme, SF adds to it the vividness of fictional presentation and the insights of astronomers, exobiologists and exopsychologists. The theme of alien life can also provoke serious discussion of the nature of consciousness and intelligence and the limits of comprehensibility. Wells' *War of the Worlds*, published in 1897, is recognized as the chief progenitor of modern stories about superior alien species, but in the same year Kurd Lasswitz explored the theme independently in *Auf zwei Planeten*. Among the best modern exemplars of such SF are the short stories "To Serve Man" (1950) by Damon Knight and "First Contact" (1945) by Murray Leinster, Hal Clement's *Iceworld* (1951), and Stanisław Lem's novel *Solaris* (1961).

SF often portrays beings who are the offspring of terrestrial humans but who are not so different in their appearance, sensibility or abilities that they constitute a separate species. The monster in Mary Shelley's novel *Frankenstein* (1818) is an important ancestor of the type, which since then has undergone considerable elaboration and transformation, especially in response to the work of Darwin and to later research in genetics. Examples of quasi-human characters in early modern SF include the sub-human Morlocks and superhuman but effete Eloi in Wells' *Time Machine* (1895) and the title figure in Stapledon's *Odd John* (1935). Writers of SF about quasi-human beings usually explain their super- or sub-human creations by referring to genetic changes induced by natural evolution, radiation, unexpected mutation, or adaptation to new environments. Quite often the new "men," although they may pose an evolutionary threat to *homo sapiens*, are treated sympathetically as the rightful evolutionary successors of a less-than-perfect present human race, or as instances of the human tendency to persecute the exceptional, including even—or especially—the superior.

Machines also appear frequently as genuine characters in SF. The traditional "robot" of more or less human appearance enjoyed its greatest popularity in older Anglo-American SF, although the word itself owes its currency in English, as well as other languages, to the very successful SF play *R.U.R.* ("Rossum's Universal Robots," 1921), by the Czech dramatist Karel Čapek (1890-1938). In recent SF the mechanical character often appears as a vast, decentralized computer with extremely high intelligence and even self-awareness, like "Mike" in *The Moon Is a Harsh Mistress* (1966) by Heinlein or "HAL 9000" in the film *2001: A Space Odyssey* (1968), based on "The Sentinel" (1951) and *Childhood's End* (1950) by Arthur C. Clarke. The figure of the intelligent, sentient machine can be employed to explore many themes: the creation of artificial life, the complexity of artificially created intelligence, the possible dangers of advanced technology, the limitations of human intelligence, and the implications of science and technology for the definition of life itself.

Isaac Asimov deals with all these ideas in his numerous robot stories (1942ff.; 1950, 1964). The "Three Laws of Robotics" which he formulated have been adopted as a convention by several other writers. Other well-known works of SF about machines include "With Folded Hands" (1947) by Jack Williamson, "Killdozer" (1944) by Theodore Sturgeon, and Stanisław Lem's recent volumes of robot stories, *Bajki robotow* [*Robot Fables*] (1964) and *Cyberiada* [*The Cyberiad*] (1965).

(iii) Plot

In SF, as in much other literature, plot serves as a source of entertaining events and as a vehicle for the portrayal of character. To fulfill these functions SF has adopted many of the traditional plot devices and structural patterns of mainstream fiction, but it has also developed some idiosyncratic approaches. Yet whatever the degree of conventionality, SF—or at least good SF—attempts above all to make science, technology, and the distinctive features of the imaginary world indispensable parts of the plot.

Writers of SF have not been loath to explore and exploit the vast expanses of space and time which science and the assumptions of their literary form encourage them to contemplate. One of the most persistent plot structures in SF is the sweeping narration of momentous events whose import can be literally universal. Multitudes of worlds and the immense depths of space itself furnish the scenic backdrop, and the course of action may extend over centuries or even eons. Memorable characters may appear, but they are far less important than the exhibition of amazing technology and the panoramic description of imaginary worlds and their histories. Examples of such fiction include both the early "space operas" and the maturer "future histories" of Stapledon, Heinlein and Asimov. In keeping with the predispositions of romance, as discussed by Northrop Frye, the rhythm of events in such SF tends to be episodic and the psychological development of character minimal. If there is a single central character, like Richard Seaton in E.E. Smith's series of *Skylark* novels (1933 ff.), he usually resembles the traditional picaresque hero.

Often SF focuses as much on the journey itself as on the worlds or times which are visited. Travel through space and time is a prominent part of SF not only because it has recurrently borrowed the devices of romance, but also because it has traditionally emphasized those areas of science and technology—astronomy, physics, mathematics, rocketry and nuclear engineering—which have transformed the extraterrestrial cosmos from a philosophical abstraction or religious "Heaven" into a real environment which might be explored like any other. Certainly it is often legitimate to interpret the journey in SF metaphorically, as an image of individual or collective human existence. Most often the journey has favorable connotations. Rather than a state of expiatory or simply meaningless wandering, it is regarded as the reflection of the energy of civilization and an apt expression of the personalities of its bravest and most intelligent representatives. But the metaphorical interpretation of the journey, even though it may be valid, should not be allowed to obscure the literal aspect of the narration. Although some writers of such SF might agree that they are commenting symbolically about life in general, most would aver that they are indeed writing about space travel itself, not merely using it as a vehicle or metaphor.

The same misconception—the inclination to seek a "real" meaning behind the objects and events the author describes—has led to the misinterpretation or exaggeration of elements of narrative content as supposedly sexual symbols. Contrary to some explications, in genuine SF the rocketship shooting through space is not—or at least is not primarily—a crude phallic image. In fact, not all spacecraft in SF are of the requisite shape. But if the rocket is indeed long and pointed, there are ample scientific reasons for the design. As the writers themselves often point out, such a shape is best suited for passage through the planetary atmosphere before or after the craft travels through "deep" space. For similar reasons, the space traveler's or rocket inventor's longing and love for space, and the description of space itself as an empty, dark vacuum rather than a luminiferous ether, cannot satisfactorily be explained merely by alluding knowingly to the concepts of psychoanalytic interpretation.[24] The argument can be generalized. SF is not "merely" a variety of traditional romance which uses modern science as a vehicle. Rather it is a form of fiction whose authors, consciously or unconsciously, sometimes tap the resources of romance in order to advance what is, at least in genuine SF, their primary purpose: the examination of imaginary worlds determined by science and technology.

SF, then, tends to emphasize the literal significance of its content. In other words, the establishment of the fictive physical reality of the imaginary world is at least as important as the exploration of its possible metaphorical implications. The accentuation of the concrete in SF has likely reinforced the preference for overt conflict, another of the basic structural patterns of the genre. Like much popular literature, and even some kinds of high-brow literature, SF is pervaded by physical conflict, often quite violent, in which good and evil are clearly differentiated. But here once again SF, in accord with its own ends, differs from the dominant pattern of recent literature. Physical confrontation between terrestrial human characters is certainly not absent in SF; yet neither is psychological and moral conflict, even within a single figure. But SF is distinguished from much other recent literature by its strong emphasis on the struggle between Man and the external world, including both inanimate objects and—an exclusive feature of SF—the inhabitants of other worlds. Terrestrial humanity may come into contact with alien life, and entire cultures may either destroy each other, attain some degree of reconciliation, or part with the recognition that they are mutually incompatible or simply incomprehensible to each other. SF is equally fascinated by the individual or collective struggle of Man to establish himself on environmentally hostile worlds or to survive in space against the inexorable laws of physics. Many short stories, particularly, revolve about the successful or often unsuccessful attempt to surmount a single technological or theoretical problem, such as the creation of a major new technological device or the threat of disaster in space or on other planets. Concentration on a single scientific or technological point, however, does not free the author from the obligation to construct an entire imaginary world and make it tangible and credible to the reader.

Despite its emphasis on concrete objects and physical action, SF does not necessarily lack all interest in the examination of personality and the effects of experience on the development of human character. Numerous works attempt to explore the nature of alien consciousness. Elaborate psychological examination of normal terrestrial human characters is not a striking feature of most SF, whether because the writers are weak in the exposition of character, as has been charged, or because SF is concerned more with other matters. In some SF, however, one encounters a particularly interesting narrative structure much like that of the traditional *Bildungsroman*, the examination of the maturation of an individual. Several of Heinlein's novels, among them juvenile works like *Farmer in the Sky* (1950) and *Time for the Stars* (1956), as well as his controversial Hugo Award winners *Starship Troopers* (1959) and *Stranger in a Strange Land* (1961), are novels of education. SF has also adapted the form to its special interest in Man the species as well as Man the individual. In works like Stapledon's *Last and First Men* (1930), Clarke's *Childhood's End* (1950), and Lasswitz' *Auf zwei Planeten* (1897), the subject of *Bildung* is all of humanity.

The "New Wave" SF authors of the Sixties, and such foreign writers as Stanisław Lem and Herbert W. Franke, have attempted to expand the structural repertory of SF by adopting—sometimes with considerable delay—several of the techniques of mainstream experimental literature, such as stream-of-consciousness narration or distortion of temporal sequence. Another narrative pattern, one encountered even in early modern SF, evidences a similar departure from "mainstream" conventionality. In some SF both plot and character may be reduced to a minimal framework or even wholly eliminated. The result is not a literature of the absurd, but rather a form of "documentary" fiction which can be used to present an imaginary world or tell the story of a scientific idea with insight, irony and sometimes humor. The typical and most effective form is the imitation of scientific argumentation to create pseudo-scientific texts, which may range from light-hearted parodies to serious investigations of the puzzling aspects of, for example, non-Euclidean geometry or the theory of relativity. A famous early example is *Flatland* (1884) by Edwin A. Abbott (1838-1926), a story of visits to worlds composed of one, two or many dimensions. Also well known are L. Sprague De Camp's short "treatise" on "Language for Time Travelers" (1938), and Isaac Asimov's series of "articles" on the imaginary chemical "thiotimoline" (1948, 1953, 1960).

Larger structural elements, especially the relation of narrated time to narrative time, are treated quite conservatively in most SF written before the last two decades, and even in many recent works. Customarily events are narrated in strict chronological sequence, although other conventions of traditional realistic fiction may be employed, such as multiple coordinate plots, the initiation of narration *in medias res*, and short "flashbacks." Such devices can be used to good effect in attacking some of the recurrent problems of SF. The "flashback" is well suited to the recapitulation of imaginary future history from a perspective located still further in the future. The same technique, and the commencement of narration in the midst of the action as well, permit the narrator to introduce masses of unfamiliar, often initially implausible background material after the reader has been drawn into the narration. But radical experiments with non-linear chronological structures are rare, except in recent SF, perhaps because such distortions can easily interfere with the attempt to establish the fictive reality and plausibility of the imaginary world. And if the author wishes to explore the paradoxes of time, the resources of his genre make it possible for him to do so in a very literal and striking manner by taking time travel as his theme.

The Literary Style of SF

The literary style of SF has often been disparaged as crude, even semi-literate, either because it is allegedly drab and simplistic, or because it is highly colored and awkwardly involute. Apologists for SF themselves concede that much SF of lesser quality warrants such disapprobation. They also point out—and students of popular literature would and do agree—that much other literature merits the same criticism.[25]

Mature SF is much less inclined to one of the two extremes usually cited by detractors of SF, that of emotional excess and linguistic extravagance. The common style of such SF gives the impression, rather, of being plain, unambitious, even artless. It is "transparent" in the sense that the reader is almost unaware of its presence or nature as a literary style.

I would suggest not only that the unobtrusive diction favored in better SF is not necessarily artless, but also that the impression of artlessness it conveys is consonant with the basic intention of SF. Like setting, character and plot, the "transparent" style facilitates the reader's acceptance of the imaginary world as a familiar and plausible place. Any inappropriate style, whatever its features, would hinder this purpose, for it is the author's vision, not the language through which it is presented, that is the chief focus of interest and evaluation. A style which pointedly called attention to itself and to the text as an artifice, whether for the sake of demonstrating the technical virtuosity of the author or of speculating about the paradoxes of fiction, would actively undermine the effort to induce a sense of fictive reality. The reader, who desires to accept fiction as reality, if only temporarily and conditionally, would thereby be reminded that he is reading "mere" fiction. Only in certain exceptional and revealing instances does SF strive to attract the reader's attention to language itself. Thus neologisms, quotation of imaginary languages, and fictive "documents" reinforce the reader's belief in the imaginary world by serving as examples of the "actual" language of that world or by claiming in effect that the text is something other than an invented narration or a piece of "literature."

The general "non-style" or "transparent" style of SF actually consists of at least two related but distinct types of diction. The language usually employed in the overall narrative framework is straightforward, moderately paced, impersonal and non-figurative. Either first-person or, more commonly, third-person narration may be used. The first-person narrator is usually a distinct figure. He, she or—if the narrator is not a terrestrial human—perhaps "it" often takes part in the action or is at least privy to important events. The third-person narrator is most often an anonymous voice whose own personality ostensibly does not "color" the reportage. In either case, setting, character and action are presented in a "matter-of-fact" tone which is neither tense and stiff nor casual and imprecise. Rather than engaging in subjective commentary or psychological speculation, the narrative voice typically relates facts, records observations, and describes objects, although the omniscient narrator reserves the right on occasion to transcribe the utterances and thoughts of the characters in language which reproduces their own emotion and manner of speaking.

The temporal perspectives assumed by the narrative persona may vary. Sometimes the narrator speaks as an interested if modest observer of contemporary events, or even a major participant in them. In more than a few instances, however, the narration is related from the more dispassionate perspective of someone who views the events he recounts from an even later time-period; if so, there are then two imaginary worlds, one enclosing the other. Whatever the temporal frame of reference, the typical narrator speaks in a manner which, though it need not lack emotion, implicitly expresses the assumption that the imaginary world, including its past, is real, precisely because it is the narrator's own world. The reader, too, is tacitly assumed to be contemporaneous with the imaginary world and the narrator. In many utopias, by contrast, and in much related early SF—Bellamy's *Looking Backward* (1887) offers a ready illustration—a narrator from the writer's own day travels to the imaginary world and then relates his experiences and observations to readers of his own time and place. Such a narrative stance undermines the effort to evoke the senses of credibility and fictive reality so vital to SF, unless the author also introduces a time-machine or similar device to establish the plausibility of the narrator's temporal journey. In more abstract terms, the forward leap in time within the text calls unwelcome attention to the fictional character of the narration by both emphasizing and confusing the distinction between the real and imaginary worlds.

When the presentation of future history warrants special breadth and detail, the narrator often abandons his "non-style" anonymity and adopts instead the stance and diction of a historian, whether scholarly or, more usually, popular. Similarly, the narrator may assume the role and speech of a scientist or historian of science when imaginary science and technology are the focus of interest. The shift in narrative strategy may not be marked in any obvious way in the text. Sometimes, however, the description of future history or imaginary science may be presented as an excerpt from an imaginary non-fictional text, such as an encyclopedia or other document. In Asimov's *Foundation* trilogy, for example, the *"Encyclopedia Galactica,* 116th ed." is the source of numerous footnotes or direct quotations. The change of roles and modes of discourse described here should be viewed less as a radical alteration than a modification and intensification of the basic narrative stance of SF. The scholarly voice merely enhances the distinctly authoritative tone implicitly present in the diction of the typical impersonal narrator, and the stylistic devices of historical or scientific discourse are often but formalized versions of those encountered in the "transparent" style. It might even be argued that the historical or scientific style in SF is itself a "non-style." It is not a literary or fictional style but rather a mode of discourse which is associated with non-fiction and therefore carries a high implicit "truth-value"; that is, of course, precisely why it is used.

Writers of SF have devised or adopted and refined a number of other characteristic rhetorical devices. Like the typically impersonal narrative voice, these stylistic techniques, which can be observed even in the choice of single words, serve to encourage the senses of plausibility and fictive reality. While not all of them appear in the works of every writer of SF, collectively they delineate a distinctive science-fictional style.

The linguistic apparatus which literature appropriates to its own ends reflects and in turn depends on the function of communication in the real world, a function which in some measure exists, and came to exist, independently of literature. The very grammatical structure of the framework of narrative fiction— usually the past tense and always the indicative mood— substantiates, presupposes, and implicitly reinforces the reader's tentative but usually benevolent willingness to believe in the non-fictional nature of the fiction. The typical narrator of mainstream realistic fiction, as Thomas Mann remarks in the Preface to *Der Zauberberg* (1924), is "[ein] raunende[r] Beschwörer des Imperfekts," an unobtrusive but loquacious voice which, using the past tense, insistently conjures and sustains the reader's belief in the "reality" of the fiction. The unkind observer might suggest that much literature capitalizes, almost parasitically, on the primary function of language—the communication of genuine information—in order to deceive the reader. But in return the reader, who is more or less aware of the deception anyway, is entertained and sometimes even edified.

If, then, the very use of the indicative past tense for narration has a rhetorical function in much "mainstream" literature, that intentionality is all the more pronounced in SF, where the imaginary world is frequently located in the future and is, by definition, always non-existent or at least clearly not identical to the "real" world. Indeed there exists no grammatical form which could represent a world which is viewed subjectively as real and past but which at the same time is regarded conceptually as hypothetical, even future. Neither "might be," "might become," nor "might have been" is or would be suitable, although SF often implies that its imaginary worlds might be more than speculations about the future. The non-existent "might come to be or become" or "might come to have been or become" would be the logical tense and mood of SF.

But to use any form except the customary tense and mood of narration would in fact undermine the intended effect of SF. A text written in the logically "correct" tense and mood—some sort of "conditional future preterite subjunctive"—would immediately stymie any effort to evoke the impressions of reality and plausibility, as would a work written wholly in the imaginary language of equally imaginary alien beings. In the former case, from the outset the reader would be prevented from indulging his desire to believe conditionally and temporarily, but nevertheless "sincerely," in the reality of the imaginary world—until such time, highly unlikely of course, that the new grammatical form had itself become an accepted linguistic and literary convention and no longer drew any attention to itself. In the latter case, that of a text written in an imaginary alien language, communication between text and reader would break down completely, unless one chooses to perceive some kind of communicated content or "meta-content" in the abstract play of sounds and signs; that, however, is not part of the intentionality of SF. Therefore SF must necessarily make use of the conventions of tense and mood employed in other narration, and in fact does so with alacrity, originality and—from the viewpoint of the aesthetician if not the "sincere" reader—irony. In other words, SF eagerly and systematically exploits the linguistic practices of realistic fiction, which in turn exploits the genuine communicative functions of language itself.

Writers of SF, as might be surmised from the foregoing discussion of general narrative stances and the particularly fragile relation between real and imaginary worlds in their form of literature, are not at all unaware of the implications of tense and mood usage. Sometimes they capitalize in elaborate ways on the conventions of past-tense narration in order to assert still more strongly the plausibility of the imaginary world. In SF, the past or past perfect tenses refer of course to the entire past time of the *imaginary* world, part of which consists of recent events which "might come to have become," including those which may transpire during the course of the narration. For the inhabitants of the imaginary world, among them perhaps the contemporaneous narrator, such events belong to the more or less distant past, while for us they are usually part of some hypothetical future time, despite the past tense used in the narration.

But sometimes the writer will exploit even more subtly and elaborately the conventions available to him. If the narrator is an inhabitant of a still later age, perhaps even a professional historian, the events he recounts may be parts of a time long past. Therefore in SF the past (or past perfect) tense may also be used to refer to a time which, from the perspective of the narrator, is a remote and, as it were, "historical" part of the "past."

Sometimes this doubly "past" time is, with regard to the reader and writer, actually still the future. Thus the inhabitants of the imaginary world, like those pictured in the opening sentences of Fredric Brown's story "Expedition" (1957), may survey the "earliest" stages, recent "history" and "present" state of manned voyages to other planets—none of which ventures, for us, have actually yet come to have become:

> "The first major expedition to Mars," said the history professor, "the one which followed the preliminary exploration by one-man scout ships and aimed to establish a permanent colony, led to a number of problems...."

Elsewhere the "historical" past tense may refer specifically to our own present time. If so, the technique has an especially ironic effect, for the radical change in perspective alienates the reader from his own supposedly real and presently-existing world. Often the author and narrator employ a detached tone of voice and an altered vocabulary to emphasize the historical distance and changed cultural perspective from which the future views our own world:

> I found myself mulling over a discussion in our class in History and Moral Philosophy. Mr. Dubois was talking about the disorders that preceded the breakup of the North American republic, back in the XXth century.... The Terror had not been just in North America—Russia and the British Isles had it, too, as well as other places. But it reached its peak in North America shortly before things went to pieces. (Heinlein, *Starship Troopers* [1959], Ch.8)

The sense of "historicity" in SF may be evoked by yet another technique, the introduction of "documents" ostensibly produced by the inhabitants of the imaginary world. Particularly popular are excerpts from archives, historical works or military communications whose source and language are "official":

But Ducem Barr waved him silent. He read the message quickly.
FROM: AMMEL BRODRIG, ENVOY EXTRAORDINARY OF HIS
IMPERIAL MAJESTY, PRIVY SECRETARY OF THE COUNCIL,
AND PEER OF THE REALM.
TO: BEL RIOSE, MILITARY GOVERNOR OF SIWENNA, GENERAL
OF THE IMPERIAL FORCES, AND PEER OF THE REALM.
I GREET YOU.
PLANET #1120 NO LONGER RESISTS. THE PLANS OF
OFFENSE AS OUTLINED CONTINUE SMOOTHLY. THE ENEMY
WEAKENS VISIBLY AND THE ULTIMATE ENDS IN VIEW WILL
SURELY BE GAINED. (Asimov, *Foundation and Empire* [1952], Ch. 8).

Diary entries, letters, newspaper articles, and laboratory notes are also frequently encountered. Such documental inserts, like scientific or historical discourse, have the appeal of an implicitly high truth-value, as well as the virtue of conveying necessary background material in concise form. The presentation of future history or imaginary science in the style of non-fictional prose can also be viewed as an extended version of the documental insert, although the author may not explicitly frame the discourse as a quotation.

The reader, who is perhaps skeptical by inclination and quite likely conversant with the conventions of SF, may choose to demand that the author offer more than authoritative diction, copious detail and intermittent documentation before he will concede that what he is reading is not just a fiction. Over the centuries writers have devised or elaborated a number of stratagems or conventions to allay such doubts. The documentary technique, for example, may be expanded to encompass the entire text, except perhaps for a short narrative introduction. Two works of early SF by Poe, "MS Found in a Bottle" (1833) and "The Balloon-Hoax" (1844), are passed off in this manner, the first as a real manuscript and the second as a newspaper article. The same ploy, and others more refined as well, are to be found in later SF. The narrator of Heinlein's *Time for the Stars* (1956), for example, explains that he is writing his narration as a journal to be read by his psychiatrist. A number of short stories, like "Expedition" (1943), by Anthony Boucher (pseud. of William Anthony Parker White), consist of a collection of imaginary documents or journal entries; so too does the classic scientific utopia *We* (1921/27) by the anti-Bolshevik Russian author Yevgeny Zamyatin (1884-1937). But perhaps the most famous work of "documentary" SF is Orson Welles' version of H.G. Wells' *War of the Worlds*. Broadcast on Halloween, 1938, the play precipitated outbreaks of mass hysteria and, apparently, several suicides. The consequent furore contributed much to Wells' decision to leave the

United States.

A closer examination of the way SF deals with imaginary science, the specific type of content which distinguishes it from other literature, yields a still more detailed picture of the rhetorical strategies of the genre and a better understanding of their function. Critics hostile to SF often dismiss its imaginary science as "fantastic." The serious author of SF, however, aims to transform the initial impression of incredibility, felt even by the benevolent reader, into one of fictive reality. The importance of the attempt to establish the plausibility of imaginary science cannot be exaggerated. At the same time, the standards of plausibility ideally applied to imaginary science and technology in SF are stricter than those by which the other features of the imaginary world are judged. The reader can be presumed to take special interest in the imaginary science, and to be more informed about science than the typical readers of most other fiction. Moreover, because science enjoys the image of being a precise discipline, the writer of SF, like the scientist, is expected to have at his command far more "hard" facts and to indulge far less in generalities than, say, the philosopher or social scientist.

The author of SF, therefore, finds himself in the precarious position of having to describe imaginary technological devices or theories with such convincing accuracy that the reader might well wonder, in effect, why the author has indeed not patented his invention or claimed credit for the theory. Such objections are not actually expressed, of course, but the skeptical stance described here is part of the relationship assumed between writer and reader in SF. The readers' columns in the Golden Age Anglo-American SF magazines amply demonstrate how carefully many readers judge the description of imaginary science, and how much those judgments affect their determinations of aesthetic value. Correspondingly, the intensity of the effort to "domesticate" imaginary science and similar types of content is reflected, in mature SF at least, in the liberal and skillful employment of a diverse stock of rhetorical devices, ranging from single words to long, carefully structured descriptive passages.

Neologisms are important in SF, for names must be provided not only for new technology but also for new places, new cultural entities, and new characters who are often alien beings. Older SF, and modern works of lesser distinction, often make do with nonsense syllables for alien words, and with vague allusions to "ray-guns," "time machines," other "dimensions," and so forth.

Modern SF of better quality employs neologisms with greater sophistication and subtlety. The writer may devise neologisms by varying actual technological terminology or by altering the meanings of common names for familiar objects, thus suggesting their further evolution in the future. A famous instance of the latter technique is Heinlein's "slidewalk."[26] An imaginary device or substance, like the notorious anti-gravity invention "cavorite" in Wells' *First Men in the Moon* (1901), may also be named for its purported inventor, just as so many real substances, natural or artificial, are named for their discoverers or inventors. Many other names for imaginary technological objects, sometimes even those of alien cultures, are devised by combining Latin or Greek words, as are in fact many genuine scientific terms.

Scientific nomenclature, whether genuine or imaginary, can be employed with particular effect in the invention of place-names. New environments, artificial or natural, are often given Latinized names. Variations on the term "Circum-Terra," used by Heinlein in *Between Planets* (1951) as a name for a giant space-station, can be found in the works of numerous writers. Latin or "official" astronomical terms, such as "Luna," "Terra" or "Sol III," are also frequently used to refer to natural celestial bodies. While the device can easily degenerate into ridiculous mannerism, when employed properly and sparingly it can contribute much to the desired effects of SF. Imaginary international terms suggest the future evolution of a unified global culture which treats science and technology in a matter-of-fact manner. Even more important are the senses of alienation and familiarization which such expressions encourage by obliterating the distinction between our own world—familiar, terrestrial, and thus "real"—and the rest of the Universe.

Writers of SF also frequently draw on analogies to our own world to devise names for imaginary places, as well as for cultural objects and institutions. Examples include Asimov's *"Encyclopedia Galactica,"* mentioned earlier, and the "I.T.T." or "Interplanetary Telephone and Televideo Corporation" in Heinlein's *Between Planets.* One of the imaginary place names in the latter novel shows how a writer may reinforce the impression of plausibility by creating a new place-name by analogy to a real terrestrial place name which itself was produced by analogy. "New Auckland" on Venus, recently settled by colonists from Earth, is named for Auckland in New Zealand, which in turn was named for the Dutch province by early explorers.

Alien or future human languages constitute one of the most

important types of neologism in SF. In some works single words or even rather lengthy utterances in imaginary languages may actually be "quoted." Alien speech is often modeled quite simply and evidently on certain actual languages. In English-language SF, at least, favorable associations are suggested typically by liquid consonants and by vowels in final position, while harsher sounds may denote threatening characteristics.[27] Writers of maturer SF tend to treat alien languages in a less obvious and mechanical manner, perhaps because they sense the danger of reducing the imaginary world to a poorly disguised allegory of our own. It is, however, quite plausible to employ the principles of linguistics to construct future human languages which have evolved from present ones. Thus in SF about future societies of terrestrial humans it is often claimed or tacitly assumed that human speech is either a streamlined version of a present language, a mixture of several tongues, or an artificially created common language such as "Basic," "Interlingua," or "System Speech." But here, as is so often the case in the narrative strategy of SF, moderation and allusiveness are virtues. Seldom does the author attempt to create and reproduce an entirely imaginary alien or human language. Rather he limits his "citations" to a few words or phrases which are especially significant and, because of the context, readily comprehensible, yet whose referents—technology, social institutions, everyday objects, or fundamental psychological concepts—are strikingly alien and therefore "untranslatable." Too many citations from unfamiliar languages might well delay the story, hinder comprehension, or undermine the sense of plausibility. It is therefore considered sufficient merely to plant the notion of the imaginary language in the reader's mind.

Quite different in theme and, consequently, narrative strategy are of course the many works of SF which introduce the still more provocative idea that alien life-forms, or distant descendants of present terrestrial life, may have developed other modes of sound production or even other physical senses which serve as bases for communication among conspecifics but are incomprehensible to us.

The special intentionality of SF has encouraged the invention and elaboration of at least one distinctive technique which can be observed in larger syntactical units. Often an imaginary element, perhaps even a neologism, is inserted into a series of "real" items of similar kind. The stratagem efficiently and subtly introduces imaginary content, above all the seemingly inconsequential details which collectively contribute so much to the impression of plausibility. Thus several actual or historical entities—people, events, objects—are followed by an imaginary one, often without interruption or comment, as though there were no existential difference between the imaginary item and the real ones:

> [An officer in the space corps] may be in the radiation laboratories at Oxford University, or studying interplanetary law at the Sorbonne, or he may even be as far away as Venus, at the Institute for System Studies.
> (Heinlein, *Space Cadet* [1948], Ch. 5)

> Among his minor accomplishments was a talent now rare,...the art of whistling.... He could reproduce the themes from most of the movies of the last two hundred years. He started appropriately with "Heigh-ho, heigh-ho, it's off to work we go,"...and switched quickly to the *River Kwai* song,...culminating with the theme from Sid Krassman's famous late-twentieth-century "Napoleon."
> (Clarke; *Rendezvous with Rama* [1973], Ch. 13)

In a common variation of the "serial" technique, a single imaginary term which stands alone is, by implicit but obvious analogy, derived from and associated with one or more real elements which themselves are not cited. Expressions like the ubiquitous "World War III" suggests the world wars of our century, while Asimov's "Second Galactic Empire" (*Second Foundation*) not only recalls earlier terrestrial empires, but implies as well the previous existence of a still imaginary "First Galactic Empire." Often such references have an ironic, poignant effect, for they suggest that even in the future Man is not perfect and tends to repeat the errors of history.

The description of a teleportation machine in the second chapter of Heinlein's novel *Tunnel in the Sky* (1955) can serve to show how the rhetorical devices discussed here can be combined to good effect in a lengthy exposition of an initially "fantastic" idea or object:

> It is useless to speculate as to the course of history had Jesse Evelyn Ramsbotham's parents had the good sense to name their son Bill instead of loading him with two girlish names. He might have become an All-American halfback and ended up selling bonds and adding his quota of babies to a sum already disastrous. Instead he became a mathematical physicist.
> ...Ramsbotham began fiddling with the three greatest Einsteinian equations, the two relativity equations for distance and duration and the mass-conversion equation; each contained the velocity of light. "Velocity" is first derivative, the differential of distance with respect to time; he converted those equations into differential equations, then played games with them. He would feed the results to the Rakitiac

computer, remote successor to Univac, Eniac and Maniac. While he was doing these things his hands never sweated nor did he stammer, except when he was forced to deal with the young lady who was chief programmer for the giant computer.

His first model produced a time-stasis or low-energy field no bigger than a football—but a lighted cigarette placed inside with full power setting was still burning a week later. Ramsbotham picked up the cigarette, resumed smoking and thought about it.

It would appear that Heinlein's aim is both to offer a seeming wealth of detail and to divert the reader's attention from the fact that devices like the "Ramsbotham Gate" cannot yet actually be described. To do so he adopts a semi-popular scientific or historical voice, and proceeds to present a wide-ranging theoretical, technological and historical account of the invention. Where, for obvious reasons, he cannot describe the details of the device itself or survey the process by which theory was transformed into workable technology, he shifts his and the reader's attention to an exciting picture of the invention in operation, adds personal anecdotes about the imaginary inventor, alludes to the highly-respected theories of Einstein, and introduces impressive-sounding scientific vocabulary, both real and imaginary.

Many of the rhetorical techniques used in SF can be viewed as specific instances of a narrative practice which is characteristic of the genre itself: the substitution of matter-of-fact allusion, whether in the form of brief remarks or protracted but—or perhaps therefore—obfuscatory descriptions, for the actual presentation of genuine, precise information about the imaginary world. The practice has the obvious virtue of economy, in that it permits the story to proceed with suitable dispatch, interrupted only, perhaps, by a tolerably short set-piece of condensed "background" exposition. It also helps deter the author, fond of elaboration though he may be, from undermining his own greater purpose by providing more details than the reader would be able to tolerate without becoming either bored or suspicious. Richard Gerber has pointed out the advantages of balancing copious concrete detail with sagacious allusion in utopian fiction and related literature about imaginary worlds.[28] Moreover, as Samuel Delany—himself a writer of SF—has remarked, the presentation of imaginary content in a matter-of-fact and allusive manner can induce a delayed sense of shock or alienation.[29] At first the reader scarcely notices the unfamiliar nature of the imaginary content; he thus accepts it almost without further consideration, and indeed desires to do so. Later—but only after he has tacitly given credence to the imaginary content—he absorbs the implications of the language which has been used and is shocked by the difference between his own world and the imaginary world.

But above all, the techniques of allusion and matter-of-factness directly further the primary goal of SF, which is the evocation of the impressions of fictive reality and logical plausibility. They do so by appealing to the reader's politeness as a good listener, to his desire to enter the imaginary world, and to his intellectual vanity as one supposedly conversant with the facts and speculations of science. The reader of course has no knowledge of "Ramsbotham Gates," "Sid Krassman's 'Napoleon,'" the "Institute for System Studies," or the "Second Galactic Empire." He has in fact never encountered any future technology, cinematic works, research institutions, or galactic empires—nor for that matter any other part of the imaginary world. By treating the imaginary world as though it were familiar to everyone but the reader, the narrator suggests that only an ignorant, uncouth outsider would need or request further information. The reader, for his part, may have certain standards according to which he judges reality and plausibility, but ultimately he does not want to spoil his own fun in the "game" of fiction. In effect, he invites and allows the writer to persuade him to accept the fiction—provided the writer exhibits particular effort and skill in presenting content which is especially implausible.

Value Judgments and Generic Classification in SF Criticism

Apologists of SF are given to quoting two lapidary utterances, one a neat epigram coined by the British novelist and critic Kingsley Amis, the other a blunter pronouncement offered by the veteran American SF writer and reviewer Theodore Sturgeon:

> "S.f's no good," they bellow till we're deaf.
> "But this looks good." "Well, then, it's not s.f."
>
> Ninety percent of all science fiction is crap. Ninety percent of everything is crap.

Literary criticism involves the formulation of value judgments and concepts of genre, whether or not they are expressed openly. The history of SF criticism is replete with disputes about the generic nature and quality of individual texts and of the genre as a whole. Even critics who agree in their primary observations may often draw quite disparate, even irreconcilable, conclusions from them. Detractors of SF frequently—and not always wrongly—note its relative weakness of characterization, the pervasiveness of simple plot structures, and a predilection for narrative prose which seems either too colorful or too plain. Some defenders of SF, among them Robert Conquest, found their counter-arguments on the reasonable request that SF deserves to be judged, as is most other literature, by its best achievements rather than its average or worst representatives.[30] Thus Heinlein vociferously accuses modern mainstream literature and criticism of neglecting or at least grossly misunderstanding science and technology. He also attacks modern highbrow writers for what he considers their obsession with "sick" characters, abnormal sexuality, and stylistic experimentation—charges which might now be leveled against his own more recent writings.[31] Yet Heinlein's arguments are not without merit, although they may be more valuable for what they reveal about the attitudes of a major writer of SF than for what they say about other literature.

Of greater consequence here are the ideas of those who maintain that SF, although its quality must ultimately be gauged against that of other literature, should first be evaluated according to its particular aims and principles. Robert Conquest and Martin Green have observed that the paramount importance given to psychological intricacy and structural or linguistic complexity in modern "mainstream" literature is perhaps idiosyncratic. In any case, they argue, SF is interested in other matters, above all the portrayal of Man's relation to the physical universe.[32]

In the preceding pages I have attempted to relate observations about science, imagination, theme, setting, character, plot and language in SF to a conception of its essential intentionality. Following the lead of Hans Robert Jauss and other proponents of receptional history and aesthetics, I have sought to detect the intentionality of SF and the mechanisms of its operation by examining the interaction which occurs among the presuppositions and aims of the author, the expectations and responses of the reader, and the text as a system of "signals" through which communication between writer and reader takes place.

SF, I have argued, makes use of the presuppositions and devices of conventional realistic fiction. The author of such fiction creates a world which exists within or through the text, and then invites the reader to become part of that world and to view it as "reality." Both the writer and the reader are quite aware—at least in their reflective moments—that the fictional world is a construct created by the text. But they choose to play a "game," as it were, and the text is their "gameboard." The "game" of realistic fiction consists in large part of the author's assertion that the fictional world does somehow actually "exist." The reader responds by provisionally entertaining that notion, at least during—and, if he is sane, only during—the process of reading the work of fiction *as a work of fiction*. But while he is of course interested in accepting the fiction as reality in that sense, his response must be cultivated. The elements of content and the rhetorical devices which constitute the text comprise the writer's "moves." The reader's defensive "countermoves" are expressed in an abiding skepticism or resistance to the author's bid for his concession of credibility. Offensively, the reader may pose an implicit demand for additional or more skillful moves on the part of the writer, who will seek to anticipate and satisfy that demand, both in the course of a single narration and in subsequent works created according to the same intentionality. As readers and writers accumulate experience—in other words, as the literary form develops—the "game" increases in complexity of rules and subtlety of strategy. Perhaps even variant subtypes of the basic game emerge and become popular, while others fade in vitality and appeal.

The "game" of SF is in part the same as that played in the reading of mainstream realistic fiction. An essential feature of the distinguishing intentionality of SF, however, is the insistence on the "radical discontinuity" (Scholes) that separates the imaginary world from our own world, even when the larger differences between text and "reality," between word and thing, are ignored. It is part of the author's purpose—and the reader's as well—that the reader confront and assimilate the alien nature of the imaginary world. The confrontation is not a simple one. Despite the manifest discontinuity, the reader of SF, like the reader of conventional realistic fiction, is still invited to accept the reality of the imaginary world during the act of reading, and will do so on proper persuasion.

But the same discrepancy between the two worlds lies at the heart of the attempt to elicit a second type of response on the part of the reader, an attempt and response which are equally fundamental to the intentionality or "game" of SF and characteristic of few if any other kinds of literature. On a level of literary play which is rational or intellectual rather than emotional or subjective, the reader is asked to accept the imaginary world as a "thought-model" or hypothetical construct which, because it is logical in its internal structure and at the very least not inconsistent with available data, can be regarded as valid and perhaps even considered aesthetically pleasing as well. The concession of plausibility occurs of course during the process of reading, roughly concurrently with the reader's essentially unreflective participation in the "reality" of the fiction. The sense of plausibility is also intended to persist after the act of reading has been concluded and the subjective impression of reality has subsided.

In a sense the interested reader of good fiction eventually loses his "game" with the writer. But in doing so he actually wins, for the "prize" for surrendering to the writer's assertions about the fiction is entertainment and perhaps edification. In fiction, as in all true games, the pleasure of play more than outweighs the tokens of defeat. But almost no one enjoys a game where the sides are unevenly matched, the play unexciting, or the players insincere. Therefore, as Hans Robert Jauss remarks, the critic "must himself become a reader again, before he...can understand and classify" a work of literature.[33] The success of the game, and indeed its very initiation, continuance and meaning, presuppose the active and sincere participation of all the players. Later, or perhaps on another level of thought whose operation is simultaneous with "naive" reading, as Richard Gerber suggests,[34] the players may of course adopt the stance of critics in order to review the quality of play or even question the very rules of the game. It goes without saying, or at least should, that the players and the kibitzers must know the rules of the game and that they not insist that it be played by other rules.

The special intentionality of SF has determined the evolution of the genre and must therefore be considered when texts are interpreted and value judgments about them are formulated. Certainly there is much SF of inferior quality, and the inept treatment of character, setting, plot and language indeed deserves criticism. But, as I have suggested throughout this chapter, "transparent" diction, conventional plots and chronological structures, simply-defined, even stereotypical characters, and fondness for detail which in much other literature might be regarded as "padding," may well characterize and serve the distinguishing intentionality of SF. The best evidence for that argument is to be found, of course, in the texts themselves. Corroboration is furnished by numerous statements of writers of SF and by evidence of a broader, comparative nature. The systematic use of the conventions of realism is characteristic of precisely those writers of SF—at least those writing before the "New Wave"—whose superiority is generally acknowledged. In the same authors one can also clearly observe the inclination to depart from convention where deviation is warranted by the intentionality of SF, as it is in the creation of imaginary words and languages, in the portrayal of new character types such as machines, alien beings, or quasi-humans, and in the close examination of mental or physical changes occasioned in terrestrial human beings by their removal from our world to other environments. It is especially significant that the ready propensity to adopt the conventions of realism, the willingness to depart from them in certain justifiable instances, and even the re-invention of many of the special rhetorical techniques of the genre can be observed in those works or traditions for which conventional middlebrow realistic fiction is not so important a part of the general literary background as it is for the "normative" Anglo-American SF, and in "mainstream" writers for whom the writing of SF is an occasional experiment rather than a regular pursuit.

In practice, of course, it is often extremely difficult to evaluate the artistic merit of individual works of SF or to assess the achievement and potential of the genre as a whole. The process of evaluation actually involves several kinds of judgment about the intrinsic quality and extrinsic worth of SF. Value judgments may be expressed about individual texts, whether they are considered specifically as SF or simply as undifferentiated literature; about SF as a genre; and, from the broadest perspective, about SF as the expression, communication and examination of ideas. If the distinct tendency to SF to adopt literary techniques whose presence in other forms of literature often indicates inferior quality is but one of many sources of difficulty which impede the formulation of legitimate aesthetic value judgments, it is also one of the most persistent and troubling. Similar problems are encountered in assessing stylistic and thematic originality and in weighing the aesthetic importance of scientific accuracy. Yet those who are not *a priori* hostile to SF and who found their opinions on some concept of aesthetic intentionality particular to it agree to a surprising degree in assigning given works or writers to one or the other extreme of the range of science-fictional quality. Although the exact order may vary, the names of certain writers, such as Wells, Clarke, Asimov, Heinlein, Herbert, Le Guin and Lem, constantly appear in formal or informal canons of better modern SF.

It is my distinct impression—and it is a reassuring one—that the application of general standards of literary quality to SF would not materially alter value judgments formulated according to the specific intentionality of the genre. The creation of good SF, then, is not directly and necessarily incompatible with the creation of good literature. But the precise relation or ratio of comparison between the two scales of quality is problematic. It is quite possible that the best SF, when compared to the best examples of other types of literature, is still only mediocre, and perhaps necessarily so. It is conceivable too that the rigorous pursuit of the special aims of SF somehow hinders the fulfilment of certain other, even more essential functions of literature—although there yet exists no precise, generally accepted determination of those requisites. More credible are the opinions of those who, like Heinlein, point out that the production of SF has been confined virtually to the last hundred years, that even in its "boom" times SF has been able to support only a relative handful of writers, and that the widespread dismissal of SF as an inferior form of literature has quite likely discouraged some talented writers from entering the field.[35]

But the study of SF involves the formulation of still another value judgment, one of a more comprehensive, extrinsic nature. It might well be asked whether SF is worth creating and reading at all. The answer depends, of course, on one's purposes, tastes and convictions. The simple value of entertainment should not be disdained lightly or, on the other hand, overvalued. Nor should one discount the argument that good SF may afford a more sophisticated type of literary or intellectual pleasure. Some proponents of SF emphasize the element of edification rather than that of sheer entertainment. They point out that SF provides information about the ever more important subject of science, that it enables us to explore the many possible shapes of the future in a hypothetical but almost tangible way, and that it prepares modern Man for the rapid process of technological innovation and consequent social change which may well characterize times to come even more than our own.[36] Such arguments, Robert Scholes would say, refer to the "cognitive function" of SF, which, like other forms of literature, can "help us to know ourselves and our existential situation." For SF, while it "offers us ... world[s] clearly and radically discontinuous from the one we know, yet returns to confront that known world in some cognitive way."[37] The alternating experience of discontinuity and cognition or re-cognition, I argued earlier, can give rise to a piquant, even shocking mixture of familiarity and alienation perhaps unique to SF.

But a reasoned apology for SF need not be so defensively utilitarian, or so intensely occupied with even more narrowly conceived extrinsic values, as are the arguments of those who tout

SF as a source of information and instruction about science. I would suggest that, in a peculiar sense, SF can be regarded as a peculiarly "humanistic" or "human" form of literature and intellectual expression. With much of the reading public, and among many academic critics as well, SF enjoys—or suffers from—the reputation of being a literature about worlds dominated by science. While that impression is understandable and in some cases justified, it involves a distortion of the essential nature of SF, at least as that intentionality can be observed in the best representatives of the genre.

SF would not be SF if science did not occupy a prominent, even preeminent place in the minds of its writers and in the imaginary worlds they create. No doubt, too, the fascination with science and technology which characterizes SF has traditionally found expression in the advocacy of a body of knowledge and a mode of experience which may now have won general if uncritical credence within the more or less educated public but have long excited the apprehension and hostility of the traditionally "humanistic" literary intelligentsia. But science in SF is not absolutely dominant; while it does not appear as the embodiment of Evil, it is not necessarily regarded as an ultimate Good, a definite Truth, or an absolute dictator of Fate.

It is in this respect, I think, as much as in any essential aesthetic features, that SF diverges from so much contemporary "mainstream" literature and yet rejoins the essentially humanistic mainstream of human endeavor, thereby reasserting its legitimacy and humanity as literature in the larger sense. Certainly many writers of fiction, as well as other observers of history and society, have foreseen the emergence of civilizations entirely governed and dehumanized by science and technology, or have perceived that specter in their own. Often they evince despair at the inconsequentiality of Man—not to mention that of God—in such worlds, and frequently they treat science as an evil in itself. But SF, or at least good SF, is not naively optimistic about science and the future. The better writers of SF have not failed to examine the dangers of science, or rather of Man's use of science; often—as in their response to atomic power and computerization—they have voiced their concerns before the rest of society was aware of any cause for alarm. In some SF the human species, the Earth itself, or other worlds are despoiled or destroyed by the misuse of science, and—most often—Man must recognize that the fault is not in his stars, but in himself.

But whether from naive over-confidence or reasoned hope, SF generally expresses an optimistic view of the future. In its qualitative assessment of science SF by no means invariably holds that Science itself is either good or evil, but rather that it is important. The source of good and evil, rather, is Man himself, and his better qualities may enable him to control science or even use it to improve himself and his world. Yet science, for all its novelty and importance, is regarded as but one more challenge to a species whose greatest strength has been not its intelligence but rather its ability to adapt to changes, among them some of its own making. Thus the characters which SF typically pictures are people who are able to live full and believable though often not idyllic lives in new environments shaped by science and technology. SF expresses a measured conviction that Man, if he constantly strives for it, can hope for salvation, or at least survival.

Kurd Lasswitz—photograph accompanying eulogy in the journal "Kantstudien"
(1911)

Chapter II

Kurd Lasswitz:
The Auspicious Beginnings of Modern German Science Fiction

CARL THEODOR VICTOR KURD LASSWITZ, the first and perhaps still the greatest writer of modern German SF, was born on 20 April 1848 in Breslau, Silesia, now the city of Wrocław, Poland.[1] He thus has the misfortune of sharing a birthday with a junior borderland German, Adolf Hitler (b. 1889), who indeed adversely affected Lasswitz' literary fortunes after the latter's death. Far more auspicious auguries for Lasswitz' life and work are afforded by his birthyear. His father, Karl, a prosperous iron wholesaler, was apparently receptive to the liberalism which figured in the many European rebellions of 1848, but he was also a practical man. In K.G. Just's words, the elder Lasswitz "translated his revolutionary enthusiasm into practical political activity as the representative of Breslau in the Prussian House of Deputies, thus reducing his utopian impulses to the realm of the humanly possible."[2] Utopianism and other progressive ideas associated with 1848 were also to play a major role in the life of Kurd Lasswitz, but they found expression in a far different way.

The young Lasswitz attended the Gymnasium Elisabethanum in Breslau, and then studied physics, mathematics and philosophy at the universities of Breslau (1866-68) and Berlin (1868-69). In 1873 he obtained his doctorate at Breslau with a dissertation entitled "Concerning Droplets Clinging to Fixed Bodies and Subject to Gravity"; the droplet theme reappears several times in his SF. But Lasswitz' scientific and intellectual interests, as his later fictional and non-fictional works amply manifest, extended far beyond the realm of laboratory physics.

Lasswitz served in France during the Franco-Prussian war, but did not see action. Then and afterward he was affected not so much by the shock of combat and suffering, or the philosophical implications of war in general, as he was by the political significance of the particular conflict he experienced, the growing importance of science and technology which it so clearly demonstrated, and the spirit of confidence which the victory reflected and in turn encouraged in his society.

After teaching for a short time at preparatory schools in Breslau and nearby Ratibor, Lasswitz spent most of his adult life, from 1876 until his retirement in 1908, as a professor of mathematics, physics and philosophy at the Gymnasium Ernestinum in Gotha. He died there on 17 October 1910 of complications resulting from appendicitis.

Lasswitz' production of scholarly and literary works was steady but not extraordinarily voluminous.[3] Except for his dissertation and some technical articles, his non-fictional writings were generally of a humanistic kind, studies in the philosophy or history of intellectual endeavor, particularly in the natural sciences. In other words, Lasswitz regarded himself as a student of knowledge or *Wissenschaft* in general, not just of its subsidiary branch, natural science or *Naturwissenschaft*. His essays on science, philosophy and aesthetics appeared frequently in such widely read but intellectually respectable periodicals as *Die Nation, Nord und Süd,* and the *Frankfurter Zeitung.* The depth and direction of his philosophical pursuits are best conveyed by the volume *Wirklichkeiten: Beiträge zum Weltverständnis [Realities: Contributions to World-Understanding]* (1900), a collection of essays about epistemology, especially the development of scientific inquiry. Other short writings are collected in *Seelen und Ziele: Beiträge zum Weltverständnis [Souls and Goals: Contributions to World-Understanding]* (1908) and *Empfundenes und Erkanntes: Aus dem Nachlasse [Things Felt and Known: Posthumous Writings]* (1920). Especially important to Lasswitz as a scientist, philosopher and writer of SF was the work of Gustav Theodor Fechner (1801-1887), a physiologist, psychologist and philosopher who wrote some early German scientific fantasy. Besides editing one of Fechner's speculative treatises and contributing an introduction to another, Lasswitz wrote a biography of Fechner and several essays about his work.

Lasswitz tried his hand at many literary forms, but it is his SF which is of greatest originality and lasting literary value. Two novellas, *Bis zum Nullpunkt des Seins: Erzählung aus dem Jahre 2371 [To the Zero-Point of Existence: A Tale from the Year 2371]* and *Gegen das Weltgesetz: Erzählung aus dem Jahre 3877 [Against the Law of the World: A Tale from the Year 3877]*, comprise the early volume *Bilder aus der Zukunft: Zwei Erzählungen aus dem vierundzwanzigsten und neununddreissigsten Jahrhundert* [*Pictures from the Future: Two Tales from the Twenty-fourth and Thirty-ninth Centuries*] (1878). At least as early as 1882 Lasswitz began to write SF short stories, some of which were soon published in the semi-popular review *Nord und Süd*. These pieces, along with others, were collected in two anthologies, *Seifenblasen: Moderne Märchen* [*Soap-bubbles: Modern Tales*] (1890, expanded edition 1894), and *Traumkristalle: Neue Märchen* [*Dream-Crystals: New Tales*] (1902, expanded edition 1907). Lasswitz' masterpiece, however, is the two-volume novel *Auf zwei Planeten* [*On Two Planets*] (1897).

Although Lasswitz was well aware of the theoretical nature of SF, he did not formally divide his literary *oeuvre* into SF and non-SF. Thus the collections *Seifenblasen* and *Traumkristalle* include a number of stories which are better classed as animal fables or traditional *Märchen* or fairy-tales. Much the same is true of the posthumous volumes *Empfundenes und Erkanntes* and *Die Welt und der Mathematikus: Ausgewählte Dichtungen* [*The World and the Mathematician: Selected Literary Pieces*] (1924). While science is the subject of several of the poems and prose works in both collections, it would be inappropriate to label as SF such pieces as "Des Astronomen Rache" ["The Astronomer's Revenge"] (*EE*, pp. 134-37) and "dx" (*WM*, p. 73). Most of Lasswitz' poetry consists in fact of occasional verse or effusive, ephemeral imitations of the German Classics and Romantics. It would also be misleading to classify as SF the early novella *Schlangenmoos* [*Snake-Moss*] (1884) and the two late novels *Aspira: Der Roman einer Wolke* [*Aspira: The Novel of a Cloud*] (1905) and *Sternentau: Die Pflanze vom Neptunsmond* [*Star-Dew: The Plant from the Moon of Neptune*] (1909). The emphasis on pure fantasy and the virtual lack of concretely described science in all three works places them outside the bounds of SF, at least as it is understood here. The same is true, despite its subtitle, of the late story "Die entflohene Blume: Eine Geschichte vom Mars" ["The Fugitive Flower: A Story of Mars"] (1910, *EE*, pp. 241-47). Still another work, the short novel *Homchen: Ein Tiermärchen aus der oberen Kreide* [*Homokin: An Animal Fable from the Upper Cretaceous*] (1902), describes the evolution of early mammals in an amusing, imaginative, but scientifically accurate fashion. But *Homchen*, as the subtitle again indicates, is primarily a modern version of the Aesopian animal fable, not a realistic exposition of an imaginary world determined by science.

Therefore it and the other works just mentioned will remain peripheral to this study.

While Lasswitz' life as a preparatory school instructor in provincial Gotha was outwardly uneventful, he was greatly concerned about political issues, the place of science in the modern world, and his own role as a scientist, educator, philosopher and writer. It is nevertheless quite difficult to determine his real vocation or *Beruf*, in the profounder sense of the word. Fritz Engel, in a rather slick contemporary review of *Auf zwei Planeten* for a Berlin-Weimar literary weekly, snidely remarks that Lasswitz "is suffered to funnel $a^2 + b^2 = c^2$ into the prep-school students of Gotha and recovers from the strain by spreading forth the wings of an unusually rich imagination and letting himself be borne upward on the full current of his thoughts."[4] Quite another picture is given in the reminiscences of Lasswitz' son Erich, who in the preface to the 1948 re-edition of *Auf zwei Planeten* recalls that his father "taught math before hundreds of grateful high-school boys [Sekundaner und Primaner] . . . in the small, intellectually active provincial court city [Residenzstadt], the best environment for him."[5]

To a certain extent both observations are correct, but neither adequately conveys the breadth and depth of Lasswitz' interests or more than hints at his true calling. Lasswitz was not merely a scientist or pedagogue, although he was a physicist and mathematician by university training and a teacher by occupation. Nor was he a professional writer of fiction, although he wrote SF— and a good deal of very traditional poetry and prose fiction—from an early age. It has been conjectured that Lasswitz had once cherished the hope of being called to a university professorship, but resigned himself to his position at the Ernestinum and turned to writing fiction as an escape when it became apparent that his original goal was unattainable.[6]

Yet his productivity, his appealingly balanced personality, and his cultural background suggest that his position at Gotha would not inevitably have conflicted with his deeper desires. Quite probably Lasswitz indeed aspired to a university post, but perhaps less for the prestige and the professional opportunities it would have offered him as a scientist than as a means for pursuing an intellectual, social and artistic vocation of a much broader nature. For Lasswitz was a descendant of classical Weimar and had deeply assimilated its ideal of humanism and its sense of cultural mission. But he was also a socially and politically conscious citizen of a modern Germany whose development owed so much to science and technology. Lasswitz neither could nor did direct his energies toward a single, narrowly defined pursuit. In all his work he sought to relate science to social consciousness, the individual human sensibility, and the advancement of culture. His interdisciplinarism and his conviction of the importance of science are evident in his scholarly writing and in his teaching. It is in Lasswitz' fiction, however, that his personality and his many interests and talents found their best, most original and most enduring expression.

Concept of Science Fiction

Much about Lasswitz' thought and art can be learned from his writings on the theory and practice of SF. He first approached the subject in 1878, in the Preface to the *Bilder aus der Zukunft*. The broader topic of science and literature is discussed in the essay "Die poetische und die wissenschaftliche Betrachtung der Natur" ["The Poetic and the Scientific View of Nature"], published in the May 1887 issue of the review *Nord und Süd*. A lengthy consideration of futurology in philosophy and fiction, "Über Zukunftsträume" ["Concerning Dreams of the Future"], also first published in periodical form, comprises one chapter of the longer philosophical volume *Wirklichkeiten* (1900). The two shorter essays "Der tote und der lebendige Mars" ["The Dead and the Living Mars"] and "Unser Recht auf Bewohner anderer Welten" ["Our Claim to Inhabitants of Other Worlds"] are Lasswitz' final word on SF. The latter appeared in the *Frankfurter Zeitung* on 16 October 1910, one day before his death; both are included in the posthumous volume *Empfundenes und Erkanntes.*[7]

In his writings on the theory of SF Lasswitz attempts to show that fiction about science is a legitimate form of art, for it expresses and satisfies basic human needs. He states that it is natural for human beings to speculate about their culture and the future of their species, because Man has an intellect and a sense of curiosity, and because "striving for improvement is the essence of human life" ("ZT", cited from *Wirklichkeiten*, 423). To these rather traditional philosophical notions Lasswitz adds the concepts and methods of modern science. He argues that the initial impetus and recurring form of conceptualization for the attempt to comprehend human existence has been Man's confrontation with Nature, especially the cosmos revealed in ever greater expanse and detail by science ("PWBN," 270-71). Science, as the German term *Naturwissenschaft* suggests, is not the mere collection of facts; it is, rather, a fundamental expression of Man's deepest philosophical, emotional and cultural drives. As science progresses from superstition to a mature and systematic form of knowledge, it contributes more and more usefully to Man's efforts to understand his world and himself and to transcend his intellectual and physical limitations. Lasswitz therefore regards astronomy, the systematic study of the Universe as a whole, as the particular "paragon of science [das Muster der Naturwissenschaft]" ("PWBN," 271); and technology he considers to be the modern expression of Man's desire to gain practical mastery over his environment, "technische Beherrschung der Natur" ("ZT", 432).

Just as Lasswitz' knowledge of philosophy enables him to explore the implications of science and technology with particular acuity, so, conversely, does his scientific training add new energy and relevance to his philosophical argumentation. As a Neo-Kantian he conceives of space and time as subjective modes of perception. As a modern scientist he also regards the two as objective, quantifiable concepts. But as a writer he views them with an eye toward their artistic potential. The course of reasoning by which Lasswitz transforms space and time from philosophical, psychological and scientific concepts into the foundations for an argument about the aesthetics of SF is truly remarkable. For him, as for all physical scientists, both space and time can be treated as dimensions—graphically as well as conceptually. The mind, consequently, can survey space, time and change under one rubric. And change, therefore, can be conceived of as a function of either space or time, or both.

These ideas Lasswitz combines with older concepts of historical and cultural development. He then employs the unorthodox but not illogical synthesis of the scientific and the traditional conceptions of space and time to formulate conclusions abut two controversial questions raised by modern science: the theory of evolution and the possibility of extraterrestrial life. One conclusion is a belief—which Lasswitz does not express without reservations—in the possibility of "a relative improvement of conditions through a gradual process of evolution [der relativen Verbesserung der Zustände durch einen allmählichen Entwicklungsprozess]" ("ZT", 425). That is, temporal change can bring about the emergence of new stages or even new forms of life; it may also—so Lasswitz' language seems to hint anyway—generate new social forms. In itself, of course, the idea of human evolution, biological or social, is not original to Lasswitz, though it was still controversial in his time as it is even now. But

Lasswitz entertained speculations about evolution which were considerably more daring than were common among the evolutionists of his time, for he looked to the distant future of the human species, not just to its past. More provocative still is his proposition that, with regard to cultural development and the diversity of life-forms, travel through the dimension of space might be considered equivalent to progression or "travel" through the "dimension" of time. It is conceivable, he argues, that elsewhere in space there exist other forms of life whose present state of cultural development might be seen to represent some possible future stage of our own. It need scarcely be said that both ideas, space-travel and cultural or biological evolution, are of great importance to SF. The opening paragraphs of "Unser Recht auf Bewohner anderer Welten" best express Lasswitz' thought about extraterrestrial life and its implications for our own culture:

> Ever since science has incontrovertibly made the Earth into a planet and the stars into suns like our own, we have not been able to lift our gaze to the starry firmament without thinking, along with Giordano Bruno, that even on those inaccessible worlds there may exist living, feeling, thinking creatures. It must seem absolutely nonsensical indeed that in the infinity of the cosmos our Earth should have remained the only supporter of intelligent beings [Vernunftwesen]. The rational order of the universe [Weltvernunft] demands that there should necessarily even be infinite gradations of intelligent beings inhabiting such worlds.
>
> To this idea might be added the profound and inextinguishable longing for better and more fortunate conditions than those which the Earth offers us. Indeed we do dream of a higher civilization [Kultur], but we would also like to come to know it as something more than the hope for a distant future. We tell ourselves that what the future can sometime bring about on Earth must even now, in view of the infinitude of time and space, have already become a reality somewhere. ("URBAW," 163)

Lasswitz' SF is, in effect, the exploration of the ideas about space, time and change which he developed over a period of several decades and recorded in his essays on the theory of SF. Thus in the *Bilder aus der Zukunft* he described superior terrestrial cultures located in the future, and prefaced his two stories with a philosophical, scientific and aesthetic discussion of his imaginary worlds. In *Auf zwei Planeten* Lasswitz actually made travel through space and progression through time virtually equivalent, in a striking manner which exploits fully both the concreteness and the imagistic resources of fiction. There he explored the confrontation of contemporary terrestrial civilization with a superior alien civilization which, although it is treated as a hypothetically or fictively real entity, also represents the possible future state of Lasswitz' own culture. The Martians' literal journey through space to the more primitive Earth, which leads to the physical encounter and conflict of the two species, is symmetrically balanced and recapitulated on the metaphorical and thematic levels by the gradual improvement of terrestrial humanity, an evolutionary journey through time whose end is the diminution of cultural distance between the two life-forms.

Lassitz did not limit his discussion of SF to broad statements of purpose and the analysis of intellectual premises. As a literary theorist and practicing writer he understood that the creation of art involved both conception and execution. In his essays he examined with considerable insight the concept of imagination and some of the literary techniques appropriate to SF—or, rather, to the new kind of literature whose nature, like its name as yet still indefinite, he sought to help determine. His ideas anticipate those of many later critics and writers of SF. Imagination and narration, for example, Lasswitz viewed as consciously methodical processes whose goal is to stimulate the impressions of plausibility and fictive reality. Like many later SF theorists he proposed that the particular concept of imagination and the choice of literary techniques it generates offered the foundation for a definition of SF as a distinct genre. In his essays, "Über Zukunftsträume" and "Unser Recht auf Bewohner anderer Welten" Lasswitz bravely attempts to distinguish SF, which he calls "the scientific tale [das wissenschaftliche Märchen]," from other fiction, especially the traditional *Märchen* or, as SF critics often describe such literature, "fantasy fiction" ("ZT," 441); the distinction is still a subject of energetic debate among students of SF.

Of equal importance to Lasswitz is the difference between SF and science itself in function and, therefore, in form of exposition as well. He suggests that it is neither proper nor possible for science, considered as a strict discipline, to speculate boldly or precisely about the future or about other worlds, for such are areas of inquiry inaccessible—at least presently—to its methods of investigation. If we wish to explore such matters, "we must turn to [the faculty of] imagination [Phantasie]"; but here imagination or fantasy "need not be unbridled," as it is in fantasy fiction ("ZT," 439). The "bridle," as Lasswitz repeatedly asserts, is to be provided not only by common sense, but even more by the concepts, methods and standards of science.

At times Lasswitz seems even to equate the science-fictional mode of imagination and argument with the scientific method itself. Like the scientist, the writer of SF thinks in terms of hypotheses, quantifiable factors, and formulas, although he enjoys greater freedom of imagination in dealing with them. In two seminal passages, written more than thirty years apart but nevertheless wholly consistent with each other, Lasswitz discusses the attempt to speculate about the future and about other cultures:

> Who can answer these questions [about the future]? Science cannot venture to do so, as long as it has not yet found the famous Universal Formula of Laplace, which will answer all questions about the past and future and enable us to perceive the mechanism of the Universe in the same manner that this mechanism presents itself to the human intellect in the motion of atoms. And yet there is a magical agency by which we can anticipate this formula and with one fell swoop lift ourselves beyond the reality which slowly works itself out in space and time with mass and energy. This magical agency which enables us to lift the veil of the future is imagination [die Idee]. Fiction [Dichtung] has the privilege of looking into the future. But if that which fiction narrates is really to inspire in us a sense of trust, then fiction must take counsel with reality and conform closely to experience. Many inferences about the future can be drawn from the historical course of civilization [Verlauf der Culturgeschichte] and the present state of science; and analogy offers itself to fantasy as an ally. (Preface to *BZ*, iii-iv)

> Now in this process fiction is much freer in its use of hypotheses than is science, whose business is to provide the objective knowledge. As long as he does not contradict the scientific knowledge of his time, the writer of fiction may expand the hypothesis in order to further those aims which he considers essential to his function. In science the hypothesis must receive its justification through the ongoing process of experience, while in fiction the hypothesis is justified simply by its psychological utility, i.e., by the effect which it creates by making objects and events vivid and plausible and by transforming them into elements of the reader's active emotional response. ("URBAW," 167-68)

The insight with which Lasswitz outlined the process of "extrapolation" and the use of "analogs"—key concepts in later theories of SF—is remarkable. His conception of the SF text as the expression of a "hypothesis" whose "data" are of the "objects and events" of the narration also points the way toward modern theories. In his earliest and latest essays Lasswitz also examines the implications of his "scientific" concept of imagination in terms of literary techniques and their intended effects. As in the passages just quoted, he emphasizes plausibility, probability and verisimilitude as principles of imagination and as goals of literary style:

We have endeavored to relate nothing which cannot stand either as probable or at least as not completely impossible according to present knowledge.... Here the difficulty of artistic representation places a natural rein on fantasy; it is essential to find the proper mean between fantastic fabulation and didactic disquisition [zwischen phantastischem Fabuliren und lehrhaftem Auseinandersetzen]. For that which is alien must be mediated to our understanding through that which is already familiar; this is not always easy and necessitates much and varied postulation [vielerlei Voraussetzung]. (Preface to *BZ*, v-vi.)

In the transformation [of speculations about science, the future, etc.] into literary form, the laws of nature and the soul may not be infringed upon without arousing the objection of the reader and interfering with the effect. For everything that occurs in a novel which is intended seriously as art must be capable of being related to our own experience, i.e., to the contemporary view of natural laws and psychology; in short, it must be explainable and plausible. An effect which occurred simply by magic and could not be explained scientifically would be just as unusable poetically as a sudden, psychologically unmotivated transformation of a character.... Our sense of veracity tolerates no postulates which directly and absolutely contradict previous scientific and psychological experience. ("URBAW," 165-6)

As the two passages show, Lasswitz was aware that in SF the plausibility of the imaginary world is suggested and judged in several ways. The sense of plausibility, and even more that of fictive reality, depend first of all on the creation of a general impression of correspondence or "sharable experience" which temporarily negates the discrepancy between the imaginary world of the fiction and our own world. The concepts and terms of literary realism are no less evident in Lasswitz' theory of SF than in those of more modern writers and critics. His notion of plausibility, like that of many if indeed not all writers of SF, also shows the direct impact of science. The scientific method, with its combination of hypothesis, projection, collection of data, and re-evaluation, is considered the model for imaginative speculation and is regarded also as a paradigm of exposition. The particular natural sciences, which furnish the preeminent categories and standards by which the real world is now observed and described, also provide many of the individual criteria according to which the validity of the imaginary world is asserted and evaluated.

Lasswitz recognized that yet another logical part of a theory about fiction based on science is the argument that science should be an essential ingredient of the imaginary world and should be made integral to the narrative:

Literature can...take as its raw material scientific knowledge itself.... The content of the scientific experience of a particular time is, after all, part of the common interest of humanity, for it is a determinant element of the present with regard to natural science and technology. The picture of the relationship of things which we form in this field is an essential element of the total content of the culture and can therefore also become the object of literary treatment. But fiction gives form to this its raw material by transforming it into the personal experience of literary characters. ("URBAW," 167)

In his essays Lasswitz mentions a number of speculative scientific and technological ideas which, he suggests, would be appropriate and challenging subjects for the new kind of fiction. Among them are extra-terrestrial life, anti-gravity, synthetic food, and differences in psychological sensibility encountered in non-terrestrial beings or in new environments ("ZT," 442, "URBAW" and "TLM" *passim*). Many of these notions are prominent themes and motifs in later SF—as they are in Lasswitz' own fiction.

Only briefly does Lasswitz speculate about some of the more specific narrative devices of SF as he envisions it. He suggests, for example, that SF might have a justifiable tendency to favor exciting plots and heroic characters ("ZT," 435-7, 440-5); but he remains silent about the finer aspects of style, even those techniques with which he was experimenting at the same time in his own fiction. Lasswitz' vagueness, or rather his caution, is understandable, for he knew well that he was investigating an embryonic form of literature whose precise characteristics were still to be elucidated by trial and error in the mutual interplay of authors, texts and readers. Consequently he devoted much of his attention to the attempt to distinguish SF clearly from other literature, to establish its artistic legitimacy, and to argue the "scientific" nature of its mode of imagination. Later writers, naturally more cognizant of the potentials and supposed limits of their genre, would consciously seek to explore and expand its boundaries, and would sometimes even venture to treat the conventions of SF in an ironic manner. Lasswitz' own SF, of course, also gives a better indication of his understanding of practical techniques.

With a century of hindsight we may choose to question Lasswitz' cultural optimism, his rationalistic psychology, and his use of the concepts and terminology of Idealist philosophy and classical aesthetics. Nevertheless, his five essays on SF should be considered landmarks in the history of the genre. Lasswitz' knowledge of science, philosophy, cultural history and aesthetics, as well as his experience as a writer of fiction, enabled him to formulate conclusions about the "scientific tale" which resemble quite closely those which form the foundations of modern theories of SF. He at least mentions, and sometimes analyzes in impressive depth, most of the questions which have occupied later theorists and critics. His understanding of science and aesthetics is in fact considerably more sophisticated than that of most writers and critics of SF during his own time and even later. Although he wrote his essays when modern SF was in its infancy and even its very name had not yet been coined, Lasswitz can be compared favorably, I think, with those later writers who, like Olaf Stapledon and C.S. Lewis, have examined the philosophical, aesthetic and scientific foundations of their form of literature with notable insight and rigor. But above all, his essays on SF show that he believed that science and technology were becoming major determinants of human existence, that the impact of science on the modern world and the future could be explored in an artistically legitimate form, and that such a literature would exhibit many affinities with traditional realism.

Medium of Publication and Contemporary Readership

The initial reception and subsequent fortunes of Lasswitz' SF were affected by the nature of his readers and by the characteristics of his medium of publication.[8] In the late nineteenth century— whether in America, Russia, Lasswitz' Germany, Wells' Great Britain or Verne's France—SF still lacked not only a single name and a firm foundation in theory and practice, but also a definite readership and regular channels of distribution. The importance of the American pulp magazine to the development of modern Anglo-American SF has often been remarked. Although Lasswitz' two early novellas and his masterpiece, *Auf zwei Planeten*, were published in hardcover, it was in a periodical medium also that his essays and mature SF short stories first attracted significant attention.

It would seem initially that Lasswitz might well have published his SF in one or more of several kinds of periodical, such as the prestigious intellectual, cultural and literary journals, the professional scientific or technological periodicals, or the very popular family magazines. In other times and places each of the three types of publication has been an important vehicle for SF. But it is apparent in retrospect that, whether because of aesthetic orientation, subject-matter, ideological proclivities or readership characteristics, none of the three varieties of periodical was truly appropriate for SF, or at least for that of Lasswitz.

Instead, whether by inclination or necessity, he chose for his SF yet another periodical medium, the review or *Rundschau.* The German reviews, whose counterparts had existed for some time in more centralized countries like Britain and France, emerged as major literary and journalistic media during the latter part of the nineteenth century in response to the need for widely-circulated but intellectually respectable national publications. Their relatively diverse fare, which typically included general-interest articles, prose fiction, book reviews, commentary on cultural affairs, and perhaps poetry and drama, appealed to a sizable readership somewhat larger than that of the highbrow cultural or scientific journals and considerably smaller, but more influential, than that of the family magazines. The best known and most widely circulated of the many reviews was the *Deutsche Rundschau* (1874-1963), whose circulation was about 10,000 in 1876; second to it was the politically and artistically more liberal *Neue Rundschau*, founded in 1890. By comparison, during the late nineteenth century the largest of the family magazines, *Die Gartenlaube*, enjoyed a circulation of up to several hundred thousand copies, the specialized cultural and scientific journals at most only a few thousand.

It was one such semi-popular review, *Nord und Süd*, which became the first major medium of publication for Lasswitz' writings and for some important early critical response to his work. An examination of the review reveals much about the probable Lasswitz readership and also helps explain why his SF, although its appeal was not insignificant, did not reach a larger audience. *Nord und Süd* appeared monthly from 1872 to 1929 and was published in Berlin. During most of the period when Lasswitz published his works in it the journal was edited by Paul Lindau (1839-1919), then well known as a journalist, theatrical director and writer of fiction and drama. It was certainly not an obscure publication, belonging in fact to the group of journals which were still major cultural influences although they ranked behind the *Deutsche Rundschau* and *Neue Rundschau.* Like most of the other leading reviews, *Nord und Süd* attempted to reach a socially, intellectually and geographically diverse audience. Within this larger readership it sought to appeal especially to the broadly cultivated reader who was more than idly interested in fields of knowledge other than his own, in matters associated with science and technology particularly, and in the concept of interdisciplinarism itself. A contemporary

American counterpart of *Nord und Süd* would resemble the now defunct monthly *Saturday Review* augmented by elements of content and form taken from *The New Yorker, National Geographic, Scientific American* and *The New York Review of Books.*

It is very likely, then, that Lasswitz' early readers were neither an amorphous mass drawn from the general reading public, nor a cohesive, highly specialized "in-group" or "ghetto" community whose chief interest was SF. They belonged, rather, to the broader range of the intelligentsia and the cultivated bourgeoisie. While doubtless many were to be found in the professions and universities or on the preparatory school faculties, others might well have been engineers, businessmen or even civil servants. While Lasswitz' periodical readership numbered among itself some professional writers, *Nord und Süd* was not the prime medium for those writers, readers and critics who were intensively and exclusively occupied with highbrow literature, whether of the Establishment or the experimental variety.

Such single factors as economic status, aesthetic tastes, intellectual level, or the exercise of science or technology as a profession seem insufficient to delineate the Lasswitz readership with any great reliability. I would suggest instead that the modest but not inconsequential body of readers which apparently constituted the central support for his SF was characterized by the active cultivation of a particular *combination* of literary, ideological and intellectual inclinations. This composite outlook was comprised of a political ideology which was definitely liberal but not radical, a more than casual interest in science and technology, and in literature a taste both for the classics and for contemporary realism. The relative weight of each trait might vary from reader to reader, but their frequent appearance together in one person was not entirely coincidental. Lasswitz' readers, it appears, were humanists who cultivated many interests, believed in the free distribution of knowledge and power throughout society, and were earnestly concerned with maintaining lines of communication among the sciences, technological pursuits, and the more traditional areas of thought and expression. In their special interests, tastes and overall intellectual constitution they were therefore much like Lasswitz himself—a similarity by no means always encountered in SF.

Lasswitz and his probable readers indeed differed noticeably from the contemporary norm, even that of the intellectual class. But they were not members of a miniscule band of outsiders whose attitudes were hostile or, much less, completely alien to the dominant outlook of the time. The conventional and not necessarily incorrect image of late nineteenth-century Germany emphasizes such distinguishing features as confident nationalism, authoritarianism, industrial expansion, economic specialization, the emergence and consolidation of certain social classes, the creation of monumental cultural institutions, and intellectual positivism. In their progressivism, interdisciplinarism, respect for the cultural heritage of the Age of Goethe, and cautious but evident positivism, Lasswitz and his readers were distinguished from the surrounding society, or at least sizable parts of it, less by their basic orientation then by their sophistication, by certain of their special tastes, and by the enthusiasm with which they advocated some of their ideals. I would even argue that the same social and intellectual factors which helped to create the less attractive features of the Wilhelmine Era also determined, to a large extent, its liberal, humanistic counter-reflection.

Both the combination of traits which typified Lasswitz and his readers, and even the close coexistence of contrary views, or rather alternative formulations of the same fundamental attitudes, can be explained in part by reference to social structure and class characteristics. The confidence in the future and the esteem for intellectual activity which might appear in either liberal or conservative forms were typical of the relatively large and growing German bourgeoisie to which Lasswitz, perhaps the larger part of his original readership, and many cultural leaders belonged. The middle class, despite its relative lack of direct political power, had gained a marked ascendancy in social institutions, economic enterprise, cultural life, and science and technology. Its values—or at least those which it espoused and whose observance soon spread to other classes—were not entirely materialistic, ideologically conservative or culturally Philistine, although it was fashionable in some artistic and intellectual circles to claim that. Among the general public, which had attained a high degree of literacy, the arts, for example, enjoyed an immense prestige which consisted at least of veneration—if not always intimate knowledge or true enjoyment—of the classical canon, particularly the literature of the Age of Goethe. Political liberalism in Germany also experienced one of its notable, infrequent periods of strength.

Other factors must also be considered. Not a small part of the interest in material progress, cultural achievement and scholarship in Lasswitz' time was directed to theoretical science and industrial technology as they affected internal social development, international relations, and even the daily life and personal consciousness of the individual. There was therefore abundant reason for the humanist to turn his attention to matters of science, even if he lacked formal education in such less traditional subjects and was not one of that growing but still relatively rare breed, the professional scientist. Conversely, scientific and technological training had not yet become so specialized that it could displace much of the traditional heavy emphasis on the humanities in the preparatory schools and universities.

As yet, then, there was little reason to be concerned about a putative schism between the "two cultures" of natural science and humanistic studies. Indeed, an all-encompassing expression of the spirit of confidence characteristic of the time was the widespread conviction that all areas of knowledge and cultural endeavor could and even should be related to one another, despite—or perhaps even because of—increasing intellectual and social specialization. The notion might appear innocuously as a reverence for all knowledge among the *Bildungsbürgertum* and as an earnest cultivation of interdisciplinary activity among certain intellectuals. It took on a more questionable and certainly less rational form in the organicism preached by such scientists as Ernst Haeckel, which harks back to the nearly mystical holism of the early nineteenth-century German *Naturphilosophen*. Certainly the admiration for intellectual generalism was conditioned by the almost universal reverence for the great minds of the Age of Goethe. It also reflected a yearning for a higher, organic synthesis which was non-rational, Romantic and, according to Ralf Dahrendorf, quintessentially German.[9] Like other and greater scientists Lasswitz was not unaffected by such currents; perhaps under the influence of Gustav Theodor Fechner, he toyed recurrently with the idea of a "Weltseele" or higher universal consciousness. But generally his interdisciplinarism, his synthesis of scientific and humanistic attitudes, exhibits a far soberer mien.

Critical Reception

During his lifetime Lasswitz received slightly more attention from literary critics, philosophers and scientists than might have been his due simply as a writer of minor artistic stature. His evident intellectual capabilities, engaging powers of fantasy, liberal sympathies, affinity for literary realism, choice of science as a subject for his fiction, and even his congenial personality appealed to a loosely-associated company of cultural observers who shared the interests and attitudes which characterized Lasswitz himself and also, apparently, the larger anonymous body of his readers. In the dozen or so years from the publication of *Auf zwei Planeten* in 1897 until shortly after his death in 1910, Lasswitz' life and works were discussed in a modest handful of essays and longer reviews.[10] Many of them appeared in the same few periodicals as Lasswitz' own SF, or at least in publications of a distinctly similar nature.

Lasswitz' early critics had sufficient literary experience and acumen to formulate an accurate estimate of the overall quality of his fiction. They expressed cordial but restrained admiration for his lively imagination and his talents as a storyteller, and they acknowledged his effort to deal with serious philosophical questions. Yet in their attempts to describe and evaluate Lasswitz' SF more precisely the early critics are often uncertain, unperceptive and inconsistent. Occasionally one even gains the impression that some of them, particularly Hans Lindau and Wilhelm Bölsche, regarded Lasswitz as a cultural curiosity or personal literary pet. Such critics, as Fritz Engel's previously quoted remarks also show, portrayed him as a congenial, apolitical scientist, teacher and historian of philosophy and science who found his place, willingly or not, in a provincial preparatory school and wrote engaging fantasies in his spare time.

It must be conceded that Lasswitz was not a writer of the highest quality and that our own greater hindsight provides us no little advantage in understanding and evaluating his work, especially as a contribution to the early development of SF. But it is quite possible, I suggest, that appreciation of Lasswitz during his own time was hindered less by any artistic or intellectual fault of his own than by certain differences, at first glance subtle but ultimately substantial, between him and his critics, even or perhaps precisely those who were favorably disposed toward his philosophical, scientific, ideological and literary attitudes—or what they took them to be. Despite all he shared with his critics, in many respects Lasswitz was both more sophisticated and less doctrinaire than his urbane critical patrons, whose partisan progressivism engendered in them a palpable inflexibility or, paradoxically, a reflex conservatism when progressivism itself—its fundamental nature and its picture of the future—was being examined by a writer who was, nevertheless, sympathetic to its immediate causes. If Lasswitz' early critics, then, were not always willing or even able to entertain his critical notions about the foundations and implications of late nineteenth-century thought, whether philosophical, ideological or scientific, neither were they generally capable of appreciating fully the significance of his experiments with an essentially new kind of literature. But superannuation, at least partial, is the general fate of literary criticism, and the merits of Lasswitz' early critics should not be ignored.

The essay "Kurd Lasswitz," a review of Lasswitz' SF and philosophical works by Raimund Pissin, a freelance writer and literary historian who was also active scientifically as the manager of his family's veterinary institute, lends support to such contentions. The piece appeared on 3 December 1904 in the liberal Berlin weekly *Die Nation* (pp. 153-4). The same journal, which most likely shared many readers with *Nord und Süd*, also published several of Lasswitz' essays and at least one other important review of his SF.

Pissin quite correctly discerns Lasswitz' Kantian background and his concern about the effects of science and technology on modern life and thought. He also acknowledges Lasswitz' efforts to give his fiction a philosophical and aesthetic justification. But in his conception of science and of speculation about the future evolution of mankind, Pissin fails to distinguish between genuine progress and the simple temporal succession of phenomena. That is, he confuses true cultural improvement with the emergence of traits which are new and possibly beneficial in practical terms, but not necessarily better from an ethical standpoint. He views Lasswitz, accordingly, as an optimist and utopian, though one of the modern, rational kind. Referring to the development of culture and knowledge, Pissin remarks, with a certain elevated and confused syntax encountered elsewhere among Lasswitz' early critics:

> Even quite early the poet Lasswitz had the urge to transport himself with bold fantasy into distant phases of this process, to times of perfection long desired, in accord with the guidelines of scientific knowledge and ethics....
> [In *Wirklichkeiten*] he marks off the outlines of his most characteristic area of creativity: shaping, in poetic form, dreams of the future [which portray] the development of mankind.... For him, technical advances of the future, [as yet only] dreamed of, are an endless realm in which to savor pure aesthetic pleasure... (p. 154).

Pissin facilely equates three seemingly synonymous terms which indeed denote quite heterogeneous concepts. As did many others in the late nineteenth century and even much later, he apparently assumes that the mere "development of mankind [Werden der Menschheit]" will automatically result in the "perfection long desired [ersehnte Verkollkommnung]" of the race and the culture, and that the realization of "technological advances of the future, [as yet only] dreamed of [erträumte technische Fortschritte der Zukunft]" is by itself a hallmark of such elevation. Quite incorrectly, I think, Pissin also considers Lasswitz' "dreams of the future" to be the uncritical expression of the same ideas. But the more perceptive of modern scientists and philosophers, among them Lasswitz, were already coming to see that the relationship between science and ethics, or as Pissin and so many others termed them, *Erkenntnis* and *Sittlichkeit*, was far from simple and that neither scientific advancement not biological evolution, whether teleological (*Werden*) or Darwinian (*Entwicklung*) necessarily implies true cultural progress.

More insight is to be found in two other early documents: the first major essay about Lasswitz' SF known to me, Fritz Engel's previously mentioned "Ein Robinson des Weltraums," written immediately after the appearance of *Auf zwei Planeten* in 1897; and Otto Jauker's eulogy upon Lasswitz' death, published in the *Deutsche Rundschau für Geographie*, 33 (1911), pp. 279-80. Both writers discuss the relation of Lasswitz' SF to the tradition of utopian thought and literature. Each notes also that in Lasswitz' fiction one encounters that notable rarity, a professional scientist who creates art for which his own field of knowledge provides philosophical foundations, thematic material, and even aesthetic concepts. While neither Jauker nor Engel uses the term "realism," both sense that in fiction like that of Lasswitz', accuracy of scientific concepts and detailed descriptions of setting and imaginary science can have an aesthetically justifiable purpose. Like Pissin, however, Engel and Jauker fail to perceive Lasswitz' critical response to his own culture.

A longer essay, "Weltphantasien," by Moritz Kronenberg, which appeared in *Die Nation* on 31 December 1898 (pp. 202-3), offers a still more sophisticated historical, philosophical and literary analysis. In his general remarks Kronenberg, like other critics, attempts to fit Lasswitz into the category of utopian thought and literature, and not without some justification. But precisely because he does not hesitate to apply careful analytical methods of literary criticism to Lasswitz' work, he is capable of considering the special functions of science and artistic imagination in the creation of SF. Kronenberg's interpretation of *Auf zwei Planeten* will be discussed in greater detail in Chapter IV.

Still more important in the history of early Lasswitz criticism are lengthier articles by Hans Lindau (1875-?) and Wilhelm Bölsche (1861-1939). Lindau, the son of *Nord und Süd* editor Paul Lindau, devoted much effort to promoting Lasswitz' fiction. The September 1903 issue of *Nord und Süd* (vol. 106) contains his review of *Nie und Immer* (pp. 413-14) and a major article, "Kurd Lasswitz und seine modernen Märchen [Kurd Lasswitz and His Modern Tales]" (pp. 315-33). A eulogy in the journal *Kantstudien* (16, No. 7 [1911], pp. 1-4) was followed nine years later by the long introduction to Lasswitz' posthumous volume *Empfundenes und Erkanntes*. Lindau's pieces are valuable sources of biographical information, if not outstanding works of literary criticism. His tone is often too encomiastic and jovial for our taste, and there is something both incongruous and improbable in his image of Lasswitz as a genial, almost childlike fantacist, a worthy descendant of Weimar Classicism, and a modern writer of serious fiction about science as well. But in several remarks Lindau at least endeavors to deal with Lasswitz as the leading German representative of a new and distinctive, but still generally unrecognized kind of fiction. Like Lasswitz himself Lindau writes of the importance of science as a source of theme and setting. He also discusses how conception and execution in Lasswitz' SF reflect a pattern of extrapolation along "lines of historical development [geschichtliche Entwicklungslinien]" (*EE*, 4-5). But Lindau offers few remarks on stylistic matters. He comments, rather vapidly, that Lasswitz' SF "is extraordinarily exciting [er spannt ungeheuer]" (*Nord und Süd*, p. 319). More insightful is his observation that convincing, unemotional narrative tone is a hallmark of much of Lasswitz' SF (*EE*, 12-13).

Lindau's summary analysis of Lasswitz' fiction echoes the latter's own view of his work. In a phrase which virtually defies meaningful translation, Lindau declares that Lasswitz' artistic development represents "Ein Fortschritt aus dem Nahen and Äusseren zum Seelisch-Geistigen und Erhaben-Fernen Inneren" (*EE*, 47). Lindau's choice of terms suggests that he was perhaps inclined to see in Lasswitz' intellectual and artistic evolution a recapitulation of what, in his own conception and that of many others, had been the maturation of Classical German literature as exemplified above all by Goethe. Lasswitz himself seems to have entertained similar though more modest notions about his own work.[11] It is even possible that he consciously sought to model his literary development on that of Goethe. But although Lindau may be essentially correct in his perception of a general "progression from the immediate and external to the spiritual-philosophical and sublime-distant internal," Lasswitz' SF evolved in a manner considerably more complex and certainly far more coherent.

The highpoint of Lasswitz' contemporary critical reception was Wilhelm Bölsche's essay "Naturwissenschaftliche Märchen [Scientific Tales]," which appeared in the *Neue Deutsche Rundschau* (9 [1898], pp. 504-14) and was later reprinted in one of Bölsche's volumes on science popularization, *Vom Bazillus zum Affenmenschen* [*From the Bacillus to the Primate*] (1900). Bölsche, because he is less reluctant than other critics to probe and to criticize, arrives at an interpretation of Lasswitz which is ultimately more complimentary because it takes him more seriously. Like Kronenberg, Engel and Lindau, Bölsche first attempts to locate Lasswitz' SF within a larger historical and generic framework. But he does not get mired in the utopian tradition or succumb to simplistic national classifications like Lindau's fatuous and tautological declaration that Lasswitz was "more German" than Verne (*Nord und Süd*, p. 319). Bölsche's comparison of Lasswitz and Verne develops two significant ideas. He remarks that SF, or as he terms it, the "scientific tale [naturwissenschaftliches Märchen], constitutes a new and reasonably well-defined form of literature, despite its ties to other genres. He also suggests that science has had a greater effect than literary tradition on the content and even the literary foundations of SF ("NM," pp. 504-6).

In his understanding of the conceptual foundations of SF Bölsche agrees with Lindau and Lasswitz, but he is superior to Lindau in his aesthetic acuity, understanding of literary history, and awareness of the importance of science in SF. He notes, for example, the delay in the assimilation of modern cosmology into literature. But his implication (p. 507) that the artistic quality of modern literature should be judged according to the degree of such assimilation is, of course, rather ill-considered. Bölsche's discussion of realism, and his evaluation of the function of precise description, scientific accuracy, and matter-of-fact narrative tone in SF (p. 506), are also more perceptive than the observations of many of the other critics. The same can be said of his ability to go beyond pleasant generalities to identify some of the scientific sources of Lasswitz' SF, especially those of *Auf zwei Planeten*. The relevant aspects of Darwin's work and of research about Mars are described in considerable and competent detail (pp. 508-9). Throughout the essay Bölsche demonstrates his awareness of the need for an "aesthetics of the future [Ästhetik der Zukunft]" which will take into consideration the new literature about science (p. 505). The fundamental principle of such a literature is to be extrapolation or, as Bölsche calls it, "scientific deduction [wissenschaftliche Deduktion]" (p. 509). Of particular value, finally, is his understanding of the attention Lasswitz devotes to formal ethical questions and philosophical concepts, an emphasis which sets his SF apart from much other (pp. 509-12). While other critics had observed the same propensity, only Bölsche attempted to relate it both to science and to the artistic intentionality of SF.

Because he was intimately familiar with science and with other SF or similar forms of literature, especially Verne's novels, Bölsche was able to appreciate the difficulties Lasswitz faced as an early creator of SF. Among the problems he mentions are the need for scientific accuracy, the dangers of superficial characterization and long-winded scientific exposition, and the lack of even a basic knowledge of science among most readers (pp. 513-14). In his discussion of artistic quality, Bölsche expresses some dissatisfaction with the actual execution, though not the basic intentionality, of Lasswitz' fiction, particularly the latter parts of *Auf zwei Planeten* (pp. 511-13). I share many of his reservations, but diagree with his analysis of the narrative logic of the novel (see below, Chapter IV).

The presence of Bölsche among Lasswitz' early critics and literary patrons raises provocative but perplexing questions about Lasswitz' relation to contemporary political movements and artistic circles.[12] Bölsche was not only a popularizer of science but also a major figure in German Naturalism, which flourished in the last two decades of the nineteenth century, especially in Berlin. From 1891 to 1893 he edited the movement's chief organ, the *Neue Deutsche Rundschau,* founded in 1890 as the *Freie Bühne.* Although more important as a critic and aesthetician, Bölsche was also a prominent member of the so-called "Friedrichshagener Dichterkreis" or "literary circle," a group of radical Naturalists located in the Berlin suburb of that name. The Freidrichshagen circle had more than a few ties to the Social-Democratic opposition against which many of Bismarck's repressive measures were directed.

In Naturalism, and especially within the Friedrichshagen circle, artistic endeavor was closely associated with the advocacy of liberal, indeed often socialist political convictions. But science and technology were of scarcely less importance to the Naturalists, who were greatly concerned with the problems of the industrial urban society, with the social implications of Darwinism, and with the effort to apply the methods and standards of "scientific" investigation to both ideology and aesthetics. A landmark of German Naturalism was Bölsche's treatise, *Die naturwissenschaftlichen Grundlagen der Poesie: Prolegomena einer realistischen Ästhetik* [*The Scientific Foundations of Literature: Prolegomena for a Realistic Aesthetics*] (1887). He also wrote an essay entitled "Ob Naturforschung und Dichtung sich schaden?" ["Whether Scientific Investigation and Literature Are Mutually Deleterious"]. Among Lasswitz' own writings on the relation of science to aesthetics, it will be remembered, was an early piece quite similar in title and thought, "Die poetische und die wissenschaftliche Betrachtung der Natur" (1887).

It is not surprising, then, that Bölsche responded favorably to Lasswitz' SF and that he published his important essay on Lasswitz in the *Neue Deutsche Rundschau.* I nevertheless hesitate to conclude that Lasswitz was closely allied to German Naturalism, whether politically, artistically, or—much less—personally. Lasswitz was located far from Berlin or any other center of Naturalism. Available evidence indicates that he was a bourgeois intellectual liberal, not a Social Democrat.[13] His literary achievement was not of sufficient quality to make him a principal figure in the history of any form of literature—except of course German SF. Moreover, Lasswitz wrote prose fiction about imaginary science and the future, while the chief literary focus of German Naturalism was drama set in lower-class contemporary urban-industrial society.

Those observations point toward deeper differences between Lasswitz and the Naturalists, disparities of the kind emphasized throughout this chapter. Although Lasswitz was beyond a doubt not oblivious to ideological questions and to the political issues of the day, he viewed both conservatism and liberalism with a detachment which neither side, by and large, was either willing or able to adopt—perhaps quite understandably. Part of his reservation can be attributed to his expansive comprehension of history and philosophy, another part to his assimilation of the ideals of the Age of Goethe, and perhaps still another to the reticent, pacific, even phlegmatic personality noted by early observers. At least as consequential in this respect was his conviction that science, rather than economic or social forces, was the principal determinant of human existence. I think it therefore more accurate if less convenient to view Lasswitz as a virtually unique, geographically and intellectually semi-isolated figure who cannot easily be associated with the major ideological and aesthetic movements of his time.

The modest handful of contemporaneous documents surveyed in the preceding pages scarcely serves to establish Lasswitz as more than a minor figure in German letters around the turn of the century. Secondary literature about him is also extremely sparse in the decades from his death to the present, and he receives little or no attention in the standard literary histories and reference works. His SF is mentioned favorably but not prominently in a few specialized studies of spaceflight literature and similar subjects which appeared in German during the Weimar Era, such as the articles "Weltraumschiffahrt, ein poetischer Traum und ein technisches Problem der Zeit" ["Spaceship-Travel, a literary Dream and a Contemporary Technical Problem"] by Karl Debus (*Hochland,* 24 [1927], pp. 356-71), and "Die phantastiche Literatur: Eine literarästhetische Untersuchung" ["The Literature of Fantasy: A Literary-Aesthetic Investigation"] by Hans-Joachim Flechtner (*Zeitschrift für Ästhetik und Allgemeine Kunstwissenschaft,* 24 [1930] pp. 36-46). Only in an obscure monograph on science fantasy, *Das naturwissenschaftliche Märchen: Eine Betrachtung* [*The Scientific Tale: A Consideration*] (1919) by Anton Lampa, is he treated as a relatively important figure. Since his works were suppressed during the Nazi Era, it is not surprising that bibliographical research reveals no critical studies for that time. Post-war German students of SF and related literature have generally devoted little attention to Lasswitz (see below).

As far as I am aware, between the years immediately following his death and the evolution of modern SF criticism there appeared only one important study of Lasswitz' fiction, and that in English: Edwin Kretzmann's useful article "German Technological Utopias of the Pre-War Period," published in the *Annals of Science* (3 [1938]:417-30). Writers and critics of Anglo-American SF, when they are aware of Lasswitz at all, have usually contented themselves with respectful but vague acknowledgments. During and after the 1930s Willy Ley (1906-1969), an emigre who had been a leading figure in German rocket experimentation in the Twenties and Thirties, did attempt to popularize Lasswitz within the Anglo-American SF community. Indeed, Lasswitz' SF may have had its greatest direct impact on the pioneer German rocket experimenters like Ley and Wernher von Braun, who revered *Auf zwei Planeten*. There is also some evidence that several other figures prominent in the history of Anglo-American SF were familiar with Lasswitz' works, among them the German-speaking Hugo Gernsback. Lasswitz, then, may well have had some indirect but not inconsequential effect on the evolution of Anglo-American SF. More recently three critics, Mark Hillegas, Franz Rottensteiner and K. G. Just, the first two of them well-known SF scholars, have published excellent essays on Lasswitz; and Rudi Schweikert has provided extremely useful background materials in the apparatus to the first modern unabridged reprint of *Auf zwei Planeten,* though the volume is difficult to obtain. Nevertheless, contrary to their opinions and my own as well, Lasswitz is still not considered a figure of any great moment in the history of SF. A popular revival of his SF is unlikely. Nor, I think, will he regain the position of prominence in the history of early SF which his works once seemed to promise and might indeed have attained under other circumstances. In many ways SF has pursued the directions Lasswitz set out in his fiction and in his theoretical writings, but it is a development upon which his direct influence was inconsequential.

Title page of Kurd Lasswitz, "Nie und Immer: Neue Märchen" [Never and Always: New Tales], Leipzig: Diederichs, 1902). Drawing by Heinrich Vogeler.

Chapter III

Lasswitz' Shorter Science Fiction: The Anthologies *Bilder aus der Zukunft, Seifenblasen,* and *Traumkristalle*

The unpretentious volume *Bilder aus der Zukunft: Zwei Erzählungen aus dem vierundzwanzigsten und neununddreissigsten Jahrhundert* was published in 1878 by S. Schottlaender of Breslau, Lasswitz' home town. It contains his first SF, the novellas *Bis zum Nullpunkt des Seins: Erzählung aus dem Jahre 2371* and *Gegen das Weltgesetz: Erzählung aus dem Jahre 3877.* The edition was modest—at most two or three thousand copies. *Bis zum Nullpunkt* was written or at least begun in 1869 and, as the last two digits in its subtitle witness, had already appeared by itself, in an 1871 issue of the *Schlesische Zeitung,* a regional periodical of limited circulation.[1] *Gegen das Weltgesetz,* then, would likely have been completed in 1877. The earlier story is about 15,000 words in length, its successor almost twice that. A brief but important preface on the writing of SF, discussed in the preceding chapter, completes the volume.

The few critics who have commented on the *Bilder* have been rather generous to Lasswitz' two youthful stories, perhaps more so than was the author himself. Both Rottensteiner and K.G. Just observe that Lasswitz, although his other SF was reissued periodically during and after his lifetime, never had the *Bilder* reprinted after the second and third printings, which appeared in 1878 and 1879.[2] Hans Lindau, in his *Nord und Süd* article of 1903, praises Lasswitz' boldness of imagination, his ability to create exciting narrations, and his expertise in using a "matter-of-fact [sachlich ruhig]" narrative tone to domesticate the unfamiliar and improbable. He also remarks that Lasswitz' descriptions of his imaginary worlds evidence an "ingenuous pleasure in [portraying] captivating concrete objects [naives Wohlgefallen am fesselnden Stofflichen]" (p. 319).

Time—changing literary tastes and the progress of both science and SF—has faded the *Bilder* somewhat. But Lindau's evaluation is essentially accurate, as far as it goes, despite his obvious and rather condescending partiality to his provincial friend. The two modern

83

critics, Just and Rottensteiner, are only slightly less appreciative. Writing with the benefit of nearly a century of historical perspective, they can also undertake to relate the stories to larger contexts, whether ideological or literary. Just, referring to German political history, goes so far as to declare that the *Bilder* "deserve a special place in the literature of the *Gründerzeit,*" the Age of Bismarck. In the earlier story, which first appeared in the same year that Germany was unified under Prussia, a "leap of time annuls the historical moment—something not without a certain boldness. The old dream of the German Reich had been fulfilled,...and in the same instant what has become fact is surpassed and called into question by fiction." Lasswitz, Just speculates, may have expressed "a hidden critique of the ancient dream [of German unification], now at last 'fulfilled.' " Just is not certain whether the critique he perceives was wholly intentional. But the Preface to the *Bilder,* he points out, shows that Lasswitz was aware of contemporary political issues, that he was able to question scientific positivism, and that he even sought to envision some of the philosophical and aesthetic problems raised by the attempt to combine science and fiction.[3]

Rottensteiner relates the *Bilder* to Lasswitz' other SF and to the larger history of the genre. In their exuberance, which he finds both appealing and excessive, the two stories "differ greatly from everything [Lasswitz] wrote later. They are rich in action [and] melodramatic, exhibit an ingenuous enthusiasm for technology, and waver in tone between seriousness and unrestrained humor.... Although they lack all literary value, these prose pieces are nevertheless extraordinarily interesting, for they already contain, in embryonic form, the central elements of many later SF stories." Like Just, Rottensteiner senses that the *Bilder* "conceal something more serious and problematical," a deeper significance which he interprets not ideologically but rather philosophically as "the conflict between pure reason and reason which acknowledges emotional values."[4]

Bis zum Nullpunkt des Seins

The events related in *Bis zum Nullpunkt* occur, as the story's subtitle forthrightly announces, exactly half a millenium after 1871. Aromasia Duftemann Ozodes, the famous performer on the "Smellodion" ("Ododion" or "Geruchsklavier"), is engaged to Oxygen Warm-Blasius. Oxygen is a scientist and "weather-manufacturer [Wetterfabrikant],... owner of a large establishment which manufactured and leased machines which artificially produced changes in the atmosphere" (*BzN,* 18-19). He is also a member of the faction called the "Temperance Party [die Nüchternen]," which advocates sober rationalism. It is an age when philosophical convictions have replaced national loyalties and economic principles in ideological disputation. In 2371, arguments about reason are pursued with passion—and conversely. Oxygen's ostensibly "temperate" ideology is actually a self-deceptive pose. His doctrinaire positivism, quick temper, and some old-fashioned male-chauvinist objections to Aromasia's professional pursuits precipitate a lovers' quarrel. Aromasia is no shrinking violet; in fact she closely resembles the forthright, intelligent and vibrant women of the classical German literature which Lasswitz and his readers so revered. Seeking to make Oxygen behave more reasonably, she and Magnet Reimert-Oberton—poet, mutual friend of the couple, and secret but honorable admirer of Aromasia—join in writing a satirical poem about him. Magnet, like Aromasia, espouses the tenets of the "Subjective Party [die Innigen]." To the humiliation of Oxygen, the two post the poem for all to read, for in 2371 incorrect thought and abnormal behavior are excoriated in public and in literary form, as they are in Enlightenment comedy. But the well-meant jest goes awry, and the tragi-comedy becomes a tragedy. Scarcely intending more than a sharp riposte to the poem, the enraged Oxygen sabotages Aromasia's "Geruchsklavier." The stench it releases during her next performance is far more than an outrageous insult to her art. There is a rush for the exits, followed by a fire in which Aromasia dies. The grief-stricken Oxygen seals himself into a new anti-gravity spaceship and catapults himself into space to seek oblivion, "out there,...where stars no longer course through space" (75). Magnet concludes the story with a philosophical reverie, in which he consoles himself with the prospect of memorializing Aromasia in a new poetic work.

The plot of *Bis zum Nullpunkt* is quite conventional, even "obviously trivial," as Kretzmann remarks.[5] A familiar story—a lovers' quarrel, differences in temperament and personal philosophy, a romantic triangle, and an unexpected catastrophe—is rewritten in a futuristic setting. Only the external details of the pattern are changed, not its basic features. The remorseful disappointed lover still commits suicide, although now he does it with a rocket instead of a pearl-handled pistol. Certainly the story has evident technical shortcomings, among them vague character motivation and the anticlimactic final passage. But the exposition of plot is not the ultimate purpose of *Bis zum Nullpunkt*. The "story" serves rather as a useful vehicle for topical satire, some rather jejune philosophizing, and, above all, the panoramic portrayal of an unfamiliar imaginary world.

To introduce or "domesticate" his fictional world and keep it at the center of attention Lasswitz employs an impressive collection of narrative devices and items of imaginary content, many of which anticipate those encountered in later SF. A richly textured background of imaginary technological objects and other futuristic ideas manifests his "ingenuous pleasure in captivating concrete objects"—perhaps it was not so ingenuous as Lindau thought. Lasswitz describes, or at least mentions with a studiously casual tone, flying machines and skyscrapers (1), covered and apparently powered walkways (2-3), weather control (18-19), extremely rapid transportation (19), artificial foods (24), instantaneous global communication (48), and the arts of the future, including of course the "Geruchsklavier" and the satirical poetic form of the "Grunzulett." The latter is apparently a facetious portmanteau combination of the sonnet, the Middle-Eastern ghasel popular in earlier nineteenth-century German lyric poetry, and the German verb *grunzen* 'groan' and adverb *zuletzt* 'last' (? "He who groans last," "le dernier cri"). But unlike the writers of much early American SF or in fact other primitive ventures in the genre, Lasswitz does not present the future as a stock of technological and cultural wonders. Instead, like those who later created maturer Anglo-American SF, he encourages the reader's sense of plausibility by describing his futuristic ideas and "gadgets" in a narrative tone which, except for a few moments of enthusiasm, is sober and almost nonchalant.

Sometimes the "matter-of-fact" atmosphere Lindau observed is created by leasurely description and concatenation of detail. For the opening paragraph of *Bis zum Nullpunkt,* which presents the all-important first view of the imaginary world, Lasswitz chooses a situation which would initially appear quite plausible to his Wilhelmine readers; to present it he employs a conventional, sedate, discursive tone with which they would also have been familiar from their habitual literary fare:

> Aromasia was sitting in the garden of her home, gazing dreamily into the blueness of the pretty summer's day of the year 2371. She followed with her glances the little dark clouds which suddenly took

shape here and there in the atmosphere and let fall a torrent of rain; or she peered out to the flying cars and aerocycles which at her feet filled the broad street in colorful hurly-burly. For Aromasia's garden was located on the roof of her house in the aery height of about one hundred meters above the ground. *(BzN, 1)*

[Aromasia sass im Garten ihres Hauses und sah träumerisch in's Blau des schönen Sommertages vom Jahre 2371. Sie folgte mit ihren Blicken den kleinen dunkeln Wolken, welche sich hier und da plötzlich in der Atmosphäre bildeten und einen Regenguss herabströmen liessen; oder sie spähte nach den fliegenden Wagen und Luftvelocipeden aus, die zu ihren Füssen in buntem Gewühle die breite Strasse erfüllten. Denn der Garten Aromasia's befand sich in der luftigen Höhe von ungefähr hundert Metern über dem Erdboden auf dem Dache ihres Hauses.]

Judged by the standards of traditional literature, the passage may not have much to recommend itself stylistically. But considered as early SF it is excellent in conception and competent in execution. Lasswitz carefully balances the familiar with the futuristic, the romantic and back-yard *Biedermeier* with the scientific. Perhaps the overt mention of the date 2371 as early as the first sentence attracts too much attention. But Lasswitz, we note, carefully places the implausible element at the end of a plausible, sober statement which otherwise contains nothing which might interfere with the reader's inclination to believe the narration. Kafka was to employ exactly the same device, admittedly with greater syntactical complexity but with similar intent and effect in the first sentence of *Die Verwandlung* [*The Metamorphosis*].

In the second clause of his second sentence Lasswitz introduces flying machines, but only quietly, after having first alluded innocuously to the weather, which in the twenty-fourth century—as we find out only later—is not solely the product of nature. To soften the surprise further he uses here the oblique dative case, rather than the more conspicuous nominative, and then proceeds immediately to a relative clause which presents additional imaginary content and leaves the reader little time for reflection and its attendant skepticism. In a work of "mainstream" literature the phrase "in colorful hurly-burly" would likely be considered both hackneyed and superfluous; here it promotes "domestication" by telling the reader something about the social impact of the flying machines. Thus rather than simply asserting the existence of aircraft, the narrator also proceeds straightaway to imply that such things are parts of everyday life in the imaginary world. In my view the final sentence, in which the narrator and author turn from directly presenting the world of 2371 to address the late nineteenth-century reader, is too explicit. The information that there are skyscrapers in 2371, delicately suggested already by the phrase "flying cars and aerocycles... at her feet" in the preceding sentence, could have been provided less bluntly in a casual amplifying phrase, or perhaps might even have been left to the reader to deduce.

Elsewhere Lasswitz is quite capable of using restrained allusion rather than detailed description to establish the "matter-of-fact" tone characteristic of SF. Weather control, in itself scarcely a trivial matter and then as now certainly improbable to the reader, is taken for granted by the inhabitants of the future. Lasswitz, accordingly, makes it the topic of a casual conversation which the reader overhears and may not completely understand at first:

> "...I'm really swamped with orders," [said Oxygen.]. "The weather is exceptionally dry and I've got my hands full providing enough water....
> "And are you absolutely sure about the weather for tomorrow?" asked Aromasia. "Convince yourself," replied Oxygen, fetching the weather-atlas from his car and opening it to the day in question. (18, 21)

Twice during the same conversation, however, Lasswitz feels constrained to offer the reader third-person explanations of weather-control in the twenty-fourth century. The length and technical tone of the interpolations conflict with the otherwise relaxed mood of the dialog, and their very presence disrupts the illusion that the reader has entered the imaginary world. It might well have been better instead had Lasswitz confined himself to a few well-chosen allusions to weather control and thereby tempted the reader to elaborate the rest of the idea for himself.

Perhaps the most striking among the techniques which Lasswitz uses to "domesticate" the reader in the imaginary world is the invention of essentially new words or the use of old words to express new meanings. The numerous and sometimes nearly untranslatable neologisms in *Bis zum Nullpunkt* include not only the previously mentioned "Luftvelocipede," "Wetteratlas," and "Grunzulett," but also "Duftaccorde" ("odorchord") (9) and "Odoratorium" ("odoratorium"), the latter obviously modeled on "auditorium"—a ready but neat play on speculative parallels between the senses which will recur in later SF. Some neologisms are even derived from others, for example the verb "luftvelocipediren" ("to aerocycle") (9) and the expression of enthusiasm "grunzulettal!" ("fantabulous!" "fansonnetalettal!")

"sonneterrific!") (21). Such constructions imply that the neologisms are not fictional inventions at all, but rather, by long-established usage or widely cultivated modishness in the imaginary world, elements of a real and continuously evolving language. The same is true of the mildly profane expression "sich zum Sirius scheren" ("go to Sirius") (34), analogous to the actual if quaint German idiom "sich zum Teufel scheren" ("go to hell"). The imaginary world, so the reader is subtly informed, is so real as to have evolved its own oaths, which—be it noted—refer no longer to religion but rather to science, the "faith" of the future.

Among the most conspicious neologisms in *Bis zum Nullpunkt* are the characters' names. "Talking" names, especially the humorous ones give to the great "Duftmeister" ("odormasters") of the fictional past (7), such as "Naso Odorato" ("Rhyno Smelt"), "Stinkerling" ("Schmelling"), "Frau Schnüffler" ("Madame Sniffaire"), and "Riechmann" ("Reekman"), strain the reader's sense of fictive reality and plausibility, although some sound more normal in German than in my fanciful English renditions. Both Just and Rottensteiner suggest that the facetiousness and patent unreality of the names in the *Bilder* indicate that Lasswitz did not take his imaginary worlds very seriously.[6] I think it more accurate to say that Lasswitz' sense of humor sometimes distracted him from his primary interest, the exploration and description of imaginary future worlds whose basic features and underlying concerns are meant to be taken seriously. In any event, not all the personal names in *Bis zum Nullpunkt,* and especially not those of the major characters, need be dismissed as amusing but misconceived pranks or evident allegories. It is possible that in selecting such names as "Oxygen" and "Magnet" Lasswitz was attempting to promote a sense of plausibility by suggesting that naming customs evolve to fit the self-image and ideals of each age, in this case one where liberalism, rationalism, and science predominate. Certainly similar naming practices have been adopted in other ages, for example the Renaissance, the Puritan Era, and the years immediately following the Russian Revolution.

Whatever the case, Lasswitz was not unaware of the import of naming-customs. It is even more significant that he included a discussion of them in the narration itself. His brief but quite informative explanation, which is managed much better than the remarks about weather-control, provides yet another indication that the imaginary world is a complex, comprehensible, and fictively real place which the narrator, already quite familiar with it, can describe to the reader in a placidly factual tone:

> Magnet Reimert-Oberton ["Rhymerd-Uppertone"]... bore, as did everyone, a dual name. In keeping with the legal equality of women, children retained the name of their mother as well as that of their father; if they married, then the daughters dropped the name of the father, the sons that of the mother, and in its stead added that of the spouse. (9)

Lasswitz' evident interest in neologisms is part of a larger attempt to exploit language and the relation between narrator and reader to evoke the impressions of plausibility and fictive reality. As I suggested in Chapter I, perhaps no aspect of the imaginary world, especially if it is located in a time far from ones own, is more implausible to the skeptical reader than the very existence of the text itself and that of the language in which it is written. The writer of SF must somehow deal with the problem, either by ignoring it studiously or by attacking it resolutely. In his early novellas Lasswitz inclined toward the latter course. Thus in *Bis zum Nullpunkt* he at least confronted the question, but he did not achieve a satisfactory solution, perhaps even to his own mind. Early in the story, for example, the narrator adds a footnote explaining the time-units used in the twenty-fourth century:

> *For the convenience of the nineteenth-century reader (for whom we are content to write), the 'hours' are taken to be such that twenty-four of them comprise a day. (20)

Such stratagems are generally counter-productive. In the present instance the footnote itself disrupts the reader's involvement in the imaginary world, and the assertion of the narrator that he is "content to write" ("wir begnügen uns") for the nineteenth-century reader raises more questions than it answers. In order to explain the existence of the note and of the narrative persona who, it now appears, has written the story, Lasswitz would have had to create a much more visible narrator or even to frame the entire text as an imaginary "document," an account written by some figure who is identified more specifically than by a vague "we" and who, for reasons which would also have to be adduced, chose to compose the text.

A few pages earlier Lasswitz had addressed a similar problem, and with even less success, by suggesting that German has survived in 2371 as a private language used among intimates:

"Wherever might Oxygen be?" complained [Aromasia] softly in the harmonious tones of the German language. For though one was accustomed to employ the newly introduced universal language almost exclusively, even in normal intercourse, one nevertheless expressed the tender feelings of the heart in the sweet sounds of one's original mother tongue. (4)

But Lasswitz' awareness of the problematic nature of both the text itself and the language of narration and dialog is more significant than his relative inability to solve those dilemmas, for it demonstrates the system and the sophistication of his concept of SF. Later writers, indeed, continued to use essentially the same techniques to approach the same problem—one which cannot actually be solved, of course, except within the make-believe confines of the "game" of SF.

Another part of the narrative strategy of *Bis zum Nullpunkt* concerns the conception and presentation of the very foundations of the imaginary world: its culture, the psychology of its inhabitants, and the processes by which it came into being. The many individual technological innovations which are part of life in the imaginary world of the story have already been discussed. But Lasswitz' purpose is not to create a scientific and technological utopia; nor is it simply to evoke in the reader a naive "sense of wonder" at science and technology. He attempts rather to examine how they can affect the world, whether in the hypothetical future or, by implication, in the present.

The inhabitants of the twenty-fourth century are themselves well aware of the importance of science and technology, and they eagerly attend the latest developments. Yet their interest is not portrayed as an all-consuming juvenile fascination, a mass preoccupation with technological spectacle, as is often the case in early SF, to the detriment of the more demanding reader's sense of plausibility. Instead, Lasswitz' characters treat the impact of science on their world as a matter of mature and lasting interest, sometimes even apprehension. Oxygen, with whose extreme positivism and pragmatism Lasswitz obviously disagrees, goes so far as to propose that civilization itself is equivalent to "the understanding and domination of Nature [die Erkenntniss und Beherrschung der Natur]" (32), especially in the sense of scientific knowledge and technological mastery. If Lasswitz was later to say much the same in his essay "Über Zukunftsträume," the phrase he used there, "technische Beherrschung der Natur," contains the explicit qualification *"technological* mastery," rather than *total* domination (see above, Chapter II). The poet Magnet, who generally speaks for Lasswitz in *Bis zum Nullpunkt,* also expresses a less radical and simplistic view that is based on a deeper understanding of science. He states that in the modern world idealism is both a feasible and necessary counterbalance to science and to the human weaknesses science reveals and fosters:

> "All this insight [into the advances of science and technology], all theoretical knowledge is powerless in the face of the force of the drive for preservation in the battle for existence, in the face of the on-goaded lust for property and pleasure and the passion of the moment. These forces could only be restrained by a power of the mind which is capable of arousing and controlling our will in an equally powerful manner." (30)

Lasswitz, like Oxygen, appreciates the contributions of science; but, like Magnet, he is also apprehensive of its threats. Oxygen's attitude corresponds to the dominant view of science in the late nineteenth century, but such ideas are not accepted so uncritically in the twenty-fourth. Even so, Lasswitz suggests, the twenty-fourth century, like the nineteenth, has not yet come to realize that an appreciation of science and technology need not exclude idealism or humanism. Consequently, the narrator remarks, Magnet is generally misunderstood by his contemporaries:

> According to our concepts he would be termed an unbearable realist; to that age [dem damaligen Zeitalter, i.e.,the future] he appeared not only an excessive idealist, but also a namby-pamby [weichlich] romantic. For he still persisted in the attitude of the poets of the twenty-third century, who in their dreams liked to transport themselves back into the Age of Steam, into those days when human beings were still constrained to lift up their eyes unto the hills. (9-10)

Lasswitz, when he addresses his assessment of Magnet to the late-nineteenth-century reader, may well also be explaining his own position as a scientist who refuses to be an absolute materialist, and as a writer who, because he cherished the past and yet wrote about the future, might easily be mistaken for a mere creator of either irrelevant, ethereal fantasies or simple glorifications of science.

The way in which the imaginary world is related conceptually to the real world constitutes not only one of the weakest but also one of the strongest features of *Bis zum Nullpunkt*. Lasswitz did not and could not solve the dilemma involved in presenting an imaginary future world as though it were real, part of the "past." But his use of analogs to construct the imaginary world of 2371 and to suggest its plausibility is impressive, especially for such an early work. The basic analog of the novella is Lasswitz' own late nineteenth century, which he subjects to a critique founded both on the ideas of modern science and on the principles of the Enlightenment and of German Classicism and Idealism. Thus the intellectual quarrel of the "temperate" and "subjective" factions echoes the nineteenth-century debates between idealists and realists. Aromasia's attempt to reform Oxygen by subjecting him to public criticism, although it may well be derived in part from Enlightenment comedy, is compared explicitly to the custom of appealing to public opinion during the later nineteenth century or, as it is called five hundred years later, "the crude Neo-Medieval Period [das rohe Neu-Mittelalter]" (3, 47). Similarly, Oxygen's weather-control business is a future version of the private or public enterprises which emerged during Lasswitz' own time to develop and exploit technology and natural resources. On a broader historical level, the "American-Chinese War of 2371" resembles the nineteenth-century wars of imperialism and exploitation (62-3).

Even some of the arts of the twenty-fourth century are clearly— sometimes too clearly—modeled on those of the late nineteenth century. Although similar imaginary devices had been discussed for centuries, the "Geruchsklavier," for example, may be a poorly-concealed and not entirely complimentary allusion to Wagner and his *Gesamtkunstwerk*. If at times the imaginary world seems too evidently a simulacrum of Lasswitz' own, it should be noted that no writer can create entirely *ex nihilo*, and that the crudity or incongruity of analogs is far more evident in hindsight. Lasswitz' use of historical analogs in *Bis zum Nullpunkt* is considerably more restrained and sophisticated than that of many other authors of SF, especially those writing in its early period, when the genre was strongly affected by the utopian tradition.

A clear indication of the sophistication with which Lasswitz constructed the imaginary world is provided by his attempt not only to present a synchronic "picture from the future," but also to describe the historical processes by which the imaginary world came about. Much SF of a more primitive nature refers only to our present age and to the future, which are viewed in the fiction as, respectively, the past and the present. Lasswitz, however, also portrays the continuum of history between the nineteenth and twenty-fourth centuries. Landmark historical events are introduced by brief but pointed allusions, a technique which enhances their plausibility, for they seem to be matters of common knowledge. The device also challenges the reader to discover—that is, to construct for himself—the meaning of the allusion; thus, as a debate about social problems between Oxygen and Magnet illustrates, it encourages him to participate actively in the exploration of the imaginary world.:

> "By your leave," Magnet interrupted him. "I must indeed acknowledge the fact that, after the great battles of the twentieth century, we have with good fortune navigated our way around the cliff of the social question in its crass form." (29-30)

Lasswitz also knows how to bolster plausibility by taking advantage of the considerable "truth-value" of the documental insert, for example the government communiqué about the American-Chinese War of 2371 (63). The insert actually constitutes a document within a document, for the narrator cites the news media which in turn have quoted the communiqué. On occasion Lasswitz also adopts the stance of the popular or scholarly historian, as he does in disquisitions on the arts of the future and their history (e.g., 4, 6-8), or in the several footnotes accompanying the text (4, 11, 20), which therefore itself appears at times to be a fictive document. Frequently, however, he simply supplies the "facts" of "past" history, and writes with a concise and initially unobtrusive matter-of-factness which avoids tedium and assures the reader that the information presented must be accurate:

> The talk of the day consisted of the conflict between the United States and the Chinese Empire, which was attempting to deny the former aerial transit rights. But the thought of war was earnestly denied, for people could not divorce themselves from the hope that the so-called "Railroad War" between Russia and China in the year 2005 was to have been the last war of the civilized world. The Chinese had been forced by that war to open up their country to European railroad traffic. But in the same year that the Central Asian Pacific Railway was completed the transportation industry suffered such an upheaval through the invention of the aero-engine that the Russian achievements soon lost their significance. (27)

The sophistication of Lasswitz' imaginary "pictures from the future" is demonstrated further by his ability not merely to dream up fantastic gadgets and new social customs, but also to envision the less obvious but often far-reaching consequences of changes in science and society. The passage just cited, in which he describes how future technological innovations affect economics and international politics, is not unique in *Bis zum Nullpunkt*. Elsewhere, as in the passage quoted on page 90, Lasswitz not only foresees the emancipation of women itself; he also speculates that it will affect naming customs—or rather, he describes how indeed it has done so in the twenty-fourth century. Similarly, flight in *Bis zum Nullpunkt* is more than a mere technological novelty; it is a part of everyday life and a cause of new social and political problems as well.

Of particular interest in this respect are Lasswitz' descriptions of the arts of the future, which are not limited to the rather facetious "Geruchsklavier" and "Grunzulett." A reference to an imaginary tragedy, *"Die letzte Locomotive [The Last Locomotive]"* by Anton Feuerhase ("Firehare"), suggests that in the future science and technology may well become conventional subjects of art, to such an extent in fact that poets may find obsolescent technology nostalgic, romantic or even tragic (12-13). Oxygen, with more enthusiasm for the idea than Lasswitz himself likely felt, proposes that science may change the very nature of art, or rather its fundamental form of expression and reception. If it is ever possible to stimulate the brain directly, he speculates, then "the physiologists will assume in the future... [the very] role which the artists now exercise" (38). Such motifs and ideas demonstrate clearly how Lasswitz, like the best writers of SF, was eminently able to conceive and describe a complex and coherent imaginary world which is different from our own not merely in its lesser material features or even in its social customs and institutions, but also in its very world-view.

Gegen das Weltgesetz

Gegen das Weltgesetz, the second novella in the *Bilder aus der Zukunft*, is almost twice as long as its predecessor. It is also considerably richer in action, imaginary science and social detail, all of which contribute much to the quality of a work of SF. Nevertheless, the story does not represent a radical new direction in theme or technique. Instead, Lasswitz attempted, with some measure of success, to consolidate and refine his previous achievement. Among the most striking resemblances between the two *Bilder* is the common theme and story-line, whose focus is the uneasy interrelationship of emotion and reason.

As Lindau noted in his 1903 *Nord und Süd* article, both "pictures from the future" relate "a love story with a quite analogous outcome. The scorned lover betakes himself into the Boundless Expanse [of space]" (323). In *Bis zum Nullpunkt* there are three main characters and the story revolves about a catastrophic lovers' quarrel between Oxygen and Aromasia; Magnet's secret love for Aromasia is of lesser consequence. In *Gegen das Weltgesetz* the love plot consists of a true romantic triangle which involves all three major characters; but this time the story ends happily with the union of the two lovers meant for each other.

Lyrica, a virtuosa on the "Gehirnorgel" or cerebral keyboard, is in love with Cotyledo. The latter is a leading botanist of the thirty-ninth century but, like Magnet, has a humanistic sensibility. The famous chemist and rationalist Atom Schwingschwang ("Forthinback") also loves Lyrica. He resembles Oxygen in his petulance, his doctrinaire insistence on rationalism, and his underlying irrationality. By 3877, exactly two millenia from the story's probable composition, there have been great advances in mathematics and psychology. The latter discipline has actually expanded into a broader science which unites aspects of physics, neurology and conventional psychology. Atom's sister, the psycho-mathematician Functionata, computes that, if Cotyledo marries Lyrica, he will become insane and die, because "in 623.7 days the molecular complex C in the cortical layer of Cotyledo's brain will disintegrate" (*GdW*, 60). If he does not marry her he can count on a happy and successful life. Functionata's prediction is based on genetic principles and on genealogical evidence that Lyrica and Cotyledo are both descendants of a certain nineteenth-century German named Schulze.

Atom seizes upon the prediction as a means to prevent the lovers from marrying, for in the thirty-ninth century marriage is contracted only when it conforms with good sense, including the information furnished by science. To defy such counsel would in fact violate an ethical "Weltgesetz" or "Universal Law," a version of the Kantian imperative now supposedly become a reality rather than a mere ideal. Cotyledo nevertheless proposes marriage, for he prefers to have Lyrica and then die rather than to live without her. Out of love for him Lyrica refuses, and then disappears with the aid of a new invisibility-inducing chemical which Atom has invented. For reasons somewhat unclear she secretly accompanies Cotyledo, who attempts to discover whether the "spirit" he senses is real or merely a hallucination engendered by his grief. While trying to replenish her supply of the chemical in Atom's laboratory, Lyrica becomes partly visible as her body removes the substance from her cells. Her reappearance occasions an exciting round-the-world flying-machine chase with Atom. Lyrica eludes him, but her craft malfunctions and she crashes into the sea near the Canary Islands.

Quite by coincidence, of course, Cotyledo and two of his friends, Proprion and the pedagogue *cum* amateur archeologist Strudel-Prudel ("Eddyblooper") are nearby recovering an ancient chest from the sea. The three rescue Lyrica, and in the chest is discovered none other than the Berliner Schulze, still alive in suspended animation. They revive him and learn that he is not the common ancestor of Lyrica and Cotyledo after all. The two are therefore free to marry, but Atom refuses to accept the verdict of changed circumstances. Acting now himself in violation of thirty-ninth-century ethics and the "Weltgesetz," he forcibly attempts to prevent the union. Cotyledo narrowly escapes Atom's machinations, and the wedding takes place. Atom seizes an experimental space capsule, launches it into space from the mouth of a half-finished giant tunnel, and dies far away from Earth.

The plot of *Gegen das Weltgesetz*, as Rottensteiner remarks, "is admittedly even more adventuresome" that that of *Bis zum Nullpunkt*.[7] He intends perhaps to imply—quite correctly, I think—both that Lasswitz did not exercise great restraint in handling the plot of his second novella, and that he was more concerned with other matters. The conventional and even trivial nature of the love story is obvious, and Lasswitz does not labor overmuch to avoid fortuitous improbable coincidences. Nor does he always succeed in controlling his satirical impulses. Thus while the idea that descent from a common ancestor may have adverse genetic effects is appropriate to the story, the appearance of Schulze himself contributes little but a few gratuitous jokes about nineteenth-century Germans.

Nevertheless Lasswitz attempts, somewhat more earnestly and capably than in his earlier novella, to relate the love-plot to the imaginary world of 3877. The impediment to the marriage of Cotyledo and Lyrica is occasioned not only by personal jealousy, as it was in *Bis zum Nullpunkt*, but also by the scientific ethics of the thirty-ninth century. Similarly, Lyrica's "Gehirnorgel" is treated much more seriously than the "Geruchsklavier" in the earlier novella. Other important plot elements, such as the invisibility-inducing chemical, are motivated less convincingly. But it is still apparent that in *Gegen das Weltgesetz* Lasswitz has become even more aware that plot in SF cannot consist simply of a perfunctory narrative framework, one adapted perhaps from nineteenth-century sentimental fiction, romance, or the fairy-tale.

In *Gegen das Weltgesetz*, as in *Bis zum Nullpunkt*, the imaginary world is the chief focus of attention, and the presentation of imaginary science and technology one of the strongest features of the piece. Among the many technological innovations Lasswitz introduces are artificial foods (26-27), commercial submarines (30-31), light-weight apparatus for individual flight (49), the invisibility chemical (55), computers (57), and voice transcribers (28). Broader ideas related to science and technology include overpopulation (18), ecological disasters (45), evolution (77ff.), geographical and climatological changes (14, 19), monumental engineering projects (91, 110ff., 159), future archeology (67), suspended animation (144), the global megalopolis with its skyscrapers (49), the prospects of interplanetary travel and communication with extraterrestrial beings (66-67), and direct control of the brain, though for benevolent purposes only (*passim*). Many of these notions, as well as the character of the mad scientist disappointed in love, are familiar ingredients of later SF.

Lasswitz makes it abundantly clear that science and technology are prime determinants of the thirty-ninth-century world, and that its inhabitants are aware of the fact. The news media of the more distant future, like those in *Bis zum Nullpunkt*, pay especial attention to matters scientific and technological (e.g., 66ff.). The "Gehirnorgel" expresses the assimilation of science into society in a more subtle and symbolical way. Most interesting of all is Lasswitz' conception of the "Weltformel" or "Universal Formula" by which, supposedly, psychological predispositions and even actual physical events can be calculated. In his Preface to the *Bilder* Lasswitz describes Laplace's "Universal Law," a seriously discussed hypothetical formula by which the precise behavior of every particle in the cosmos might be calculated, as a conceivable but highly unlikely method of understanding the world, including the shape of the future (see Chapter II). Like the "Gehirnorgel," the imaginary theory expresses Lasswitz' conviction that science was profoundly affecting the human condition and was becoming the dominant category of understanding. In his SF and in his other writings he clearly wished to make his readers aware of such ideas.

But however much Lasswitz entertained the notion of a new

discipline which might develop a "Weltformel," he questioned both the "state of the art" and the uses to which hyper-mechanistic theories might be put, either in the thirty-ninth century or even more, by implication, in his own time. As his essays and other fiction show, Lasswitz was not hostile in principle to the idea that science could contribute to the material benefit and the formal study of mankind. But his knowledge of science and his humanistic background caused him to view with considerable skepticism the often extravagant claims being made by the proponents of such embryonic disciplines. These doubts Lasswitz makes a fundamental part of *Gegen das Weltgesetz.* The story demonstrates that a true "Weltformel" and "Weltgesetz," scientifically-founded principles which would explain and, ideally, govern human conduct, would have to involve something more than an impersonal method of calculation. If one insists on seeking to defend the ridiculous plot of *Gegen das Weltgesetz,* the improbable but nearly tragic complication of the course of true love occasioned by Atom's jealousy and abetted by Functionata's misapplied science, then it is here that some justification is to be found. Although there is no substitute for a strong plot, the theme is advanced quite capably in the debates of the characters and in the finer details of language. Even the oath "Heiliger Laplace! [Holy Laplace!]" (46) may be intended to express Lasswitz' skepticism, in his characteristically humorous way. The phrase indeed clearly shows the prevalence of mechanistic thought in the everyday life and speech of the imaginary world—and possibly also, by its suggestion of profanity, resistance to the same idea.

To "domesticate" the imaginary world of *Gegen das Weltgesetz* Lasswitz again employs virtually the full range of stylistic devices distinctive of SF. The use of "talking" names and of neologisms for imaginary technology is essentially the same in both stories and therefore needs little further discussion. Of particular interest are the participle "lustfliegend" ("pleasure-flying") (74) and the related but almost untranslatable compound noun "Spazierschwimmer" (135), no doubt modeled on the real word "Spaziergänger" ("stroller"); both imaginary terms refer to individual air travel, which is not only a technological reality in 3877 but also a leisure-time activity. "Stundenblatt" ("hourly [newspaper]") (91), the future term for "newspaper," is patterned on the actual "Tageblatt" ("daily" or, in the original etymological sense, "journal"); the alteration suggests very succinctly the rapidity of communication in the thirty-ninth century.

Often familiar words are given new meanings or used in new contexts which, despite their allusive brevity, reveal much about the imaginary world. Thus in a passing reference to the "Saugrohr" ("drinking straw" or "tube") (66), we learn that in the thirty-ninth century food is artificial. It is mixed at the table instantly, though not wholly without culinary artistry, and then ingested through tubes—an idea which reappears often in later SF. When Lyrica, wearing her personal flying apparatus, rushes quite literally "im Fluge" ("flying") from her apartment (95), a subtle but effective alteration in meaning gives new life to a hackneyed idiom.

As formalist critics would put it, the change "makes strange" the form and content of the expression. It thereby reinforces the readers's sense of plausibility, for the phrase is no longer a worn hyperbole but rather a simple statement of fact. Lasswitz' skilled use of brief allusion to attract attention to the ostensibly trivial aspects of the imaginary world can also be observed in references to the pastimes of the thirty-ninth century (49), its calendrical system (99), courtship and wedding customs (69-70, 156), and even to such matters as the future equivalents of the handshake and verbal salutation (13, 63).

To introduce imaginary science and technology, and other features of the thirty-ninth century as well, Lasswitz also employs long, detailed description, somewhat more capably here than he did in *Bis zum Nullpunkt*. Many of the distinctive stylistic devices discussed in Chapter I can be found, for example, in the explanation of the metallurgical and chemical properties of the miracle substance "Chresim" and its application in the atmospheric "swimming" apparatus:

> The material of the swimming apparatus consisted of a platinum-silicium-carboxide compound, a complexly constructed substance which, with its extraordinarily low specific gravity, united the properties of platinum with the transparency of glass and the flexibility of rubber but which also, like the latter, could be tempered. Because of its utility this substance bore the name "Chresim" (from Χρήσιμος, 'useful') and found the most varied applications in industry. The "aeronatabelt" [Luftschwimmgürtel], a completely transparent, internally vacuous bell of Chresim surrounding the body, held it in equilibrium. Toward the front the apparatus closed off in the shape of a wedge and served simultaneously as a shield against the air being cut through with the greatest velocity. From it hung down two stirrups in which the feet found a support-point, while a large propeller (of tempered chresim) located at the back imparted to the machine a velocity whose direction could be controlled at will through skilled movements. Motive power was provided by a container full of liquid oxygen which had been compressed

at a very low temperature by an immense pressure until it condensed, and which now could be employed as a long-lasting source of power. Everyone, of course, had gone through his aero-natation school [Luftschwimmschule] ... (49-50)

Lasswitz' efforts to make imaginary science and technology plausible in *Gegen das Weltgesetz* demonstrate a better conception of the recurrent technical problems of SF and a greater practical skill in attacking them than is apparent in *Bis zum Nullpunkt*. Adjectives like "complicirt" ("complicated") and "geschickt" ("skilled"), or adverbs like "natürlich" ("of course"), actually provide little explicit information. But where the writer himself necessarily lacks precise knowledge about the devices or ideas whose general nature he has been able to imagine, such words fulfill the important function of suggesting that the concepts or objects described do exist and that knowledge about them has been conveyed.

Another and more recondite strategem, one which Lasswitz employs with considerable skill in *Gegen das Weltgesetz*, involves the corroboration of imaginary technology by reference to scientific theories which themselves are often imaginary as well:

... Functionata... was working leisurely on the integration-machine.... The labors of the greatest masters had advanced it to the point that enormous calculations, which otherwise would have filled out the life of an individual, could be carried out by the integration-machine in but a few hours and without any exertion of thought. The method of symbolic notation made it possible to transform the work into a mechanical task and to solve any given system of differential equations through complicated combinations of the mechanism.... (57-8)

The same purpose is served by "documentary" reference to scholarly writings and to the history of imaginary science, as in the introductory lecture on cultural history delivered by Strudel-Prudel, headmaster of the "Psycháon" or "Gehirnschule" ("Cerebral Academy"). Lasswitz greatly enhances the effect of the "historical" discourse by framing it as a lecture rather than merely offering it as a statement of the narrator:

"In the year 3614 Molekulander discovered the artificial synthesis of protein, and in the year 3616 there appeared, under the title *Complete Theory of Cerebral Functions*, the immortal work of a lady who bore the curious name 'Schnuck' ["Lambkin"]." (26-27)

In *Gegen das Weltgesetz*, as in *Bis zum Nullpunkt*, the

imaginary world and its history are obviously patterned on certain actual historical analogs, again especially those of Lasswitz' own time. Even though he looks two thousand rather than a "mere" five hundred years into the future, he surveys the intervening time-span with even greater detail than is to be found in the earlier story. Thus an entire chapter is devoted to Strudel-Prudel's history lecture. According to him, and presumably Lasswitz too, the nineteenth century, and even more the thirty-ninth, are characterized by the rapid progress of science and by a conflict between liberalism and reaction, although in the future the particular issues of contention have changed. The resemblance between the two periods is ascribed to the recurrence of similar historical processes whose nature is much better understood in 3877 than it was in 1877. While Lasswitz of course intended his picture of 3877 as a commentary on 1877, the thirty-ninth century is not simply an allegory or disguised picture of the late nineteenth century. In his elaborate presentation of the imaginary world and in his assertion that history is governed by certain "laws of periodicity [Gesetze der Periodicität]" (26) discovered only shortly before the thirty-ninth century, Lasswitz cultivates the assumption, appropriate to the intentionality of SF, that the imaginary world is indeed a "real" world in its own right.

Topical satire is of less interest to Lasswitz in *Gegen das Weltgesetz*, and therefore he is able to concentrate more of his—and the reader's—attention on the examination of the imaginary world itself. More evident, accordingly, is his ability to envision and investigate the wider consequences of science and technology, including some of their less beneficial effects. More apparent, too, is his comprehension of the notion that the inhabitants of the future, even though their world is a descendant of ours, will be concerned with ideas and issues quite different from those of our time. Lasswitz shows how technology is not simply a tool controlled by its creators, but rather inevitably changes society and individual consciousness. He also explores some of the possible deleterious consequences of science, such as overpopulation (18) and climatological change (14, 19). Most provocative of all, perhaps, is the notion that the future will see major changes in human psychology. The point is embodied most plainly in the "Hirnschule" and "Gehirnorgel," and is implied also by the arts of the thirty-ninth century (31ff.). The same idea is expressed in references to consciousness-altering devices (74), advances in neurology (74ff.), and possible differences in the categories according to which time, space and sense impressions are perceived (25-6, 34-5, 66-7).

While *Gegen das Weltgesetz*, like its predecessor, voices a critique of positivism, excessive rationalism, and unwarranted confidence in science, Lasswitz occasionally neglects to perceive some of the problems which might well emerge in his imaginary world even as he himself conceives it. With poorly concealed fascination and little fear of geological catastrophe he describes a project to drill a hole directly into the core of the Earth (110ff.). Without further deliberation he also remarks that the technology of the thirty-ninth century serves to strengthen family ties, demonstrating therefore that "here, too, it was apparent how material progress had as a consequence advancement in morals and ideals" (64). The idea was already being much questioned in Lasswitz' own time, and Lasswitz himself, as I have already noted, entertained reservations about it. Another provocative subject, thought control, is discussed at length (82ff.), but Lasswitz, as Rottensteiner notes, does not explore its disturbing implications.[8] The sinister aspects of the idea will later be a major theme in SF, from the worst movies to Huxley's *Brave New World* and Orwell's *1984*. But similar optimism was commonplace in Lasswitz' time, and is often apparent in SF, even much later.

Compared to *Bis zum Nullpunkt*, *Gegen das Weltgesetz* represents not a qualitative change but rather a certain quantitative improvement in Lasswitz' literary skills and his understanding of the intentionality of SF. In the second novella, as in the first, he several times reveals his awareness of the problematic aspects of SF, especially those which pertain to its special principle of verisimilitude. His logical mind is still troubled with the fundamental and possibly unresolvable dilemma of SF: how and why the reader is given—in the form of a literary text to boot—a picture of the future, and what the narrator's role is in that experience. Accordingly, early in *Gegen das Weltgesetz* Lasswitz, or rather the narrator—and in the *Bilder* it is indeed often difficult to make the distinction—feels constrained to address to the reader a remark about the terminology used to describe the imaginary world:

> Here we shall have to request forgiveness if the expression now and then does not precisely suit the real occurrence [den realen Vorgang]. The language of the nineteenth century, in which we must speak of course, is simply not always capable of following the newly-won insights of the future. (6)

A similar statement introduces the "Phonograph" or voice-transcriber: "We take the page and read—to our amazement in the

German language, though in stenographic signs" (28). Such passages may well constitute improvements on similar remarks in *Bis zum Nullpunkt*. But they still say either too much or too little, for they raise questions about the status of the narration which are not satisfactorily answered. By referring to the difference in language between the nineteenth and thirty-ninth centuries, by trying to explain how the narration has come to exist, and by allowing the narrator to speak momentarily as more than an anonymous, impersonal voice, Lasswitz seeks to anticipate and allay the reader's doubts about such matters. But his explanations are awkward, and the narrative persona who emerges briefly in them is not a viable personality.

Similar difficulties are occasioned by Lasswitz' use of footnotes and parenthetical remarks addressed to the reader, although he indulges in them less here than in *Bis zum Nullpunkt*. Fairly effective are a footnote giving the equivalent of the thirty-ninth century unit of currency (4), and a remark that Strudel-Prudel "used the customary universal language" (13) in his lecture on the history of the future. But sometimes, as in a note on time-units, Lasswitz feels it necessary to continue the digression with laborious amplifications or polemic remarks aimed directly at the reader as an inhabitant of another time:

> *One pentade equals five days. One year equals 73 pentades. This arrangement has the advantage that the time-space of the week (pentade) divides into the year without a remainder. (99)

The footnote shows of course that Lasswitz was eager to reinforce the reader's belief in the imaginary world, but he undermined his own purpose by misunderstanding the nature of the effort to evoke the senses of plausibility and fictive reality. Instead of trying to argue that the pentadic calendar would be superior to our own, Lasswitz might well have portrayed, as effectively as possible, its actual use in the imaginary world. But footnotes of any kind, like other momentary remarks to the reader, strongly tend to disrupt the illusion that the writer and reader are directly observing the imaginary world. That deleterious effect can be forestalled only by resolute measures which leave the reader in no doubt about the status of the narrator and the nature of the text itself. The writer may choose, for example, to make the entire narration an identifiable part of the imaginary world by framing it as a "document" produced by an inhabitant of that world. Generally, however, it is better to ignore such problems completely, or more accurately, to anticipate and counteract the readers' doubts by the use of an impersonal, omniscient and impeccably accurate narrative voice which has no need to address the reader personally or to offer him special explanations. That in fact is the stratagem Lasswitz pursues throughout most of the *Bilder* and in the better part of his other SF.

The *Bilder aus der Zukunft* are certainly not flawless. Despite his bold imagination and his evident descriptive skills Lasswitz is not a first-rate practitioner of realistic prose, especially in his management of dialogue. A more serious shortcoming, one more harmful to his development as a writer of SF, is Lasswitz' overindulgence of his playful sense of humor and his impulse to satirize contemporary institutions and customs. While such sallies of wit are in themselves neither reprehensible nor uninteresting, they interfere with the attempt to establish the imaginary world as a plausible and fictively real environment. Equally injurious to that purpose are Lasswitz' awkwardness and inconsistency in defining and conveying to the reader the relation between the real and imaginary worlds as it is created by the process of narration and the text itself. Yet another problem, one which continued to trouble Lasswitz and which has subsequently plagued many other writers of SF, concerns the integration of the story-line, especially the love-plot, with the larger exposition of the imaginary world or "thought-model." Such weaknesses are to be found of course in many other writers of SF, especially among those writing as early as Lasswitz. They are far outweighed by the facts that even in his first works Lasswitz was quite evidently seeking to accomplish the basic intentionality of SF, and that he already possessed an impressive command of the stylistic requisites of the genre. The *Bilder aus der Zukunft* are landmarks of early SF. Created by a youthful writer, they show a promise which Lasswitz later realized more fully.

"*Seifenblasen* and *Traumkristalle*"

The anthologies *Seifenblasen* (1890, enlarged edition 1894) and *Traumkristalle* (1902, enlarged edition 1907) contain most of Lasswitz' smaller fictional pieces, as well as three poems and the essays "Selbstbiographische Studien"["Autobiographical Studies"] (*Sb*, 274-88) and "Schiefe Gedanken" ["Out-of-true Thoughts"] (*Tk*, 197-207). Together the twenty-six stories, which vary in length from about 2000 to, in one instance, almost 10,000 words, cover a period of more than twenty years in Lasswitz' literary career. The compositional history of the stories is somewhat uncertain. "Apoikis" (*Sb*), presumably the earliest, was written during or before 1882, and several of the pieces in the enlarged edition of *Traumkristalle* were apparently composed only shortly before the revised volume was published in 1907.[9]

In their length, treatment of theme, and narrative stance the stories differ greatly from the *Bilder aus der Zukunft* and from *Auf zwei Planeten* as well. Some cannot even be classified as SF, as Franz Rottensteiner points out.[10] Nevertheless, Lasswitz' short stories should not be regarded as constituting a discontinuity between the two early novellas and the mature novel. Certainly that argument is not unequivocally supported by biographical and chronological evidence. *Bis zum Nullpunkt* was written between 1869 and 1871, when Lasswitz was still a student or, in the midst of his studies, was serving in the Franco-Prussian War. He wrote the very similar *Gegen das Weltgesetz* as late as 1877. By that time he had taught two years in Breslau and Ratibor, before assuming his duties at Gotha in 1876, where he apparently wrote all of his short stories. Moreover, the publication of *Auf zwei Planeten,* also written at Gotha, preceded that of *Traumkristalle* by five years. Lasswitz in fact continued to write short stories until the year of his death.

Such evidence does much to call into question the conjecture, advanced by Lasswitz' contemporaries Lindau and Engel, his one-time pupil Hans Dominik, and the modern critics K.G. Just and Rudi Schweikert, that Lasswitz wrote his SF primarily to console himself for his failure to obtain a university professorship. In fact his literary career began at least as early as his student days. The same chronological considerations, the great dissimilarities among the stories themselves, and the striking differences between them and Lasswitz' other SF also make more difficult another task, the evaluation of the position of Lasswitz' short stories within his literary development. Since many of them cannot be classified as SF and, as Franz Rottensteiner aptly remarks, are not of lasting literary value,[11] I will not discuss each story in detail here. I hope rather to use analyses of certain important stories or groups of similar pieces to examine how Lasswitz' shorter fiction contributed to his evolution as a writer of SF—a process which began with the *Bilder aus der Zukunft* and which, furthered by his theoretical investigations of SF, culminated in *Auf zwei Planeten.*

The shorter fiction of Lasswitz' middle years constitutes a vital but notably indirect contribution to that literary development. Hans Lindau, in his early *Nord und Süd* essay, stated that the stories "were created not for the sake of some [abstract] idea, but rather from a joy in 'painting' [nicht um der Idee willen hergestellt worden sind, sondern aus Lust am Malen]." Lasswitz' approach to his stories, Lindau added, "has a reassuringly quieting note, [for] he who uses the idea as a point of departure easily lapses into a kind of picture-postcard brushwork, [because] freedom is lacking" (328). The assessment may be valid with regard to the modest scale of Lasswitz' ambition and achievement in individual pieces. But Lindau does not adequately express the collective import of the short stories. He also fails to appreciate the nature and sophistication of Lasswitz' artistic intentionality.

Seifenblasen includes three poems, "Unverwüstlich" ["Indestructible"] (1878), "Epilog" (1885), and "Prolog," the last of which was written perhaps as late as 1890. In them Lasswitz, with his characteristic combination of earnestness and jest, expressed the conscious intent or, as he put it, the "Programm" (*Sb*, 1, line 9) which motivated his efforts. To explain his writing he elaborates— perhaps even belabors—several aspects of the "Seifenblase" or "soap-bubble" image. The metaphor, he suggests, has aesthetic implications: the stories represent attempts to imitate in literary form the delicate, shimmering and perfectly rounded shape of the soap-bubble, and they should be viewed as ethereal, playful, but not entirely inconsequential creations (*Sb*, 1, ll. 17ff., 3, ll. 1-24, 4, ll. 9-16). If the soap-bubbles eventually burst and leave only a spot of lye, it is because their creator—the poet is by implication also a chemist and parlor magician—has not achieved the proper mix (*Sb*, 4, ll. 17-20). Lasswitz also insists that his literary soap-bubbles be regarded from a scientific perspective. One ought to realize that they consist, so to speak, of fat and alkali; the author advises his readers therefore to "study in advance a chemistry text" in order to appreciate them better (*Sb*, 2, ll. 1-4). The same idea, that the kind of literature which Lasswitz creates cannot be understood without reference to science, is also expressed in the earlier poem "Unverwüstlich," where scientific terminology is mixed with the traditional language of love poetry.

In the most general terms Lasswitz reformulates the soap-bubble image into a statement—one which recurs throughout his theoretical writings on science and literature—that the modern world requires a correspondingly modern form of artistic imagination and expression:

These days, our fantastical bent to show,

Th' unmodern trifle we do abhor
Of mounting the Muses' winged steed to go
A-riding in romance's land of yore.
Quite other means suit modern times now,
With the lofty state of aeronautical lore:
A wave of the hand, and on our frothy Montgolfière
Freely we swim in the glistening atmosphere. (*Sb*, 3, ll. 25-32)
    [Um heut'gen Tags phantastisch uns zu zeigen
Verschmähen wir den unmodernen Tand,
Das Flügelross der Musen zu besteigen
Zum Ritt in der Romantik altes Land.
Ganz andre Mittel sind der Neuzeit eigen
Bei der Aëronautik hohem Stand:
Ein Wink, und auf der Schaum-Montgolfière
Frei schwimmen wir im Glanz der Atmosphäre.]

In 1890, and much less a decade earlier when he wrote his first short stories, Lasswitz could not have known precisely his future evolution as a writer of SF. But the "Prolog," despite its playful stance, reveals an interest in speculative science and technology, a desire to integrate science with art, and a concern for developing literary forms appropriate to that venture. All three are consonant with Lasswitz' other fiction and with his own writings on aesthetics.

It is these ideas which provide the proper perspective from which to examine the pieces in *Seifenblasen* and *Traumkristalle*. I would suggest that the stories, whatever their value as individual works of literature, collectively represent a process of trial-and-error experimentation in which Lasswitz pursued and achieved a better understanding of the conceptual foundations of SF, its stylistic requisites and tendencies, and thus its proper generic bounds. To advance that thesis it is not necessary to over-interpret the "Prolog" and the other poems, or to indulge in specious deterministic and teleological arguments which treat *Auf zwei Planeten* as the inevitable end-product of a conscious process of self-development.

Lasswitz' earliest SF and his essays on science and literature show clearly that from the beginning he possessed a fairly distinct notion of SF and that he also intended to realize it in some if not all of his literary endeavors. The tendency to experiment cautiously and systematically with the intentionality of SF is evident in the two *Bilder aus der Zukunft*, which resemble each other closely in theme, plot and technique. Finally, the existence of *Auf zwei Planeten* proves in retrospect that Lasswitz, during the very time when most of the short stories were written, somehow acquired the abilities which enabled him in effect to reformulate into a far maturer work the ideas and techniques already adumbrated in the *Bilder aus der Zukunft*.

(i) Experimentation with the Utopia and Imaginary Voyage

SF has long been associated, though not always legitimately, with the utopian tradition. Lasswitz' own utopian affinities, philosophical and literary, are evident throughout his writings. "Apoikis" (1882), the earliest story in *Seifenblasen*, is a delicate, poignant epistolary tale which recounts a modern European's visit to a hidden island in the Atlantic which harbors an ideal society evolved by a colony of Greeks whose ancestors had left Athens after the execution of Socrates. The piece is a sterile literary atavism which looks backward to an idealized past, rather than offering a direct critique of modern civilization or the exploration of a reasonably plausible future world, as had the *Bilder aus der Zukunft*. Although some interesting imaginary theories and devices are introduced, the unimportance of science and technology in "Apoikis" also makes it difficult to classify the story as SF. But in writing it Lasswitz may well have gained additional experience in conceiving and describing imaginary societies different from his own, and in maintaining a factual, calm narrative tone.

Lasswitz did not repeat his early miniature *tour de force* in the traditional utopia. He did, however, continue to explore the opportunities offered by narratives about distant, radically different environments and by the imaginary voyage, a literary tradition closely related to both utopian writing and SF. "Stäubchen"["Dust-Speck"] (1889, *Sb*) and "Auf der Seifenblase" ["On the Soap-Bubble"] (1887, *Sb*) are stories about tiny but complex inhabited worlds. In the latter Lasswitz describes in detail the imaginary land and society of the "soap-bubble people" or "Saponians" ("Saponier"). The wry pun on *homo sapiens* suggests that Lasswitz intends to satirize our own species; indeed the Saponians arrogantly take as their racial or species cognomen the epithet "the Thinking Beings" ("die 'Denkenden' ") (*Sb,* 16).

Science figures in the story in several essential ways. The narrator and his companion, the congenial inventor Onkel Wandel, are able to visit the soap-bubble world and observe its transient existence only by means of Wandel's invention "Mikrogen," which radically reduces their size and retards their sense of time. The narrator, at pains to establish his veracity by confessing his occasionally limited knowledge, claims not to know whether "Mikrogen" is a device or a chemical.

On the soap-bubble the two visitors find themselves in the midst of a controversy about theology, philosophy and science. The Saponian rulers, who espouse as dogma the notion that their world is unique, solid and composed exclusively of the two elements fat and alkali, have accused the scientist Glagli of blasphemy and treason. Glagli has advanced the heterodox theory that the soap-bubble world is only one of many, that it is hollow, and that it consists of not two but four fundamental elements—fat, alkali, glycerin and water. Siding with Glagli, who refuses to recant and is threatened with being boiled in glycerin, the narrator and Onkel Wandel barely escape to their own world. The narrator regrets that he cannot substantiate his story with documents because in his precipitous departure he has had to leave behind a ponderous manuscript record of his observations (*Sb*, 16-17). Such apologies are a rhetorical device common in SF, utopian literature and the imaginary voyage.

Like "Stäubchen," "Auf der Seifenblase" is obviously an imaginative transformation, both playful and serious, of Lasswitz' dissertation on droplets. It reflects even more his long occupation with the history, philosophical foundations, and methodological weaknesses of science. While the story might legitimately be termed a scientific fantasy or romance, it is not genuine SF, despite the prominence of imaginary science and the systematic effort to envision and describe a manifestly different world. The world which Lasswitz creates in the story simply cannot be viewed as subjectively real or plausible; nor, perhaps, was that his intent. He makes it too evident that what he offers is a kind of parable about our own world, although it does indeed deal with science in an imaginative way. Thus Glagli's name and his predicament constitute a reference to Galileo whose transparency, perhaps greater still than that of the pun on "Saponier"-*homo sapiens*, makes it impossible for the reader even to pretend to view the soap-bubble world as a fictively real environment. Likewise, the humorous, breezy narrative frame or introduction, which treats the visit to the tiny world as the amusing result of an afternoon spent with an avuncular, eccentric inventor, hinders the impressions of plausibility and fictive reality, or at the very least does nothing to encourage them.

(ii) *Marchen* and the Nature of Imagination

Lasswitz' fondness for the *Märchen* ("fairy-tale" or "fable") is evident in the *Bilder* and in the utopian stories just discussed. It is even more apparent in a number of fanciful narratives such as "Prinzessin Jaja" ["Princess Yesyes"] (1892), "Tröpfchen"["Drop-let"] (1890), "Musen und Weise" ["Muses and Sages"] (1885) and

"Der Schirm" ["The Umbrella"] (1893) in *Seifenblasen*, "Jahrhundertmärchen" ["Tale of the Century"], "Das Lächeln des Glücks" ["Fortune's Smile"], "Weihnachtsmärchen" ["Christmas Story"] and "Der Gott der Veranda" ["The God of the Veranda" in *Traumkristalle,* and "Die Unbeseelten" ["The Soulless Ones"] (1908), "Die Entflohene Blume" ["The Fugitive Flower"] (1908) and "Frauenaugen" ["Women's Eyes"] in the posthumous anthology *Empfundenes und Erkanntes.* These pleasant but literarily undistinguished tales are set in never-never lands inhabited by traditional fairy-tale characters, allegorical entities, or personified natural organisms and philosophical concepts.

It would be extremely questionable to describe most of Lasswitz' *Märchen* and similar narrations as SF. Nevertheless I think that his experimentation with the form and his investigation of its conceptual presuppositions contributed to his development in the genre. Lasswitz' writings on aesthetics show that he was much concerned with the proper nature and, more particularly, the necessary limitations of fantasy or imagination in SF. And certainly his early critics also sensed some sort of kinship between his works and the older tradition. Like Lasswitz himself, they frequently sought to describe his fiction by using the term "Märchen," sometimes with qualifying adjectives like "modern" (Lindau) or "naturwissenschaftlich" ("scientific"—Lampa).

In any case, several of Lasswitz' *Märchen,* whatever his reasons for choosing the form, incorporate types of content or examine ideas related to science and therefore to SF. Some, like "Prinzessin Jaja," which tells of an attempt to formulate and answer "the most useless question in the world" (*Sb*, 25), use the *Märchen* vehicle to explore epistemological themes. In other tales, like "Der gefangene Blitz" ["The Captive Lightning-Bolt"] or "Morgentraum" ["Morning Revery"] in *Traumkristalle,* scientific ideas and technological objects appear in personified form, just as animals, plants or spirits are given human traits in the Aesopian fable or the traditional *Märchen.* Whatever the intrinsic quality of his *Märchen* and whatever pleasure he may have had in writing them, Lasswitz may well have gained from such ventures the insight that abstract philosophical concepts cannot be introduced into SF with no more than a perfunctory narrative framework. Nor, he may have learned, does it suffice merely to offer animations of technology. Experimentation with the *Märchen* form, as with the utopia and imaginary voyage, seems also to have given Lasswitz a better understanding of the fundamental nature of imaginary worlds in SF. Such environments are neither exact copies nor idealizations of the real world; even less are they totally independent constructs which the reader neither can nor wants to see as "real" worlds.

(iii) Short Stories about Imaginary Science and Technology

In the *Bilder aus der Zukunft* and in *Auf zwei Planeten* Lasswitz attempts a panoramic portrayal of futuristic worlds shaped by science and technology. By contrast, the focus of "Psychotomie" ["Psychotomy"] (1885), "Der Traumfabrikant" ["The Dream-Manufacturer"] (1886), and "Mirax" (1888) in *Seifenblasen*, and of "Die Fernschule" ["The Tele-School"] and "Der Gehirnspiegel" ["The Cerebroscope"] in *Traumkristalle*, is confined to a single scientific idea or technological device. "Psychotomie" and "Der Gehirnspiegel" describe innovations which make it possible to "dissect" or gauge emotions objectively. They offer fanciful variations on the microtome and the ophthalmoscope (*Augenspiegel*), actual German inventions of Lasswitz' own time. The longer story "Mirax" recounts the attempted " 'application of the theory of evolution to the artificial generation of the cosmic psyche' ['Über die Anwendung der Entwickelungstheorie auf die künstliche Züchtung der Weltseele']" (*Sb*, 208), as the great future-scientist Mirax' pioneering work is entitled. Lasswitz may have incorporated into the story a satire of both Marxism and its adversaries. The title of "Der Traumfabrikant" echoes a motif of *Bis zum Nullpunkt*, in which Oxygen is a "Wetterfabrikant" ("weather manufacturer"). Similarly, "Die Fernschule" represents a variation of the "Hirnschule," the futuristic educational institution described in *Gegen das Weltgesetz*.

The general narrative pattern of such stories is familiar from much other SF. Lasswitz simply recounts, in a casually anecdotal manner, the invention and employment of imaginary science. But once again, although he sought to "bridle" his fantasy by tempering it with the content and methods of science, he did not integrate the two in a manner wholly consonant with the intentionality of SF. Although he describes his imaginary science with great industriousness and makes it the central ingredient of the narration, the devices and ideas he imagines are much too fanciful to be taken seriously. As Lasswitz himself seems to feel, they are whimsical caricatures rather than legitimate extrapolations of science. The characters themselves are unrealistic, flat, stereotypical figures whom the narrator views with sovereign amusement. And Lasswitz does not succeed in presenting as fictively real environments the imaginary worlds which form the settings of the stories—if indeed that was his intent. His narrative stance is characterized by satire, mirth and a desire to indulge in recondite jests about science. The incongruous approach may well indicate a lack of skill; but it is likely too that Lasswitz did not regard his creations with utter seriousness.

It would appear retrospectively that in writing such stories about imaginary science, and in his *Märchen* about science as well, Lasswitz learned through both error and partial success that the synthesis of science and fiction into SF involves a special kind of conceptual and technical integration. As he seemed to have sensed in a simple but effective way in the *Bilder aus der Zukunft*, SF does not consist merely of the transformation of science and technology into fairy-tale characters, the narration of amusing stories about fanciful devices or theories, or the inclusion of actual or easily-foreseeable scientific ideas within a more or less traditional love story—the last being one of the larger atavistic flaws of "Die Frau von Feldbach" (*Tk*). Lasswitz may have come to think also that some sciences, like astronomy, physics, chemistry and engineering, are more readily suited than others to the aims of SF, at least at certain stages in their development. Other areas of science and technology may not have progressed sufficiently to provide the rich but still manifestly incomplete corpus of factual material which is the foundation for successful imaginative expansion in SF. Or they may lack the provocative philosophical implications and the potential for the creation of powerful symbolical associations and descriptive effects which can contribute so greatly to the impact of the narration. As his aesthetic essays show, Lasswitz was theoretically aware of those ideas, and throughout his literary career he created some works at least which correspond far more closely to what, even from the Preface to the *Bilder aus der Zukunft*, he had understood to be the nature of SF.

(iv) "Aus dem Tagebuch einer Ameise"

Throughout his short stories one can observe Lasswitz using and varying—not always for the better—the rhetorical devices which were already introduced in the *Bilder aus der Zukunft* and which were to be employed so effectively in *Auf zwei Planeten*. The pieces in *Seifenblasen* and *Traumkristalle* abound in neologisms, pseudo-scholarly accounts of future history, and, of course, lengthy descriptions of imaginary science. Lasswitz also experimented with many approaches to the vexatious matter of integrating imaginary science, plot action, and the progressive evocation of the unfamiliar fictional world. The problem is evident in the *Bilder*, and in most of his later short stories Lasswitz seems to have found no way of dealing with it which was satisfactory—even to himself. Also of paramount importance, it should be reiterated, is the attempt to determine and, through appropriate narrative techniques, to establish the relation of the imaginary world to the real world. Here also Lasswitz experimented, wavered, and—if he is to be judged in hindsight according to the intentionality of SF—often erred.

Yet not all the short stories need be viewed as salutary but in themselves less than successful experiments. Despite its title, "Aus dem Tagebuch einer Ameise" ["From the Diary of an Ant"] (1890), by far the longest of the stories in either *Seifenblasen* or *Traumkristalle*, shows Lasswitz' many strengths to especially good advantage, along with some of his characteristic weaknesses.

The story, like many SF texts, is presented as a document. In a short introduction replete with pseudo-scientific and pseudo-historical detail, a human "editor" who is a student of entomology explains how the diary was found and the language of the ants discovered and deciphered by the famous entomologist Antenna. The ant language, transmitted through the insects' feelers, "is based on ether-waves of 800 to 2000 trillion oscillations per second," which Antenna was able to detect, decelerate and record by means of a "fluorescence microscope" (*Sb*, 98-9). The editor notes certain difficulties in idiom which have made the translation of the diary a demanding project. He then refers the reader to "Antenna's original work which, in Latin, has appeared with Antwind Bros. in Humburg [Gebrüder Emswind in Flausenheim]" (*Sb*, 99).

The diarist's prissy diction and his alternately avuncular and testy tone have a *Biedermeier* air which was no doubt familiar, amusing and therefore credible to Lasswitz' readers. In the course of recording his response to a book on the *"Life and Activity of Humans"* by the controversial ant-thropologist Sssr (*Sb*, 99-100), the narrator—himself an ant, of course, but of the conservative persuasion—offers an elaborate picture of ant society. He subsequently participates in a dangerous but successful expedition to study the human beings, whom the ants consider inferior in intelligence, social consciousness, and ethics. Yet the ants themselves, as the narrator unintentionally reveals by his own statements, suffer from many flaws and misconceptions about the nature of the world and themselves. As the story unfolds certain ants, including the narrator, entertain doubts about the correctness of their science. But in the end, as winter arrives and the ants "creep into [their] winter-cell[s]," such misgivings are put to rest (*Sb,* 139).

The actual plot of the story consists of the initial encounter between human beings and an alien species as viewed from the perspective of the latter. The theme is a mainstay of utopian literature, the imaginary voyage, non-fictional travel literature, and SF as well, although the "alien" as narrator appears far more frequently in SF. In "Aus dem Tagebuch einer Ameise" Lasswitz also explores, in a circumscribed fashion, another topic which appears so often in SF, including his own: the inadequacies, so often exacerbated by overconfidence and cultural egocentrism, of science itself as a body of supposed "facts" and as a mode of obtaining knowledge. Viewed more broadly still, the story examines the concepts of morality, intelligence and emotion—in short, the fundamental aspects of the idea of humanity itself.

Many of the narrative devices characteristic of SF, such as the spurious document and pseudo-scientific diction, are to be found in well-developed form in "Aus dem Tagebuch einer Ameise." Lasswitz also gives free but, in this instance at least, not inappropriate rein to his talent for creating neologisms or altering the meaning of existing words. The technique, although it often has a humorous air, underscores the alien nature of the imaginary world. It also shows how language and outlook mutually affect each other, often to the detriment of clear and impartial understanding. Time, for example, the ants reckon not by our system, but rather by units which combine "sun" with some cyclical activity important to them; thus "Eggsun," "Larvasun," "Pupasun," "Wingsun," "Preysun," "Weddingsun," and "Wintersun," which appear with apparently diurnal numerals as the headings of the diary entries. Lasswitz may also be spoofing incidentally ancient Germanic month-names, which a few Germans of a philological and nationalistic bent periodically sought to revive.

Also amusing but significant is the ant-narrator's use of idioms which have been altered to correspond to the physiology and world-view of the ants. He says not "lay hand," but rather "mandible" ("Kiefer") to something (*Sb,* 112), not "hold one's tongue" ("den Mund halten"), but rather "feelers" ("Tasten") (*Sb,* 136). Similar in nature, but more sophisticated in form and even more directly related to the central theme of the story, are a number of neologisms which transpose "man" or "human being" with "ant" or "animal." For the narrator the word "antly" ("ameisenlich") (*Sb,* 103) has the same meaning that "human" ("menschlich") has for us. Other examples include the disparaging phrase "only a human" ("nur ein Mensch") and the species-characterization "non-reasoning human" ("ein unvernünftiger Mensch") (*Sb*, 103), the verb "de-antify" ("entameisen") (*Sb*, 111) for the actual *entmannen* 'unnerve, emasculate' or perhaps for *entmenschlichen* 'dehumanize,' and the exclamation "Let us guard ourselves against degeneration into humanity!" ("Hüten wir uns vor dem Vermenschen!") (*Sb*, 112). It is not surprising, therefore, that the ants also subscribe to a different cosmology and theology; thus their deity is the "Primal Ant" ("Uremse") (*Sb*, 102). They assume, moreover, that human beings lack reason and social consciousness, and they find love and individualism incomprehensible, immoral or ridiculous.

Lasswitz also uses the term "red ant," in itself not a neologism of course, in an intriguing manner. Ssrr's revolutionary study of humans is interesting and intelligent, the narrator remarks, "but written from a red-ant perspective of course" ("zwar rotameisenlich geschrieben") (*Sb*, 100). Later the diarist responds to the red ants' proposal to send an expedition to the humans with the utterance "Let the red ants pursue their politics of adventurism [Abenteuerpolitik] by themselves!" (*Sb*, 103). Obviously Lasswitz is formulating the general features of his imaginary situation in accord with actual entomological information. It is quite possible, however, that he also wishes to suggest that in his own society scientific truth, or at least valid insights into the nature of mankind, might be found among certain "red" thinkers who were shocking "respectable" circles. But whether from discretion or his fundamental distrust of dogmatism, Lasswitz does not glorify the "red" views of Ssrr. The story, it should be noted, dates from 1890, the year in which Bismarck's anti-socialist laws (1878) were repealed.

Numerous works purporting to be SF have adopted the insect world as an actual setting or as an "analog" for the creation of alien beings. But if it is indeed SF—and here I have serious reservations—"Aus dem Tagebuch einer Ameise" does not belong to the main current of the genre. Nor is the story flawless stylistically. It is, first of all, too long; certain ideas and devices lose their effect by over-repetition, and far too much space is devoted to the trite love plot between the two humans whom the ants study. Once again, too, Lasswitz cannot resist the temptation to indulge in topical satire or to give his characters unrealistic "talking" names, like that of the human entomologist Antenna. Such elements, as always, detract from the impressions of plausibility and fictive reality. But in its theme of "First Contact" between alien cultures, its critical examination of knowledge, science and the nature of humanity, and in its systematic use of certain narrative devices, the story exhibits many of the essential features of the characteristic intentionality of SF. Indeed, if one concentrates on these fundamental aspects and momentarily disregards such incidental matters as Lasswitz' over-indulgence of satirical impulses and his occasional tendency to treat the imaginary world less than seriously, it becomes apparent that, in its presuppositions, theme and technique, "Aus dem Tagebuch" is of a kind with *Auf zwei Planeten* and much other SF. In writing a rather fanciful story about the encounter of insects and human beings Lasswitz may have gained the insight that the same ideas and techniques might better be employed in a more serious investigation of the meeting between Man and extraterrestrial "humans."

(v) "Aladdins Wunderlampe," "Die Universalbibliothek" and "Wie der Teufel den Professor holte"

Among all of Lasswitz' short stories, "Aladdins Wunderlampe" ["Aladdin's Magic Lamp"] (1888) in *Seifenblasen* and "Die Universalbibliothek" ["The Universal Library"] and "Wie der Teufel den Professor holte" ["How the Devil Fetched the Professor"] in *Traumkristalle* stand most directly in the line of Lasswitz' development as a writer of SF and are therefore most pertinent to the early modern history of the genre. The three stories evidence clearly conceived, impressively innovative approaches to the impetus to create systematic "thought-models," the effort to delineate the proper nature of imagination in SF, and the attempt to select scientific content appropriate to such literature. It is scarcely surprising, then, that Willy Ley chose "Aladdins Wunderlampe" and "Wie der Teufel den Professor holte," along with the less impressive "Psychotomie," for translation and publication in the prestigious *Magazine of Fantasy and Science Fiction* three decades ago, and that more recently Franz Rottensteiner reprinted the latter story and "Die Universalbibliothek" in *Polaris* (1973), his important German collection of SF and critical essays.[12]

"Die Universalbibliothek" playfully explores what would now be called a cybernetic theme: the notion that it might sometime seem possible and feasible to generate, by random computer printout, a library containing all knowledge, including even that of the future.

The idea, which recurs frequently in later SF, is developed in one of Lasswitz' favorite narrative frames, a congenial conversation between a late nineteenth-century German professor and his visitor. But the "Universal Library" remains literally—and literarily as well—a mere parlor speculation, and quite necessarily so. Aside from basic technological difficulties, the professor explains, two great impediments make the project unrealizable. Even if one presupposes radical miniaturization, the library would require a space far larger than the known universe. In any case the sequence of apparently coherent information might suddenly be interrupted by gibberish. And far worse, it would also be impossible to distinguish fact from falsehood. Although the story was likely written around the turn of the century, Lasswitz' picture of the resulting chaos exhibits many dadaistic tendencies, as indeed do other of his speculations about language and knowledge:

> "... but the worst thing really comes," [said the professor] "when one has found an ostensibly rational volume. You want to look up something in *Faust*, for example, and then indeed you actually strike upon the volume with the correct beginning. And when you've read a ways, suddenly it continues 'Hickory, dickory, dock! [Papperle, happerle, nichts is da!], or simply 'aaaaa'.... Or a logarithmic table begins, but here too one doesn't know whether it's correct. For in our library there is not only everything that is correct, but also everything incorrect. And one dares not let oneself be deceived by the titles. Perhaps a volume begins: *History of the Thirty Years' War* and continues: 'When Prince Bluecher had wedded the Queen of Dahomey at Thermopylae..." (*Tk*, 143; Lasswitz' ellipsis in the middle and at the end)

In "Wie der Teufel den Professor holte" Lasswitz offers a brief rendition—not his only one—of the Faust theme.[13] The milieu is Wilhelmine, the subject of contention between Man and Devil theoretical physics. Another parlor gathering hears, from the professor himself, how he had been confronted and "fetched" by the Devil. Congenial and quite "human," the Devil here is the professor's *Doppelgänger*, for "each is his own devil,... and [the Devil] fetch[es] each after the manner in which he views the world" (*Tk*, 154). The professor of science and the Devil, accordingly, embark on a journey through "a hundred thousand trillion kilometers" of space. Their vehicle is not the magic cape used in Goethe's *Faust*, but rather a "space-automobile" ("Weltraum-Automobil" or "Weltautomobil") made of "Stellit" (*Tk*, 154, 156). (A substance of the same name but quite different proprietorship appears in *Auf zwei Planeten*.) Because the two travel at speeds far faster than that of light, the professor and the Devil can observe, in reverse order of course, events of the past as they overtake light rays emitted from them long ago. The idea was not yet wholly untenable when Lasswitz wrote the story.

In banter with his skeptical guests the professor relates the lively interchange with the Devil which has convinced him that his experience was not a dream, but rather, as his obfuscatory terms would have it, a real but "metaphysical" experience of either a "scientific-cosmological" ("naturphilosophisch-kosmologisch") or "ethical-noological" ("ethisch-noologisch") kind (*Tk*, 165). The traditional disputation with the Devil is versed as an argument about the very scientific possibility of just such an experience. The meta-dispute revolves about the nature of reason, the notion of existence, and the concept of infinity, all considered both as traditional, abstract philosophical ideas and as foundations of modern physics. According to contemporary science, the professor explains to the Devil, whose knowledge of physics is somewhat outmoded, space is curved and therefore finite. The Devil, pleased that the finitude of the universe might make it possible for him someday to destroy everything, magnanimously releases the professor. Quite conveniently the "Weltraum-Automobil" has returned to the vicinity of the Earth, for at its enormous velocity it has rapidly circumnavigated the universe while seeming to travel in a straight line—a feat often repeated in later SF.

In "Aladdins Wunderlampe" a scientist whose museum has purchased an old lamp from the Middle East has reason to believe that he actually possesses the legendary magic lamp. Showing it to his parlor guests, he causes the genie's voice to be heard, only to find out that the genie may grant solely those wishes which do not upset the course of past or future history and which do not contradict the laws of science accepted at the time the lamp's possessor summons the spirit. The lamp and the genie are therefore virtually powerless in the late nineteenth century, which believes that the universe is governed by a highly-oriented, inviolable system of physical causality. In one way the story might be interpreted as a comment on the difficulty of creating literature about imaginative science in an age of realism and mechanism, although Lasswitz himself argued that such fiction was possible. More significant, I think, is the broader view of science which underlies the story. In "Aladdins Wunderlampe" Lasswitz expresses—in a whimsical manner, to be sure—his earnestly skeptical response to scientific positivism, or at least its excesses. But perhaps whimsy, as the literarily more gifted mathematician-fantasist Lewis Carroll had discovered somewhat earlier, was a mode of discourse particularly suited to the informal but critical examination of the immense innovations in theoretical science which were beginning to upset long-established positivist attitudes. Here and elsewhere in his writings Lasswitz even goes so far as to entertain the idea that the actual nature of the physical world changes in accord with the evolution of human beliefs about its appearance and structure. But solipsism, or even radical relativism, it might be suggested, is likely incompatible with both science and SF if it is taken seriously, which it is not in the present story.

Lasswitz' scientific imagination and his ability to pursue some of the most fundamental and most abstract concepts of science are represented in their most daring form by "Aladdins Wunderlampe," "Die Universalbibliothek," and "Wie der Teufel den Professor holte." The stories are much like the "metaphysical fiction" which Scholes and Rabkin, in their study of SF, describe as "a certain kind of speculative tale based on scientific or philosophical ideas... [and involving] speculation about the nature of the universe which goes beyond the bounds of known science."[14] To Poe and Jorge Luis Borges, two of the chief practitioners of "metaphysical fiction" mentioned by Scholes and Rabkin, we might add Olaf Stapledon, Lewis Carroll, the Edwin Abbott of *Flatland* (1884), several writers of modern SF, and, I would suggest, the Lasswitz of these three stories.

Nevertheless, the literary skill of the stories does not match their ambitious scientific and philosophical content, and may also make it questionable to view them without reservation as SF. It is of lesser consequence that Lasswitz once again devoted too much attention to gentle satire of late-nineteenth-century manners. For each of the stories he also chose the anecdotal framework which he used in much of his other short fiction, and in one he also included the device of the "story-within-a-story." Therefore such challenging ideas as the computer-generation of theoretically infinite information, the seeming paradoxes of post-Newtonian physics, and the relativistic, even solipsistic implications of science itself are treated, not as the foundations of fictively real imaginary worlds, but rather as the hypotheses, idle pipe-dreams, or even tall tales of congenial academics. The fiction, therefore, is not itself a "thought-model," as in genuine SF, but rather a framework or vehicle for the discussion of a "thought-model." Exposition of ideas is substituted for fictional exploration of them as hypothetical realities. The deficiency, if the term is justified, is difficult to explain, and hindsight must not be permitted to cloud fair appreciation. In his playful literary moods, and in his more speculative moments as a serious scientist, Lasswitz was able to entertain heterodox aesthetic and scientific notions and to express their dual idiosyncrasies in whimsies like those discussed here. But in his background and his heart he was literarily a realist and scientifically a moderate positivist who was most comfortable when he could explore in his fiction, without indulging in the ironies of literary form or scientific theory, the hypothetically real implications of science and technology for human life.

Whatever its explanation, Lasswitz' reluctance to explore his ideas about science without the disrupting mediation of an ironic or playful stance is perhaps the most serious flaw of his short stories, if they are being considered as SF. The patent unreality of the utopian stories and imaginary voyages, the sterile conventionality of the *Märchen*, the choice of ants as fictional characters, and the anecdotal framework Lasswitz adopts in so many of his stories all interfere with the reader's ability to approach his fictions in a manner consonant with the intentionality of SF. The flaw, however, does have favorable long-range implications. I would suggest that Lasswitz, after his first two novellas, felt a definite uncertainty about the relation of the imaginary worlds of fiction to what he considered, for reasons which are admittedly understandable and reasonable, to be the "real" world—that is, his own. Therefore he proceeded with some caution. Sometimes he portrayed highly fantastic environments in narrations which, as an anchor for both writer and reader, pointedly employ the more particular devices of realism. In other stories bold speculations about science and the universe are debated by familiar characters, some of them much like Lasswitz himself, within a prosaic late-nineteenth-century setting.

Lasswitz' cautious attitude can be ascribed, in part at least, to his own profound comprehension of the intentionality of SF, which made it clear to him that the imaginary world had to be conceived and described in such a manner that the reader could be induced to regard it as real and plausible. At the same time, as he was also well aware, the intentionality of SF strongly encourages the writer to select for his imaginary worlds two types of environment, extraterrestrial worlds and the future, which are difficult to entertain, and to describe, as realities. The reconciliation of fantasy, realism and science in literature did not come easy to Lasswitz, nor has it to most writers of SF.

In his short stories, then, Lasswitz undertook—consciously or not—what might be called a strategic retreat from the confident frontal approach to the creation of SF which characterizes the *Bilder aus der Zukunft*. Limiting his experimentation to pieces of more circumscribed length and scope, he attacked in turn one or a few problems of conception, content, form and style posed by the intentionality of SF. In terms of generic categories, he explored the advantages and disadvantages of certain more established literary forms, such as the utopia, the imaginary voyage, the semi-fictional exposition of science, and fantasy fiction or the *Märchen*, all of which have long been associated with SF but still differ significantly from it. In doing so he improved—often through the experience of failure—certain of his basic literary skills, such as the establishment of an integral relation between plot and the exposition of the imaginary world; he learned to curb his penchant for humor and satire where it interfered with his larger purpose; and he also refined his command of a number of the specific stylistic techniques and narrative practices which, as his theoretical investigations and earlier literary experience had indicated, were apparently useful in SF. Most important and most arduous of all his achievements, however, was a better understanding of the function of science in SF and of the way the imaginary world and the real world are related in it. It is understandable, therefore, that the short stories are uneven in quality and often transcend the bounds of SF, for such missteps and deviations were ultimately not unprofitable. After two decades of practical experience and theoretical investigation, and after having struck upon an especially appropriate theme, Lasswitz achieved a solution to the intentionality of SF. The result was *Auf zwei Planeten*.

Front cover of Kurd Lasswitz, "Auf zwei Planeten," edition of early 1920s

Chapter IV

Auf zwei Planeten:
Early Masterpiece of
German Science Fiction

*Yet most of these worlds were really no worse than our own. Like us, they
had reached that stage when the spirit, half awakened from brutishness
and very far from maturity, can suffer most desperately and behave
most cruelly.*

Olaf Stapledon, *Starmaker* (1937)

CONNOISSEURS OF SF would call *Auf zwei Planeten*,
Lasswitz' masterpiece, a story about "First Contact," the initial and
often crucial confrontation of terrestrial mankind with other "men."
First Contact is an archetypal theme and plot of SF, and constitutes
one of its particular contributions to the thought and literature of
the modern world. *Auf zwei Planeten* might be described equally
well as a descendant of the Homeric epic, for it is a story of war and
of individual excellence. But Lasswitz does not merely retell the
Iliad and the *Odyssey*; his perspective is modern, philosophical and
scientific. The novel portrays the conflict of two cultures and
examines its effect on the lives of individuals and on entire
societies—their history, philosophy, social structure and
technology. The conflict occurs not because of a woman, but rather
because human curiosity and the technology of space flight bring
into contact two races which differ radically in psychology and
cultural level. The two are incapable of comprehending each other,
and sometimes even themselves, until a process involving hate,
love, and the acquisition of understanding has followed its course.
Thus *Auf zwei Planeten* is also a novel of education, not only that of
individuals but especially that of entire cultures. In fictional form
Lasswitz examines the nature of superiority, the value of
knowledge, and the meaning of humanity—questions which
occupied him throughout his life as a scientist, philosopher,
educator and descendant of German Classicism and Idealism.

Lasswitz began *Auf zwei Planeten: Roman in zwei Büchern* in

November 1895 and finished it on 11 April 1897.[1] The novel was first published in October 1897 by the Emil Felber Verlag in Weimar and Berlin. Soon the publisher was advertising that it was available for a price of eight marks "at all book stores and from all itinerant distribution agents [Kolporteure]."[2] *Auf zwei Planeten* continued to enjoy a modest success, including publication in a one-volume "popular edition" (*Volksausgabe*) in 1913. By 1930, when the last pre-Hitler edition appeared, at least 70,000 copies had been printed—a considerable number for that time, as Franz Rottensteiner remarks, but not enough to qualify *Auf zwei Planeten* as a true bestseller.[3]

During the National Socialist Era *Auf zwei Planeten* was banned as "democratic."[4] But soon after the war, in 1948, a new abridged edition in popular format and with modern illustrations was published by the rather obscure Cassianeum Verlag in Donauwörth (Swabia). The new edition coincided with the hundredth anniversary of Lasswitz' birth, but no doubt its appearance owed much to the growing popularity of SF in general and to the increasing worldwide interest in rocketry after the war, an interest which could now be pursued openly in Germany. Other abridged German editions of *Auf zwei Planeten* appeared in 1958, 1959, 1969 and 1972. Rudi Schweikert's edition of the entire text (1979), though already no longer readily accessible, represents a landmark in the modern appreciation of Lasswitz. Nevertheless, in its popularity with German readers of SF *Auf zwei Planeten* ranks well below the novels of Hans Dominik, the *Perry Rhodan* series, and the translated works of many foreign authors.

In the years immediately following its first German publication *Auf zwei Planeten* was translated into a number of European languages. Although translations "into all... civilized tongues" had been advertised as early as 1897,[5] it was not until much later that the novel appeared in French or English, the languages of Verne and Wells. Only in 1971 did the Southern Illinois University Press publish the first English-language edition, a translation of the abridged German edition of 1948 with a few passages added from the 1969 edition. A paperback edition was issued the same year under the Popular Library imprint (New York). Hans Rudnick, a Shakespearean scholar and professor of English, was the translator. The well-known SF critic Mark Hillegas added an afterword, and Wernher von Braun contributed an epigraph. While the earlier "indigenous" Anglo-American SF community knew something of Lasswitz, the translation apparently had to wait until interest in older, lesser known writers among both critics of SF and the broader readership had reached a state where the venture was feasible.

Upon its publication in 1897 *Auf zwei Planeten* received a modest amount of attention, especially in the liberal press.[6] With some overstatement the publisher's advertisement in the endpapers to the second impression (1898) claimed that "no book more interesting has ever been offered to the reading public." There was frequent mention of the novel's exciting plot, which may surprise us now with our taste for even faster action. Science, too, has advanced so far since 1897 that we wrongly but inevitably fail to appreciate fully the scope of Lasswitz' imagination. Many of his contemporary reviewers, for their part, were unable—perhaps understandably so—to grasp the wider import of the novel. The early critics usually treated it as an entertaining piece of humanistic, politically liberal fantasy. Generically *Auf zwei Planeten* was classified as a hybrid mixture of several more or less related types of fiction such as the utopia, the robinsonade, and literature about modern science and technology. Almost always the early critics overlooked the profounder philosophical and ideological questions which the novel posed about its own time.

One early reviewer, however, did offer a solid descriptive analysis of *Auf zwei Planeten* and a perceptive discussion of its generic status. In his review, "Weltphantasien" ["Cosmic Fantasies"] (*Die Nation*, 31 Dec. 1898, pp. 202-204), which was published just one year after *Auf zwei Planeten*, Moritz Kronenberg observed that the novel represented a clear departure both from the traditional utopia and from fiction about actual science. Therefore, he suggested, it deserved to be recognized as an impressive example of a new genre. While conceding the author's weakness in characterization and other conventional literary skills, Kronenberg acknowledged Lasswitz' ability to present a well-rounded and plausible thought-model, remarked with approval his emphasis on philosophy and ethics, and pointed out the difficulties involved in the attempt to join science and literature. These are still the topics which one must consider in interpreting and evaluating *Auf zwei Planeten*.

Plot Summary

Auf zwei Planeten begins when a balloon expedition attempting to reach the North Pole for the first time is marooned on a mysterious island exactly at the Pole.[7] The island is the advance base for a Martian expedition to Earth. The three explorer-scientists, Josef Saltner, Karl

Grunthe and Hugo Torm, are nearly killed when their balloon is caught in the Martians' "abaric field," the area of variable artificial gravity within which the Martian landing craft—veritable space shuttles—commute between the land base and the permanent space station located over the Pole. Grunthe and Saltner are rescued by the Martians. Torm is feared lost but will appear later after many hardships. (Chapters 1-5)[8]

The Martians, who call themselves "Nume" and their planet "Nu," are not bug-eyed monsters or Wellsian giant insects, but rather "humanoids," as SF customarily calls such beings. They have a greater spiritual and, perhaps, physical beauty than Earthmen, as is indicated by their slightly bigger eyes and foreheads—a motif by no means unique to *Auf zwei Planeten*. Ethically, culturally and technologically the Martians are of course greatly superior to terrestrial humans. But Earthmen and Martians are similar enough that the races can be mistaken for each other. Even interbreeding is possible; Grunthe and Saltner soon deduce that Friedrich Ell, the independently wealthy German scholar and scientist who sponsored their expedition, is the offspring of one such union. Ell, the reader learns later, is the son of the explorer All, who was stranded on Earth a generation earlier. Through the balloon expedition he hopes to re-establish contact with his father's civilization, about which he knows much, though only indirectly. Among the Martians are the females La and Se. Beautiful, personable and intelligent, they are not quite the mysterious, ravishing but often rather vapid princesses of Edgar Rice Burroughs' novels and so much early pulp SF.

From La, Se and the other Martians Grunthe and Saltner learn the language of the aliens and something of their advanced technology. Although the Martians treat them politely, they are generally regarded as primitives, or almost even as pets and laboratory specimens. But the two Earthmen maintain their dignity and that of terrestrial humanity by their physical courage, intelligence and strong individualism, and by their own ethical excellence, which, unlike that of the Martians, rests on emotional as well as philosophical foundations. (Chapters 6-14)

The prospect of serious conflict between Martians and terrestrial humans soon emerges. When a new crew arrives to resupply the polar base, the Martians importune Grunthe and Saltner to return with them to Mars. The two have good reasons—scientific curiosity and romance—to undertake the journey. But the obduracy of the Martians in insisting that the Earthmen accompany them borders on the denial of individual freedom, the sacred foundation of the aliens' own ethics. The Martians begin to seem less than perfect, and indeed their contact with Earth brings out in them some unattractive atavistic traits which, they had confidently assumed, had been eliminated through progressive evolution. Despite their claims of innate honesty, the Martians can practice deceit. Indeed their effort to lure Grunthe and Saltner to Mars is motivated by their desire to prevent the explorers from revealing their discovery until the Martians wish their presence known. The Martians also exaggerate their altruism in order to conceal their real goal on Earth, which is the exploitation of its energy resources. It still appears, however, that the Martians are far superior to terrestrial humans, as is suggested by their advanced ethical concepts and cultural development, which are examined in detail. Saltner willingly agrees to go to Mars, but Grunthe feels it is his duty to return to Europe and report the discovery so that Earth can determine its proper response to the Martians. He sustains his resolve only with considerable argument; but the Martians' ethical sense is still so powerful that they are incapable of forcing another human being to act against his will. (Chapters 15-20)

On their way to Mars the Martians leave Grunthe in Germany and establish contact with Ell, of whose existence they had previously known nothing. Ell and Saltner depart with the Martians; they are joined by Torm's wife Isma, who hopes to search the Polar area for her husband before the Martian spaceship leaves Earth. Ell, as befits his dual ancestry, is to be trained as the chief intermediary between Mars and Earth. (Chapters 21-24)

Although relations between individual Martians and Earthmen remain friendly, those between the two cultures deteriorate steadily. Dangerous misunderstandings occur, and the Martians become more and more convinced that Earthmen are barbarians and can therefore be treated as non-humans unprotected by the laws of Martian ethics. Their condescending attitude, abetted by their greed for Earth's energy resources, reveals more and more the uglier, all-too-"human" side of these extraterrestrial "human beings." During the search for Torm, impulsive belligerence and imperfect communication bring about a clash between the Martians and a British warship, a confrontation which might easily have been avoided. The Martians restrain their superior weapons, but their strong temptation to use them with full force bodes ill, should they conclude that Earthmen are not ethical and rational beings. The behavior of the Englishmen, although justified in part as the assertion of their own rights, does not encourage such an estimation. Blood is shed, and the Martian captain Ill expresses his fear that a disastrous conflict is inevitable: "The humans are insane.... I hear that the human beings have named our planet after the god of War. We wanted to bring peace, but it appears that our contact with this wild species is throwing us back into barbarism" (26: 415). (Chapters 25-26)

The next major section of *Auf zwei Planeten* is set mostly in space or on Mars. Because of the emergency caused by the skirmish, Isma must go to Mars along with Saltner, Ell and the Martians. Public opinion on Mars, despite the Martians' implicit cultural condescension, still favors reasonable treatment of Earth. In their travels and inquiries the three from Earth learn much about Martian society, technology and psychology. During this "utopian" interlude, however, the main action proceeds apace on both planets. Tensions between the two civilizations are exacerbated by the Martians' underestimation of terrestrial human worth and by recurrent news of unfortunate incidents on Earth. On Mars an anti-Earth or colonialist-imperialist party emerges and gains greater influence on Martian foreign policy. Ell himself assumes some of the Martian arrogance, for he is sincerely convinced that Martian culture, even if it must be imposed by force, would be beneficial to the development of Earth. A relationship of both attraction and hostility between Ell and Isma Torm adds to the plot interest and expresses in personal form the interaction of the two planets. (Chapters 27-38)

On Earth First Contact has also caused great problems. Human stubbornness and human dignity inspire opposition to the aliens. England refuses to make amends for the incident in the Arctic and is occupied by the Martians. Other nations begin to wage war over the remnants of the British Empire. The Martians seize upon the occasion to justify the declaration of a protectorate over the Earth, which is established after short and futile resistance. At first the Martians occupy and pacify only the belligerent states of Europe. But their protectorate, administered by Ell, becomes ever more arrogant and oppressive as they carry forth their program of "economical, intellectual [and] ethical education of mankind" (46:294). They resort more and more to police-state methods, including brainwashing and behavior modification conducted in facilities which serve simultaneously as "laborator[ies], school[s], and penal institution[s]" (49:348). At the same time the Martians exploit Earth's atmospheric and solar resources, sometimes using forced labor (43:248). Their difficulties in adjusting to terrestrial climate, and the recalcitrance of the natives as well, add still more to their exasperation and overreaction. (Chapters 39-49)

In the final section of the novel events unfold rapidly in several settings. The occupation becomes a tyranny, and Ell, who now sees the mistake of forcibly imposing Martian culture on Earth, departs in near despair to lend his support to the pro-Earth faction on Mars. In America, not yet occupied, a secret resistance movement is organized; it is based both on improvements of Martian technology and on a genuine advancement in intellect and moral will stimulated by cultural contact with the Martians. Just before the suspicious Martians move in full force against Earth, the rebels strike. Though they can scarcely hope to defeat Mars itself, they gain a decisive tactical advantage on Earth. The polar base and space station are seized, and an armistice is negotiated. The Martians agree to leave Earth, with the stipulation that there will be no contact between the two planets, except for light-beam messages, until Mars determines its policy. On Earth there is considerable suspicion that the Martians may try to recoup their losses or even undertake a genocidal war. When technical problems hinder communication between the two sides as direct negotiations resume, it appears that strife may again break out, perhaps needlessly. While spaceships from each planet hover near each other in the Earth's stratosphere, the captain of the terrestrial ship, and Ell, now the leader of the Martian peace mission, must step onto their decks—a slight anachronism, perhaps—and shout the final messages of peace to each other face to face. The strain is too much for Ell, and he dies, but the conclusion of peace and the mutual recognition of the human status of the two races is symbolized by the union of La and Saltner. (Chapters 50-60)

Structure

The structure of *Auf zwei Planeten* is subtle and complex, and exhibits significant resemblances to certain novelistic and dramatic patterns with which Lasswitz would have been familiar. Most evident initially is an alteration of interconnected subordinate and coordinate plots which characterizes many nineteenth-century "mainstream" novels, for example those of Dickens and, in Germany, Gustav Freytag. But in its deeper structure, the manner in which the idea of "humanity" is examined and expressed through the action of the novel, *Auf zwei Planeten* seems to be patterned on the model of classical drama, especially as it was reformulated in Germany during the Age of Goethe.

The fundamental action of the novel is, of course, the encounter between Earthmen and aliens. Grunthe's and Saltner's personal contact with the Martians constitutes the first of the coordinate plots. The two remain together until Chapter 20, after which Grunthe returns to Germany and Saltner goes to Mars. The romance between Saltner and La commences early in the former sequence of events and continues throughout the novel; it is a major focus of narrative interest in Chapters 6-38 and 50-60. Grunthe appears less often after he and Saltner separate, but he remains active as a participant in the resistance to the Martians which takes place on Earth in both the private and public spheres; he is therefore most evident when Earth is the scene of narration, that is in parts of Chapters 1-26 and 39-60. Isma's search for Torm begins in Chapter 23; her broader role as a major figure in the conflict of Martians and Earthmen continues from then until the end of the novel. Torm himself, after he vanishes at the North Pole, is also the center of a lesser sequence of events. But most of his adventures occur offstage and are presented only indirectly, either in quotations from his messages or in retrospective summaries, as in Chapter 44. During much of the fourth section (Chs. 39-49), however, Torm does appear in person as a fugitive from the Martians and as Ell's chief adversary. Throughout the novel Lasswitz introduces lesser subplots, short framed narrations, and detailed descriptive passages. Among them are Saltner's melodramatic rescue of his mother from the vindictive Martian official Oss (Chs. 48, 49, 55, 56), Jo's tale of early space travel (Chs. 13-14), and the descriptions of Martian landscape, history and culture which constitute important parts of Chapters 27-38.

In the first three major sections of the novel (Chs. 1-38) the coordinate plots are developed in longer segments. After the Martian occupation, when the two races are interacting at close quarters and in many places at once, the coordinate plots alternate more rapidly. Seldom, however, does the exposition of events result in confusion or disorientation. In novels of lesser quality the use of multiple plots can degenerate into a sequence of contrivedly interrupted cliff-hanging episodes which serve more to create momentary excitement than to further the presentation of a larger action. Lasswitz develops his coordinate plots coherently, bringing each to an appropriate preliminary resolution before moving to another, until he has laid the foundation for a final denouement which unites the several sequences of events and expresses the overall theme. He avoids discontinuity and stagnation by carefully integrating and overlapping the coordinate plots and the groups of characters who participate in them.

The nearly constant physical presence of the Martians also contributes much to the structural unity of *Auf zwei Planeten*. Not only does their virtual ubiquity concretely bind together the several coordinate plots; it also keeps in the reader's mind the novel's fundamental question, the nature of "humanity." Considered collectively, the actions of the Martians also constitute a distinct major plot-sequence, which consists of their momentous program to explore, "civilize" and exploit the Earth. Therefore the Martians themselves, or at least Mars as a setting, figure in every chapter. But it is Earth and its inhabitants with which Lasswitz is ultimately concerned, and therefore it is within the realm of terrestrial humanity that the overall action of the novel must be developed and resolved. Thus we see the Martians by themselves only seldom, as in Chapters 3, 32, 46, 50 and 57. But each instance, we note, is significant in that it either enables the reader—who is after all a terrestrial human—to understand the Martians better, or else portrays a key moment in the Martians' gradual comprehension of our race.

The internal or "dramatic" structure of *Auf zwei Planeten* is less concerned with the exposition of plot than the development of *character*, in the fullest and most reflective sense of the word. External, seemingly incidental conflict is transformed and deepened into a confrontation of fundamental attitudes which is fought out between entire cultures, among individual characters, and even within the soul of a single person. The "happy end" of *Auf zwei Planeten*, which presents the reconciliation of the two cultures and the union of La and Saltner, may indeed echo the form of comedy; but such elements are not at all inconsistent with the structure of classical tragedy, in which understanding, rather than necessarily death, is the culmination of the action. Ell's acquisition of knowledge, his suffering, and his death are of course important elements in the dramatic pattern of *Auf zwei Planeten* and can be viewed as "tragic" in a certain sense. But behind the archetypal motifs Lasswitz employs lies a mighty dramatic theme, one which, it may be admitted, demanded a mightier book than he may have had the technical ability to write. In his science-fictional "thought-model," his very realistic but still ideal exploration of the theme of "First Contact," Lasswitz strove to picture a process of conflict, nemesis and recognition which might afford—to the novel's characters and the reader as well—a deeper insight into the nature of the Universe and of humanity.

Lasswitz' self-acknowledged debt to the classical heritage, ancient and German, has been evident throughout this study. The five major parts of *Auf zwei Planeten* can indeed be considered equivalent to the acts of a classical drama. "Act I" (Chs. 1-14) describes the first encounter, initially accidental and innocuous, between Martians and terrestrials; it also provides necessary background material about the Martians. In "Act II" (Chs. 15-26) the actual conflict between the two cultures commences and becomes more and more serious. The figure of Ell offers hope for reconciliation, but also shows how Martian and terrestrial traits can conflict within one person. The skirmish with the British warship gives Ill occasion to voice the fear that catastrophe is inevitable. "Act III" (Chs. 27-38) is sharply delineated structurally, conceptually, and even spatially, since it is set on Mars. The description of the technologically and ethically superior Martian civilization expands the philosophical dimension of the action. Equally important is the exposition of concrete events. The gradual hardening of Martian policy toward Earth points to the catastrophe of Martian occupation, which begins in Chapter 39. The same movement is expressed on the personal level in Saltner's and Isma's break with Ell and in the temporary estrangement of La and Saltner. At the center of the act, however, is the philosophical, ethical and emotional conflict which takes place within Ell; it is a *Seelendrama* in the classical tradition. Ell's decision to side with Mars, and the subsequent Martian program of civilization and exploitation, are set forth in "Act IV" (Chs. 39-49), which describes the disastrous effects the Protectorate has on the terrestrials and then on Ell and the Martians themselves. "Act V" (Chs. 50-60) consists of the successful rebellion against Mars and the ultimate reconciliation of the two planets which is achieved after the nature of humanity is fully comprehended. The recognition that a previously misconceived necessity can thwart human—or rather, Martian—plans is followed by the overall resolution of the action, which involves the death of one main character and the union of the other two.

The highly dramatic structure of *Auf zwei Planeten* is carried out in the treatment of time and in the alternation of sections which introduce new events and those which present necessary background material. The action extends over a period of four and a half years, which is divided almost exactly into halves by the nadir of the narrative, the imposition of the tyrannous Martian Protectorate. But approximately four-fifths of the novel's actual page-length is devoted to the first two years. The leisurely pace of the first part of *Auf zwei Planeten* enables Lasswitz to introduce the imaginary world thoroughly to the reader. Thus the first three sections or "acts" (Chs. 1-38) encompass a relatively short span of time, from 19 August (1:4) to autumn of the first year. Although many important events transpire, much of the narrative is occupied with the presentation of the landscape, people and institutions of Mars. Subsequently time moves more rapidly, heightening the dramatic tension. The next major temporal interval comprises perhaps twenty-two months, from some time before October of the first year (39:194) to the second anniversary of First Contact, when it appears that the encounter of the two races has ended in utter catastrophe (44:272). The action of the eventful but short final section extends over two and a half years. The Martians' departure from Earth after their limited defeat occurs in August, four years after their presence on Earth became known in Europe and two years after the total occupation began (59:507, 511; 60:532). While the final resolution comes to pass a few months later, in December (60:532), the additional time does not obscure the marked symmetry of the bisected four-year interval which begins with the first encounter of the two races and concludes with the temporary cessation of communication between them.

Lasswitz makes it clear that the temporal framework of *Auf zwei Planeten* is not due to mere caprice, time-honored literary tradition, or some mystical notion of immutable cosmic laws that determine, with mathematical precision, the timing of human behavior. Rather it is science, in the form of physical laws governing the motion of planets, which dictates the temporal structure of the novel and thus, as Lasswitz carefully implies, exerts a vital influence on Man and his environment:

> The eleventh of December was anticipated with especial apprehension. On this day the opposition of Mars and Earth took place; there occurred the configuration in which the two planets were closest to each other. At the opposition at the end of August four years earlier the presence of the Martians on Earth had been discovered; the opposition in October two years ago had brought the victory of the Antibat [anti-Earthling] Party. Thus people imagined to themselves that the next opposition, in December of that year, must distinguish itself through some sort of calamitous event. (60:531-2)

Lasswitz' formulation of the relationship between celestial phenomena and terrestrial events should not be mistaken for an expression of astrological beliefs. Nevertheless, he does attempt to exploit some of the rich symbolical effects which art has long found in astrology and in the metaphorical elaboration of astronomy. Thus the word "Opposition" should not be understood merely in its astronomical sense. Celestial events, according to Lasswitz, may indeed bring about disaster on Earth, not because they inevitably make themselves known through a "calamitous event" but rather because Mars is an actual world whose inhabitants are quite capable of traveling to Earth and attempting to impose their will on it. The opposition of Mars and Earth does not in itself subject Earth to mysterious threatening forces; it is an actual astronomical configuration which, according to the established science of the time, offers the best physical circumstances for travel between the two planets.

In *Auf zwei Planeten*, then, there are actually two temporal rhythms, one spanning exactly four years and the other four years and four months. The first, based on the natural or sidereal year, is familiar to all who live on Earth and therefore of course appears frequently in literature. In both life and art, including *Auf zwei Planeten*, the sidereal or calendrical anniversaries of important events are noted and themselves may well become the occasion of significant happenings. The pattern is strongly reinforced by the recurrence of the seasons and the life-cycles that follow them. The second temporal rhythm—scarcely an archetypal pattern or even a familiar fact—corresponds to the period of twenty-six months between oppositions of Earth and Mars. Yet both rhythms—and Lasswitz doubtless wanted his readers to recognize the fact—are based on astronomical events. The annual cycle marks the recurrence of the same configuration of Sun and Earth against the background of "fixed" stars. "Opposition," however, is a more abstract and, as it were, extraterrestrial concept. It denotes the astronomical configuration in which two planets lie on the same radial line from the Sun and are thus nearest each other in their orbits. The two concepts reflect different cosmological systems and different subjective world-views as well. The juxtaposition of temporal rhythms and the cosmological concepts they express is, I think, essential to Lasswitz' purpose in *Auf zwei Planeten*. The annual or sidereal cycle implies a qualitative distinction between the Earth and the celestial bodies, which serve merely as points of reference. The concept of opposition treats the planets, including the Earth, as bodies of a similar nature. Thus, as the characters of *Auf zwei Planeten* learn, both Mars and Earth might well be actual environments or worlds harboring intelligent life.

Not only the temporal structure of *Auf zwei Planeten*, but also the very events which comprise its action depend on science. The encounter of the two cultures could not have come to pass without the technology of space travel, nor would the Martians' presence have been discovered without the employment of innovative technology. Similarly, the Martians' expedition to Earth is occasioned not only by the progress of science, which had made that venture a "vital cultural undertaking" (8:111), but also by a technological crisis, the shortage of oxygen and energy on Mars.

Many of the lesser events in *Auf zwei Planeten*—Isma's search for Torm, the Martian military victories, the use of the "Retrospektiv" apparatus to investigate the past, and the Martians' pursuit of Saltner in the mountains (Chs. 49, 55)—are possible in their given form only because of technology, imaginary or real. Finally, the resolution of the conflict between Mars and Earth is intimately associated with science and technology. The communication of peaceful intentions is to occur by means of intense light beams. Ironically, the apparatus fails, nearly bringing about an even more disastrous catastrophe, genocidal war. That the final bridge between the two races must be created by face-to-face communication between human beings without the mediation of technology adds an important ingredient to the meaning of *Auf zwei Planeten*. Lasswitz suggests thereby not only that science and technology exert an inescapable physical, philosophical and ethical influence on the world, but also that human excellence, responsibility and sacrifice are meaningful and indispensable, even—or especially—in an age of Science.

Characterization

The characters in *Auf zwei Planeten* may be divided into three categories: terrestrial humans, Martians, and—*sui generis*—the half-Martian, half-terrestrial Ell. Characterization, and particularly the use of dialogue to convey psychological subtleties, are perhaps the weakest feature of *Auf zwei Planeten*. The terrestrial human figures do not emerge as especially profound personalities. In some respects they are in fact conventional literary types—perhaps in part intentionally so. Nevertheless, Lasswitz pays careful attention to psychological motivation, and in some places seems aware of the stereotypical aspects and human foibles of his characters, whom he views with a certain detachment and even quiet humor. Here, as in the management of theme, plot and imaginary science, *Auf zwei Planeten* represents a considerable improvement over Lasswitz' earlier SF.

The terrestrial human figures in *Auf zwei Planeten* recall some familiar types of nineteenth-century German literature, especially of middle-class ("Biedermeier") fiction and the regional novel. Saltner—honest, congenial, somewhat loquacious, but not a weakling—is the personable, occasionally blunt Tyrolian. He is a trained scientist, but he also possesses native wit. His colorful personality is entertaining and provides a healthy contrast to the drab scientists typical of much other fiction, including not a little SF. Saltner's mature and nobly passionate love for La, a member of the alien and supposedly superior species, helps to advance the fundamental theme of the novel by demonstrating a vital aspect of experience which was heretofore unfamiliar to the Martians but is nevertheless, as they eventually must concede, profoundly human. On a broader thematic level, Saltner embodies one of the two reasonable responses to First Contact which Lasswitz describes in *Auf zwei Planeten*, that of open but not craven acceptance.

Karl Grunthe, the reticent but not insensitive North German, is Saltner's complement, but not his contrary. What Se says of Grunthe, with a touch of racial condescension which she will later abandon, could apply equally well to Saltner and to Isma Torm too: "He is one of the Earthmen [who would have been] worthy of being born on Mars" (54:435). Grunthe espouses the other reasonable approach to First Contact, that of innate caution reinforced by the recognition that the organic unity and integrity of one's own culture must be maintained, even if some features of the alien culture are accepted.

The figure of Isma Torm, like those of the female protagonists in the *Bilder aus der Zukunft*, suggests Lasswitz' debt to German Classicism. Isma belongs to the lineage of Lessing's Minna von Barnhelm and Goethe's Iphigenie. A person of considerable intellectual power and intuitive moral excellence, she is a touchstone of what is ethical and reasonable. She is also a woman of tenacious but not implausibly placid marital loyalty. Indeed, Isma does not lack earthier feelings. During Torm's long absence and her continued association with Ell she is strongly attracted to the latter, both intellectually and physically. The erotic tension of the Isma-Ell subplot and the possibility that Ell may violate his Martian ethics to possess Isma prevent her loyal search for Torm from becoming too unrealistic and sentimental. Like the Saltner-La romance, the relationship between Isma and Torm demonstrates the fundamental worth of terrestrial humanity. When the Martians, claiming political exigency, obstruct Isma's noble urge to rejoin her husband, the reader receives a clear signal that the Martian ethical system is not ideal, not totally "humane." It is flawed both by its overemphasis on rationality and by a hidden element of selfishness.

Of Hugo Torm we do not see much, since he is stranded near the Pole in Chapter 2 and reappears only much later, in Chapter 42. Torm is an Odysseus, but with a different kind of enemy. After the Martian invasion he returns secretly to Germany; there is a price on his head for having used force against a Martian in his escape. Torm helps to lead the rebellion against those who have overrun his homeland; and, again like Odysseus, he must also rescue his wife and reassure himself of her fidelity.

Lasswitz' protrayal of terrestrial human beings in *Auf zwei Planeten* is at least adequate, especially since much of the novel is concerned with matters other than intricate psychological analysis of such figures. A harder task, and yet one where he may have succeeded better, is the creation of alien characters. Later SF, following the development of science itself, has generally been more skeptical than Lasswitz was about the probable degree of similarity between terrestrial and alien life-forms. Recent research, of course, has made the notion of humanoid Martians, or perhaps any Martian life at all, virtually untenable even in SF. But both the close resemblance of the two races and the superior cultural level of the Martians were compatible with the science of Lasswitz' time, especially the well-publicized research of Schiaparelli and Lowell. Moreover, the similarity in physique and mental faculties contributes greatly to the novel's overall theme of First Contact, for it seems at first that there is little which would make the two races or species incompatible. Yet the very facility of rudimentary interaction leads to the discovery of subtle but fundamental cultural, emotional, ethical and philosophical differences which must be resolved, if indeed they can be, through confrontation, conflict and the reconciliation of the tenderest emotions.

Whatever the philosophical considerations which motivated Lasswitz' conception of the Martians, they still serve the purposes of characters in a work of fiction and can be discussed accordingly. Like the terrestrial humans, the Martians range from briefly sketched stereotypes to fairly complex individuals. The loftiness of Martian intellect and ethics does not preclude differentiation among personalities, and in fact such variety furthers the impression of plausibility. His lesser Martians, however, Lasswitz models on obvious terrestrial stereotypes—a practice which may also encourage the sense of plausibility. Ill's wife Ma, for example, is the Martian counterpart of the typical German bourgeois *Hausfrau*, and indeed she is given an archetypal name, the Indo-European root syllable for "mother" (Chs. 28ff.).

Other notable examples of sentimental type characterization of Martians are the old spaceship captain Jo, who spins yarns of the days when Martians were Martians and spaceflight new and dangerous (Chs. 13-14), and the unnamed miner from Mari, near the Gol Desert (Ch. 37). The miner questions Saltner, whom he takes to be a Martian "astronaut," about the recents news from Earth:

> "So tell me then,...is it really true what's in the newspapers so much, that there are 'Nume' there? I mean like us, rational?"
> "Oh, they may have at least some rationality."
> The miner shook his head. "It won't be much, probably.... Otherwise why hadn't they come to us already? We folks here, you know, don't really believe that much is to be gained there. We think the government is just talking big now because next year are the elections to the Central Council. So people are saying if we go to Earth, we can grab the sun with our hands there, so to speak; we'll get so much money there that everyone will receive double the state subsidy." (37:169)

The sentiments and language of this ordinary Martian-in-the-street resemble those of the *Stammtisch* habitués in Torm's home town of Friedau (Ch. 43). Here, as in the portrayal of Jo as well, the tone may be too sentimental, too *Biedermeier*, and the Martian figure too stereotypical for our own taste. But the passage combines subtle humor with serious exposition of theme. Lasswitz does not employ terrestrial stereotypes as models for Martians merely to lighten his task in creating characters, or to gain the reader's emotional participation by appealing to maudlin sentimentality. Instead, stereotypes, particularly those of the upright salt of the Earth or Mars, are rather a means—but one of several—which he uses to express the idea that human is human, wherever it occurs.

The more important Martian figures in *Auf zwei Planeten* are modeled less overtly on terrestrial patterns, but they too are somewhat typecast, and with good reason, for every Martian must represent millions of unseen members of a race with which we are totally unfamiliar. Ell's uncle Ill, for example, can be quite strict with terrestrials when, as the leader of the Martian expedition and later a high official in the Martian Protectorate, he must do his duty. But in private he is cordial, reflective and fatherly; his character is thus estalished as both "human" and "humane."

The idea that two species so different as Earthmen and

Martians might still both be human is expressed with particular clarity in the characters of Se and, especially, La. Lasswitz seems to have patterned La, like Isma, after the noble female figures of German classical literature, to which he added touches of late nineteenth-century sentimentalism. La is the essence of goodness and warmth. We are encouraged to feel that she, like Isma, would be noble by nature, even if she did not possess the advanced ethical sense of the Martians. She is therefore very similar to some terrestrials. But despite her warmth she lacks—or so it seems initially—the earthy, Earthly, human element of sensuality and, consequently, the ability to fall in love. But La's experience of love and humanity in Saltner, and her observation of Grunthe's nobility as well, change her attitudes about Earthmen and love.

Women who think themselves above love but then succumb to it have appeared countless times in literature. But when the woman is a Martian, the convention is no longer trite, because the reader has no previous knowledge of Martian nature. The relationship between La and Saltner, with the Martian Oss and, at one point, Ell himself as frustrated rivals, provides story interest and later contributes directly to the successful terrestrial rebellion. But above all the union of the two symbolizes the reconciliation of Mars and Earth and thus helps to demonstrate the ideas of universal humanity and the worth of terrestrial human beings.

By far the most important alien figure, and perhaps the central character in the entire novel, is Ell. It is he who mediates between the two worlds and to whom the title alludes, as his own musings toward the end of the novel reveal: "Was not his homeland on two planets...?" (57:474). In his ancestry, his loyalties and his psychological constitution Ell is half terrestrial and half Martian. In intellect and ethical sense he is utterly like the Martians, but unlike them he feels love instinctively and emotionally. His passion for Isma, whose physical aspect is evident despite Lasswitz' Wilhelmine discretion, and his hard-won restraint of that illicit desire as well, do much to establish his humanity in both the terrestrial and the universal senses. The same features concretely illustrate the central themes of interplanetary reconciliation and the recognition of terrestrial "Numenheit."

Ell has always known he is part Martian. Even before First Contact, we are told, he often expressed his frustration at terrestrial imperfection with the sardonic and cryptic exclamation, " 'Ko bate, poor humans, you don't understand!' " (7:94). His dual nature becomes a tragic dilemma when his love for Isma cannot be fulfilled and when his loyalty to Mars and his sincere belief in the benefits of its culture cause him to take the Martian side. He must break with Saltner and Isma, and temporarily violates some of the laws of both terrestrial and Martian ethics, especially the principle of individual freedom (33:136). After serving as Martian Protector in Germany, Ell realizes that the project was wrong, harmful to both cultures. His death is, to him, probably a surcease from unbearable personal frustration and disillusionment, but it is not a sign that the two cultures and the two types of human nature they represent are irreconcilable. Indeed, Ell's death is a necessary part of the conclusion of peace between the two planets.

The character of Ell is brilliantly conceived and often touching. It is presented more capably than many other such hybrid characters in SF. But ultimately the characterization is somewhat unconvincing. There is in Ell a certain detachment and lack of warmth which keep us from fully empathizing with him. Perhaps Lasswitz, particularly in the second half of the novel, was too occupied with the ever-accelerating plot and the complex subject of humanity to develop Ell's own pathos sufficiently. Yet a thorough psychological exploration of the figure would have done much to further the investigation of the nature of humanity which lies at the center of *Auf zwei Planeten*.

Still, Ell is a sympathetic figure whose portrayal obviously lay close to Lasswitz' heart and evoked not a little of his own admiration and compassion. It is quite possible even that in the character of Ell Lasswitz has limned a half-veiled and of course somewhat idealized self-portrait. The conjecture is prompted by evidence more substantial than the fact that Ell's name is pronounced exactly like the initial letter of the author's own name. Ell lives and works in his observatory, yearningly occupies himself with the idea of life on other planets, and even compiles a lexicon of the Martian language. K.G. Just, following early biographical sources, notes that living in a house which the previous owner, an eccentric, had constructed as an observatory was one of Lasswitz' most important childhood experiences.[9] Lasswitz' lifelong interest in extraterrestrial life is expressed most overtly and powerfully in his novel about Mars, which includes the essentials of a basic lexicon and brief grammar of Martian. In any case, except where his personal interests and weaknesses cause him to err in pursuing Martian ideals and policies too vigorously, Ell expresses many of Lasswitz' own ideas and views the world of *Auf zwei Planeten* from a perspective which is distinctly superior to that of the other characters, if not quite as omniscient as those of the narrator and the author himself.

Imaginary Science and Technology

Auf zwei Planeten is inconceivable without science. As I argued earlier, science is more than an abstract concept or broad philosophical theme in the novel; it is an integral element of the action and structure of the narration. Yet the role of science in *Auf zwei Planeten* does not end even here. The imaginary world which constitutes the setting of the novel abounds with technological objects and scientific ideas, from the most mundane gadget to complex theoretical notions, all of which are carefully thought out and described. Science and technology, however, do not obtrude unnaturally in *Auf zwei Planeten*, as happens in much SF. Lasswitz, moreover, does not simply present imaginary science and technology with a take-it-or-leave-it air, nor does he introduce theories and gadgets merely to inspire a sense of wonder in the scientifically inclined reader. Instead, he makes such content essential to the exposition of theme and the evocation of the imaginary world. He incorporates technology and theory into the texture of the story by explaining them in detail, by examining their wider implications, by showing their function in society, and by making them part of the plot. These practices ultimately increase our sense of wonder, of course, but they also "domesticate" the reader in the strange new world. That Lasswitz even attempted to integrate science and technology so fully with the rest of the novel is part of the excellence of *Auf zwei Planeten*. That he accomplished his purpose without seriously hindering the progress of the action, a problem endemic in SF, adds still more to his achievement.

Lasswitz considered astronomy "the paragon of science," and indeed an astronomical event is the prime mover of the novel. As Mark Hillegas notes, the several spectacular oppositions of Mars which actually occurred in the late nineteenth century no doubt intensified Lasswitz' interest, and that of his readers as well, in the notion of extraterrestrial life, especially as it might exist on the nearby planet which seemed to resemble Earth in many respects. It is likely, as Hillegas himself remarks, that Lasswitz drew much of his information about Mars, real or speculative, from the same sources which inspired H.G. Wells' *War of the Worlds* (1897) and so much other SF.[10] The well-publicized work of Giovanni Schiaparelli (1835-1910) and Percival Lowell (1855-1916), much of it conducted during the favorable oppositions of 1877 and 1892, produced a wealth of new information about the physical features of Mars.

Neither astronomer hesitated to advance ideas which, to some extent, exceeded the bounds of cautious, objective interpretation of verifiable data. In 1877—the year in which Lasswitz most likely wrote *Gegen das Weltgesetz*, which alludes to attempts to communicate with Mars—Schiaparelli announced his discovery of "canali" on Mars; the word was easily and willfully misinterpreted to mean artificial "canals" rather than simply "channels," the more accurate rendition. In 1895 Lowell published the first of his speculative books about Mars. For decades to come, writers of SF made industrious use of both the factual information and the provocative hypotheses advanced by Schiaparelli and Lowell, until modern research made virtually untenable the idea of life on Mars, or at least that of higher forms somewhat like those existing on Earth. And for decades each close opposition of Mars incited the larger public to speculate about life on Mars, to entertain—with fascination or panic—rumors about landings of flying saucers, and to consume more SF.

Lasswitz' essays on science and SF, especially "Der tote und der lebendige Mars," show that he was quite familiar with contemporary research about Mars and speculations about its possible life-forms. But while he adopted the basic concepts of Schiaparelli and Lowell, the many details he added independently provide the tangibility vital to the sense of plausibility. Original and essential too was Lasswitz' philosophical development of the theme furnished by science, for it was he who determined the precise nature of both the Martians' superiority and their attitude toward alien cultures. The giant, insect-like Martians who terrorize Earth in Wells' *War of the Worlds*, which appeared in the same year as *Auf zwei Planeten* and was also heavily influenced by the same sources, show very well how the Schiaparelli-Lowell vision of alien civilization could serve as a powerful inspiration for writers of SF and yet leave them ample latitude to develop their own ideas. Hillegas, incidentally, argues conclusively that "there was no influence, direct or otherwise, of one story upon the other.... Any influence... would be *Auf zwei Planeten* on Wells' later writings, notably *A Modern Utopia* (1905)."[11]

Since *Auf zwei Planeten* is set in the near future, almost all of its imaginary science and technology is the creation of the Martians. Most spectacular are space ships and space stations which employ the anti-gravity substance "Stellit" (8:110) and the propellant "Repulsit" (12:187). The Martians also have laser-like devices which they use for long-distance communication (24:382). Among their other technological innovations are fluorescent lighting (18:277), photoelectric relays and amplifiers (16:244), mobile homes (27:10), plastics (11:164-66), artificial foods (6:83, 9:120-24, 43:247), wheelless vehicles which glide on thin films of water (27:13), various automatic machines which perform everyday tasks (Ch. 9), and xerocopiers and instant cameras (10:134-36).

Several of the Martian "gadgets" could have been foreseen easily in Lasswitz' own time, at least by the more imaginative scientist or inventor, and in fact some of them soon appeared. Many new ways to use electromagnetic radiation, for example, were suggested by the widely publicized work of Hermann Helmholtz (1821-1894) and Heinrich Hertz (1857-1894). Similarly, the foundations for the chemistry of synthetics had already been laid in Germany by intensive laboratory research and the giant chemical industry. Other of Lasswitz' imaginary devices, such as lasers, are much more recent developments; the direct use of lasers in long-distance communication is still largely experimental. Still speculative in our own time, but not inconceivable theoretically, are some Martian technological innovations, for example weapons which employ strong magnetic forces (45:283-84) or which induce nerve paralysis (25:391).

Modern physics, however, seems now to substantiate the impossibility or extreme improbability of some of Lasswitz' imaginary science and technology, above all anti-gravity, velocities faster than light (12:186-87), and the "Retrospektiv" (29:47-50), an instrument which recaptures light rays and thus permits a look into the past. The development of physics proceeded so rapidly in the late nineteenth and early twentieth centuries that within ten years of the publication of *Auf zwei Planeten* many of Lasswitz' theoretical assumptions had been called into question, if not yet totally abandoned. But as far as I can determine, none of his imaginary scientific ideas or technological devices directly contravened the accepted theories of his time. Indeed, such notions as anti-gravity and faster-than-light travel have continued to appear in SF, because modern science, it may still be argued, has not yet incontrovertibly established their impossibility, and because, in any case, many writers (and readers) of SF are unable or unwilling to forego those time-honored devices.

The Schiaparelli-Lowell vision of Martian civilization, as I remarked earlier, has provided the impetus for many works of SF, of which *Auf zwei Planeten* is but one early though impressive example. Not only the basic theme of contact with a superior

Martian civilization, but also many of the details of scientific theory and technology which Lasswitz incorporated into the novel, can be found in later SF. Paralysis beams, space stations, anti-gravity, automatic machines, ray guns and artificial foods are indeed the stock in trade of the genre. Certain Martian social customs as well, such as eating in strict privacy, are also not unique to *Auf zwei Planeten*. Even closer correspondences can be found. An alien beverage described in Robert A. Heinlein's *Have Space Suit—Will Travel* (1958, Ch. 10), also a novel of "First Contact," closely resembles the fatty-textured synthetic cocoa of *Auf zwei Planeten* (9:123). Lasswitz and Heinlein also devise the same neologism and present it to their readers in similar statements. The narrator of *Auf zwei Planeten* remarks that certain conditions on Mars are due to causes of a "geographic [kind], or, as we ought to say in the case of Mars, 'areographic' [areographisch]" (8:108). In Heinlein's *Red Planet* (1958) one character declares he is considering the study of "areography"; the author-narrator adds a note explaining the term (Ch. 1).

Such correspondences, however striking, should not be taken as indisputable evidence of Lasswitz' influence on later SF authors. Most if not all of them can plausibly be ascribed to common use of the Schiaparelli-Lowell hypothesis, to other contemporary research, or to familiarity with the recurrent motifs of utopias and imaginary voyages. With regard to tabus associated with eating in SF, it might also be suggested that the inversion of familiar circumstances or customs is one of the genre's characteristic means of creating the features of an alien culture and causing the reader to view his own world in a new light as well. Yet it is still quite possible that, in one way or another, *Auf zwei Planeten* has furnished later writers of SF with scientific themes and motifs. As Wernher von Braun and others have remarked, the novel provided much inspiration for the German rocket experimenters whose work was in turn of considerable importance to later SF.[12] In some cases Lasswitz' influence may have been more direct. There is ample evidence that Hugo Gernsback and Willy Ley, who provided many writers of Anglo-American SF with story ideas and scientific information, regarded Lasswitz' works as worthy of emulation in both content and style. Among "Golden Age" writers Arthur C. Clarke, for example, has professed a knowledge of *Auf zwei Planeten*,[13] and Heinlein, who had at least some knowledge of German, knew and admired Ley. It would be unlikely indeed that Ley did not tell him something of Lasswitz, whether or not Heinlein actually read *Auf zwei Planeten*. Further investigation of the matter would, I think, prove rewarding.

Philosophy and Ideology

As a novel about "First Contact" *Auf zwei Planeten* lies squarely in the main current of SF. But the nature of humanity, the theme Lasswitz sought to explore through that vehicle, is also a fundamental subject of mainstream literature. In *Auf zwei Planeten* the concept of humanity is examined with a philosophical prolixity and rigor which are scarcely typical of most other SF but characteristic of Lasswitz as a professional philosopher and descendant of German Classicism and Idealism. But *Auf zwei Planeten* is not a dry treatise presented within a perfunctory narrative framework. The exploration of philosophical ideas is carefully integrated with science, the exposition of the imaginary world, and the development of the plot. And for Lasswitz, here as in the rest of his work, an essential part of philosophical inquiry concerns the nature and proper behavior of political institutions—a subject which, he quite probably felt, had suffered from a notable dearth of reasoned deliberation. Admittedly, *Auf zwei Planeten* is not a blatantly partisan work, especially when compared, for example, to the drama of German Naturalism. But nevertheless the novel expresses a well-reasoned political statement, a fervent dedication to liberal moderation whose subtle formulation and humane tone should not be mistaken for a lack of either deliberate ideological commitment or personal engagement.

In *Auf zwei Planeten* it is not Man, the supposed crown of creation and clever *homo faber*, who invents space flight and discovers other beings. Instead, they come to him first, and it is therefore the superiority and the "human" status of Earthmen which are called into question. Especially during the "Protectorate" in the middle sections of the novel, the Martians' claim to dominance is founded largely on their superior intellect and science—the same criteria of material advancement and cultural achievement which Western civilization had invoked to justify its domination of other societies. But Lasswitz' Martians, it seems, are indeed also morally and philosophically superior. Therefore the outcome of the inquiry into the nature of humanity and cultural superiority depends on ethics and philosophy rather than on simple technological and intellectual sophistication.

Lasswitz was a recognized neo-Kantian, and his Martians are also Kantians—but with some intriguing differences vital to the meaning of *Auf zwei Planeten*. The Kantianism of the Martians is neither an ideal nor a systematically pursued rational philosophy. It is, rather, part of their innate psychological constitution, a reflection of their advanced evolution. It is their natural behavior to follow the principles of what to us are rationalistic and utopian ethics—until, that is, their contact with another culture and their attempt to exploit Earth's resources for their own benefit and to educate its people to their idea of "humanity" confound their vaunted but insufficiently examined ethical principles and leads them to the verge of genocide.

The fundamental principle of Martian ethics is illustrated at length early in the novel, when Se explains to Saltner why the Martians cannot simply force the Earthmen to go with them to Mars:

> " 'Force'? How do you mean that?... 'Can?' I don't know, I don't rightly understand you, my dearest friend. But surely one can do only that which is not wrong. Your language is so unclear. Do you see this handle? You say that I can turn it, and mean that I have the physical possibility to do that. But if I turn it, then the seat will sink under you; therefore I can't turn it, that is, I cannot want to. This moral possibility or impossibility you simply cannot express any other way. Could it happen with you on Earth that you would rescue people from the water and then take their lives? And taking away freedom, is that not still worse? (17:266)

For the Martians, freedom, in both the moral and the physical senses, is a fundamental concept and treasured personal right. They are constitutionally incapable of contravening the will of another "human" being. The principle has not merely an abstract moral force, which would indeed be insipid and ineffective in a work of fiction, but rather actual physical power. But "will," as Se tries to explain to Saltner, is to be understood as genuine mature volition, not as spontaneous, self-serving caprice:

> "By 'will' you understand just all kinds of emotional forces which are merely individual urges. These we can overpower [bezwingen]; against *this* will we can detain you.... Now, if you... want to leave here just because you prefer returning home to going to Mars, then you will be hindered. If, however, it is a matter not of your individual will, but rather your ethical [sittlich] will, your free determination as a person [Persönlichkeit], or whatever you call what we term 'numanity' [Numenheit]—then there exists no power which can hinder you." (17:267-68)

Lasswitz strove to make the nature of Martian ethics

conceptually clear and to relate abstract principles to social customs and casual behavior. But he does not explain just how, in practice, the Martians can reliably discern and evaluate the motives of others. Perhaps our difficulty in comprehending and believing such ideas indicates something about our own imperfect nature. But the vagueness with which Lasswitz—and the Martians themselves— approach this crucial distinction is essential to the meaning of *Auf zwei Planeten* as an examination of the nature of humanity in the context of cultural First Contact.

Martian Kantianism has a grievous flaw, one which could not have been anticipated before the Martians encountered another race. The Martians automatically assume that other beings who are apparently intelligent, civilized and physically similar to themselves are "human." Heretofore the assumption has proved satisfactory, since all such beings had been Martians—a trivial case, logically speaking. But the implicit contrapositive of the same proposition, which does not become evident until First Contact, is that a being who is not a Martian is not human. The reasoning is flawed, as even the principles of formal terrestrial logic show, but the belief becomes common among Martians in Lasswitz' novel, just as it has frequently governed the attitudes of one culture toward another on Earth. The rights of others, the Martians conclude, must be respected only when the other beings are recognized, by Martian standards of course, as human—possessed, that is, of intelligence, reason, genuine will and morality. Otherwise they may be treated as we ourselves treat lesser animals: not brutally or inhumanely, it is supposed and claimed, but not equally either. Should a person or an entire race show by its behavior that it is not rational—again, according to Martian standards—then the ethical imperative no longer applies.

In *Auf zwei Planeten* Lasswitz shows how a manifestly excellent civilization, misled by a conceit in the universal validity of its own standards of judgment and by a cupidity it attempts to conceal even from itself, can disastrously misjudge the nature of another culture. Quite probably he was genuinely interested in investigating the possible consequences of an actual future encounter between Man and extraterrestrial beings. But Lasswitz also offered his own late-nineteenth-century culture a highly critical evaluation of its own behavior toward other peoples. And to emphasize his critique he made Western civilization itself the victim, not the perpetrator, of imperialism and colonialism.

As I suggested earlier, then, *Auf zwei Planeten* is not a placid philosophical treatise or, much less, a utopia, despite its grand scientific theme, serious investigation of ideology, and examination of the idea of humanity. Rather than stating his argument outrightly, Lasswitz carefully substantiates it by integrating it with the development of plot and character. He is especially careful to show that terrestrial humanity, the "underdog," has much to offer, even to the Martians. The resolution of the action depends directly on the interplay between Martian and terrestrial psychology and philosophy as functional determinants of behavior. In more concrete terms, the action revolves about the question whether the Martians can be made to see that Earthmen, while not as advanced as themselves, are "human" beings, or whether they will regard them as subhuman creatures who can be ignored, exploited, or even exterminated.

We can gauge how Lasswitz sought to express his philosophical ideas in concrete form and thus to integrate them into the action of the novel by observing in detail how he treated two essential aspects of human behavior: love and language. So much has the Martians' ethical philosophy become an instinctive part of their culture—at least until it is thrown into confusion by later events—that they extend the principles of reason and freedom even into the realm of love, which Earthmen consider to be governed, for good or ill, by passion. La explains to Saltner that love, in the Martians' view, should be subordinated to reason, so that it does not lead to a denial of freedom. Thus initially she doubts the very possibility of love between Earthmen and Martians (20:312-14). But her attitude changes during the course of the novel. After Saltner has rescued her from a crevasse, La tries to tell Se that "Earthmen are not just amusing beings [ein Mensch ist doch nicht bloss komisch]" (11:163). Her feelings caution her against callousness, for Earthmen, as she has already sensed, might have thoughts and beliefs which ought to be taken seriously.

La and the other Martians do not yet have a clear understanding of the emotional nature and power of love, nor do they fully comprehend Earthly ways. But La is fascinated by Saltner and the new emotions he expresses and excites. "Who can know how Earthmen's hearts may feel?" she muses. "Perhaps the Earthmen were much stronger in their feelings than in their intellect [Verstand]" (11:162). In the middle sections of the novel she tries to live without Saltner, and then recognizes that she cannot. Love, the source of a new kind of experience and knowledge provided by contact with Earthmen, requires a reassessment of the concept of humanity (52:407-08).

Saltner's feelings toward La, and the constancy of Hugo and Isma Torm as well, show that love is both a valuable quality of all humanity and one of the special contributions which terrestrial humanity can make to the Martians. The tragedy of Ell's life and his passion for Isma, which reflect the unfortunate duality of his nature and loyalties, echoes the theme in a minor mode. Although for a time Ell feels some affection for La, his great passion is and always has been for Isma, who is married happily—on the balance—to his old friend Torm. The emotion of love itself is not ignoble or reprehensible, but the direction it takes in Ell is ethically wrong, by both terrestrial and Martian standards.

Relations between Earthmen and Martians are also greatly complicated by problems of language, which in turn reflect profound differences in attitude. Lasswitz' imaginary Martian language will be discussed in detail shortly; of particular relevance here, however, is a single linguistic feature: the use of the terrestrial and Martians words for "human." Only SF can confront us with men who are not "men," men who may even consider Earthmen not to be "men." Since the Enlightenment and the voyages of discovery which preceded it, the idea that all men are "human" has enjoyed widespread acceptance, despite some barbarous relapses. As their physical nature shows, they are all members of a single species inhabiting a single world. But "human" also has an implied philosophical and ethical sense which refers to membership in a group of beings who are superior to other forms of life. The discrepancy between the biological and the philosophical or moral senses of "human" has always provoked discussion. Modern science, which has established the existence of extra-terrestrial life as a serious possibility, if not a probability, adds a new dimension to the word and idea "human."

From the terrestrial point of view, men in *Auf zwei Planeten*—terrestrial men, that is—are of course "men" ("Menschen") and Martians are "Martians" ("Martier"). But to the Martians, an Earthman is a "Bat," a being from Earth, which they call "Ba"; a true "human being," according to the Martians, is—or at least always has been heretofore—a "Nume," a being from "Nu" or Mars. The quality of "humanness" or "humanity"—in standard German, "Menschheit"—the Martians call "Numenheit." (Since *Auf zwei Planeten* is written in German rather than Martian, "Numenheit" is actually a hybrid term; we are not given the "real" Martian word in its "true" form.) Before science made space travel possible, the

Martians had defined "Numenheit" only according to geography (or rather "areography"), and for good reason. It had been empirically valid to say that all Martians were human beings ("Nume") and, conversely, that all human beings were Martians ("Nume"). "Bat," and thus, for a Martian speaking German, "Mensch," would "translate" better then as "Earthling," "Earthbeing," or simply "Earthman," with distinct connotations of "sub-human" or "savage."

Before the development of space travel, the Martian concept of humanity had involved no conceptual paradox or logical fallacy, and therefore no terminological difficulties. First Contact confronts the Martians with the question whether men—"Bate"—might also be "Nume." Despite its supposed perfection, their intellectual and ethical equipment cannot adequately fathom that totally new experience, contact with the humanoid ("numenoid"?) aliens of Earth; nor can their language, whose evident paradoxes and contradictions Lasswitz cleverly uses to point up those of the concepts behind the words. The impressions the Martians gain from their initial encounters on Earth, amplified and distorted by their selfish interests, encourage them to consider Earthmen subhuman. The first terrestrials they meet, the Eskimos near the Pole, do not seem to them to be "Nume." The admirable behavior of Saltner and Grunthe changes the Martians' first impressions somewhat, but they nonetheless remain skeptical. Their tendency to regard Earthmen as non-human is reflected in their linguistic habits, as recorded with some modification to fit the actual language of narration. The Martians habitually refer to Grunthe and Saltner as "the poor Earthmen [die armen Menschen]" (e.g., 6:79, 86). Grunthe recalls having heard Ell, in moments "when he could not get across one of his strange ideas, when he wished to express his sympathy with the lack of understanding in men," mutter the words, "Ko bate, poor men, you don't understand [ko bate, das versteht ihr nicht, arme Menschen]" (7:94).

Despite Ell's and the Martians' benevolence, expressions like "ko bate" and even the word "bat" by itself are the fictional equivalents of such phrases as "the poor benighted heathen" current in Lasswitz' own time. So too are the attitudes behind the terms. At first, the Martians are inclined to regard the Earthmen as though they were "children,... whose foolishness [Thorheit] one lovingly excuses [nachsieht] while one educates them to higher understanding [zu besserem Verstandnis erzieht]" (11:157). Even Se, one of the more perceptive of the Martians, initially regards

Saltner and Grunthe as animals, though cute ones:

> The Martian woman laughed again while regarding [Saltner] pleasantly, as one expectantly looks at a curious animal. (6:76)

> "How is the 'Bat':" [she asked La].... Have you fed him [or "it"] already? [Hast du ihn denn schon gefüttert?]" (7:92)

La, Se, and—much more slowly—the other Martians gradually learn that Earthmen are not totally lacking in "Numenheit." Chapter 11, appropriately titled "Martier und Menschen," explores at length the linguistic and conceptual paradoxes of "humanity." The Martians are somewhat perplexed by the existence of Ell, which implies that "Nume" and "Bate" are similar enough, at least in physical nature, to produce offspring who, moreover, apparently deserve to be recognized as "Nume." Grunthe and Saltner are only mildly disturbed by the Martians' superiority, partly because the technological and intellectual advancement of the other culture is so evident. The Earthmen soon reassert their dignity, but the relative disparity between terrestrials and Martians is not left in doubt by Lasswitz or his characters. In Chapter 11 "Mensch" is used by the aliens in a distinctly pejorative sense, and subsequently the meaning of the word is restricted, among Martians, to "Earthman," with a clearly implied connotation of inferiority.

La does not follow the practice, for when Saltner rescued her from the crevasse she saw that terrestrial humans had their own virtues and came to realize, "after she had first accustomed herself to the very idea, that an Earthman could fall in love" (11:161). The vixenish Se, however, reminds her of the differences between the two species; she uses "Mensch" in an emphatically contemptuous way: " '... But he's just an Earthman! It's terribly funny when the fellow tries to be so cute and lovable! [... er ist ja bloss ein Mensch! Es ist doch furchtbar komisch, wenn der sich Mühe giebt, so recht liebenswürdig zu sein!]' " (11:162). In Se, who will later learn to appreciate terrestrials, such condescension is amusing; but it foreshadows uglier versions of the same attitude among other Martians.

As relations between the two planets deteriorate, the terms "Mensch" and "Nume" are differentiated even more radically. Impatiently the Martians explain their intentions; their benevolent tone is still at least partly sincere, but their words are also chosen to disguise their colonialistic ambitions:

"Now the motivations which occasion us to establish contact with the terrestrials are of a purely idealistic character. Here it is not possible for us briefly to convey them to you in a way that you, as terrestrials, might understand them. We are Nume. We are the bearers of the culture of the Solar System. For us it is a sacred obligation to make accessible, to terrestrials as well, the result of our hundred-thousand-year-long cultural labor, the blessing of 'numanity'." (19:294)

["Was uns aber nun veranlasst, die Menschen selbst aufzusuchen, das sind Beweggründe rein idealen Charakters. Es ist nicht möglich, sie Ihnen, als Menschen, hier in Kürze zum Verständnis zu bringen. Wir sind Nume. Wir sind die Träger der Kultur des Sonnensystems. Es ist uns eine heilige Pflicht, das Resultat unsrer hunderttausendjährigen Kulturarbeit, den Segen der Numenheit, auch den Menschen zugänglich zu machen."]

The lack of tolerance and caution with which the Martians introduce their culture to Earth causes the terrestrials to behave in a most un-numenlike way. Consequently, the Martians question even more the rights of terrestrials to the status of "Numenheit," which has been granted provisionally to Grunthe and Saltner as individuals. Caught in a position not unadvantageous to their ulterior purposes, the Martians feel more and more justified in forcing Earth to follow their dictates and submit to their educational programs. Lasswitz has Ell refer to their mission as the "economic, intellectual, [and] ethical education of Mankind [wirtschaftliche, intellektuelle (und) ethische Erziehung der Menschheit]" (46:294). To German ears the phrase clearly echoes the hallowed language of Lessing's "Die Erziehung des Menschengeschlechts" ["The Education of the Human Race"] (1780) and Schiller's "Briefe über die ästhetische Erziehung des Menschen" ["Letters on the Aesthetic Education of Man"] (1795). One should note also that in German "Erziehung" refers to the rearing of children as well as the education of the mind. Ell's words could scarcely be more ironic or more chilling as a description of how idealism can distort the meaning of the idea of humanity, especially when it masks—even from the idealist himself—self-serving intentions. Whatever its ideals, the Martian program is pursued in a way that makes it an inhuman perversion of the ideas of intellectual excellence, ethical maturity, and independent cultural development expressed by "human" and "humanity." It is not surprising, therefore, that the motto of the "Terrestrial Human Confederation [Menschenbund]" formed to resist Martian tyranny is "Numanity without Nume! [Numenheit ohne Nume!]" (53:417).

The phrase "Erziehung der Menschheit" is but one instance

where Lasswitz' use of language reveals much about the foundations and intent of the philosophical argument he advances in *Auf zwei Planeten*. One of his most admirable traits is the ability to assimilate, appreciate, and yet deeply question the attitudes and monumental achievements of earlier thinkers, especialy those of his own culture. Lasswitz was thoroughly familiar with Kant and the German Classics and Idealists. Using the terminology and concepts of those thinkers, he called into question the social, ethical and philosophical arguments of Kant, Goethe and Schiller, or at least the misinterpretation of their ideas. Rationalism and idealism are not rejected out of hand in *Auf zwei Planeten*, but the dangers which attend them—monomania, pride and self-deception—are made exceedingly clear.

The philosophical and ethical argument Lasswitz constructs so carefully serves as the foundation for an equally deliberate examination of more specific social and ideological questions. The novel offers a critique of three ideological attitudes current in the late nineteenth century: imperialism, utopianism and liberalism. Most readily apparent is the attack on imperialism, which Lasswitz views as a consequence of flawed reasoning, a perverted sense of humanity, cultural egocentrism, self-delusion and, not least of all, greed. Like Wells in *The War of the Worlds*, Lasswitz chose to set his novel about Mars in the immediate future and to cast aliens, rather than advanced terrestrials of some distant future, in the role of superior beings who attempt to dominate a supposedly inferior race. Thus, with a sure grasp of irony and an accurate sense of the resources made available by the basic generic presuppositions of SF, Lasswitz created an imaginary world in which the "civilized" Europeans, in a direct reversal of roles, find themselves the victims of imperialism, colonialism and a program of "civilization."

The Martians' defeat of imperial Britain illustrates Lasswitz' attitude toward one specific manifestation of imperialism in his own time. But far more important to his ideological critique are the Martians themselves as cultural and economic imperialists. Lasswitz does not hesitate to call the reader's attention to the historical and political models or "analogs" on which the imaginary world is based. As the philosophy, policies, and even the diplomatic language of the Martians show, nineteenth-century European imperialism is indeed the overall pattern for the contact between Earth and Mars. The chief features of both versions of imperialism, in Lasswitz' view, were the threat to the cultural integrity or even physical survival of the "inferior" race, and the potential lapse into barbarism of the supposedly more advanced culture.

An analog of lesser importance in *Auf zwei Planeten* is the conquest of the American frontier, a process of course not unrelated to the larger pattern of European imperialism. Lasswitz, who once remarked that he read stories about Indians,[14] uses the confrontation of Indians and Europeans mainly to illustrate the incomprehensibility of advanced technology to more primitive societies. More than once Grunthe and Saltner express their mystification when faced with Martian technology by comparing themselves to Indians marveling at the white man's science, his "medicine": "Here we're just playing the role of wild Indians, and what we don't comprehend is simply—medicine" (11:158; see also 33:114). Although genocide is a real danger in *Auf zwei Planeten*, that aspect of the American frontier analog is not emphasized. Other less important analogs would be obvious to the German reader: the expansion of Roman rule into ancient Germania, and French domination of Germany in recent centuries.

It is understandable that Lasswitz would criticize European imperialism. He was a humanitarian, a liberal and also, one might suspect, a German who might well have resented the colonial empires of other powers. Yet he does not excoriate the British or French by writing jingoistic future-war fiction in which his own country merely replaces the enemy as top dog. Nor does he even insinuate that Germany should enter the competition for empire. Lasswitz' attack is directed without reserve at imperialism itself, which he views from the perspective of an ideological liberal and descendant of Kant and Schiller who was deeply disturbed by the distortion of the ideals of rationalistic ethics and the true education of humanity into instruments that serve greed and that ultimately corrupt those who wield them.

But Lasswitz is not satisfied simply with an attack on imperialism. Such condemnations, often shallow and unrealistic, characterize much of the futuristic literature of the time. The rest consists largely of ideologically contrary but equally inane dreams of successful imperialism. Just as he criticizes Kantianism while still remaining a Kantian, so Lasswitz—although he was an optimist and genuine progressive—takes political utopianism and progressivism to task. He shows how those beliefs, if based on insecure foundations or applied incautiously, can easily metamorphize into reactionism, repressive policies and relapses in the evolution of civilization.

Lasswitz' Mars exhibits many utopian features, as his early

critics noticed. But it is also the perversion of utopia. Thus *Auf zwei Planeten* anticipates the idea, expressed by many in the twentieth century, that a realized utopia might easily degenerate into a dystopia where departures from the supposedly ideal status quo, including further utopian speculation, are discountenanced. But Lasswitz does not bias the argument in his favor from the outset by envisioning an imaginary society which is clearly a nightmare even on first impression, like the totalitarian societies which other thinkers foresaw or actually observed. Judged by reasonable standards, his Martian society is indeed more advanced than terrestrial civilization in many significant ways. To emphasize the utopian aspects of Martian culture Lasswitz employs the same motifs and stylistic devices found in traditional utopias. There are travelers' reports, formal disquisitions on politics and government, and frequent allusions to customs and cultural objects which concretely demonstrate the superiority of Martian civilization. But unlike the creators of true utopias, Lasswitz warns against the dangers of believing that perfection has been attained; he even questions the very idea of perfectibility. His Martians, as *Auf zwei Planeten* persistently asserts, are real beings, not abstract ideals. He argues that, although human beings can progress toward true "humanity," a culture which assumes that it has reached perfection is dangerously susceptible to behavior which in effect transforms utopia into dystopia.

In evaluating liberal progressivism and utopianism Lasswitz did not hesitate to question certain ideas associated with science itself, which for many liberals was an important area of knowledge, sometimes almost an object of veneration. Lasswitz obviously believed in the validity and value of scientific and technological pursuits. Nevertheless—or perhaps therefore—he shows in *Auf zwei Planeten* the dangers inherent in the automatic equation of technological sophistication and excellence of theoretical inquiry with cultural and moral superiority. The Martian missionary-exploiters find it most tempting to justify imposing their will on the exasperatingly benighted heathens of Earth by an argument which assumes and asserts that specious but attractive equivalence. Lasswitz' critique of liberalism that is founded on an unexamined, condescending, positivistic faith in science and technology is most trenchant at the point where the Martians' sense of cultural mission is rapidly turning into a program of repression in which science and technology will be useful tools. The Martians' official protestations of benevolence echo the pronouncements of sincere liberals as well as the self-justifying prevarications of hypocritical capitalists:

> "The terrestrials will have nothing to fear from us, as soon as they have learned to understand us. We have no need of the inhabitants of Earth; we come to them in order to bring them the blessings of our civilization." (19:293)

Lasswitz is most cautious in assessing the relation of technology to cultural excellence. Quite reasonably he perceives that, in an approximate way, technological advancement is a presupposition and therefore an index of cultural development. But he is aware of the gross errors and flaws of Western civilization, especially as they have appeared in its contact with other cultures. For Lasswitz such faults stem, in large measure, precisely from the highly advanced philosophy and technology of Western civilization, which encourage it to assume that it is more advanced than it actually is.

Auf zwei Planeten, like any other literary work of more than trivial merit, should not be interpreted willfully as a period piece, a tendentious vision, or a timeless statement. Lasswitz was far too sophisticated an observer of cultural history and a writer of SF to cast his writings as serious prophecies. His SF is, rather, a sometimes optimistic, sometimes admonitory exploration of hypothetical future worlds. But historical hindsight allows us to credit the Lasswitz of *Auf zwei Planeten* with a certain visionary perception of some of the dangers which were inherent in the German culture of his time and which later contributed to the disasters of recent German history. In his mature SF novel Lasswitz quietly but incisively examines how a highly developed civilization can adopt a policy of economic and cultural imperialism and even approach the brink of genocide precisely because of its confidence in the superiority of its foundations and its faith in its sacred mission to educate other cultures after its own pattern. The Mars of *Auf zwei Planeten*, even though Lasswitz treats it as a real extra-terrestrial culture like those which our species might sometime encounter, can also be taken to represent Western civilization in general and Germany in particular. While neither he nor anyone else in 1897 could have envisioned the Third Reich as an inevitable historical event, Lasswitz identified certain traits in German society and thought which involved dangerous misconceptions and contradictions. Extrapolating those features from the past and from his own time, when the politically unified "land of poets and thinkers" had become imperial Germany, he imagined a future in which dystopia is averted only at the last minute through a difficult process of understanding and reconciliation.

It would be incorrect, however, to view Lasswitz as a doctrinaire skeptic or pessimist. In his critique of imperialism, idealism, intellectual positivism, science and rationalism itself he is not as extreme as other thinkers have been. His restraint, which sometimes borders on ambivalence, may well be attributable both to his ability to see the many sides of an argument and to the fact that he was affected, inevitably, by the attitudes of his own time, including some of what we now consider to be its prejudices. Lasswitz retained an evident reverence for the ideas of Lessing, Kant, Goethe and Schiller, and he was not immune to the confidence in reason and the belief in the ultimately beneficial nature of science and technology which were characteristic of the late nineteenth century. And he necessarily lacked the experience of twentieth-century history which inspires our own skepticism.

Lasswitz' argument, consequently, is moderate, but it is not indecisive. He indeed believed in the gradual improvement of mankind, and at the conclusion of *Auf zwei Planeten* mankind—both "Menschen" and "Nume"—has indeed progressed significantly. But, Lasswitz avers, man should improve organically, by his own faculties and at his proper pace. Great advancement must be accompanied by even greater critical awareness, for such progress can lead to dangerous relapses—as both Kant and Schiller themselves had warned, and as Lasswitz' own time and ours have demonstrated.

As a philosopher and historian of philosophy Lasswitz was eminently prepared to investigate the general concept of humanity. As an observer of the cultural and political life of the late nineteenth century he was also troubled, as I have suggested, by the absolutism, imperialism and colonialism of his time, and by the distorted ideas of humanity and progress which were being used to justify them. The subtlest point of his argument, I think, is both expressed and made possible by the close resemblance between Earthmen and Martians. The latter can be viewed as embodiments, in deceptively ideal form, of some of the better traits of terrestrial humanity, whether present or future. Their behavior, therefore, represents a critique of the conduct of civilized terrestrial mankind in its dealings with supposedly inferior cultures—either those on Earth in the present or, hypothetically, those which we might sometime encounter elsewhere in the universe.

By creating a race of extraterrestrial beings embodying our own ideals Lasswitz can offer a critique of imperialism which is broader, more systematic and less subject to accusations of nationalism than would have been possible had he written a "mainstream" realistic novel or a "future war" story about aliens. Yet the Martians should not be reduced to simple allegorical figures which are taken to represent the imperialism of Lasswitz' own time or that of some subsequent period in the development of terrestrial humanity. Within the fiction the Martians are real beings, and they and their world are matters of independent interest. For Lasswitz was a modern scientist and writer of SF who seriously contemplated the possibility that extraterrestrial life might exist, if not on Mars then elsewhere. He grasped the implications that idea might have for traditional concepts of culture and humanity, and he also wondered whether there might occur a real First Contact which could interfere with the proper development of terrestrial humanity.

The two functions of the Martians, or the two ways according to which we are invited to interpret them, are not inconsistent with each other. Rather, as Lasswitz himself might argue, the Martians resemble European imperialists and erring social meliorists not simply because they are directly modeled on such figures—true, of course—but because the distinctive features of cultural egocentrism are likely to appear wherever two races of different levels of advancement, yet neither of them perfect, encounter each other. Lasswitz thus reaps the benefits attendant on the peculiar relation between real and imaginary worlds in SF, and yet avoids its disadvantages. The real-life targets of his criticism are evident, and yet his fiction presents a genuine thought-model which seriously explores new situations brought about in some way by science.

Science-Fictional Technique

In its stylistic features, as in its plot, characterization and theme, *Auf zwei Planeten* is an impressive piece of SF which achieves reasonably satisfactory solutions to many of the technical problems apparent in Lasswitz' other works. The tone of narration is notably calm, even dispassionate, and the narrative voice almost never wavers from that stance to emerge momentarily as a truly identifiable personality who explicitly addresses the reader. Far rarer than in Lasswitz' earlier SF are parenthetical remarks, notes or references to "we" or "the nineteenth-century reader," intrusions which would remind the reader that what is narrated is in fact mediated by a narrator and a fictional text.

Occasionally Lasswitz adopts the stance of the omniscient, impersonal "future historian," as he does when describing the history of Martian interplanetary flight. The device, as I suggested in Chapter I, is merely a variation or intensification of the impersonal narrative voice and is extremely useful in SF. One of but many instances of the technique can be found in the narrator's brief sketch of the history of Martian interplanetary flight:

> The investigation of the Earth, the discovery of the interplanetary path to it, and the ultimate occupation [Besitzergreifung] of the North Pole comprise an extensive and important chapter in the cultural history of the Martians.
> The transparency of the atmosphere on Mars had early made its inhabitants excellent astronomers. Mathematics and science had reached a height of development which shimmers before us terrestrials as a distant ideal. The more the aging Mars aggravated the living conditions of the Martians by its relatively small water supply, the more magnificent had been the efforts through which the Martians developed the technique of dominating nature [die Technik der Naturbeherrschung].... (8:102)

Admirable examples of another distinctive stylistic feature of SF, the depiction of imaginary environments or of familiar landscapes viewed from new perspectives, are also encountered often in *Auf zwei Planeten*. In Chapter 27, for example, Lasswitz presents a lengthy description of Mars as Isma Torm—and with her, the reader—sees it for the first time from the space station situated over the Martian South Pole:

> It was summer at the South Pole of Mars, and therefore approximately two-thirds of the planet's disc, seen here from the axis outward, appeared illuminated, while one third lay in deep darkness. On the illuminated portion one could now survey the southern hemisphere as far as the tenth degree of Martian latitude. As the space ship descended this horizon narrowed more and more, while as a consequence of the closer approach the image of the planet gained in expanse and the details emerged ever more distinctly. Because of the thin, transparent, cloudless atmosphere the configuration of the surface lay clearly before the eye as far as the margin of the visible plane. In the vicinity of the Pole and toward the terminator there extended wide regions, in coloration gray trailing off into blue-green: the *Mare australe* of Earth's astonomers. The Pole itself was free of ice, but to the west of it, between the dark land areas, there still lay long expanses of snowy areas up to the eightieth parallel. Ill pointed out two large, extended areas, which glistened deep red in the sunshine to the north between the sixtieth and seventieth parallels, as the deserts Gol and Sek.... This deep red color predominated in the rest of the visible disc, but was interrupted in several places by broad and extensive gray areas. All these dark places were connected amongst themselves by dark bands which proceeded in straight lines through the light areas. The light areas are [sic] partly sandy, partly rocky upland plateaus, dry and almost unvegetated

regions in which are located only sparse settlements for obtaining mineral riches. By contrast, the dark areas, whose territory is penetrated by dampness and covered with a luxuriant vegetation, are thickly populated....

Ill pointed to a spot near the northern boundary of the vegetated region,... toward which... an especially large number of dark bands converged.

"There is Kla," he said, "the seat of the Central Council; there we will live for the time being...." (27:7-9)

The passage conveys a wealth of detail, much of which, like the indications of latitude, is precise and even quantitative. Particular attention is given to the thin, nearly transparent atmosphere, the dry maria or "seas," and the "canals," features in which Mars differs radically from Earth, at least according to the science of Lasswitz' time. Martian "areographical" names are adduced in the matter-of-fact manner which, common in other SF, contributes much to the impression of authenticity. Likewise, the casual tone with which Lasswitz describes the artificial objects in the landscape makes the existence of Martians seem almost a matter of course. The momentary lapse into present tense ("The light areas *are...*") suggests that Lasswitz himself might have surrendered to the same conviction in the midst of creating his imaginary landscape.

Best among Lasswitz' descriptions of landscape, however, is the view of Earth from the nearby Martian space station:

They [Earthmen and Martians] stood in a mysterious twilight which was illumined only by the reflection of the moonlight at the one end of the gallery and by that of the earthlight on the ceiling above them.

Deep-black lay the sky about them, above them, to the sides, at their feet. On the black background shone the stars with a clearness never seen before, as a thousand quietly glowing points....

In the center, at their feet, hovered the Earth, a shining disc. It [or "she"] had the form of the waxing moon after its first quarter, but one also perceived the part not illuminated by the sun, for the light of the moon cloaked it in a feeble shimmer. The entire disc of the Earth appeared at a visual angle of sixty degrees and thus filled precisely the third part of the sky beneath the horizon. The terminator cut the Polar Sea in the vicinity of the mouth of the Yenisei, so that the largest part of Siberia and the west coast of America lay in darkness. The glaciers on the east coast of Greenland shone brilliantly in the light of the midday sun, and Iceland, a gleaming white speck, rose from the dark currents of the Atlantic Ocean. The western portion of the ocean and the American continent could not be distinguished. Above them rested a seldom-broken cloud layer whose upper side reflected the rays of the sun with blinding whiteness.... By contrast the entire map of Europe, at least in its northern part, lay in favorable light before their enraptured gaze. The air there, under the influence of an extended high-pressure zone, was perfectly clear and pure, so that one distinctly perceived the northerly

"Dort ist meine Heimat"—"There is my homeland."
Drawing by W. Zeeden from abridged centenary edition (1948) of Kurd Lasswitz, "Auf zwei Planeten."

"Der Glo hatte sich bis dicht uber die Station gesenkt"—*"The Glo has descended until it was right over the station."* Drawing by W. Zeeden from abridged centenary edition.

islands and peninsulas and the deeply incised ocean-bays. Beyond, the shapes of the plains became blurred in a bluish-green atmospheric shade, but for a sharp eye the ranges of the Alps and even the Caucasus flashed up as fine clear lines. The border of the illuminated portion of the disc shimmered in more subdued light, and only on the terminator did a few clear points of light denote the setting of the sun for the snowy peaks of the Tienshan and Altai.

In profound silence the Germans stood, completely immersed in the sight which until now had been granted to no human eye. Never before had they been so completely aware of what it meant to be swirled through space on the tiny grain called "Earth."...

Saltner drew [La] to himself and spoke: "And there, my Earth—isn't it beautiful?" (15:230-32)

The passage easily bears comparison with the best of such descriptions to be found in later SF. Lasswitz presents a view of our own planet as seen from nearby space, a vantage point only recently attainable in reality. He carefully points out the heretofore unfamiliar features of the extraterrestrial environment, such as the blackness of the airless medium, the brilliance of the stars, and the dim moonlight reflected from the dark limb of the Earth. By stating that the globe "hovers at [the observers'] feet" he also emphasizes the relativity of directional orientation which prevails beyond the perceptible influence of planetary gravity. Lasswitz then turns to smaller geographical features which, though familiar in themselves, are now viewed from a new perspective. The spectacle of Earth as a single body hovering in space, upon which the remotest places can be seen at the same time, impresses Lasswitz' characters—as it later did other astronauts, both fictional and real—with a sense that the world is indeed a unit. And, by describing the Earth as waxing gibbous, Lasswitz underscores the fact that it, like the moon or other planets, is indeed an astronomical body. The detailed, scientifically accurate picture does much to further the theme of *Auf zwei Planeten*, the idea that First Contact obviates provincial differences among Earthmen and requires them to realize that they must reckon with the possibility that "humanity" may have a larger meaning. And yet somehow, as Saltner's rhetorical questions suggests, Earth is nonetheless special. While Lasswitz' efforts to convey delicate emotions are sometimes awkward, as may be true here, the alternation of precise, impersonal description with an appeal to emotion is quite effective.

Similar care in the evocation of setting and presentation of significant detail is evident when Lasswitz describes imaginary science and technology. The collection of solar energy, for example, is vital to Martian civilization, and is a prime factor in the Martians' effort to establish a base on Earth. Lasswitz pictures at considerable length the giant energy station located in space near Earth:

> ...The ring, one-half Earth's diameter above the pole, was exposed uninterruptedly to the solar radiation. The energy emitted from the sun was picked up and collected by an enormous number of plane elements located in the ring and on the upper surface of the flywheels. On the surface of the Earth terrestrials employ mainly only the heat and light of the solar energy. But here in empty space it became evident that the sun emits incomparably greater quantities of energy, especially rays of very large wave-length, such as electric, as well as those of still much smaller wave-length than those of light. We notice nothing of that, because for the most part they are absorbed already by the outermost layers of the atmosphere and are re-radiated back into space. Here, however, all these quantities of energy, which would otherwise have been lost, were collected, transformed, and, in appropriate form, reflected to the island at the North Pole. On the island, in conjunction with the radiation directly picked up there, they were employed in a series of magnificent achievements....
>
> Firstly, a portion of this workpower was used to generate an electro-magnetic field of the most enormous strength and expanse. The entire island with its 144 circular stations represented, as it were, a gigantic electro-magnet which was fed by solar energy itself. The construction was laid out in such a manner that the lines of force concentrated themselves about the ring and the latter was kept hovering against gravity....
>
> It would have been impossible to erect such an apparatus any place else on Earth than in the extension of its axis of rotation, that is, over the North Pole or the South Pole. For, aside from deeper-lying difficulties, at any other location the shifting of the surface of the Earth due to its daily rotation would have offered insuperable obstacles to the establishment of equilibrium between gravity and the electromagnet.... (3:41-42).

The Martian energy accumulators are apparently based on theoretical information actually available to Lasswitz, for example the research in electromagnetism conducted by Helmholtz, Hertz, Maxwell and Faraday. But Lasswitz' vision of the technological implementation and social effects of that research advanced beyond the speculation of his own day and sometimes even the capabilities of modern technology, although the idea of large-scale collection of solar energy in space is now taken seriously.

Whenever possible Lasswitz suggests how the Martians have realized in their technology ideas only intimated by terrestrial scientific theory. When, as in the passage just quoted, he cannot provide such hard information—an understandable problem—he does not hesitate to resort to the rhetorical stratagems characteristic of SF. Pseudo-scientific "double talk" is used with technical skill and judicious restraint. Thus the space station is maintained in its position in space by "a series of complicated and most ingeniously conceived control apparatuses [eine Reihe komplizierter und höchst scharfsinnig ausgedachter Kontrolapparate]" (3:42). Neither the noun "control apparatus" nor the modifiers "complicated" and "most ingeniously conceived" indeed say anything definite about the actual mechanisms they are supposed to explain, but such terms sound impressive if they are not overused.

Lasswitz also introduces confident analogies between imaginary and actual technology to persuade the reader that information has been provided when in fact it has not. We are told, for example, that the island energy accumulator constitutes, "as it were [gewissermassen] a gigantic electromagnet." Diversion of the reader's interest from the specific features of imaginary technology to an exciting description of its actual operation is yet another subterfuge which Lasswitz employs with some effectiveness. And if, lastly, he distracts the reader's attention from the details of imaginary science and technology to an examination of their wider social and philosophical implications in the imaginary world, he thereby adds credence to the idea that science and technology are not merely offshoots or superstrata, but rather determinants of human life. Even—or especially—the mundane social consequences of imaginary technology are not ignored; in his description of the Martian transportation system, for example, Lasswitz includes mention of such everyday matters as currency and routing, and he is fully aware that these seemingly unnecessary details may contribute much to the reader's sense of plausibility (36:158ff.).

Still other of the special rhetorical stratagems of SF discussed in Chapter I, among them smaller-scale devices like the "serial" technique, can be observed in *Auf zwei Planeten*:

> Here [in the Gol Desert] there dwelled culturally backward groups of the
> planet's population, some still even pursuing agriculture,... but most
> active in mining and in the solar energy collection facilities. (27:19-20)

To establish the plausibility of his imaginary technology, the "solar energy collection facilities [Strahlungs-Sammelstätten]," Lasswitz introduces the imposing compound neologism—without interruption or special attention—in conjunction with "agriculture" and "mining," two concepts and terms already quite familiar to the reader. Indeed, agriculture is considered "even" ("sogar") a vestigial pursuit, since Martian food is artificial. The series is preceded and followed by short, matter-of-fact comments which further reinforce the plausibility of the imaginary technology by explaining its place in Martian history and society. Lasswitz does not employ the "serial" technique frequently in *Auf zwei Planeten*, or elswhere in his SF, but the example discussed here demonstrates a fine command of the device. It is significant also that Lasswitz' understanding of the intentionality of SF led him to devise independently a stylistic device which reappears constantly elsewhere in the genre.

Lasswitz is also aware that offhand, even supposedly trite words like "of course" or "naturally," which in themselves have nothing to do with imaginary content, can contribute much to the sense of plausibilty:

> The alternation of counter-gravity and earth-gravity [produced by the Martian generators] extended, however, over the entire field, with the consequence, naturally, that the exploration party's stricken balloon was also subject to the variations of gravity. (4:50)

Since the reader has no prior knowledge of "abaric fields," there is nothing at all "natural" about the expression "naturally" ("natürlich"). But the word helps to make the unfamiliar seemingly familiar by creating a bond of intimacy and confidence between reader and narrator. Other words or phrases used in a similarly casual and allusive manner also serve to provide background information without slowing the pace of the narration, or at least to persuade the reader that he knows something which he actually does not and can not know:

> Jo [the veteran Martian spaceship captain] greeted Saltner in his open and, with regard to Martian notions, rather blunt manner and gave the names of his companions. (12:171)

Rather than describing the customary manner of Martian salutation, still unknown to the reader, Lasswitz alludes to Jo's idiosyncratically "open," "robust," "blunt," or even "rough" ("derb") version of the greeting. The technique assumes, or rather instantly creates, the presupposition that the reader is actually in a position to judge Jo's behavior as a divergence from the norm; that in turn rests on the tacit assumption that the norm, and by implied extension the rest of the imaginary world, in fact exists.

A passage from the concise "Cultural History of the Martians [Kulturgeschichte der Martier]" presented in Chapter 8, which is subtitled "The Lords of Space [Die Herren des Weltraums]," illustrates to particular advantage Lasswitz' ability to "make strange" the familiar world and at the same time make a strange world familiar with a single, in itself unobtrusive word or phrase. Using the appropriate historical tone, the narrator characterizes the significance of Earth for Mars:

> After the surface of the planet [Mars] had been completely explored and settled, the attention of the Martians, in accord with the nature of things, directed itself more strongly than ever beyond the bounds of their habitat toward their neighbors in the solar system. And what here could captivate them more mightily than the shining Ba, the legend-enshrouded Earth, which, now as morning-, now as evening-star, outshone all the other stars of their black sky? (8:104)

The historical and astronomical perspectives are unambiguously Martian. We are reminded that the sky of Mars is darker than Earth's, and that, on Mars, Earth appears as a morning and evening star, just as Venus and Mercury do for terrestrial observers. The term "in accord with the nature of things" ("naturgemäss") reinforces the plausibility of the exposition of Martian cultural history by suggesting, even more strongly than would "naturally" ("natürlich"), that the Martians' curiosity about their neighbors in the solar system is a consequence of certain natural laws about which the reader, ostensibly, needs no further information. The epic epithet "legend-enshrouded Earth" ("sagenumwobene Erde"), one of several such expressions in *Auf zwei Planeten*, has even profounder implications which affect the reader all the more because Lasswitz does not spell them out. By representing our own Earth as a distant, mysterious planet, the phrase subtly but effectively insinuates that Mars, not Earth, is the familiar world, that its civilization is so advanced that it has long spun legends about Earth, and that the other planets, among them Mars for us, are mysterious but real places, not insubstantial specks of light in the sky. All three ideas are intimately related to the notion of encounter between alien civilizations which is one of the fundamental themes of SF. Perhaps no other single passage in *Auf zwei Planeten* better argues that Lasswitz was aware of the intentionality of SF and of the stylistic resources which might be used to further it.

One of the most interesting features of *Auf zwei Planeten* is Lasswitz' imaginary Martian language. Naturally not everything the Martians say can be quoted in Martian, yet the reader knows they speak a different language. For the sake of plausibility, therefore, the reader must know something of the Martian language and must be told how communication is first established—a favorite theme of "First Contact" stories. Lasswitz includes scenes in which the characters point at objects and recite Martian and German names for them (e.g., 6:75-82). Such interludes appear frequently in SF and may well be modeled in part on the description of encounters between Europeans and exotic cultures in travel journals, robinsonades, Western stories and utopias. Lasswitz also furnishes his explorers with a basic Martian-German lexicon, which they discover after being stranded at the North Pole. The device is not a patently improbable contrivance, for Ell, in keeping with his mission to unite the two cultures, had compiled the dictionary and concealed it in the expedition's equipment.

But the reader's sense of plausibility is advanced most by observation of the Martian language in use. While Lasswitz does not indulge in a full-scale linguistic treatise, he provides enough examples of Martian that one could almost construct a basic Martian glossary and grammar. Or rather, the reader is sufficiently convinced that it would be possible to do so. Since the relatively few examples of Martian actually given are simple and clearly systematic, he is persuaded that what he does not hear is the same as well.

Martian is a very concise language, the result, Lasswitz seems to imply, of a higher intelligence and of millenia of linguistic evolution. Monosyllables predominate, and articles, cases and most declensions are absent, except in a few nouns. The singular and plural of "Earthman" and "Martian" are, respectively, "Bat"/ "Bate" and "Nume"/ "Nume", which indicates at least two types of noun formation. But "Ba," the word for "Earth," appears in unchanged form as a nominative, genitive and dative, and as the subject of an optative verb; thus "Sila Ba! Long live Earth! [Es lebe die Erde!]" (27:13), and, on a sign in the "terrestrial museum" on Mars, " 'Corsan ba,' 'collections from the Earth [Sammlungen von der Erde]' " (29:51). The grammatical form of "Nu," the Martian word for "Mars," is similar. We see it in unchanged form as a simple nominative, as a subject of the optative expression "Sila Nu!" (27:13), and as the object of a preposition "Vel lo nu, spaceship to Mars [Raumschiff nach dem Mars]" (15:229). This last phrase enables us to deduce information about Martian prepositions. "Lo" appears to mean "to," or rather "toward"; an earlier phrase "Bate li war,...terrestrials in the abaric field [Menschen im abarischen Feld]" contains the apparently related preposition "li," meaning "in" (3:47). As for verbs, although complex utterances are rare, there may be a distinction between singular and plural in conjugation. Copulative verbs, however, are apparently optional, as in Greek, Latin, the Slavic languages, and several non-Indo-European tongues.

Although other Martian utterances are not easy to analyze linguistically, they do have an appearance of systematization, and the reader is told explicitly what they mean:

> "E najoh. Ke.... Bate li war. Tak a fil."
> "Attention! Disturbance! What has occurred?... Terrestrials in the abaric field. Shut down as quickly as possible.
> [Achtung! Was ist vorgefallen?... Menschen im abarischen Feld. Abstellen so bald wie möglich]" (3:47)

> [Se exclaimed,] "It's just too funny!" "Fafagolik?" Saltner attempted to reproduce the strange sounds. (6:76)

> [Ill introduced himself.] "Ill re ktorh, am gel Schick—Ill, family-name Ktohr, from the clan Schick [Ill Familie Ktohr aus dem Geschlechte Schick]." (22:346)

The last of the utterances just cited confirms the general absence of noun declension in Martian, but does not tell us much more, unless by "am gel" Lasswitz intends to imply that Martian represents a hypothetical later stage of German—"*aus dem Geschlecht*." Certainly the suggestion is consistent with the subtle but unmistakeable equation of Martian civilization with an ideal of German culture, a theme present throughout the novel.

The rest of the Martian vocabulary cited in *Auf zwei Planeten* consists mostly of scattered concrete nouns and names of both persons and places. "Pik," for example, is a stimulant (12:172), "Eck" and "Thekel" are units of currency (36:158-59), and "Lis" a synthetic textile made of crystal filaments extracted from "Dela," mussel-like organisms (11:166). "Gragra" (46:306), a Martian childhood disease, may hint at the terrestrial "pellagra." The "Ro-Wa" (5:59) is a lily-like flower, and "Boff" (31:72) a kind of fruit. Certainly the mention of such mundane items helps to make the Martian language, and therefore Martian civilization, more real. We might also expect to find Martian expressions for more important things. The words for "Earth" and "Mars" have already been discussed. The Sun is called "O" (6:81), perhaps a verbal icon. "Ba" (13:193) and "Glo" (16:253) are the names of spaceships; the word for "spaceship" itself is "Vel" (3:49), which suggests root words for "fly" or "speed" in the Indo-European languages. The capital city of Mars is "Kla" (27:9); a small desert town is "Mari, Sei" (36:159) in the "district [Bezirk] Hed" (37:164). Two of the 154 Martian federated states are "Berseb" and "Hugal" (33:108), two deserts are "Gol" and "Sek" (27:8), and the desert people of Mars are called "Beds" (27:20). Personal names are numerous and seem to be differentiated according to gender. Masculine names, such as those of the major characters "Ell," "Ill" and "Hil," end in consonants, diphthongs or apparently long vowels. The less frequent feminine names, such as "La," "Se," "Ma" (28:24) and "Blu" (29:40), all end in vowels.

Such bits and pieces, like the linguistic remnants of early Germanic languages scattered among classical sources, may seem mysterious and unpromising, but they are more useful than might be expected. Whether or not Lasswitz intended the reader to fathom every possible similarity, it is obvious that to a large extent the imaginary Martian language is modeled—intentionally, necessarily, and at least somewhat openly—on real languages. Of particular importance, as I have already suggested, is German. The names of Ell, his father All, and his uncle Ill, for example, exhibit a pattern of ablaut, assonance and alliteration among kin, prominent features of ancient Germanic naming practices. The distinction of gender in personal names by consonantal or vocalic ending is Indo-European. But Lasswitz is careful not to overemphasize the similarity between German and Martian, for to do so would undermine the impression that the Martians are fictively real beings.

Other Martian words seem to be patterned after more exotic non-Indo-European languages. As befits their desert provenance, "Gol," "Berseb" and "Hugal" might well be Near-Eastern, as seems to be the case also with "thekel," the currency unit, which suggests "shekel." "Bed" appears very much an abbreviation of "Bedouin." "Gol," however, might allude—instead or as well—to Mongolia, and the name of the other desert, "Sek," may be intended to suggest words for "dry" in the various Romance languages. The name of the desert town "Mari" may be borrowed directly from the actual Mari, an ancient Babylonian city of some importance which is mentioned in Biblical sources.

As might be expected, the influence of Greek and Latin on Lasswitz' imaginary Martian language, especially its scientific and technological terms, is also very evident. Sometimes he provides names for new objects merely by creating nonce words from Greek and Latin. Thus we encounter "abarisch" (3:47), "diabarisch"

(8:107) and "Abariker" (12:189), which have to do with anti-gravity; "Stellit" (8:110), "Repulsit" (12:187), "Teletyt" (13:199) and "Nihilit" (38:180), all imaginary substances or energy sources; and "Anthygrin" (46:300), apparently a medicine. We are not told the "real" Martian names, unless, as is not very likely, those given are supposed to be the alien terms as well. It might be objected that the practice may make it difficult for the reader, who is presumably more familiar with Greek and Latin than with non-Indo-European languages, to believe in the fictive reality of the Martian language and thus that of the Martians themselves. But neologisms coined from Greek and Latin do have the virtue of being more or less readily comprehensible. They also sound "scientific," for it is almost traditional—in SF and in actual practice—to devise names for scientific and technological innovations from Greek and Latin roots.

The Greek and Latin connotations of the words the Martians apply to themselves and their planet are still more intriguing. "Nu," as Lasswitz' early reviewer Moritz Kronenberg suggested, may be derived from the Greek "nous," meaning "intellect" or "reason." "Nume" may be intended to suggest, in addition, both Latin "numen," meaning "god" or "divinity," and Greek "noumenon," a true ideal or entity perceived by the rational faculty, as opposed to a physically apprehended, transitory and perhaps illusory "phenomenon."

Mathematics is proverbially the language of science, and in SF it can be a subject of considerable interest, for the reader, because of his scientific inclinations, may tolerate or even desire more attention to mathematics than the general reader might think appropriate. Lasswitz satisfies the reader's curiosity about alien mathematics with a mathematical system which, although its exposition is briefer than that of the Martian language, is equally clever and systematic in conception. Just as he does not interrupt his narration with long quotations in Martian or formal discourses on the language, Lasswitz does not overwhelm the reader, as he had in the *Bilder aus der Zukunft*, with abstruse calculations or disquisitions which have nothing to do with the action. Accordingly, information about Martian mathematics is often provided incidentally by the Martians themselves. Thus, for example, they find it necessary to give the Earthmen terrestrial equivalents of their own time units:

"When will [the departure] take place?" [asked Grunthe.]

"64, 63 [i.e., 64.63]" replied Jo.

Grunthe looked at him inquisitively.

"Median Martian Longitude [Mittlere Marslange]," added Jo.

"But you have to recalculate all the measurements for the gentlemen into their terrestrial system of computation," began La. "They can't adapt themselves to our method of measurement that fast. The departure is tomorrow at 1,6 [i.e, 1.6], that is, according to your chronological reckoning, at three o'clock." (12:180)

Lasswitz was aware that there is no real reason why our own modern decimal system, with its admixture of older duodecimal and sexagesimal systems, and, more recently, binary reckoning, should be universal. But instead of positing a completely regularized decimal or "metric" system, Lasswitz adopts a base whose arithmetical virtues—ease of fractional factoring, for example— have long made it popular with a minority of mathematical reformers. Martian reckoning, as Grunthe and Saltner deduce (9:128), is purely duodecimal, and Lasswitz repeatedly but not tediously reminds the reader of the difference. Often, for example, he alludes to quantities which, when translated into base-12, become "round" numbers rather than seemingly odd or random figures. Thus Martian spaceships and their crews almost always appear in multiples or simple fractions of twelve: 6, 12, 48 and 60 Martians (5:67, 12:175, 12:179, 12:180), 144 spaceships (20:311, 33:104), and 3456 crewmen (39:199). The last number is 2×12^3, which would confirm that the Martians also employ a place-system based on increasing powers of the root.

Temporal units are also strictly duodecimal (9:127-28). The Martian day is divided into twelve hours, and parts of a single hour are apparently rendered as duodecimal fractions in which the numeral 6 after the "duodecimal point"—a comma in German, of course—represents the fraction 6/12 or, in decimal notation, .5; thus "1,6," "11,6," and "9,6" (12:180, 15:219, 20:302). Lasswitz offers still more detail to flesh out his imaginary world and to challenge the reader fond of mathematical puzzles. What initially appears to be a hundredth, or rather a hundred-forty-fourth, of the basic Martian time unit, namely the difference between "29,36" and "29,37," is stated to equal about ten minutes (36:153). It is conceivable that the whole number in such expressions refers to the day of the year, and that the numbers after the duodecimal point/comma denote fractional parts of the day. Terrestrial astronomers actually employ such a system, though of course they use ten as the base. If the Martian temporal system is in fact duodecimal, there would be 144 (12^2) rather than 100 (10^2) such fractional parts. Since the length of the Martian day, in terrestrial units, is 24 hours and 37 minutes, or 1477 minutes, each fractional unit of Martian time would in fact correspond very nearly to ten minutes (1477/144). The reader who puzzles out the details of Martian mathematics thus uncovers a neat consistency which encourages him to give credence to the imaginary world. Yet nowhere is the imaginary mathematics either explained or defended—digressions which mar Lasswitz' earlier SF. The subtlety and restraint he exhibits in introducing Martian mathematics is a mark of the skill with language—whether real language, Martian, or, as the structuralists would call them, the "meta-languages" of symbol and mathematics—which he had gained by the time he wrote *Auf zwei Planeten.*

*   *   *

In the preceding pages I have argued rather insistently that *Auf zwei Planeten,* by virtue of its literary qualities and level of conceptual sophistication, deserves to be regarded as a premier work of SF. It was here that Lasswitz found not only the right mode and tone of narration, but also a theme and plot appropriate to the premises and aims of serious SF. Theme, plot and the exposition of the "thought-model" are well integrated in *Auf zwei Planeten,* and almost every incident and detail contributes to the whole. Part of the excellence of the work can be attributed to Lasswitz' choice of an eminently appropriate theme, part of it to the improvement in general literary skills and to the greater insight into the intentionality of SF which he had gained from his previous efforts. *Auf zwei Planeten* can bear comparison to the best SF of its time, including that of H.G. Wells. And, although it has suffered from the problems of obsolescence to which SF is particularly subject because of its special content, the novel can still compete with the best works of modern SF.

I would also maintain that *Auf zwei Planeten* deserves more favorable consideration simply as a work of literature. It is, however, not difficult to understand why it has been relegated to obscurity by "mainstream" critics. The novel is marred by some genuine artistic shortcomings, and indeed its prohibition during the National Socialist years disastrously undermined the popularity— steady if at most only modest—it had once enjoyed. Yet some of the blame for the neglect of the novel must rest with the critics themselves. In evaluating the meager critical response to *Auf zwei Planeten* and to the rest of Lasswitz' SF, one encounters, as I observed in Chapter II, the same problems which are manifest throughout the study of SF: perplexity about the fundamental generic nature of SF, uncertainty about its relation to the dominant current of literary realism, and, sometimes, prejudiced contempt for all SF. Thus Ernst Alker, for example, in his standard survey of nineteenth-century German literature, cites *Auf zwei Planeten*— though not without some appreciation of the novel's intrinsic qualities—as a demonstration of the inability of much German literature of the time to come to grips with reality.[15] Whatever the merits of Alker's overall assessment of late nineteenth-century German literature, his evaluation of *Auf zwei Planeten* is inaccurate in its severity, if not indeed in its entire tenor. As I have maintained, the novel does offer some incisive criticism of European civilization and German culture. Admittedly, it would appear that Lasswitz' primary purpose in *Auf zwei Planeten* was not to examine, in detail and from an ideologically committed perspective, the more immediate features of Wilhelmine Germany, at least not in the manner of, for example, Naturalist drama. But the novel does investigate very thoroughly another kind of reality, that of the future, one of whose possible versions must needs in time become the present. And it was clearly Lasswitz' aim in his presentation of the imaginary world to evoke in the reader the senses of reality and plausibility, impressions not at all inconsistent with the aesthetic tenets of realism.

If in fact *Auf zwei Planeten* is characterized by conventional realism, it also exhibits forthright, even bold experimentation. Both are to be found in the way Lasswitz treats themes and types of content which few if any other writers had previously examined, at least in the same way. To present a hypothetical but subjectively real imaginary world, and to investigate the nature of humanity in the light of modern science, Lasswitz adopted many of the narrative habits of realism, as does in fact much SF. But since his subject-matter was not drawn from contemporary reality, the world of "sharable experience," the result was something other than just another second-rate "mainstream" realistic novel. *Auf zwei Planeten* also constitutes an early modern attempt to express the facts and speculations of science in *fiction*, rather than in some other form. Yet it has been precisely these innovative features, I think, which have kept the novel from being appraised more seriously and favorably. *Auf zwei Planeten* had to seek recognition from critics who—understandably enough, perhaps—were not prepared to perceive that SF, like every other type of fiction, must be judged both by general aesthetic values and by standards which take its own nature and merits into account.

Such deliberations, however, impinge on matters of personal taste and raise the questions involved in evaluating the relative worth of various kinds of writing. Alker may be right in his judgment of *Auf zwei Planeten* and supposedly similar non-traditional novels; it is also conceivable, as I speculated in Chapter I, that the aesthetic presuppositions and tendencies of fiction about science conflict with certain requisites of art which are absolute and universal, though as yet only vaguely determined. But until the unlikely time that these highly problematic issues are resolved, I consider it justifiable to describe *Auf zwei Planeten* as an excellent work of SF and, at the least, a much underrated piece of literature.

Hans Dominik. From the author's autobiography "Vom Schraubstock zum Schreibtisch" (1942). After a drawing by W. Nus.

Chapter V

Hans Dominik:
Science Fiction for the Masses in Weimar and National Socialist Germany

Most famous—or notorious—among writers of German SF, and certainly most durable, is Hans Dominik. Between 1921 and 1940 he produced sixteen SF novels; their total hardcover circulation during his lifetime exceeded two million copies.[1] The various postwar paperback re-editions of Dominik's novels issued by the Weiss Verlag and Heyne Verlag have maintained his place on the mass market. No other German SF, in fact, has enjoyed such currency among the general public in Germany except perhaps the *Perry Rhodan* series of the last two decades. It should be noted, however, that the shorter *Perry Rhodan* novels are produced by a stable of house authors and that their circulation is aided by intensive promotional efforts aimed at a readership which is not only more prosperous than that of Dominik's time, but also, thanks to the influx of Anglo-American SF after 1945, even more receptive to SF.[2]

Dominik's work, therefore, deserves attention for its sociological significance, whatever value it might have as literature or, specifically, as SF. I confess, however, that I find the undertaking rather distasteful. In their style, quality of imagination, and scientific content the novels are inferior to the SF of both Lasswitz and several other of Dominik's lesser-known contemporaries. Moreover, Dominik's ethical principles and political opinions, although such matters should not directly effect aesthetic evaluation, are disturbing, even odious. In many ways he was shallow-minded and ignorant, yet pompously opinionated about literature, science and politics. He was also a racist and chauvinist whose attitudes and works easily lent themselves to the aims of National Socialism.

Hans Dominik was born in Zwickau on 15 November 1872 and died in Berlin on 9 December 1945.[3] His father, Friedrich Wilhelm Emil Dominik (1844-96), was a bookseller and editor of periodicals in both cities. In his autobiography of 1942, *Vom Schraubstock zum Schreibtisch* [*From Bench-vise to Writing Table*] (= *VSS*), Dominik recalls that as a child he was fond of playing with mechanical things. His strength in school was science, his weakness "philosophical trivia" and the "dead languages" (*VSS*, 23). From

1888 to 1890 he attended the Gymnasium Ernestinum in Gotha, where he studied mathematics under Lasswitz. Besides offering interesting details about the latter, his recollections reveal something of his own political and intellectual inclinations:

> The teachers in Gotha, too, were to a large extent strange birds and eccentrics [Typen und Originale]. The one who stood out most was probably our mathematician Kurd Lasswitz, who became known among the broader public especially through his utopian novel *Auf zwei Planeten*. For my father's magazine *Zur guten Stunde* [*For the Pleasant Hour*] he wrote clever technological stories [geistreiche technische Märchen], and in addition was a philosopher and wrote ponderously learned philosophical works. His life was tinged by a certain tragicality. Originally he wanted to devote himself to the career of a university lecturer [Hochschuldozent], but had become impossible in Prussia because of his freethinking views [freisinnige Anschauungen] and so had fetched up in Gotha as a preparatory school professor. His jokes and bon-mots passed from mouth to mouth and could no doubt fill a hefty volume. (*VSS*, 26)

Dominik returned to Berlin in the summer of 1890 and in the spring of 1893, at the age of twenty, graduated from the Königliches Luisengymnasium. He then began practical training in railroad technology and attended courses in electrical and mechanical engineering at the famous Technische Hochschule (Institute of Technology) in Berlin-Charlottenburg. Although his first interest was electrical engineering, training in the more traditional areas was still required for government certification and for employment in the newer speciality. (*VSS*, 28-38)

In the fall of 1894 Dominik augmented his professional education with a brief steamship voyage to New York as a volunteer engineer trainee. He had studied English privately for two years, and was quite interested in America as a land of technology. In early 1895 the elder Dominik's business collapsed and his health failed. Although his formal training was still incomplete, Dominik obtained employment as a technician working on the design, construction, and installation of power plants at the Cologne office of the Allgemeine Elektricitätsgesellschaft (AEG), a leader in electrical engineering. (*VSS*, 44-72)

Dominik's curiosity about America and his desire to study recent American progress in electrical engineering resulted in a second and longer trip to the United States in 1897. He gained access to prominent society through his acquaintance with Oswald G. Villard, with whom he had attended the Kaiserin-Augusta-Gymnasium in Charlottenburg. Villard, who later became the owner and editor of the *New York Evening Post,* was the son of Henry Villard, the railroad magnate and leader of the German-American community. Among those whom Dominik met through the Villards were Carl Schurz and the wife of Thomas Edison. Although Schurz was a Forty-Eighter and a liberal force in American politics, Dominik admired him for his efforts to promote close relations between Germany and America. (*VSS,* 73-78)

Dominik visited the Edison power plant in New York but was not impressed. A trip to Schenectady, where he heard much about labor troubles and saw a concentration of industry greater than any in Germany, affected him far more and apparently caused him to reconsider a tentative plan to take up residence in America. He then traveled by way of Buffalo and Cleveland to Detroit, and thence to the smaller factory cities of Michigan. He later recalled his Midwestern experiences rather fondly in some of his novels, such as *Wettflug der Nationen* and *Atomgewicht 500,* parts of which are set in Detroit and Bay City, Michigan. Dominik found the Midwest clean and pleasant, an appealing contrast to the evils of the Eastern cities, which he described in his autobiography as "Jewified metropolises [verjudete Grossstädte]" (*VSS,* 45). Once again he was tempted to remain in America, but decided to return to Germany. (*VSS,* 78-85).

In his autobiography Dominik quickly passes over a third trip to America, and other information about it is sketchy. During the early part of the century his publisher August Scherl had financed an experimental monorail project for which Dominik served as a technical advisor. Sometime shortly before World War I, apparently, Scherl sent Dominik to America, along with Scherl's son Richard, to offer his pet idea to J.P. Morgan, after—or perhaps even while—the project was discussed with Krupp. Dominik states only that "neither in Europe nor in America was it possible to achieve a practical exploitation of the invention" (*VSS,* 163-64). *Vom Schraubstock zum Schreibtisch* was published in 1942, at a time when Dominik may well have considered it imprudent to recount in any detail what might have appeared to be a lapse of devotion—on Scherl's part if not his own—to the interests of the Fatherland.[4]

In 1898 Dominik accepted employment as an electrical engineer with the Union-Elektrizitäts-Gesellschaft, like AEG a major electrical company. It was a boom-time for electrification in Germany, and electrical engineering was a frontier of technological research, a subject of no little public fascination, and an arena of international competition. Although Dominik's ambition was to advance to the directorship of some municipal utility system, the project reports he wrote were so good that Union-EG transferred him to its promotional department. While he regarded the move as a professional dead-end, however remunerative it might be, subsequent job changes, including employment with the Siemens AG, seemed always to involve a return to technical writing (*VSS*, 87-100). Dominik's association with a certain Professor Budde, director of the Siemens plant at Charlottenburg, improved his attitude toward writing about science. Budde wrote technical texts but also composed "scientific ramblings [naturwissenschaftliche Plaudereien]" for the popular press (*VSS*, 100). Another colleague, Dr. August Raps, entertained similar interests in short-range technological fantasy and extrapolation (*VSS*, 102).

Dominik's promotional responsibilities with Siemens grew as the firm recognized his talent for expressing technical concepts in lively language. Although he felt a certain frustration of his technological ambitions and capabilities, economic circumstances precluded a return to engineering. These professional and practical considerations, his long-time desire for financial independence, and an interest for literature which he had maintained since childhood, encouraged him to venture into full-time free-lance writing. With evident satisfaction Dominik later remarked that the choice, although it involved some initial risk, turned out to have been the right one. (*VSS*, 108-11)

Indeed, Dominik prospered from the very beginning of his literary career. By the turn of the century he was writing technical articles and semi-fictional popularizations of modern technology for several major German newspapers, among them the *Norddeutsche Allgemeine Zeitung* and the *Berliner Tageblatt*. As titles like "Aus den Memoiren einer Taschenuhr" ["From the Memoires of a Pocket-Watch"] suggest, these "technical short stories" ("technische Kurzgeschichten") or "tales" ("Märchen"), as Dominik calls them, were often cast in the form of fantasies or whimsical narrations written both to entertain and to educate the general reader. Somewhat more traditional in narrative structure were several stories about futuristic technology which appeared between 1907 and 1933 in *Das neue Universum* [*The New Universe*], a science-popularization annual aimed at the juvenile audience.[5] Dominik also employed a less fictional mode of technological journalism modeled, he says, on the "causeries scientifiques" of Henri Parville (1838-1909), a popular French technological writer (*VSS*, 114-15).

Dominik's short works, as is readily apparent, resemble the science popularizations and "naturwissenschaftliche Märchen" of Lasswitz, Gustav Theodor Fechner (1801-1887), and Dominik's near contemporary and fellow Berliner Wilhelm Bölsche (1861-1939). Nevertheless, he does not acknowledge any debt to his German predecessors and contemporaries, or to the many American and English writers of such semi-fiction.[6] (*VSS*, 111-16)

Dominik's growing reputation brought him further commissions to write promotional material for German industry. Soon he was also editing technical journals, delivering lectures, and contributing to various magazines about industrial technology and automobile racing. In 1910, financially secure, he married. (*VSS*, 116-28, 165-75)

Dominik continued to set the course of his literary career according to the conditions of the popular press and his personal relations to those who controlled it. The *Berliner Tageblatt* was owned by the Mosse family, the largest publishing house in Berlin. Dominik was dissatisfied with his lack of a standing contract with Mosse, and, as he adds in his autobiography, he also wished to dissociate himself with what he termed "the leading German newspaper of world Jewry" (*VSS*, 130). In 1905 he joined the publishing house of August Scherl, at first as a writer of scientific essays and technological reportage for Scherl's daily paper, the *Berliner Lokal-Anzeiger,* and for the giant illustrated weekly, *Die Woche*. Dominik was already acquainted with several members of Scherl's editorial staff who had at one time worked for his father (*VSS*, 136-38). Scherl differed from Mosse so much that Dominik later characterized his new employer as "the antipode of the Mosse Verlag" (*VSS*, 128). His association with the Scherl Verlag under Scherl himself and under the latter's successor Alfred Hugenberg lasted for the rest of his life (*VSS*, 127-49, 162ff.). Its larger implications will be discussed in detail later.

Shortly before the beginning of World War I Dominik began to write novels. In his autobiography he states that his first, *Glück auf!* [*Come Up Safe!*] (1912), a story about mining, was written at the instigation of an old schoolfriend who composed popular novels for serial publication in newspapers (*VSS*, 167).[7] But none of Dominik's early novels, and not all of his later ones, can be classed as SF. While he frequently chose technological themes, the technology itself is not imaginary. Instead, he fictionalized the more exciting aspects of actual modern science; the plot structures are conventional and the settings sometimes derived from his travels in America.

Nevertheless, Dominik considered these works "a good preparation for the major SF novel [Vorschule für den grossen technischen Zukunftsroman] to which [he] was to turn only a decade later, after the Great War" (*VSS,* 171).

World War I put an end to the publication of Dominik's articles in Scherl's papers, although he continued to write serial novels and to edit a journal about lighting technology. Because of his age and a progressively debilitating spinal condition he was not called up for service until January 1917, and then was classified as fit for reserve duty only (*VSS,* 194-96). During the War he and Scherl's ne'er-do-well son Richard, who was later disinherited, worked privately on a "Strahlenzieler" ("ray-focuser"), a primitive form of radar (*VSS,* 189ff.). Nothing actually came of the invention, at least at Dominik's hands. In his fiction, however, there is frequent mention of such devices. (*VSS,* 182-215)

After the War Dominik returned to full-time writing. He also worked for a time as "technischer Dramaturg" or "director of theater technology" for the Deutsche Lichtbildgesellschaft, which made a series of films popularizing present and futuristic tehnology (*VSS,* 216-18). The early Twenties represent a decisive turn or rather a new stage in Dominik's literary career and in his association with his chief publisher. Since the end of the War, he later wrote, he had been pondering the idea of showing, "in the form of a novel, the tremendous possibilities for the future which new scientific knowledge was opening up to a literally fantastic extent." The new "technological-futuristic novel" ("technischer Zukunftsroman") was to differ from Dominik's earlier fiction in its particular combination of form and content: imaginary rather than actual science and technology presented in full-length novel format. Dominik's efforts were encouraged by Ludwig Klitzsch, the general director of the Scherl Verlag. In scarcely six months during 1921 he wrote his first true SF novel, *Die Macht der Drei,* which appeared initially as a serial in *Die Woche.* The editorial board of the magazine, Dominik reports in his autobiography, was hesitant to publish the novel because of its supposedly untraditional subject and style. Nevertheless *Die Macht der Drei* was a notable success in serial form and soon thereafter, in 1922, was reissued in hardcover. (*VSS,* 221-22)[8]

The novel was followed by a stream of "technische Zukunftsromane" which Dominik produced at an average rate of nearly one a year for almost twenty years. His SF novels, with date of first hardcover publication in parentheses, are: *Die Macht der*

Drei: Ein Roman aus dem Jahre 1955 [*The Power of the Three: A Novel from the Year 1955*] (1922); *Die Spur des Dschingis-Khan: Ein Roman aus dem 21. Jahrhundert* [*The Trail of Genghis Khan: A Novel from the Twenty-first Century*] (1923); *Atlantis* (1925); *Der Brand der Cheopspyramide* [*The Burning of the Pyramid of Cheops*] (1926); *König Laurins Mantel* [*King Laurin's Cape*] (1928); *Das Erbe der Uraniden* [*The Legacy of the Uranids*] (1928); *Kautschuk: Ein Roman aus der Industrie* [*Caoutchouc: A Novel of Industry*] (1930); *Befehl aus dem Dunkel* [*Command from the Dark*] (1933); *Der Wettflug der Nationen* [*The International Airplane-Race*] (1933); *Das stählerne Geheimnis* [*Secret of Steel*] (1934); *Ein Stern fiel vom Himmel* [*A Star Fell from the Sky*] (1934); *Atomgewicht 500* [*Atomic Weight 500*] (1935); *Himmelskraft* [*Heavenly Power*] (1937); *Lebensstrahlen* [*Rays of Life*] (1938); *Land aus Feuer und Wasser* [*Land of Fire and Water*] (1939); and *Treibstoff SR* [*Propulsion Fuel SR*] (1940). All but three of the novels were published by the Scherl Verlag, either under its own name or that of "E. Keils Nachfolger;" Scherl had acquired the Keil interests in 1904. The "Eggerth" series (*Wettflug, Stern* and *Land*), three novels about a father and son of that name, appeared in Leipzig with Koehler & Amelang or its successor Hase & Koehler.

While he was turning out his SF Dominik carried on his non-fiction journalistic work and wrote a few other novels as well (*VSS,* 245-89). A cardiac condition and his worsening spinal affliction seem not to have interfered seriously with his productivity until his last years. The events of 1933 heartened him, and in his autobiography, published three years before his death in 1945, Dominik looked forward to the end of the war and of technological secrecy. He would then be able to write fiction about the newest developments in technology and "to glimpse, at least from afar, the dawn of the coming age, the Age of Energy" (*VSS,* 292).

With regard to his early scientific education and subsequent literary career Dominik resembles many other writers of SF, including Lasswitz and more than a few authors of "Golden Age" Anglo-American SF. In such figures a youthful fascination with natural science and mechanical things was followed by formal scientific or technological education, perhaps some professional work in research or industry, and then, without systematic literary training, a transition to fiction writing. The adoption of a literary career seems often to be the immediate result of mere chance, restlessness, financial exigency, or even a lack of professional success in the sciences. Dominik's explanation that his own entry into serious literary activity was motivated to a large degree by financial considerations is probably both sincere and accurate, as is his claim that it was also the natural continuation of an early interest in literature. But I am tempted also to ascribe his change of careers to a lack of first-rate technological ability, combined with the evident fact that his employers and publishers found that the talent of writing skillfully about science and technology for a general audience was even scarcer than technological aptitude itself. Thus an unfulfilled ambition to be a great scientist or inventor, like the heroes of his novels, may have caused him to be dissatisfied with his actual position, secure but prosaic, as an electro-engineering technician or technological journalist. But however one judges his novels or his talents, Dominik was also inspired, as other writers of SF have been, by an innate artistic impulse, an avid interest in science and technology, and a desire to express the importance of science in the modern world.

The Scientific, Technological and Social Milieu

Dominik lived, worked and wrote in Berlin between 1890 and 1945, the most eventful and significant period in the cultural and political history of the city itself and of the unified Germany of which it was the capital. His SF, however, was not the product of that Berlin which, as the national and international center of prestigious cultural institutions, avant-garde artistic movements, and liberal politics, is so familiar from the reminiscences of emigres and the studies of cultural historians and literary scholars. It was, rather, the new technology, reactionary ideology, and mass culture of early twentieth-century Berlin and Germany which in large part determined the content and form of his writings.

Dominik's Berlin was the technological and scientific capital of a new Reich quite conscious of the immense effect industry and science had come to have on its growth, internal unification, and international prestige. By 1871, when superior armaments and transport helped Prussia defeat France, Germany was beginning to think of itself as a country of technologists and scientists as well as the proverbial "land of poets and thinkers." During the subsequent decades the excellence of German theoretical and applied science and—welcome or not—the image of the industrial metropolis became prominent parts of popular and intellectual consciousness Technological wonders were evident everywhere: a modern, genuinely effective German navy, a department store with thousands of lights, the cinema, rapid communications, mass transit, new chemicals, medical advances, even flight.

In Dominik's time chemistry, metallurgy, engineering, and, somewhat later, aeronautics were the prestigious areas of German science, within the intellectual and professional communities as well as in the popular view. Dominik was trained in two of these fields, mechanical and electrical engineering, and worked professionally in the latter. He wrote newspaper reports and popularizations about contemporary happenings in all of them and helped to organize public spectacles which featured futuristic mass transit and the first demonstration of powered flight in Berlin.

Another recent development then affecting mass consciousness and ideology in Germany was the growth of giant corporations within the larger context of the authoritarian and paternalistic industrial state. The very names of such huge firms as Krupp, Siemens & Halske, Bayer & Hoechst, Bayrische Anilin- und Sodafabrik (BASF), Thyssen, and the Allgemeine-Elektricitäts-Gesellschaft, for which Dominik himself worked, attest that the corporate expansion which took place during and after the latter decades of the nineteenth century was intimately associated with science and technology, as was the emergence of state-controlled enterprises like the railways. Dominik's training, location, and dual career in engineering and technical journalism afforded him the opportunity to observe those processes from a close if not impartial vantage point.

Both the growth of theoretical and applied science and the relation of business to the state in Germany exhibit certain distinctive tendencies and accents which are in turn reflected in popular consciousness and, in many forms and at many levels of sophistication, in ideological thought as well. It is not excessive, I think, to speak of a distinctly German version of the modern ideology of science and technology discussed in Chapter I. Many among the masses and the classes indeed associated the successes, the future triumphs, and even the very existence of modern Germany with science and technology. At the same time, repelled by other manifestations of modernity, they often looked nostalgically, and with a good deal of idealization, to the rural, pre-industrial, feudal past which was still, in Germany more than in other industrialized Western nations, part of recent memory. The National Socialists represented but one egregious instance of this curious yoking of opposites, which was also to be found on the left.[9]

The political, economic, and industrial development of Germany, while it engendered severe tensions, also nourished two related and even more broadly espoused notions, both of which expressed and furthered the aims of social integration and national aggrandizement. One was the close and benevolent cooperation, if not the virtual coalescence, of business and government. The other was the organic incorporation of the citizen—whether aristocrat, intellectual, official, private bourgeois, proletarian, or agrarian—into an all-encompassing structure, for his own good and that of the state. Government, business, the media, many intellectuals, much of the citizenry, and the Church (or at least the Protestant Church) helped to promote and sustain a climate in which all but the poorly organized and often politically naive dissenters felt that individual lives, business enterprises, social institutions, and governmental policies ought to be, and indeed were, closely allied entities which contributed to the social and cultural unity and development of Germany. The individual was expected—and often expected himself—to behave as an integral and socially responsible member of his society, though not as a politically active citizen.

Patriotism and the desire for social stability are not unique to Wilhelmine Germany, nor are burgeoning science and technology, corporate expansion, strong central government, and hand-in-glove cooperation between state and business. But in their institutional structures and in their popular self-images many other industrialized and politically centralized countries have maintained—for better or sometimes worse—at least the semblance of a greater degree of personal independence, private enterprise, and the restriction of government to legislative, executive, and judicial functions. It was the well-cultivated sense or even myth of communality which was distinctly German. Whatever the true nature of their society, many Germans believed, or at least ritually assented to the notion, that Germany, in its integration of citizen, commerce, and state, was a unique form of society. It was—or at least should be—neither an Eastern despotism nor, as was insisted with similar vigor, a Western "democracy" or contractual society, but rather a true community; not a *Gesellschaft* ("society"), but rather a *Gemeinschaft* ("communality"), as Ferdinand Tönnies (1855-1936) formulated the contrast in his famous study *Gemeinschaft und Gesellschaft* (1887). The concept of *Gemeinschaft*, like that of science and technology, came to assume the dimensions of an ideology or myth. In its widely attractive mixture of rationality and mysticism, of pre-capitalistic idyllicism and technological modernism, and of conservatism and radicalism, the dominant ideology or self-image of the new industrial society emerging in Germany evidences a pattern of polarities and a yearning for organic synthesis which, according to Ralf Dahrendorf, is characteristically German.[10] Unfortunately, such beliefs, relatively innocuous in themselves, later did little to discourage the spread of National Socialism, which had evolved its own patchwork combination of political reactionism and millenial futurism, of bucolic nostalgia and fascination with technology, and of irrationality and pseudo-science.

Dominik's Concept of SF

Dominik's SF was shaped not only by the larger historical, ideological, and scientific environment, but also by his concept of SF or, as he called it, the "technological-futuristic novel" ("technischer Zukunftsroman"). Although he lacked formal literary training and was little concerned with theoretical aesthetics, he evolved a conception of SF which was reasonably definite in its overall intentionality. But Dominik was no more an innovative stylist than he was an aesthetician; nor, apparently, did he desire to be one. Fortunately, however, his grasp of the principles of realistic prose fiction exceeded his abilities as a literary theorist. He adopted—simply and, if one judges success by popularity, capably— the same conventions of realism which typify most recent *Trivialliteratur.*

Accordingly, Dominik derived many of his aesthetic principles and stylistic techniques from the conventional middle-brow fiction and journalism of the decades around the turn of the century. As his models he mentions Dumas *père,* Kipling, Verne, and his own maternal grandfather Theodor Mügge (1806-61), a prolific but minor writer of realistic regional novels (*VSS,* 114, 167-68). All were good story-tellers who worked with exciting plots, exotic landscapes, and a conventional prose style whose intended function was description and narration rather than artistic experimentation and psychological introspection.

In his autobiography Dominik thus barely touches on the more complex theoretical aspects of realism and dwells instead on those minute matters of practical technique whose mastery gave him an evident sense of self-satisfaction:

> I learned...that in the novel one can also work [operieren] most successfully with letters and telegrams, but that the technique must be used with moderation. It became clear to me that "logic" is one of the chief requisites of the novel. The reader will always detect an illogical plot and will not forgive the author....

> Another task, by no means easy, is the invention of apt names for
> the characters of a novel.... A name in a novel has to be created with
> hard conceptual work. After all, in its content and sound it is supposed to
> be as it were a label for the figure in question and even in itself betray
> something about its nature. (*VSS*, 169-70)

The trivialities Dominik discusses here accurately characterize the
general nature of his literary product, a *Trivialliteratur* whose only
claim to distinction is its description of imaginary technology. Thus
the most evident features of his SF, other than imaginary science
and technology, are its marked preference for clearly outlined and
psychologically unambiguous characters, easily recognizable and
emotionally evocative settings, and frequent doses of adventure and
suspense—all presented in a language which gains, maintains, and
rewards the reader's attention and credence by its mixture of
forthright blandness and highly-colored, contagious emotion. The
purpose of such stratagems, in *Trivialliteratur* and—it must be
conceded—in much other literature as well, is to provide
entertainment and perhaps edification. What distinguishes the one
from the other, according to many critics, is the primitive style,
insipidness of psychological characterization, crudity and
unaptness of emotional appeal, trivialization of thought, and
reinforcement of simplistic, conventional attitudes which are found
in *Trivialliteratur*.[11]

Dominik's "technischer Zukunftsroman," then, is
fundamentally a sub-genre of realistic fiction. The same, I argued in
Chapter I, might be said of most SF, even its better examples, for SF
has its own reasons to emphasize detailed description, linear plot
chronology, simple characterization, and the impression of rational
imagination. But, as I also remarked, SF is distinguished from other
fiction by its particular content, namely imaginary science and
technology, and by the way in which, ideally, author and reader
view the imaginary world. Dominik's observations on these
matters, although not very profound, indicate both that he indeed
intended science to be the focus of interest in his SF, and that he was
at least vaguely aware of the concepts of "extrapolation" and
"thought-model:"

> I was [in the early years of this century] in the fortunate position of
> being able to follow, from beginning to end, the developmental efforts of
> a newly emergent technology; and today, after forty years, I must say
> that indeed rarely has something so captivated me as this struggle of the
> inventive human mind with the power of nature [dieser Kampf
> menschlichen Erfindergeistes mit der Naturkraft]. (*VSS*, 107)

I had immersed myself ever more deeply in the revolutionary discoveries which were in the process of giving our physical-chemical picture of the world [Weltbild] a quite different stamp.... [S]ince the end of the War I had been turning over in my mind the idea of treating, in the form of a novel, the tremendous possibilities for the future which new scientific knowledge was opening up to a literally fantastic extent [die Idee, die ungeheuren Zukunftsmöglichkeiten, welche die neuen naturwissenschaftlichen Erkenntnisse in geradezu phantastischem Ausmass eröffneten, in Form eines Romans zu verarbeiten].... [But the] narration which would come about thereby indeed had to become so fundamentally different from everything otherwise customary in novels. Those were the reservations I immediately expressed to Ludwig Klitzsch [the general director of the Scherl Verlag] when he suggested that I write a novel of technological content. He listened to my objections and then opined, "Precisely that could be the right thing. The World War has so frazzled everyone's nerves and gotten us all so bent out of shape [umgekrempelt] that 'peaceful novels' of the traditional sort ['ruhige Romane' der hergebrachten Art] no longer suffice us. We need a new form in our pleasure reading [Unterhaltungsliteratur] as well." (*VSS*, 221)

Further information about Dominik's concept of SF can be gleaned from his few comments on more specific points of novelistic craftsmanship. He evidently felt that portraying the "struggle of the inventive [i.e., technological] human mind with the power of nature" and exploring "the tremendous possibilities for the future which new scientific knowledge was opening up" might be accomplished most easily, if not most subtly or profoundly, with relatively simple techniques that permit and encourage the reader to focus his attention on content rather than literary style. If such was not his considered opinion, it was at least the practice he adopted. Yet his naive remarks also show that he was somewhat cognizant of several of the perennial problems which face the writer of SF. Among them are the integration of story interest with the scientific or technological "gimmick," the introduction of necessary but potentially tedious scientific or historical background information, the need for a plot structure which is coherent and creates narrative tension, and the careful but concise evocation of the imaginary world as a setting for action and characterization. (*VSS*, 168-71)

Dominik's ideological views are apparent in all his novels, as they are in his autobiography, and his concept of SF, like that of so many other writers, is quite amenable to the inclusion of ideological statement. The facile association of revolutionary scientific advances with exciting social and political developments in *VSS* shows how easily an interest in exploring the future, even if science and technology are ostensibly the original and main subject, can lead to the introduction of political themes, especially if the writer is already so inclined. Thus Dominik describes how he came to see, more particularly, that in SF science can be both an object of genuine interest and a vehicle, even a metaphor, for ideological content:

> Thus a geological theory furnished the practical motivation for the advance into the unknown deep and provided further the possibility of associating political consequences of great extent with an engineering project undertaken ostensibly only out of sheerly scientific interest. That is the history of *Secret of Steel* [1939]. (*VSS*, 277)

Dominik's concept of SF has much in common with those of other writers. As his autobiography clearly shows, he believed that science and technology were major determinants of the modern world, and he wished to explore, or rather expound, that theme in the imaginary worlds of his SF. But Dominik's formulation of his aims as a writer of SF, with its emphasis on "struggle" and "tremendous possibilities," is crude and hyperbolic; moreover, the actual literary product does not realize its creator's own aims, at least as SF, though certainly it achieved gratifying success as popular literature. In effect Dominik's works represent a mixture of two kinds of primitive SF: the detailed, often didactic exposition of "hard-core" technology, and the sensationalization of science with the narrative devices of "mainstream" adventure fiction. Like the "gadget" stories, "space operas," and "gosh-wow!" SF being written in America at the same time, Dominik's novels concentrate on exciting technology and favor fast, sweeping action. Yet for all his theoretical intentions and his interest in futuristic science and technology, his works, when compared to much other SF, contemporary or even earlier, exhibit a distinct conservatism or even paucity of scientific and technological imagination. The imaginary technology which he envisions could have been foreseen by any competent scientist, and in fact much of it had already appeared in still earlier SF. Theoretical discussion is usually inept, when not wholly absent. But perhaps most telling of all for the experienced reader are the facts that all his novels are located in the near future, and that only part of a single novel, *Das Erbe der Uraniden,* is set elsewhere than on Earth.

Medium of Publication

Dominik's medium of publication and the disposition of his initial popular readership determined the lineaments of his SF as much as did his literary intentionality, and they have largely governed its fortunes in literary history.[12] As a writer of popular literature for a great commercial publishing house which was interested in making profits and in advancing certain attitudes and values, he was more dependent on the artistic, economic, and ideological demands of his medium than many writers of "serious"—and often unprofitable—literature are, or at least like to think they are. It appears that Dominik did not find such strictures onerous. The SF he created in accord with his general notion of literature and specific concept of SF is unmistakably his own. But his personality, scientific interests, literary tastes, and ideology seem to have harmonized easily with the convictions and desires of his publishers and, quite evidently, those of his readers as well.

Most of Dominik's SF novels and many of his other works were published by the Scherl Verlag, which was owned successively by August Scherl (1849-1921) and Alfred Hugenberg (1865-1951), both prominent German conservatives. Scherl, like his fellow tycoon Alfred Krupp, was a colorful personality, eccentric or in some respects even pathologically neurotic, as Hans Erman observes.[13] He was born in Frankfurt am Main, where his father, a small-time editor and publisher, had taken refuge after the unsuccessful liberal revolution in Prussia. Early poverty contributed to obsessive ambition, a distinct paranoia, and a mania for prominence in public life. Like many others who were affected by the events of 1848, Scherl subordinated liberal ideas to a yearning for national unity and strength. For him, as for the Prussian government since the time of Frederick the Great, the good of the people was not an end in itself but rather a prerequisite of a strong state; the function of the citizen, conversely, was to contribute to the advancement of the state.

Scherl's literary tastes, his policies as a publisher, and other of his public enterprises reflect these attitudes. The proper relation of the publisher to the reader, he believed, consisted neither of condescending advocacy of "serious" literature nor of purely commercial provision of entertainment. The publisher, and through him the writer, should both satisfy the demands of the masses and yet attempt to contribute to the betterment of the reader. In his early years Scherl's notion of the proper product comprised literature which appealed to the reader who was weary of futile politics and desired adventure and sensationalism or, alternately, the personal assurance and social affirmation afforded by the bourgeois idyll. After the unification of Germany Scherl also emphasized national citizenship and practical education. His profitable but not merely self-serving devotion to popular literature of a more elevated kind is reflected in his acquisition (1904) of *Die Gartenlaube,* for many years the leading German "family magazine," and in long-time sponsorship of educational publications, loan libraries, and popular education programs.

Scherl also took an early and abiding interest in technology, which he valued for its own fascination and for the contribution it could make to the aggrandizement of Germany. He had the first linotype in Germany, and could thus influence the consciousness of the mass readership still more. His weekly magazine, *Die Woche,* was the first mass periodical in which photographic content predominated; founded in 1899, it was for some years the largest publication of its kind in Germany. Scherl also sponsored the first exhibition of powered flight in Berlin (1909), and promoted an experimental monorail project. Such ventures were not simply publicity gimmicks, but rather also attempts to inspire Germany to further greatness and to encourage it to develop the technological requisites of a politically strong and culturally advanced society.[14]

Clearly there was a place in Scherl's publishing enterprises for the works of writers who, like Dominik, actively espoused or were at least willing to cater to the publisher's ideological outlook, concept of literature, and, perhaps not least of all, his interest in technology. It was no disadvantage to publisher or writer, of course, that Scherl's—and Dominik's—ideas were shared by many German readers.

Dominik established himself as a professional writer with the Scherl Verlag during the first years of the century, but his SF novels were published after a change of ownership which occurred when Scherl's progressive eccentricity had involved the house in serious financial difficulties. In 1914, at the urging of both government and the business community, the "Deutscher Verlagsverein," a consortium of publishers and business leaders controlled by Alfred Hugenberg, bought the Scherl Verlag in order to keep its pro-government publications from falling into the supposedly untrustworthy hands of Jewish publishers in Berlin.[15] Hugenberg was a Rhineland mining capitalist, director of the Frankfurt Berg- und Metallbank, and from 1909 to 1918 chairman of the board of Krupp. In 1916 he acquired outright control of the Scherl interests, and subsequently enlarged his media empire with the purchase or foundation of news agencies, advertising companies, and the renowned cinema enterprise Universum-Film AG (Ufa).

The change of ownership did not materially affect the policies of the Scherl Verlag or at all diminish Dominik's association with it. Hugenberg's literary tastes and, at least in these earlier years, his political views did not differ significantly from Scherl's. Dominik, for his part, continued to explore the "tremendous possibilities" of what he considered highly futuristic technology and to promote the same political ideas he had always espoused. Even had Hugenberg lacked an interest in technology he would not likely have interfered lightly with the success of one of his most popular and profitable house writers. Often, in fact, Dominik introduced motifs or themes which favorably reflected certain of Hugenberg's own ideological and technological concerns. Geology, mining, and subterranean engineering projects, for example, appear frequently in the novels. Another important theme is the organized German colonization of new land, whether in Asia, on newly-emerged continents, or on Venus. One of Hugenberg's pet interests was the promotion of German settlement in Eastern Europe. This so-called "Deutsche Ansiedlungsbewegung" expressed both nationalistic sentiments and the urge to conquer nature through science and technology. Dominik's flattering portrayal of German scientists, technologists and industrialists also harmonized with the attitudes of Scherl and Hugenberg, and may even owe some of its details to the two figures, who shared with each other, with Dominik, and with many other Germans an appreciation of technology and a belief in the social responsibility of the commercial entrepreneur.

An examination of Hugenberg's political activities sheds a good deal of light on Dominik's own views and on the political function of his novels, especially during the Nazi Era—a subject which will be discussed in detail in the next chapter. Hugenberg played a prominent role in the National Socialists' rise to power—a role he perhaps adopted only with misgivings and may well have come to regret later. During the Weimar years he was, as head of the *Deutschnationale Volkspartei* [German-National People's Party], a leading figure in those nationalist and conservative circles whose common goal was the destruction of the Republic. As Hitler's influence grew Hugenberg came into closer contact with him— sometimes as an adversary, often as an ally. In 1929, for example, the two made common cause against the Young Reparations Plan; similarly, in 1931 the organizations headed by Hugenberg, Hitler, and other leaders of the "National Opposition" joined together in the "Harzburger Front." The Front disintegrated amid the squabbling over right-wing strategy in the 1932 elections for

Presidency of the Reich. Yet for a while Hugenberg could delude himself into thinking that he was the spokesman of a movement which the Nazis had joined, rather than the reverse.

While Hugenberg was a prime agent in the efforts which German capitalistic and aristocratic reactionaries made to turn Hitler to their own ends, no doubt he shared many of Hitler's ideas and antipathies, though not his racial anti-semitism. Certainly his actions contributed to both the undermining of the Weimar Republic and the enhancement of Hitler's power. The latter's association with Hugenberg and other powerful capitalists, for example, gave him greater access to German industrial circles and their resources than he had enjoyed previously. As a reward for his support or a concession to his residual political power Hugenberg was allowed to serve as Minister of Economy, Food, and Agriculture in the first Hitler cabinet, formed in early 1933. Under increasing pressure he resigned his post a few months later.

Hugenberg, like Dominik, clearly believed in the close integration of business, state, and individual. But he would have had ample cause for dismay when, after 1933, the National Socialist state undertook a gradual but eventually thorough program to bring under its effective control, or even directly absorb through the Party organization, all economic and cultural institutions, including the media. Hugenberg found it prudent to transfer to Party control some parts of his business interests, such as his news bureau and Ufa. In exchange his newspapers, periodicals, and book-publishing facilities, including the Scherl Verlag, remained—but only for a time—relatively untouched, although their publications of course conformed to National Socialist policies. Under Hugenberg's increasingly nominal direction the Scherl Verlag continued to prosper, and to publish Dominik's novels. In 1944, however, it too came under complete government control, as had almost all other media before it. Hugenberg's long association with German conservatism and his exclusion from power after 1933 leave room for debate about the degree of his active, intentional complicity in the rise of National Socialism as a political party. But there is no doubt that he shared many aims and attitudes with the National Socialist movement, that his publishing empire served its causes, and that, as he once wrote to Hitler, it was his "life's wish that the task commonly undertaken on 30 January [the formation of the first Hitler cabinet in 1933] would lead to a happy conclusion."[16]

Probable Readership

The general nature of Dominik's probable readership can be
ascertained more readily than that of Lasswitz'. Unlike the latter,
Dominik did not write for a small group of humanistically educated
and politically liberal readers who were also interested in science.
Nor did he publish his works in a medium which specialized in SF,
as Anglo-American writers began to do during the late Twenties.
From the very first he directed his SF at the mass reading public,
and he succeeded in capturing a sizable portion of that audience.
None of his novels was a failure with the public. Indeed, although
his fiction is seldom mentioned by literary critics, even students of
popular literature, in terms of copies sold Dominik ranks very high
among all German writers active in the period between 1915 and
1940 surveyed by Richards.[17] Moreover, many of his novels
achieved a phenomenal circulation in a relatively short time, and
there is every indication that their popularity persisted or even
increased in the later war years. Thus if by 1936 there had appeared
1,305,000 copies of Thomas Mann's *Buddenbrooks* (1901), which
Richards lists as the greatest best-seller of the time, within but three
years there were published 188,000 copies of *Treibstoff SF* (1940)—
not even Dominik's most popular novel. In the eleven years after its
first publication Mann's famous novel *Der Zauberberg* (1924),
ranked 214th by Richards, sold only 135,000 copies; for a Dominik
novel that would be a somewhat mediocre figure. Among German
SF Bernhard Kellermann's *Der Tunnel* (1913) is the only
contemporary work to surpass Dominik's novels in popularity. With
358,000 copies printed by 1940 it ranks fortieth in Richards' list, but
was Kellermann's only venture into SF. Publication statistics of *Die
Macht der Drei* (1922), but the first and perhaps not even the most
popular of Dominik's novels, suggest that it was, year for year, only
slightly less popular and perhaps even more durable. Any estimate
of the size of Dominik's readership should also recognize that his
novels were serialized in the mass press before publication in
hardcover, and that more than one reader had ready access to each
newspaper and book copy, for the novels were often stocked by the
commercial lending libraries which were popular at the time.

It is as difficult as it is desirable to determine more precisely the
distinctive characteristics of Dominik's contemporary readers and
to ascertain their reasons for favoring his SF novels over other
literary fare. One might surmise initially that the typical Dominik
reader, if such there indeed was, may have been either a Dominik
"fan" specifically and exclusively, an aficionado of SF in general, or

else merely a consumer of *Trivialliteratur* who did not distinguish rigorously between Dominik's SF and other reading material. A cautious assessment suggests that a combination of the first and last of these suppositions, though still not wholly accurate, is the most plausible. In more precise terms, it would appear that the Dominik readership was not composed primarily of a specialized group interested specifically and intensely in SF itself, without regard to content, style, or author. Rather, most of his readers seem to have been consumers of popular literature who came to find that his fiction, in its larger features, satisfied their desire for a familiar form of entertainment and expressed congenial political and moral ideas, while offering in addition new elements of content consonant with the special interest in science and technology they either already possessed or soon cultivated.

That conjecture is supported by evidence of several kinds. In Dominik's time there was neither a single German term for "science fiction" nor a specialized medium for the publication of such literature in Germany. Even had the latter existed, it is quite likely that Dominik would still have preferred to publish his novels in serial form and then in mass hardcover editions. In any case, the overall difference between Dominik's novels and other kinds of literature, in medium of publication and therefore, by implication, in readership, was certainly far less distinct than that between Anglo-American SF and "mainstream" literature of the same time, or between Lasswitz' SF and the mass literature of the Wilhelmine era. It should be observed also that the popularity of Dominik's SF appears not to have directly increased that of other contemporary SF in Germany, although from time to time other works of a similar nature, like Kellermann's *Der Tunnel,* were able to appeal in their own right to the mass audience.

But above all stands the evident fact that Dominik had a large and regular personal following. He succeeded in appealing to multitudes of readers of popular fiction who closely identified the writer with his work and chose their reading matter accordingly. So much could the Scherl Verlag count on the sales appeal of his fiction, even that of his earlier novels, that the first printing of, for example, *Der Brand der Cheopspyramide* (1929) numbered 15,000 copies. By 1940, 70,000 copies of the novel—in fact one of Dominik's less popular works—had been printed. At the end of his career Dominik was enough of a celebrity that, despite war-time plant and paper shortages, 15,000 copies of his autobiography were in print by 1943, but one year after its publication.

According to Walter Nutz the typical writer of mass fiction enjoys a curiously anonymous or impersonal kind of popularity. The reader of such literature either buys works of the same kind without regard to the name of the author, or else buys the works of a single author without regard to content.[18] The Dominik reader, however, not only prized certain definite features in his novels, but also associated them explicitly with the author's name. Although there is a dearth of statements by individual readers—a source of documentation which is available for Anglo-American SF of the same time—the import of popular advertisements of the Fifties is clear:

> Who, whether young or more mature, does not reach enthusiastically [mit Begierde] for Dominik's excitement-laden novels of the future! Much of what he so prophetically envisioned has already reached fulfilment—one more reason to re-experience in reading the breath-taking portrayals.
>
> Millions of readers devour Hans Dominik's novels of the future, pursue enthralled his plausible [glaubhaft] portrayals, loose themselves from this reading only with difficulty.... The furious development of technology makes the seemingly impossible possible.[19]

By mixing the novel element of futuristic technology with the conventional features of popular fiction, Dominik was able to solve what one student of recent mass SF, Dieter Hasselblatt, has described as the fundamental problem of producing and marketing popular literature: the constant need to offer new and exciting fare while still catering to the reader's equally insistent demand that the literary product he buys and consumes will remain, like any other mass-produced item, reassuringly uniform from purchase to purchase.[20] It is virtually certain, too, that Dominik's SF appealed more precisely to the ideological sympathies of many of his readers as well. Therefore, especially after 1933, it served a political function of a nature more specific than the reinforcement of general social values often noted by students of *Trivialliteratur.* During the War years most of Dominik's novels continued to appear in sizable editions. Although there is evidence that the publication or circulation of two of them was "restricted," though not completely denied, by the Nazi censors, the point should not be over-valued. It would appear that rather than being judged actually subversive in any real sense, they were simply considered to be not directly conducive to the goals of National Socialism. Such was in fact the lot of several works by otherwise quite "respectable" writers.[21]

Indeed, the patent fact that most of Dominik's novels were

reprinted in large editions, even when publishing facilities were becoming ever more scarce, argues cogently that the National Socialist government found his works to be of some use in channeling public opinion. One of their chief merits would doubtless have been their escapism, which became especially valuable when military reverses were becoming commonplace and reading was one of the few remaining forms of entertainment. It was particularly advantageous, however, that the escapist elements in Dominik's SF were combined with enthusiastic nationalism, overt racism, and glorification of the German "leader-type," the idea of *Gemeinschaft,* and the work of German scientists and technologists.

I would also contend that during the latter years of the War Dominik's novels could well have abetted the desperate hope for a secret German superweapon ("Wunderwaffe"). The present lack of explicit documentation which might show that the government directly exploited that aspect of Dominik's fiction as a matter of conscious and explicit policy is, in my opinion, of little significance. However precisely or imprecisely the regime formulated, recorded, and carried out its literary policy, its overriding aim was to limit publication to those works which directly furthered its purposes. It is indeed quite possible that the very vagueness or even incompetence with which Dominik treats such subjects as rocketry, jet flight, and nuclear physics—a matter I shall take up in detail in the next chapter—directly contributed to the usefulness of his fiction during the Nazi period. After 1933, and especially during the Forties, when the military was conducting its secret work on the V-rockets, jet aircraft, and atomic weaponry, any substantial, informed discussion of such matters would have been most unwelcome.[22]

Critical Reception

What little response Dominik's novels have elicited from literary critics and historians has been almost entirely negative. The popular appeal of his SF is conceded, and is sometimes recognized to depend on his facility in the techniques of *Trivialliteratur* and on his ability to capitalize on the exciting features of the technology of the present and near future.[23] A few critics, such as Rudolf Majut, Alice Carol Gaar and Susanne Päch, have devoted some attention to the recurrent themes and motifs in his work.[24] In an essay which appeared shortly before the present study went to press, Wolfgang Braun drew conclusions about technology and ideology in *Die Macht der Drei* which I find very congenial.[25] But as yet there has been no serious attempt to argue that Dominik's SF possesses any great literary merit. The ideological aspects of his novels have been roundly condemned, most notably by Manfred Nagl.[26] Yet perhaps the best estimate of Dominik's SF was offered as early as 1930 by Hans-Joachim Flechtner, who wrote within the larger context of "fantastic literature." In his capsule analysis he noted in Dominik's novels the combination of sensational technology, extremist ideology, and exciting but conventional literary realism which appealed to the undifferentiated mass readership.[27]

Some later writers of German SF, such as Freder van Holk (pseud. of Paul Alfred Müller) and the creators of the *Perry Rhodan* series, resemble Dominik in their reactionary political attitudes, treatment of technology, choice of settings, and rough, sensationalistic prose. Horst Heidtmann has even argued quite plausibly that in the early post-war years East German writers of SF could scarcely have avoided "the influence of Dominik and his fellows, which is to be ascertained especially in the consciously or unconsciously borrowed aesthetic structures; of course the Dominik model was 'refunctionalized' ideologically."[28] Most recent German SF of better quality, however, has looked elsewhere for thematic and stylistic inspiration. Non-German writers, readers, and critics, among them particularly those associated with Anglo-American SF in its early years and "Golden Age," have paid Dominik even less attention. *Air Wonder Stories,* edited by the German-speaking immigrant Hugo Gernsback, published one of his pieces—and it is important to note that it was a non-fiction work—in 1930, eight years after Dominik had established his popularity in Germany as a writer of SF.[29] Indeed, other German writers of SF, including Otto Willi Gail, Friedrich Freksa, and Lasswitz himself, received far more attention and certainly more respect from the Anglo-American SF community.[30] Dominik's nationalism, of course, was not congenial to Anglo-American readers; nor, apparently, were his literary style and imaginary science considered more than mediocre, scarcely worthy of notice or, much less, emulation. And, as I suggested earlier, the Anglo-American "space operas" which appeared in the Twenties and Thirties were far bolder than Dominik's novels in their treatment of setting and technology, and certainly no worse in their style. The maturer English-language SF of the Thirties and thereafter, while it took not a little of its inspiration from German science, found nothing of value in the kind of SF represented by Dominik's novels.

Chapter VI

Dominik's Science Fiction Novels: The Future Glory of Germany and Its Technology

But this collapse can not be the end. We think back to the severest times of our history. We think about the dreadful devastation of the Thirty Years' War, which seemed, as Treitschke puts it, to announce the downfall of the German name and yet became the beginning of a new life. We think of the rebirth of German morality and German power, in which our people has more than once lifted from the profoundest misery and abjectest humiliation. Amidst all the distress and oppression of the day we direct our gaze to the broad horizon of the future; we believe in the indestructibility of the German essence and the inalienable role of the German people in the ascent of mankind.
Karl Helfferich, *Der Weltkrieg* [*The World War*] (1919), closing passage of volume 3.

Dominik's SF novels do not differ from one another in any fundamental way. His purpose, as he remarked at the end of his career, was always to "treat... the tremendous possibilities for the future which new scientific knowledge was opening up" and to portray the "struggle of the inventive human mind with the power of nature." Although there is some variety in his selection of scientific and technological material, he seldom ventures far from physics and chemistry and the associated branches of applied science, especially engineering. The choice of content affects the literary features of the novels in only a very limited way. In their length and manner of narration, as well as in their ethical and ideological stance, all sixteen novels are essentially identical. Dominik wrote the first one, it should be recalled, after two decades of experience in technical journalism and fiction; the format he adopted for it was never greatly altered, for it satisfied his publishers, his readers, and, apparently, Dominik himself. In the following examination of Dominik's SF I will therefore analyze his novels collectively, illustrating my arguments with references to whatever novel most clearly and conveniently exhibits the particular feature being discussed.[1]

A summary of a single novel, however, provides a useful preliminary orientation, and Dominik's first, *Die Macht der Drei*, can serve as a ready example.[2] The hero of the novel is the German Silvester Bursfeld; his loyal companions are the Swede Erik Truwor and the Indian Soma Atma. Working mostly in their secret laboratory in Sweden, the three develop a marvelous energy source first discovered by Silvester's father. The invention can power airplanes, focus huge amounts of energy at great distances, and even transmit words and images, The chief antagonist of the three is the ancient enemy of Silvester's father, Dr. Edward F. Glossin, who covets the love of Jane Harte, Silvester's betrothed and later his wife. Glossin, once the protegé of Cyrus Stonard, the dictatorial American president, is now the latter's globe-trotting factotum and the *eminence grise* behind the dictator's plans to dominate the world. Since the new energy source obviously poses a threat to the scheme, Glossin seeks to destroy the three. He employs his strong hypnotic powers to abduct Jane, and then incites a British commando attack on their laboratory. But the raid fails, for the three escape by themselves hypnotizing their attackers, who report them dead. Jane is rescued and brought to safe seclusion. The three use their power to halt a war between Great Britain and the United States and then impose world peace. Glossin attempts to save himself by engineering Stonard's fall from power, but later shoots himself when he realizes that his political schemes and amorous dreams have been thwarted. Silvester and Erik must die to secure victory, yet at the end of the novel the reader knows that the memory of the Three will live on in Silvester's heir, soon to be born, and in the worshipful recollection of their fellow men.

Character and Plot

The characters and plot-lines in Dominik's novels are derived—one is tempted to say that they are lifted bodily—from conventional popular literature, especially that of lesser quality. Character and plot serve not only to maintain the reader's interest and to express and affirm dominant social beliefs, as is their general function in *Trivialliteratur,*[3] but also to further the intentionality of SF as Dominik conceived it. Invariably the center of action is a young, more or less mature male, like Silvester Bursfeld in *Macht,* Georg Astenryk in *Befehl,* Ronald Lee in *Erbe,* Walter Uhlenkort in *Atlantis,* or Hein Eggerth, who appears in *Stern, Land,* and

Wettflug. Such figures are heroes in the popular sense of the word. In their "struggle... with the power of nature" they exhibit physical strength and moral probity, overcome natural obstacles, roundly but fairly defeat the villain, and succeed—chastely, to be sure—in love. Dominik's heroes are distinguished from those of other low-brow literature only in their superior scientific knowledge and their mastery of futuristic technology. Not infrequently the heroes are accompanied by lesser versions of themselves. Thus Silvester Bursfeld has his two companions Erik Truwor and Soma Atma, and Marian Heidens is Georg Astenryk's "loyal friend, helper, servant [getreuer Freund, Gehilfe, Diener]" (*Befehl*, 22).

Dominik seldom describes at length the physical appearance or psychological constitution of the hero. He prefers instead to show the hero in action, which is the essence of his nature. While the heroes are rather featureless as individuals, they can be described collectively in some detail. The hero is, above all, Germanic, and in fact usually German. The trio of Aryans in *Macht*—the main hero a German, one of his companions a Swede, the other an Indian—expresses Dominik's racial views quite clearly. The typical Dominik hero or sub-hero is, of course, tall, well-built, and handsome. Erik Truwor, for example, is "blond, blue-eyed, of Nordic type [blond, blauäugig, vom nordischen Typus]" (*Macht*, 40). But it is less important that the hero's eyes be blue than that they be clear and perceptive, so that the reader may marvel when they "fasten upon the altimeter" (*Stern*, 6) or take in an entire situation at a single glance. Whether engaged in physical combat or technological operations, the hero's hands are as skilled as his eyes, and excellence of eye and hand is exceeded only by mental acuity. The minds of even the hearty, extroverted heroes, like Hein Eggerth are impressively quick and subtle. The more intellectual heroes, like the scientist Dr. Wandel (*Atomgewicht*), the inventor Ronald Lee (*Erbe*), or the capable man of the world Georg Astenryk (*Befehl*), are distinguished by the quality of true genius as well.

Among the novels there is some variation in the age, psychological makeup, and intellectual endowments of the heroes, and even in the extent to which the plot depends directly on them. Hein Eggerth, for example, is quite young, especially in *Land* and *Stern*, and he is not a creative scientist. In the three "Eggerth" novels the hero therefore plays a lesser role in large-scale political and social developments; the plot, especially the development of new technology, is carried to a greater than usual degree by an ostensibly subordinate figure, Hein's father, the inventor-capitalist

Professor Eggerth. Dr. Hegemüller in *Treibstoff* and Dr.Wegener in *Geheimnis* are, by contrast, somewhat older, more intellectual, and more introverted than the typical Dominik hero; and in *Macht* Erik Truwor and Soma Atma enjoy a prominence far greater than that of the customary sub-hero. But Hein Eggerth, Dr. Hegemüller, Dr. Wegener, and Silvester Bursfeld are still quite evidently the heroes of their respective novels.

The variations among Dominik's heroes are slight in comparison to their essential similarity, for the functions that they are created to fulfill and the ideas that they are intended to embody are always the same. Dominik alters or rather supplements the characteristics of the conventional hero of popular romance and sentimental adventure fiction only enough to make science and technology a special aspect of his heroism. Moreover, heroes of a radically different nature—aliens, quasi-humans, or machines— have no place in his novels, even though such figures had already appeared often in other SF.

Besides Jane Harte in *Macht*, the company of Dominik's SF heroines includes Christie Harlessen (*Atlantis*), Hortense van der Meulen (*Erbe*), Maria Witthusen (*Spur*), and Anne Escheloh (*Befehl*). Sometimes a lesser heroine, such as Ronald Lee's sister Violet in *Erbe*, accompanies the principal heroine, accenting her personality and experiencing, in a smaller way, her tribulations and triumphs. The heroines, like the heroes, are all Germanic, and most of them are German. As the description of Maria Witthusen shows, their appearance corresponds to Dominik's image of their ideal national type: "Light-blond hair framed the delicate forehead, beneath which there sparkled light-blue eyes [lichtblondes Haar umrahmte die schmale Stirn, unter der lichtblaue Augen erglänzten]" (*Spur*, 45). While the heroine may understand much about science and technology, as does Hortense van der Meulen, she does not actively participate in the action. Instead, like a rag doll she is seized and threatened by the villain and then rescued by the hero. When not in danger she may be seen, like Jane Harte-Bursfeld, in a picture of German domestic bliss, waiting anxiously but confidently for her hero and quietly spreading joy among all those around her (*Macht*, 181-83).

The heroine's purpose, then, is to further the love plot and to inspire in the reader the emotions of chaste delectation and indignant trepidation. The type abounds in other SF, especially early pulp SF, which so often borrowed the techniques of romance and melodrama readily available in popular literature. Maturer SF sometimes departs from this pattern to portray women who have complex personalities and who act independently. Such figures are absent in Dominik's novels. So too are more exotic female characters, not only those from other terrestrial cultures but also extraterrestrial female characters, like the Martian princess and her kin, who embody a different approach to the attempt to integrate romantic interest with science. There are also no female villains in Dominik's novels, or even any instances of the *femme fatale*.

While almost every Dominik novel has a love plot, overt sex, as might be expected, is absent in his SF. Salaciousness was irrelevant to his science-fictional purposes, as he conceived them, and was also inappropriate to the assumed tastes of his audience—a factor perhaps even more decisive. Occasionally, however, one encounters passages, admittedly rather tame ones, which express romantic sentiments somewhat more passionately, though still indirectly, or which seem to hint at less conventional sexual proclivities. Dr. Glossin in *Macht*, for example, exhibits distinctly voyeuristic and sadistic behavior when he has Jane in his power (e.g., 104-05).

In most of his novels Dominik creates villains fit to oppose his heroes and threaten his heroines. The villains, such as Dr. Glossin (*Macht*), Guy Rouse (*Atlantis*), Robert Canning (*Erbe*), and Turi Chan (*Befehl*), are stock characters, the embodiments of evil, who contrive to obstruct the hero. They are motivated essentially by simple nefariousness, twisted ambition, and envy. Sometimes, too, they are the agents of hostile nations—for Dominik a wide category indeed. But their villainy is supplemented by a motive appropriate to SF: they wish to steal and exploit the hero's scientific discoveries and inventions, or at least frustrate their beneficial effects.

None of the villains, of course, are Germans. Some, like Turi Chan, or Hidetawa and Yoshika in *Wettflug*, are stereotypical wily Orientals. Others, less exotic but more plausible, are Caucasians, like Robert Canning, the embittered inventor and disappointed lover in *Erbe*. Dominik's ideological convictions and scientific or pseudoscientific interests enabled him to vary the basic stereotypes to a modest extent, sometimes in an interesting way. Some of the more enigmatic and satanic villains, like Dr. Glossin or the Orientals, employ mysterious mental powers in their attempts to trap their intended victims. Many of the villains also make use of their own secret technological devices, or of those they have temporarily seized from the forces of good. Occasionally one also encounters quasi-villains, all-too-human figures who have somehow turned bad and often regret their weaknesses and misdeeds. One such character is Awaloff in *Erbe*, who has erred in aiding the Russian Communist regime and suffers at the hands of the principal villain Canning. Even the latter, at the end of his life, is plagued by regrets, although his protestations of remorse may well be mere set speeches (*Erbe*, 309-12). Variations in the stereotypical villain, however, are relatively insignificant in comparison to the range of possibilities open to *Trivialliteratur* and to SF, even in Dominik's own time. Perhaps because he was too unimaginative, or else too preoccupied with what he considered to be the evils of his own time, Dominik did not create any non-human villains, whether alien, quasi-human, or mechanical.

Two other figures play roles of some importance in Dominik's SF, although they are never leading characters. Closely related to the villains, in their evil ways, their opposition to the hero, and in their embodiment of Dominik's racial and ideological attitudes, are a number of African, Oriental, or even American despots. Among them are the black dictator Kaiser Salvator Augustus, ruler of central Africa in *Atlantis*, the central Asian potentate Toghon-Khan in *Spur*, and the dictator Cyrus Stonard in *Macht*. A counterbalance to the despot, in many novels, is furnished by the figure of an older and wiser man who aids the hero in some way. The type ranges from the prosaic Professor Eggerth of *Land, Stern*, and *Wettflug*, who is the inventor of the "St" planes flown by his son Hein, to several guru-like figures who, like the reclusive Johannes Harte in *Atlantis* and the mysterious Germanic sage Weland Gorm in *Erbe*, emerge from mountain monasteries or other refuges with special powers or secret knowledge. The older, wiser men do not astound the world by openly performing marvelous deeds, as do the young technological protagonists or the slightly older scientists. But they are indispensable to the heroes' success, and contribute much to the evolution of the plot and the creation of sensationalistic effects.

The supporting cast in Dominik's novels consists of various bit players and of nearly faceless crowds who are essentially parts of the scenic backdrop rather than active characters. Like the major figures, the minor players are often identified merely by name. Dominik, as he noted in his autobiography, paid careful attention to the selection of names for his characters, even if he spent little or no other effort on establishing their personalities (*VSS*, 169-70; see Chapter V). Thus identification according to national or ethnic identity is important in the delineation of almost all the figures. It is perhaps even more significant than class membership or adherence to the forces of good or evil, for in a certain sense national or "racial" origin, according to Dominik's world-view, is the prime determinant of personality and behavior. Therefore both narrator and characters often substitute the national identification for the name of the character, and the stereotype supposedly suffices to convey personality and explain behavior:

> At the door [Dr. Wandel] nearly collided with the Irish lab worker [Laboratoriumsdiener] MacGan. Astonished, the son of the Emerald Isle [der Sohn der Grünen Insel] watched him stride hurriedly on. "The German seems to be in a bad mood today...."
>   Poor Dutchman [*sic* in original], you don't have an easy time of it with the Yankees, thought the Irishman to himself. (*Atomgewicht*, 12)

Chief among the foreign national types are the Americans, among whom Dominik differentiates several subtypes. The names or brief phrases which he employs to describe incidental characters reflect his racial beliefs and national biases, the impressions he gained from his travels in the United States, his distorted or caricatured notions of standard American stereotypes, and his association of Anglo-Saxon culture with technology. In *Atomgewicht,* for example, the aristocrat Henry Chelmesford, clearly of English descent, is president of United Chemical, and another Anglo-Saxon, Phil Wilkin, is an assistant laboratory scientist. Menial laboratory tasks are performed by the Irishmen MacGan and O'Brien. Although Dominik was a white supremacist and anti-semite, only in a few instances, as in *Spur,* where there is an unsuccessful Negro rebellion, does he refer specifically to other American ethnic groups. In Dominik's conception America was first of all a land of Yankee technologists, industrialists, and capitalists. Otherwise it is at best a land blessed by the presence of German ethnic or racial cousins but misguided in domestic governance and foreign policy. The notion of America as the "melting pot" appears seldom in Dominik's novels, and such genetic and cultural mixture, it need scarcely be said, is regarded unfavorably.

The other national or racial groups prominent in Dominik's SF are the Slavs and Orientals. They furnish individual characters— almost always villains—and undifferentiated masses which often appear against sweeping Trans-Uralic or Asian landscapes. Both groups represent what is exotic, "abnormal" (as defined by comparison to European civilization), and, most of all, threatening. For obvious reasons Western Europe, especially Germany, has in its collective historical consciousness often combined the Slavs and Orientals into a single Eastern threat, a jumble of Huns, Golden Hordes, and so on. Dominik adopts the popular image, although occasionally he tends to see the particular threat of Russia as the ideological danger of Bolshevism, while the Oriental peril is something inexplicable and absolutely evil. Dominik's anti-Bolshevism, his fear of Orientals, and his selection of historical "analogs" as well, can be seen very plainly in the opening scene of *Erbe*, where a future air battle between German-led European forces and the "Russian-Manchurian" alliance is described explicitly as a "Second Battle of the Catalaunian Fields " (*Erbe*, 5-10; see below).

Other nationalities and racial groups play roles of considerably lesser importance. Surprisingly, Dominik is not particularly hostile toward the French and British; in fact, he pays very little attention to them at all. In his future world the British Empire is in decline, Britain's industry has been outstripped by that of America, and the correction of the injustices of Versailles is usually a part of past history, not a cause of dramatic struggle in the present. Other nations or races receive still less attention, although the use of Africa as a setting in novels like *Atlantis* permits Dominik to express his racial opinions. The order of finish in *Wettflug* would seem to embody his attitudes toward the various major nationalities. Germany and America, ethnically and technologically the two superior countries, place first and second in the jet-plane race, while Russia and Japan are utterly defeated. Italy, England, and France, who had been Germany's adversaries in Europe and had once held leading positions in science and technology, achieve only mediocrity.

The most blatant national or racial type in Dominik's SF is, of course, the German. In analyzing the German characters, however, one must take into account the disparity in viewpoint which, at least ideally, separates Dominik and his original readers (and perhaps some of his modern "fans" as well) from readers and critics who do not share his ideology or perhaps even his national background. It is of some interest that Dominik occasionally differentiates among regional or, as some German nationalists expressed the notion, "tribal" German types. In general, however, he ignores such distinctions in favor of a single idealized conception of the "German" or even "Germanic" type. Even more significant are differences that have to do with the very belief in stereotypes and with the distinction between those which are viewed favorably and those which express pejorative judgments. For most of us Dominik's

German characters are crass, one-dimensional, and therefore implausible stereotypes. Manifestly constructed according to oversimplified, patently false idealizations, they demonstrate the author's crudity of thought and literary skill. But for Dominik and his loyal or "sincere" readers, such figures seem to embody real traits and therefore can or might be encountered in actual life. Although they represent the larger group to which they belong, they also remain individuals, characters who are considered plausible despite their superiority, or perhaps precisely because of it. In short, stereotypes are not stereotypes, for those who believe in them.

The examination of stereotypes in Dominik's SF reveals much about his ideological convictions. It also affects our understanding of his novels as the focus of literary experiences. Thus the non-involved reader may regard Dominik's heroes and heroines with amusement at their triteness and distaste for their deeds and beliefs. It may well seem to be the villains who, although they are closely modelled on the stereotypes of romance and melodrama, possess the greatest individuality among the major characters; and we note indeed that some villains, like Dr. Glossin in *Macht*, actively participate in more of the action than do even the heroes. But for Dominik and his original readers the centers of attention and admiration were the heroes and heroines. They, and the lesser German figures as well, were viewed as magnificent but still plausible individuals who embodied those features whose recurrence among other Germans, if perhaps in less perfect form, supposedly made it possible and legitimate to categorize millions of individuals collectively.

In devising the plots of his SF novels Dominik also borrowed heavily—for us, nearly to the point of unconscious caricature—from romance, melodrama, and adventure fiction. The characters, clearly divided along lines of right and wrong, participate in sequences of action consisting of physical events which are often of worldwide importance. The specific purpose of such events, as I have argued earlier, is to demonstrate the spectacular nature of science and technology and to portray the heroic personality of the technologist. On a broader level, the plot-action in Dominik's novels, as in other *Trivialliteratur*, serves to evoke in the reader a sense of awe at the grandiose happenings he witnesses, and yet also to encourage him to identify with the characters and to feel that he is directly involved in the events he is privileged to observe so intimately.[4]

It would appear that for Dominik and his readers the

accomplishment of such purposes required little complexity of structure or characterization. Typically, the action of the novels lasts a short time, perhaps a year, and there are no major hiatuses or chronological inversions in the narration. The exposition of psychological states is almost non-existent, the development of personality minimal at most; the latter is limited to the lovers' recognition of their love, for example, or the villains' occasional and essentially conventional confessions of failure and expressions of remorse. Therefore the plot reaches its resolution not by a significant development and interaction of personalities, but rather through the removal of physical obstacles, the defeat of opposing persons and forces, and the benevolence of fate. Usually the narration ends with a romantic union and the prospect—often literal, as in *Erbe*—of more worlds to conquer. At the very least, as in *Macht*, the plot is concluded by heroic death accompanied by some nobly consoling element. Both types of ending have essentially the same sentimental effect on the reader.

With regard to action and setting, Dominik apparently believed that more is indeed better. Either he could not or would not base the plot structures of most of his novels on larger divisions like chapters. Instead, there are dozens of short segments set apart from each other only by spaces in the text, although thousands of miles and a change of characters may separate one episode from the next. In *Macht*, for example, there are forty-seven episodes which vary in length from less than two pages to more than a dozen. Quite likely the extremely disjointed form of the novels owes something to the popular German newspaper serial novel, and indeed some of Dominik's works first appeared serially in Scherl publications. For his scenic backdrops Dominik employs much of the globe. Major settings of action in *Macht* are New York, Washington, London, Lord Horace Maitland's castle in Britain, Colorado, Sweden, the Rhineland, Australia, the North Pole, and even Trenton, New Jersey. Incidental settings include Naples and Berlin, and several episodes occur during flight. The theme of geological cataclysm enables Dominik to create spectacular new terrestrial landscapes in *Atlantis* and *Land*. Space itself is a setting in *Treibstoff* and *Erbe;* in the latter novel—and only there among Dominik's works—part of the action takes place on another planet, Venus.

Despite the nearly dizzying sequence of events and rapid alternation of settings, every Dominik "technischer Zukunftsroman" is composed of three basic fields or realms of narration. There is a "private" realm, which consists of individuals and their personal interactions, a "public" realm, which has to do with economics, politics, and society as a whole, and a "scientific" realm, in which technological objects and scientific ideas are presented. The private realm, in most of Dominik's novels, is concerned with personal heroism, love and villainy. In *Macht* the private action, most of whose events are set in Trenton, Lord Maitland's castle, Colorado, and the Rhineland, centers on the romance of Silvester and Jane. Much of the tension stems from Glossin's attempts to destroy Silvester and have Jane for himself.

The public realm in Dominik's novels is comprised of a course of events that affect the fate of the world on a grand scale. Typically there are copious descriptions of high government policy sessions, boardroom debates, business coups, battles and crowds. In *Macht* the action of the public realm consists of Stonard's attempt, aided by the machinations of Glossin, to aggrandize his power, followed by conflict with other governments and then the intervention of the Three. Most of the events of the public realm occur in Washington, London, Lord Maitland's castle, and Australia.

The focus of narration in the scientific realm is the discovery of new science and its employment in spectacular deeds. In *Macht*, quite obviously, the development of the energy source, its protection from Glossin, and its use to impose world peace comprise the action of the scientific realm. The Three and, once again, Glossin, are the chief actors, and most of its events take place in Sweden and at the North Pole, until the Three make their invention known and employ it all over the world.

To a certain extent each of the three realms is distinct from the others, for each contains certain characters, settings, and sequences of events which are not directly related to those of the other realms. Most of the individual episodes are devoted to a single realm as well. Therefore, the rapid shift of narrative focus from one realm to another, which occurs every few pages, usually involves a change of subject, characters and setting. Yet the three realms are not entirely independent of one another. Certain figures are common to more than one realm; some, like Glossin, have vital roles in all three. Much the same can be said of settings; in *Macht*, for example, Lord Maitland's castle figures prominently in both the private and public realms. Often, especially toward the end of a novel, the ever-accelerating action will expand to encompass all three realms as a conclusive resolution is prepared.

The basic structural principle discussed here reveals much, I think, about Dominik's approach to literature in general and to SF in particular. For several reasons it was to his advantage to establish the three realms as distinct entities, but also to integrate them with one another. Separation of the realms permits the use of three well-defined, easily comprehended coordinate plots which can be interrupted and alternated to generate suspense. But Dominik had sufficient insight and experience to understand that, even on general aesthetic principles, some overall unity of action was necessary. The integration of the three realms and the central importance given to the scientific realm as the novels approach their resolutions also express his special intentions as a writer of SF. The exploration in fictional form of the great potential of science and the workings of the inventive or technological mind, he understood, demanded more than the mere description of imaginary science, or even more than tales about marvelous inventions. In his imaginary worlds Dominik, like other writers of SF, wished to show how science and technology, although they were interesting in themselves, were matters of extreme importance to society, history, and individual human lives. The nature of his imaginary worlds, the stylistic means with which he sought to carry out his science-fictional intentionality, and the degree of success he achieved in the attempt are the subjects of the rest of this chapter.

Ideology and the History of the Future

In his SF Dominik devotes considerable attention to the larger social and political features of the imaginary world. His vision of "future history" remains essentially the same from novel to novel. All the novels are set in the near future, within a century or so after Dominik's own time. Sometimes he even provides exact dates. *Macht* (1922), for example, is set in 1955 (subtitle), *Atlantis* (1925) in 2002 (pp. 8-9) and *Spur* (1923) in 2006 (p. 69). Occasionally there appears some character, like the old man in *Macht* (pp. 153ff.), who can recall the past, including events which for readers of our time have still to occur. Or perhaps the narrator, or even one of the characters, will simply refer to the "past" in a casual way which suggests that the first few decades of the twentieth century are recent enough that their major events are still familiar, but distant enough to be part of "history."

Unlike many writers of SF, both good and bad, Dominik does not apply his imagination to the more distant future. Nor does he venture to conceive of any change in the physical appearance or biological nature of the human species. As the preceding discussion of characterization and structure shows, the psychological nature of individuals and even their everyday customs and pursuits—manners, emotion, courtship, family life and business—also remain much the same in Dominik's visions of the future. But there have been momentous changes in social institutions and political conditions, and in science and technology as well of course. While some variation in these features can be detected among the novels, the differences can usually be ascribed to the choice of temporal setting. There is, however, no indication that Dominik set out to create systematically a unified "future history" as a common background for his novels. Rather the nature of the future remains essentially the same from novel to novel because his notion of literature and SF, his view of his own world, and his hopes for the future were in equal measure static and simplistic.

Dominik's expositions of future history and political conditions touch on almost the entire globe, in a manner which often ignores distinctions of less than continental size. In the East there is danger, either from atavistic chaos or new and highly regimented aggressive powers. Although he portrays the threat of an industrialized and communist Russia in several novels, most notably *Erbe*, the East is generally pictured as a vast semi-anarchic, semi-feudal land ruled either by nomad chiefs or by despots, as in *Spur*. The image of the East as a land of sub-human masses which recurrently threaten European civilization with either chaotic devastation or barbarian authoritarianism has long been a part of German historical consciousness. In Dominik's time the fear was reinforced by both the Russian Revolution and the emergence of Japan as a major power. An equally powerful alternate historical image is that of Eastern Europe and Asia as a vulnerable land of brutish peasants or uncivilized nomads eminently suitable for colonization by the civilized nations, above all Germany. The notion reflects the long-time German dream of *Lebensraum*, the actual history of German settlement east of the Elbe, beginning in the Middle Ages, and renewed attempts to encourage Germans to settle in Eastern Europe in Dominik's own time (see Chapter V). Both images, of course, provided Dominik—and other writers as well—the opportunity to generate novelistic excitement and suspense, and to stimulate nationalistic feeling by picturing Germany as the daunty defender or even beneficent disseminator of civilization.

Only occasionally does Dominik refer to political conditions in South America and Africa. The countries of South America are unchanged politically, except for some stabilization in government and an increase in German immigration; the latter is viewed not as the flight of dissatisfied, undesirable, or disloyal elements, but rather as an expansion of German influence by capable emigrants who, like those in *Erbe*, retain their ties to the parent culture. In South America there has been some progress in industrialization, and some of the South American countries described in *KLM*, for example, have used their resources to attain a measure of independence from Yankee domination. At one point in *Erbe* Dominik refers to the "United States of South America [Vereinigte Staaten von Südamerika]" (166). It is not clear whether the nation is a new continental federation or, less likely, an extension of the United States of Brazil which existed in Dominik's own time.

Where Africa is mentioned peripherally or, as in *Atlantis*, even appears as a major setting, greater changes are evident. In accord with Dominik's political dreams and racial attitudes, the great colonial empires have weakened and begun to disintegrate. As I remarked earlier, Britain and France themselves, as well as other Western European countries, receive little attention in Dominik's SF. In Africa colonialism—one regrets having to admit the occasional if fortuitous accuracy of Dominik's vision—as given way to semi-civilized, volatile, native despotism, poorly disguised by a few showy engineering projects and made ludicrous by the despots' shabby imitation of the lapsed customs of European monarchs and ancient Roman emperors.

Of all foreign countries America is most prominent in Dominik's SF. For him the United States, the destination of his early travels, was the pre-eminent land of technology, the home of millions of German immigrants still tied to their parent culture, and the epitome of ideas and institutions which he regarded with contempt, disgust and fear. In his novels the mutual alienation of government, business and citizenry in America provides the prime counter-example to the German society of the future. Dominik's picture of the United States or, as it sometimes appears, the future "North American Union [Nordamerikanische Union]" (*Macht*, 84) is based not on any supposition of radical change, but rather on a systematic and actually rather tame extrapolation of tendencies which he believed could be perceived in early twentieth-century America. In Dominik's vision of the future, therefore, American foreign policy is unprincipled and imperialistic. On the local level government is ineffective, on the federal level often dictatorial—in both instances, Dominik would probably have said, because of too much popular democracy. The American business community is viciously capitalistic, feeling no responsibility to state or society.

The quintessential American businessman is the conniving corporation president Henry Chelmesford (*Atomgewicht*) or the adventurer-entrepreneur Guy Rouse (*Atlantis*). To promote his own gains the latter does not quail even before the prospect of diverting the Gulf Stream, a project which threatens the destruction of northern European civilization. American technologists view their efforts not as contributions to a greater community and historical purpose, but simply as jobs or as opportunities to achieve personal glory and financial gain.

On occasion Dominik does credit the common people of America with a sense of racial solidarity and a cultural consciousness which maintain old-fashioned values in some persons and enable the undefiled populace to resist the attempts of their leaders to carry out policies detrimental to northern Europe (*Atlantis*, 38). In *Das stählerne Geheimnis* Dominik treats America even more favorably, envisioning it as a land which in its organically harmonious social fabric and sense of racial integrity has come to resemble somewhat his ideal of Germany. The unusual charitability might be explained in several ways. Germany as a nation plays little or no part in the novel. Dominik may therefore have been freer to resort to a convention of considerable power and long standing in literature, namely the almost universal tendency to identify exploration and technological innovation with America and, to a lesser extent, Britain. One notes that in much German adventure, technological and science fiction the protagonists, including the admired heroes, are not Germans but rather Americans.

Dominik was not unaffected by such images and apparently could entertain them when his initial choice of setting and characters did not dictate that entire nations appear as heroes or villains. As I remarked in the previous chapter, his experience of America included both New York, which he saw as a mercenary, degenerate and racially mongrelized center of Yankee capitalism, and the Great Lakes region, which he viewed as the sound German and Anglo-Saxon heartland. Also, like many Germans, Dominik regarded America as a country which had indeed been the enemy of Germany in one war but which, as a former adversary of Great Britain and home of many Irish- and German-Americans, should have been Germany's ally and might sometime—the novel was published in 1939—become her partner in the battle against the English, Slavs and Orientals. But *Das stählerne Geheimnis* remains merely an exception which illuminates all the more a glaring rule to the contrary. Most often, indeed, Dominik pictures

American society as hostile to Germany in its external relations and, in its internal constitution, as an agglomeration of isolated, alienated individuals, social groups, and institutions which lacks any unifying concept of *Volk*, state or duty. Thus even though it remains a world power in the immediate future, America must ultimately lapse into internal conflict and fail in competition with a healthier and more organic society.

Of far greater moment in Dominik's novels, especially their public realm, is the nature of that society, the Germany of the future. The chief characteristics of the future history of Germany, as he imagines it, are national resurgence, attainment of international prestige and respectability, the creation or re-creation of a sense of social communality, and the exhibition of scientific superiority and traditional heroism by individual Germans. Such observations, in themselves, are of course rather fatuous. In the years after World War I—and not only then—the same concerns often lay uppermost in the minds of both the masses and classes in Germany, whatever their ideological persuasion or sophistication (see Chapter V). But two points should not be overlooked. For some reason Dominik and his readers found the exploration of those issues in futuristic fiction to be of some considerable value. Moreover, both author and contemporary reader approached them from a nationalistic, conservative, reactionary or—I realize the dangers of such facile equivalences—fascistic perspective which is presumably rare in "lasting" literature and foreign to modern literary criticism.

The broader genesis or historical "analog" of Dominik's future Germany—and there may well be more than one analog—will be discussed shortly. Perhaps more apparent initially are several concerns or modes of thought which are transferred to the futuristic realm of narration. In Dominik's "future history" Germany has surmounted the humiliations and unnatural restraints of the Treaty of Versailles and has reassumed its rightful position as the political, economic, intellectual and perhaps even military center of Europe. In some novels Germany leads a loosely united federation of European states, a "European Confederation [Europäischer Staatenbund]" or "United States of Europe [Vereinigte europäische Staaten]" whose "central administration [Zentralregierung]" is located in Bern (*Atlantis,* 10, 61, 34). Although individual Germans demonstrate distinct superiority of character and intellect, Germany does not dominate the entire world, militarily or even politically, and apparently has no desire to do so. The processes which are to lead to German resurgence and the emergence of the

European confederation are not described in detail. In *Macht* the characters look back on the years immediately after World War I, when the novel was actually written, as a time of shame which has now been wiped out. Nothing more is said, ostensibly because the characters themselves are familiar with the details as a matter of course.

Dominik's picture of future German society shows how the German nation and its institutions will be equal to the task of achieving Germany's rightful, superior position in Europe. The relation between government, business, industry and private life in the Germany of the novels can be characterized as an informal but pervasive and effective integration which creates a whole greater and more important than the mere sum of its parts. Such harmonious concert supposedly reflects the nature of the German spirit; it is expressed in an immediate sense of communality or *Gemeinschaft* and as an innate principle of social behavior. State, commerce and the individual always act in accord with the concept of organic society, not because they are forced to do so, but because such behavior is ethically good, practically beneficial, and—for a German—constitutionally natural.

The relationship between the German government and the "European Settlement Company [Europäische Siedlungsgesell-schaft]" in *Spur* illustrates the harmonious cooperation of business and government, or even the obliteration of the distinction between the two. The company is a commercial enterprise but also exercises—in Dominik's view quite properly—the legislative, administrative and military powers of a state. Indeed its ultimate goal is the creation of a new German society on "unoccupied" soil. Quite likely it is not so much the various British and Dutch colonial companies which served as Dominik's models, but rather the Teutonic Order and the secular companies which in the late middle ages promoted German settlement beyond the Elbe and Oder, or even more likely the organizations for German "colonization" of Eastern Europe supported by his publisher Hugenberg.

Professor Eggerth's conception of his role in society as a German entrepreneur and technologist exemplifies the social or rather "*Gemeinschafts*-consciousness" of the outstanding reflective individual. But the notions of German excellence and communality, as well as the specific theme of German scientific and technological superiority, are demonstrated at their most visceral level in the hero. His success—in his own view as well as Dominik's—is not merely the triumph of an individual. It represents, rather, that of the society and race, just as the nefariousness and ultimate failure of the villain express the nature of his race or that of the nation which seeks to benefit from his schemes. It is not simply his personal property which the hero develops, employs and protects, but rather the prized scientific and technological resources of Germany.[5]

In this and the preceding chapter I have discussed the ideas of social *Gemeinschaft*, national resurgence, technological excellence and the defense or expansion of territory as features of Dominik's own thought and as aspects of both popular and intellectual consciousness in Germany during this time, especially after World War I. As James Joll has noted, contemplating a still broader context, each nation collects and transforms certain historical events or periods into myths which become ingredients of general consciousness and consequently influence the way the nation responds to the present. The overall pattern of Dominik's historical myths—in other words, the body of "analogs" which are the basis for extrapolation in his SF—is a familiar one. It consists in fact of the same radical alternation of utter, seemingly undeserved, externally-occasioned catastrophe with dazzling expansion and triumph which, Joll suggests, characterizes German historical consciousness in general.[6]

Dominik, effectively combining his sense of the dramatic requisites of fiction with a desire to satisfy his own dreams and those of his readers, sets his novels in a time when the cycle of history is well into its ascendant but still below its zenith. Implicitly symmetrical, the pattern also permitted Dominik and his readers to entertain the immediately assuring thought that the rapid decline evident in the wild fluctuation of actual history in recent times was nearing its nadir or had even reached it. The period of felicity in Dominik's future history re-creates and echoes—with obvious idealization, of course—what many readers must have regarded as highpoints of past German history: the heroic age, the First Reich of the Middle Ages, perhaps the "Northern Renaissance" of Luther, Dürer and Hans Sachs, perhaps too the limited gains of the much-heralded *Zollverein* or Customs Union (1832), and, most likely, the *status quo ante* (WWI) *bellum* of the Bismarck-Hohenzollern Second Reich which was founded in the year before Dominik's birth and lasted until he was forty six. In the future, correspondingly, Versailles is a bygone moment of disaster, just as, to the Wilhelmine Era, the catastrophe associated with the events at Canossa during the Middle Ages and the ascendancy of France from the Thirty Years' War to 1815 represented humiliations which had been obliterated in the course of time by the workings of history and the heroism of the German nation.

One of the—to us—more trivial features of the imaginary future history that Dominik creates in his novels provides particularly enlightening information about his own view of history and about the probable expectations and responses of his readers. In *Erbe* he employs a historical analog which, if it is not totally unfamiliar, may well appear strange, particularly to contemporary non-German readers. At the beginning of the novel Central and Western Europe, led by Germany, defeat the "Russian-Manchurian" forces near Chalons, France, in a huge air battle which Dominik explicitly terms "The Battle over the Catalaunian Fields [Die Schlacht über der Katalaunischen Ebene]" (*Erbe*, 10). The name alludes to the actual battle of the Catalaunian Fields (or Campus Mauriacus), a historical event familiar to every German schoolboy, at least in Dominik's time. There, in 451 A.D., Attila and his Huns were defeated by the Visigoths, Franks, Burgundians and other Germanic tribes under the command of Aetius and Theodoric I (reg. 419-451); the latter, it should be noted, has often been confused in the popular mind with the nearly legendary Theodoric the Great (454?-526), just as the several invaders from the East have frequently been jumbled together, sometimes under the collective term "Huns." Dominik's rather clever turn of phrase—the battle takes place not *on* but *over* the Catalaunian Fields near Chalons—reminds the reader of the futuristic nature of the battle and thus of the entire imaginary world.

Perhaps the selection of historical "analog" is not as inconsequential a matter as it might seem initially. Dominik's attitude toward things "Germanic," whether past, present or future, was as adulatory as it was distorted, and he shared the widespread German hostility to the Latin nations, especially France. Nevertheless, in creating his future history he did not use, as have so many other nationalistic German writers, a far more familiar "analog," the *Hermannsschlacht* or Battle of the Teutoburger Wald (9 A.D.), in which the Germanic tribes, as yet culturally "undefiled," routed the legions of Rome. He chose instead a historical model which appealed to a German self-image nobler, more grandiose, and more imperial than the bitter defiance of isolated, semi-savage tribes living on the peripheries of civilization. In the opening scene of *Erbe*, and elsewhere in his SF where the German nation or race defends its own territory or extends its sway over Eastern Europe, Asia, new land masses or even Venus, Dominik wished to portray

Germany as the modern equivalent not of primitive, tribal forest-dwellers or, even less, an army of Huns. Instead, the Germany of the future was to resemble that of the late Roman or early medieval past, which was regarded as the defender and extender of European civilization, the legitimate successor of the Roman Empire, and nevertheless still the quintessence of Germanic virtue. In terms more impartial and abstract, Dominik created—consciously or, more probably, unconsciously—a vision of the future in which there was no need, for him or his readers, to choose between two traditional, powerful and often contradictory images of Germany. The first, attractive to many Germans of Dominik's time but also disturbing to most foreigners and some Germans as well, features the actual or putative political unity and military glory of Germany under such heroic, even mythic, figures as the Carolingians, Barbarossa, Frederick the Great, Bismarck and—then and even now, it must be said—Hitler. Viscerally less powerful, but more flattering to the German moral, intellectual and cultural self-image, and certainly more respectable to other nations, was the picture of Germany as "the land of poets and thinkers."

As far as I have been able to determine, Dominik was not politically active. Nor apparently did he become even a nominal party member during the National Socialist period. When Hitler came to power, Dominik was over sixty years old and a semi-invalid; he also owed no small loyalty to his publisher Alfred Hugenberg, leader of the rival but decidedly conservative and nationalistic *Deutschnationale Volkspartei.* Even so, as I suggested in the preceding chapter, many of the ideas expressed in Dominik's autobiography and novels are consonant with the tenets and goals of National Socialism. Certainly the regime felt it had sufficient reason to continue reissuing his works in large editions, even in the later years of the war. It is intriguing, therefore, that Dominik's "future history" does not blatantly picture a *Führer.* Nor does his SF even strongly express the desire for such a leader—at least not overtly. The new Germany is apparently a descendant of the Weimar Republic; in *Stern,* for example, it bears the name "Deutsche Republik" and is governed by a system of ministers and, presumably, parliament, which Dominik does not describe at any length but seems to regard with favor.

Such features, however, would not necessarily have made his novels ideologicaly suspect to the National Socialists or useless for their purposes. The vision of future German history in Dominik's SF adds an air of respectability to German resurgence by presenting it

as a legitimate, natural and organic historical development, just as
the Nazi regime sought to establish itself at home and abroad as the
rightful successor and natural fulfilment of the past, as well as the
expression of the free determination of the German people. It might
be noted also that tyranny lies in the eye of the beholder. For
Dominik, dictators are figures like Cyrus Stonard in *Macht* and
Salvator Augustus in *Atlantis*, or Woodrow Wilson and Franklin D.
Roosevelt in the real world.[7] Unlike usurpers of power in decadent
democracies or despots ruling backward societies, a strong leader in
a resurgent Germany would be, for Dominik, merely the natural
personification, formulator and executor of the enlightened
collective will of the people. The end of *Macht*, accordingly, looks
forward to a time still grander than the fictional "present," when
there will come "one... who with pure heart and hands will reach
for power" (359). While passages of such explicitness are rare in
Dominik's SF, the *Führerprinzip* is by no means absent. It is
evident, above all, in the nature of his heroes and in their
relationship to the lesser characters and the entire societies they
lead.

The ideological aspects of Dominik's SF can be analyzed not
only with regard to those who directly influenced its attitudes and
controlled its publication, but also with reference to those who, in
great numbers, chose it as their reading material. For the typical
contemporary reader the future worlds of Dominik's novels
satisfied, in an indirect and vicarious but powerful way, certain
political, aesthetic, even moral desires. The Germany of the future
has regained all the qualities which he and his readers valued in
their own image of the ideal Germany, such as diligence, loyalty and
scientific talent. It has also surmounted the immediate political
obstacles which he and many other Germans considered to be major
problems of their own time. Dominik also pictured the yet more
distant future which lies even beyond the time he described in his
novels with a still greater degree of optimism and expectation
similar to that with which in his autobiography he looked forward to
the end of World War II and the coming "Age of Energy" (*VSS*, 292)

But Dominik seldom emphasizes the military might of
Germany as a single power in the future. Nor does he portray the
imaginary world as an absolutely ideal environment, a finished
society. Social utopias or future-war stories would indeed have
provided him and his readers no little immediate gratification, but
the euphoria would have been followed by depression occasioned by
renewed contemplation of the actual present situation. Dominik

aims instead at a subtler and more enduring sense of satisfaction. By contrasting his own culture to the materialistic, militaristic, morally weak, and imperialistic countries of the future, above all the United States, he evokes and invokes the image of a Germany which in its inner strength and international probity is far nobler than the self-righteous powers that—in but the most recent of their perfidies—joined forces to defeat Wilhelmine Germany and impose the Treaty of Versailles.

The image of a confident, stable but not all-powerful or totally utopian Germany caters to the desire for ideological wishfulfilment. It also serves purely "literary" purposes, above all the maintenance of plot-tension—a matter not to be ignored in popular fiction especially. Dominik's vision of "future history" leaves room for entertainment, in the form of exciting and inspiring descriptions of the way in which individual Germans are still able to contribute significantly to the further improvement of their homeland and its international status. There are still battles to be won, scientific and technological ideas to be developed, and opportunities for the demonstration of personal excellence. Nobility indeed triumphs in Dominik's future worlds, but only after a struggle which makes victory not only sweeter but also more plausible.

Science and Technology

Dominik's novels would scarcely differ from the multitude of ideologically conservative popular novels of the same period were it not for the pre-eminent role he accords imaginary science and technology. Science is the focus of the most important of the three realms of narration described earlier, and the mastery of science and technology—and only that—distinguishes the heroes of Dominik's SF from the traditional heroes of romance, melodrama and adventure fiction encountered elsewhere in German popular literature. The fact, finally, that the novels deal with *imaginary* science virtually dictates that the setting of the narration be the future, rather than the past or present, as it is in other fiction.

Indeed, it is only with respect to the scientific realm that any significant variation is to be found among Dominik's novels. Here one can discern three relatively distinct plot variations, which effect in turn modest but characteristic alterations in the overall narrative structure. The round-the-world jet-plane race in *Wettflug der Nationen* (1933) exemplifies a primitive and very episodic type of plot structure that consists of competition among several adversaries seeking to achieve some spectacular technological goal.

At the center of attention are the deeds of the uncomplicated, extroverted hero Hein Eggerth; almost equally prominent is the description of the wondrous technological gadgetry he wields. Romance and personal or political intrigue are of relatively minor importance in *Wettflug*. So too are even the theoretical background of the revolutionary stratospheric airplanes and the examination of the creative scientific personality, represented by the lesser figure of Hein's father, Professor Eggerth. In *Wettflug* the super-plane has in fact already been invented when the novel begins, and most of the narrative tension is derived not from political events of world-wide import, from the machinations of the villain, or from the description of a scientific discovery, but rather from the race itself and the conquest of physical obstacles it involves. Dominik, with his competent command of the devices of popular literature, intensifies the excitement with a poorly-motivated but, for his readers, apparently effective complication. For most of the novel the Eggerths' marvelous "St" planes, which enter the race intentionally late or disguised as more conventional aircraft, fly at reduced speeds and make frequent detours to help less proficient competitors. Only toward the end of the novel do they reveal their true power to a breathless world.

Treibstoff SR (1940) exhibits a similar if not quite so primitive theme and sequence of events, namely the race into space. Dominik describes, if somewhat sketchily, the theoretical and experimental development of spaceflight technology, some—but by no means all—of which was then still highly speculative. The basic research is considered to be almost as heroic as the "actual" flight into space and the protection of the rocket-engine design from the Japanese secret agents, which comprises the rest of the plot. It is tempting to think that *Treibstoff*, published in 1940, constitutes an improvement in structural and thematic sophistication over the earlier *Wettflug* (1933). But the second "Eggerth" novel, *Ein Stern fiel vom Himmel* (1934), written only a year after *Wettflug*, concentrates even more than the later *Treibstoff* on theoretical science and the personalities of the experimental scientists, as do many of the other novels of the Thirties or even such early works as *Atlantis* (1925). Close study of the theme of spaceflight competition in *Erbe* (1928) and *Treibstoff* also reveals a lack of development, or even a regression, in conceptual and structural abilities (see below). *Erbe* deals with flight to Venus, not merely into space near Earth; it is more impressive than *Treibstoff* not only in its spatial dimensions and audacity of scientific imagination, but also in the author's treatment of plot and character. It would appear, then, that the quality of a given novel depends less on Dominik's innate skills as a literary stylist than on felicitous selection of scientific content and theme.

Considerably more sophisticated in narrative structure and treatment of science than the "competition" novels are several works which recount the story of scientific or technological discoveries and examime some of their wider consequences. In *König Laurins Mantel* (1928), *Befehl aus dem Dunkel* (1933), *Atomgewicht 500* (1935), *Himmelskraft* (1937), and even *Macht* (1922), superiority in science and technology is not merely a source and symbol of national glory as demonstrated by victory in heroic competition. Instead, science and technology are viewed—by the author and by the characters themselves—as vital contributions to economic, political, and sometimes military advancement. The center of attention, therefore, is not the hero who performs stupendous though not immediately practical technological deeds, but rather the individual scientist, research team and society which produce the new science, put it to good use, and protect it from those who whould misuse it—a matter extremely important to Dominik. Social questions, villainous intrigue and international politics thus have a larger function here than in the competition novels.

The "competition" and "discovery" plots each have their advantages and disadvantages. Certainly the "competition" plot attempts less. It merely tells the story of an exciting technological event; most of its effect is derived from the description of fantastic technology and the portrayal of the spectacular figure of the hero, whose personality is based almost entirely on scientific brilliance or mastery of technology. Nevertheless such characters and their deeds would likely have been not only exciting but probably also quite plausible to the contemporary reader, who was familiar with actual but nearly legendary exemplars of technological genius and persistence like Edison and Lindbergh. The "competition" novels make a simple point, but they make it with a certain effective bluntness.

The "discovery" novels, by contrast, attempt to afford a broader perspective on science and a deeper look into the methods and personality of the scientist or inventor. Often, however, the narration becomes mired in ideological polemic or the complications of the villain's machinations and the sentimentalities of the love-plot. Besides performing great feats with technology, the hero is made to play a major role in public events and in a love story as well;

he saves not only his beloved, but also his country. To the reflective reader, at least, it may seem quite improbable that one person should be so diverse and prolific, and that so much—perhaps even the fate of the world—depends on one who was heretofore occupied with quiet scientific pursuits. Maturer SF often chooses protagonists or at least narrators of far more prosaic stature. Such figures can add much to the reader's sense of plausibility, and they advance the idea that imaginary science and technology can be exciting enough in themselves without the spectacle of a larger-than-life hero or the distraction of an unmotivated love-plot. Nevertheless, the prominent location of the heroic scientist or technologist at the center of action in all three realms, private and public as well as scientific, expresses quite succinctly the importance of science and technology.

Most ambitious in scope is the third variety of scientific plot, which is concerned with cataclysms affecting large parts of the Earth or even the entire globe. The type is exemplified by *Spur* (1923), *Atlantis* (1925) and *Land* (1939); cataclysmic events are also of considerable importance in the spaceflight competition novel *Erbe*. The cataclysm—an earthquake, a change in climate, or the precipitous emergence of new land masses—may be caused either by Nature alone or by human technology, but science always figures prominently in its genesis, explanation and containment. Much other SF, both primitive and mature, describes the collapse of civilizations, the destruction of entire planets, or even the end of the Universe. By comparison, the scope of Dominik's cataclysmic novels is limited. Only our own planet, or perhaps just a part of it, is affected, and the cataclysm is never an utter catastrophe, for neither Dominik nor his readers could countenance a truly unhappy ending. The relatively modest scope of the cataclysm saves Dominik's novels from the gross implausibility of some "space operas." On the other hand, he is never able to attain the dramatic and pictorial effects achieved in such classic works of grand-scale cataclysmic SF as *When the Worlds Collide* (1933) by Edwin Balmer and Philip Wylie, *Last and First Men* (1930) and *Starmaker* (1937) by Olaf Stapledon, or the epic collection *Cities in Flight* (1950ff.; 1969) by James Blish.

Dominik manages the "cataclysmic" plot just as well or poorly as he handles the simpler "competition" and "discovery" patterns. The broader scope of the cataclysmic plot, while it maintains the immediate excitement of the "competition" or "discovery" plots, does enable him to establish a greater degree of unity between the scientific theme and the private and public realms of action. Thus the imaginary world and its events are more plausible. The hero, rather than instigating happenings of global importance, merely participates in them, though his role is not inconsequential. Events in high government circles, the workings of science, and acts of individual excellence are all believable parts of the portrayal of widespread cataclysm. Therefore one does not feel so much that technology is merely the vehicle for an exciting plot, or that the public realm exists merely to entertain the reader with glimpses into the workings of commerce, goverment and history.

Dominik's treatment of cataclysm also reveals much about his attitude toward science, nature, and Man's place in nature. In many of the "cataclysmic" novels the cataclysm is initiated by human beings who use science and technology in ignorance or defiance of nature's laws and human moral principles. In *Atlantis*, for example, the American capitalist Guy Rouse commences on a venture to blast a second Central American Canal with atomic explosives—a project still being seriously proposed until a few years ago. The explosion triggers a displacement of land masses in the Isthmus, which diverts the Gulf Stream, threatens the climate and civilization of Northern Europe, and raises Atlantis as well. In *Land* a project to release geothermal energy leads unexpectedly to tremendous volcanic activity and the creation of new land. Dominik's formulation of the cataclysmic events is clearly motivated in part by narrower ideological considerations, either the desire to condemn American capitalism or the wish to give vivid expression to the notion of *Lebensraum*. But the statement of immediate political themes is only one facet of a still larger idea which has both intellectual and moral implications. The cataclysm brought about by technology must also be contained and combatted by technology. Man must act to correct his errors, and science can be used to help solve the problems Man creates with science.

Equally important, however, is the Earth's eventual but inevitable reassertion of its own equilibrium to overcome the disturbance wrought by human technology. The process, and the state of equilibrium itself, are viewed as manifestly and inherently good. Dominik's attitude very much resembles that of most other writers of SF and, I think, most scientists as well. Nature is orderly and, at the very least, not malevolent. Knowledge, in general, is good, although Dominik occasionally invokes the warning, encountered in so many fictional portrayals of scientists, from *Faust* to the worst SF movies, that "there are some things Man is not meant to know." Technology itself is ethically neutral; Man's own moral constitution and intents govern the effects of his use of science. Such, anyway, are Dominik's considered judgments. He is not a consistent or profound thinker, and, like many scientists and writers of SF, he often lapses into attitudes which reflect a much more positivistic stance, even a strong tendency to glorify and mystify science and technology.

Cataclysm is also the vehicle for still broader ideological or philosophical statement in Dominik's SF, as it is in much other literature, for science is not only a discipline which seeks to analyze nature objectively; it can also be used as a metaphor for the expression of value judgments about human life and social institutions, as Dominik remarked in his autobiography (*VSS*, 277; see above, pp. 191-2). Equilibrium is, supposedly, a neutral concept of physics that is employed to describe a state and process of observed and measured in nature. But in Dominik's SF, and certainly elsewhere also, equilibrium is viewed not only as an ideal state in nature, but also as a morally, ideologically and even aesthetically desirable condition in human affairs as well. In *Atlantis*, for example, Johannes Harte uses his long-distance energy concentrator to repair the damage caused by Rouse's atomic explosion in the Isthmus. Dominik expresses the equivalence of natural and human realms by employing an anthropomorphic image; it should be observed that the thoughts of Harte and the statements of the narrator are virtually indistinguishable from each other:

> Once more yet! murmured [Harte's] lips.... Until the wound is sealed, the earth's body healed. Order in the world [Weltordnung]... [Dominik's ellipsis]...
> The canal-bed, there it lay again,... unhindered path for the world-economy. The wounds of the earth, struck by criminal hand, healed. (*Atlantis*, 266, 286-87)

The metaphorical expansion of geological concepts and the notion of equilibrium encourages still more general conjectures about Dominik's relation to literary tradition and about his view of his own ideological affinities. Considering the myriad connotations of the word "nature," it is scarcely surprising that the concepts of science have been used as metaphors in moral and ideological statements, or that, conversely, science is constantly plagued—or enriched—by the injection of value judgments. In any case, as is shown by, among many other examples, the Vulcanist-Neptunist controversy of the eighteenth and nineteenth centuries, the association and confusion of scientific, ideological and ethical concepts is not original to Dominik; nor, on a more specific level, is his treatment of the concept of geological evolution, whether or not he was much aware of the literary tradition of which he was a part. His resolute rejection of geological and thus, by implication, social cataclysm suggests that he regarded himself as a conservative or even perhaps a gradualist, although in our view he was an ideological reactionary with distinct fascistic sympathies. The discrepancy is revealing, for fascism, despite its appeal to conservatives and reactionaries, promised a new world-order which, it was often stated, would come about through revolution. The broad emotional appeal of that idea in Germany during Dominik's time need scarcely be mentioned. It should be noted, correspondingly, that in his SF Dominik does not absolutely reject even the very mention of cataclysm; on the contrary, he gives both natural and social cataclysm prominent place, and beneath or beside the expression of abhorrence is a certain fascination with it.

Like most writers of SF, Dominik favored certain areas of science and technology as sources of content for his fictions. Chief among his interests were the geosciences, physics and chemistry, and flight. Sometimes, as in those novels which, like *Spur* and *Atlantis*, are panoramic in theme and setting, the focus of interest includes several fields. But usually a single scientific or technological theme predominates in each novel, as the titles themselves—for example, *Land aus Feuer und Wasser, Atomgewicht 500,* or *Wettflug der Nationen*—often indicate. Often, too, there is a distinct and, it would seem, natural correspondence between the various kinds of scientific content and the types of scientific plot structure discussed immediately above. Thus the two novels in which flight is most important, *Wettflug* and *Treibstoff,* are essentially "competition" novels; physics and chemistry are the major subjects of many of the "discovery" stories, such as *Atomgewicht.* Even more obvious is the focus on the geosciences in the "cataclysm" narratives. The correspondence is not exact or inevitable, in Dominik's novels or in other SF. But the recurrent association of a certain kind of science and technology with each of the three variant types of plot structure demonstrates that scientific content can have a considerable effect on narrative form in SF.

Dominik's selection and treatment of scientific and technological content is not merely a matter of sober, "scientific" objectivity. Most of the ideas explored in his SF can be traced directly to his professional training, early employment, and personal interests in mechanical or electrical engineering and aeronautics. Similarly, each theory or device has something to do with areas of science and technology which, in the first several decades of the twentieth century, were subjects of greatest interest among the general public, and often in professional circles as well. Often Dominik had received his early training or was active as a technical journalist in the same fields. Far more difficult to weigh is a third factor: the aesthetic and mythical implications of science and technology. For Dominik—and not for him alone, of course— each area of science and technology, besides constituting a realm of objective inquiry and knowledge, was also imbued with mythical connotations or might find expression in certain archetypal situations. Some of these associations Dominik had absorbed from popular culture, some from his formal education, and some from literature, including earlier SF. Through his description of science, his creation of character and plot, and sometimes his very choice of individual words, he sought to envelop science and technology with a mythical aura. Not unrelated to the element of myth in Dominik's world-view and fiction is, lastly, the ideological aspect of science. He writes about *German* scientists and *German* science, with constant reference to what he considers to be their innately and specifically "German" nature.

These observations suggest two tentative conclusions. Dominik did not attempt to explore a wide range of scientific and technological ideas or, much less, the nature of science itself. Nor did he search out the more recondite and speculative areas of theoretical and applied science. Instead he wrote about the science and technology which were most accessible, interesting, and believable to him and his public, and which possessed the added virtue of being spectacular. The tendency shows Dominik's kinship with Jules Verne, but it is by no means characteristic of all SF. Whatever motivated his selection of scientific and technological raw material, Dominik did not fail to transform it, adding or emphasizing various kinds of personal, figurative, or even—loosely speaking— symbolical significance. Many of these meanings, admittedly, may be offensive to the present-day reader, or perhaps just improbable, alien, or even obscure. But both the limited range of Dominik's imagination and the ideas he associated with science and technology must be considered when one examines his SF novels as an expression of his own attitudes, as a communication addressed to his readers, and as examples of SF.

(i) Geosciences

The geosciences furnished Dominik with several important

scientific motifs and plot elements, above all the theme of geological cataclysm, whether natural or caused by man. Terrestrial or cosmic cataclysms palpably affect Man's very existence and sometimes even that of his world. Such events, or simply the prospect of their occurrence, have a profound conceptual and emotional impact which has found frequent expression in philosophy, religion and myth, as well as in literature. Dominik assiduously invests cataclysmic events and the figures involved in them with grandiose mythical characteristics. The classical myths are expressed, for example, in the very title of *Atlantis*,[8] and the Biblical tradition of Eden and the Promised Land is echoed in those novels, such as *Erbe*, where new land is explored and colonized. Dominik also alludes to the mythological and heroic Germanic past in his portrayals of cataclysm; thus refugees leaving Northern Europe as Rouse's canal venture begins to make its climate inhospitable are described as "a new migration of peoples [eine neue Völkerwanderung]" and as a new wave of Vikings (*Atlantis*, 183, 316).

Although the geosciences were not a major part of Dominik's formal education or his professional activity as a technician, he had many opportunities to appreciate their significance and several cogent reasons, not all of them strictly scientific, to incorporate them into his SF. By the last few decades of the nineteenth century the geosciences and the attendant applied disciplines, whose essential growth as systematic pursuits began only in the late eighteenth century, had reached an impressive and fertile level of achievement and further promise. Everyone, from factory worker to intellectual, knew that the present was an age of coal, oil and—increasingly—gasoline power. Concrete symbols of the age were the railroad, the automobile, and, as Henry Adams remarked in his autobiography (1906), the dynamo. The geosciences and related areas of technology had played a key role in such developments, and in Germany their importance was understood perhaps especially clearly. The mining and processing of coal, iron ore and potash had become major industries in Germany and vital factors in German political and military power, as the Austro-Prussian, Franco-Prussian, and First World Wars made evident. The public eye had been caught by a number of spectacular feats of civil engineering, like the Suez and Panama Canals or, closer to home, the subway and the Spree River tunnel in Berlin. Then as now there was also much sensational talk of a Channel Tunnel. Even the more theoretical or academic of the geosciences, such as paleontology and seismology, had inspired, among both scientists and the lay public, spectacular and at times controversial speculations about the structure, age and creation of the world and about Man's place in its history.

Dominik's journalistic pursuits and his relations with his publisher would have amplified any innate interest he might have taken in the geosciences and therefore would certainly have affected his treatment of geology and the related areas of industry and engineering in his SF. It is quite likely, for example, that the experiences he gathered during the early years of the century while covering the construction of the Berlin subway and the river tunnels for Scherl provided inspiration and background material for the descriptions of subterranean engineering projects in *Atlantis* and other "cataclysmic" novels (*VSS*, 140-43). Not to be discounted, however, is the literary influence of Verne's works, for example *Voyage au centre de la terre*, of the best-selling novel *Der Tunnel* (1913) by Bernhard Kellermann, or possibly even of Lasswitz' *Bilder aus der Zukunft*. Of similar importance were the technological interests and activities of Dominik's publisher Alfred Hugenberg. Accordingly, mining and refining figure prominently in *Land, Atlantis, Spur* and *Geheimnis*. In several of the "cataclysm" novels, and in *Erbe* as well, Dominik capitalizes on the more sensational aspects of geology to inflate the idea of German colonization of new land into fictional projects even more grandiose than those envisioned by expansionists like Hugenberg.

It is quite probable, however, that in its thematic repertoire Dominik's SF would have been much the same without Scherl and Hugenberg. Novels like *Land* and *Atlantis* provide an excellent opportunity to observe how ideology and scientific content interact with each other in SF and how that interaction is so complexly affected, even in Dominik's works, by the aesthetic presuppositions of SF. In imbuing the geosciences with ideological significance Dominik emulates—probably without much direct knowledge—far greater writers. Voltaire, for example, wrote a major philosophical poem in response to the catastrophic Lisbon earthquake of 1755, and Goethe, in his poem addressed to "The the United States [Den Vereinigten Staaten]," expressed a vision of the peaceful evolution of American society, which he correlated—quite erroneously—with the absence of volcanic rocks in America. But Dominik's use of the geosciences to convey ideological concepts reflects, far more strongly I think, the historical consciousness and concerns of the contemporary society. Among those ideas or images, as I remarked earlier, were the desire for new territory, the fear of encroachment from East and West, and even an overall sense of German history as a succession of unexpected catastrophes—emotions and attitudes countered by an equally strong yearning for synthesis, equilibrium and organic development.

The generic presuppositions and literary traditions of SF may also have encouraged Dominik to write about the geosciences and to invest them with ideological meanings. Exploration of new territory, on Earth or elsewhere, is a major theme of SF, and it virtually demands political treatment, usually utopian or dystopian. The contention that Dominik's selection of particular geological themes or patterns was influenced by the German political environment is strongly reinforced by the observation that Anglo-American SF writers portray geological cataclysm and the settlement of new land according to their own culture's predominant historical and ideological analogs. Cataclysmic threats to the climate, so obvious in Dominik's SF, are therefore of relatively lesser importance in Anglo-American SF. And the settlement of new land, in American SF at least, typically follows the popular myth of American westward expansion, which is seen not as the establishment of systematically planned, racially "pure" proprietary colonies or even commercial ventures in new territories, but rather as an organic, natural process involving the fusion of immigrants of many nationalities and the emergence of self-governing communities.

Another geoscientific motif in Dominik's SF illuminates particularly well his use of contemporary science and its relation to his German nationalism. *Das stählerne Geheimnis* (1934) is based on the theory of continental drift or, as it is now called, plate tectonics, first formulated by Alfred Wegener (1880-1930). Wegener proposed that the continents are masses or "plates" of lighter material floating on a molten foundation of heavier matter. As the present coastal outlines of the Americas, Europe and Africa have long hinted, the continents were at one time joined into one or a few "supercontinents." The hero of *Das stählerne Geheimnis* is another Dr. Wegener, a geoscientist who profitably employs his namesake's theories and thus vindicates them; the Wegener theory is also mentioned in *Atlantis* and *Land*. During Alfred Wegener's own lifetime his theories, widely publicized and popularized in such writings as *Die Entstehung der Kontinente* [*The Origin of the Continents*] (1915, 4th ed. 1929), were rejected almost universally by geoscientists, particularly outside Germany. The repudiation was based on scientific grounds then quite cogent and reasonable. But Dominik may have found the theory of continental drift attractive for at least two reasons. Wegener's theory gave new life to notions of ancient continents like Atlantis or Mu, ideas which have long held a particular fascination for followers of the occult, including some writers of SF or pseudo-SF; similar notions were entertained by National Socialist geoscientists. Moreover, for Dominik the figure of someone like his contemporary Wegener, whom he describes not merely as a scientist but instead specifically as "the German scholar Wegner [*sic*]" (*Atlantis*, 39), would illustrate especially well how a particularly "German" idea or science is rejected by the rest of the world but triumphs in the end. That Alfred Wegener himself died on an expedition to Greenland probably increased his appeal to Dominik, who sought to portray scientists and technologists as heroic figures. Undoubtedly Dominik would be pleased to know that the theory of continental drift, albeit with considerable modernization, has finally gained a wide and rather spectacular acceptance in recent years. But it would be incorrect, I think, to attribute his partiality toward Wegener and his ideas to any genuine scientific acumen.[9]

(ii) Physics, Chemistry and Engineering

At least as important as the geosciences in Dominik's SF are chemistry, physics, and the related areas of engineering. They are the chief subject of *Atomgewicht 500, König Laurins Mantel, Himmelskraft, Lebenstrahlen, Stern* and *Macht*. In many novels, such as *Erbe* or even the "cataclysmic" *Atlantis*, their role is subordinate but far from insignificant.

Dominik clearly viewed the physical sciences in a mythic way. In ancient cultural traditions there are indeed myths—the stories of Prometheus, Daedalus and Faust, for example—which can be interpreted as referring in some way to what we now call physics, chemistry and engineering, even if that was not originally their main import. But in comparison to the geosciences or to the idea of flight, which have their ready counterparts in ancient, universal fears and dreams, the physical sciences are relatively lacking in immediate emotional impact and mythical associations, in large part, I think, because of their traditionally abstract nature. Only recently, as it has become abundantly apparent that the physical sciences can furnish the means to greatly alter the condition of humanity, or even destroy it, have they, and the individual figures of the theoretical scientist and technologist as well, become of importance as subjects of art and nascent myth.

Dominik strives energetically to create the impression that the physical sciences are exciting and portentous, both by making them the essential factors in events of great significance, and by surrounding them with an aura of mystery, mysticism and legend. Sometimes he makes explicit use of actual myths, as in the figure of Weland Gorm in *Erbe*, whose very name alludes to the Germanic myth of Wieland or Weland the Smith. At the same time, however, Dominik seeks to show the reader that the marvels he describes are not miracles, but rather the products of rational science, and that science is a natural and plausible part of the everyday world. The result is a disconcerting, sometimes unintentionally amusing oscillation between the conventional bourgeois world and the realm of myth, between the scientist as a rational human being, essentially similar though notably superior to his fellow man, and the scientist as superman, a reincarnation of ancient heroes, possessor of arcane knowlege, monomanic seeker of truth, and, sometimes, tragic hero.

Other and more prosaic factors having to do with the status of the physical sciences in Dominik's time also influenced his treatment of the subject. The pattern of classification adopted here—the close association of physics and chemistry, and the relation of both to engineering—is not arbitrary, for it fits Dominik's way of thinking, and, to a certain extent still, even our own.[10] But that categorization, and with it widespread interest in physics and chemistry, are scarcely to be found except in recent times. It was only after the mid-nineteenth century that theoretical and practical work in the physical sciences became a truly vital focus of attention in scientific circles, and that their content, principles and methods came to exert a strong influence on other areas of intellectual inquiry, including political science, theology and aesthetics. The general consciousness did not remain unaffected by the practical consequences and even the conceptual implications of the physical sciences. Progress in physics and chemistry encouraged two ideas which are important here. Theory and practical application came to be viewed as intimately related pursuits, each making possible advances in the other; the close association of "R & D," now almost a truism, has by no means been a commonplace throughout history. Secondly, as physics and chemistry expanded their purview into both microcosm and macrocosm it became more and more apparent that the two disciplines were overlapping areas of a single larger realm of inquiry which dealt with matter and energy in all their various contexts. Our own age has maintained the same synthetic approach, and has even enlarged the borders of the physical sciences to incorporate many areas of biology and even some aspects of psychology.

The circumstances outlined here affected all the scientifically advanced countries, including Germany. Metallurgy and chemistry, particularly the development of synthetics, have been special glories of German science and technology since Friedrich Wöhler's synthesis of urea (1828), the foundation of systematic organic chemistry by Justus Liebig (1803-1873), and the growth of the mining and smelting industries during the nineteenth century. Not Marconi, but rather Heinrich Rudolf Hertz (1857-1894), who discovered radio waves (1887-88), is celebrated in Germany as the inventor of the radio, just as Werner von Siemens (1816-1892) is given credit for the dynamo. In many quarters of German society, as I pointed out in the foregoing chapter, it was—and is—common to ascribe a goodly measure of Germany's economic, military and cultural prestige to excellence in the physical sciences, both theoretical and applied. Physicists, chemists and medical scientists like Robert Koch (1843-1910), Rudolf Virchow (1821-1902), and Hermann Helmholtz (1821-1894), as well as Hertz and Siemens, gained a certain status as culture heroes.

Dominik's treatment of the physical sciences reflects their status in the Western world and their particular role in Germany. The close relation between research and development is a basic presupposition of the novels which, whether it is tacitly assumed or described at some length, is never questioned. There are no theoretical discoveries which are not exploited technologically, and no technological device is created without much difficult—if sometimes only vaguely described—theoretical work. Dominik assumes and portrays a similarly intimate kinship between physics and chemistry. In *Atomgewicht*, for example, the theme of atomic power is developed with reference to both chemistry and electrical theory, and in novels like *Himmelskraft* and *Treibstoff* chemical or metallurgical invention is described not as a matter of the simple creation of new products by the fortuitous, intrepid combination of substances, but rather as a process in which knowledge of physics is essential.

Dominik's commodious concept of the physical sciences serves his literary purposes well. In envisioning spectacular technological devices, he places far more emphasis on the wondrous nature and **versatility of the inventions** than on the particular sciences on which they are founded. Frequently they can do many different things, some related to physics, some to chemistry, and some to electrical engineering. An example is the energy source in *Macht*. Another is to be found in *König Laurins Mantel*, where Dr. Arvelin devises a chemical which induces invisibility by altering the laws of optics, thus creating a modern scientific version of the mythical King Laurin's Cloak.

Dominik gives special attention to chemistry and metallurgy, as befits their prestige in his society. Wondrous substances are not unique to his novels, but most other SF is much less preoccupied with them. In *Erbe*, for example, metallurgy is described as an index of general technological progress; the inhabitants of the future sense that they "stand on the threshold between the Age of Steel and the coming Age of Light Metals" (194). Not the least part of the "legacy of the Uranids" is their super-light alloy, created from two atmospheric gases. Miracle metals were a pride of German science, and one of Dominik's major non-fiction works, *Vistra, das weisse Gold Deutschlands: Die Geschichte einer weltbewegenden Erfindung* [*Vistra, Germany's White Gold: The Story of an Invention That Shook the World*] (1936), describes the invention of an actual super-light alloy. His fictional physicists and chemists, like Dr. Wandel in *Atomgewicht* and Professor Raps in *Macht*, also conform to the predominant conception of such figures and the recognition of their contribution to Germany's political and cultural position. Particular emphasis is placed on the strong social consciousness of the scientist, the exploitation of basic scientific research to benefit industry, and the effect of technology on society and politics. To emphasize the distinctly German features of his German scientists, Dominik contrasts them to the unscrupulous Asians or to the over-individualistic, even avaricious American scientists and technologists.

Two aspects of Dominik's treatment of the physical sciences deserve further notice for what they suggest about the direction and scope of his imagination and even about his knowledge of science. Concepts and devices related to electrical engineering appear frequently in the novels, but almost always as elements in larger ideas or inventions having to do with other areas of science. Similarly, few of Dominik's major characters are explicitly identified as electrical engineers, and in fact most are geoscientists, physicists, chemists or flight technologists. The lack of emphasis is puzzling, of course, since Dominik was an electrical engineer and, it would seem, injected considerable personal wish-fulfilment into his heroic figures. But perhaps his very familiarity with electrical engineering encouraged him to view his own area of expertise more

Hans Dominik. From the author's preface to a reprint of his first novel, "Die Macht der Drei" (1922).

as an established discipline than as a new, wide-open pursuit suitable for adventurous imaginary fiction. Quite likely he would have been more aware of the difficulties involved in creating imaginary concepts and devices in his own field than in others.

By contrast, when dealing with physics and chemistry Dominik focuses his attention on the more orthodox areas of speculation, such as atomic power and the creation of new elements, both of them ideas already widely familiar at the time. Even so, his use of available information is not particularly impressive. Theoretical explanations and technological descriptions are often vague, and there seem to be certain inconsistencies, as in the conception of nuclear fission and the creation of super-heavy artificial elements in *Atomgewicht*, which would have raised objections even in Dominik's own time. He also studiously ignores the more esoteric— and for other writers of SF more challenging—speculative aspects of contemporary physical science, such as relativity and quantum physics. Only tentative explanations for these discrepancies can be proposed. The spectacular vision of atomic power and the transmutation of elements, in contrast to the abstractions of relativity and quantum physics, may have appealed more strongly to Dominik's mythic conception of science and to his preference for sensational effects. He may also have felt a certain aversion to the so-called "Jewish" or "decadent" physics of Einstein and Planck, and indeed to any physical concepts which, because they emphasized uncertainty and randomness, would have conflicted with a world-view based on absolute values, destiny and the power of the will. It is even possible, finally, that Dominik lacked sufficient knowledge of recent work in theoretical physics to explore the subject in his SF. These issues will be taken up again at the end of the present chapter.

(iii) Flight

Flight is of great importance in Dominik's SF. It is the main subject of four novels, *Erbe, Treibstoff, Stern* and *Wettflug*, and receives much attention in many of the others, such as *Land* and *Macht*. Since flight, along with the related subjects of astronomy and cosmology, is also a major theme of most SF, Dominik's treatment of the topic offers a favorable occasion to evaluate his skill and vision according to some of the genre's prime criteria.

The many mythical associations of flight and the appearance of the theme in literature before SF are familiar matters, and Dominik does not hesitate to capitalize on the mythical tradition. His aeronauts and astronauts have the aura and power of culture heroes, and he seeks to portray flight itself as a transfiguring, transcendental experience, an event which may powerfully affect the society as well as the individual. While Dominik was undoubtedly aware of some of the classic literary works about flight which were written during and after the Renaissance, or even in ancient times, the most important literary inspiration for his portrayal of flight seems to have been the Verne of *De la terre à la lune* (1865) and *Autour de la lune* (1870). Like Verne, Dominik sets his novels in the near future, concentrates on technological details rather than theory, and envisions flying machines as the creations of private individuals who amaze the world by revealing their inventions in some spectacular and often not immediately practical way.

Yet the chief impetus and source of raw material for the theme of flight in Dominik's SF is to be found not in literature but rather in the realm of contemporary technology and theoretical science. As a technician Dominik would naturally have paid heed to aeronautical developments, especially since he lived in the main technological center of Germany. His interest in flight can be observed as early as the first decade of the century, when he was involved in August Scherl's project to bring a Wright Brothers representative to Berlin to conduct the first demonstration of powered flight in Germany. He also wrote for journals of automobile technology and racing, an area which at the time shared with aeronautics many participants and technological issues. Dominik's training in mechanical and electrical engineering would have encouraged him to concentrate his attention on certain immediate problems in the practical technology of flight, such as fuel composition, structural materials and aircraft design. Not the least factor in his avid interest in flight would have been the international competition to attain superiority in aeronautics, for practical military purposes as well as national prestige. In view of Dominik's professional and political orientation, for him aeronautics was clearly a fit subject for the heroic portrayal of German technological excellence.

Serious SF depends heavily on the science of its own time, especially those areas of investigation and application, I would suggest, which are neither too established and mundane to be exciting and conceptually provocative, nor too wildly speculative or theoretical to be tangible and plausible. Dominik wrote his SF during a crucial period in the development of flight theory and technology. In the early years of the century the great promise of flight was becoming more and more apparent, but so too was the complexity of the research and engineering which would be needed to advance it beyond the stage of abstruse theoretical speculation or, on the other hand, basement workshops and daredevil pilots. It is understandable, then, that seldom in the early decades of the century did anyone except a few specialists, whose work was often discounted, make the distinction between atmospheric and space flight which has subsequently become almost a matter of course. In atmospheric flight the aircraft, which is always subject to Earth's gravity, flies by propeller or jet thrust against the air; wing lift is used to gain or maintain altitude. Oxygen for combustion and breathing comes from the atmosphere. In true space flight, as many SF authors take pains to explain, reaction alone provides the power, and the spacecraft is able to venture far beyond the terrestrial atmosphere and gravitational field. Therefore oxygen must be carried for both crew and engine, if the latter is powered by chemical combustion rather than some other source of propulsion.

The distinction outlined here was vital to the actual advancement of both true space flight and atmospheric flight, including jet-propelled air travel. It is also of great importance to SF. Space flight involves radically different, usually far more complex problems of theory and engineering, matters which the successful author of serious SF must be able to understand and convey. Similar obstacles—and likewise opportunities for artistic effect—are offered by the great differences in philosophical and psychological implications between atmospheric and space flight. The latter at least potentially introduces far greater physical dimensions than atmospheric flight, and thus effects a considerable alteration in visual and conceptual perspective. The immense distances traversed, the time involved in such journeys, even at great velocities, and the vast number of new worlds that can be visited by travel through space expand the spatial and temporal scope of thought and narration. At the same time the Earth, if it does not recede beyond visibility and memory, is seen as a single body, a small round sphere rather than a giant flat surface. The space traveler is also freed from the Earth's gravity. The experience, as several astronauts have described it recently, and as writers of SF had already conceived it vicariously for decades before, can bring about a revolutionary, sometimes even mystical alteration in one's understanding of the individual, society and even God. Part of the intent of SF is to explore such ideas.

The three "Eggerth" novels, *Wettflug* (1933), *Stern* (1934) and *Land* (1939), provide the most detailed picture of imaginary atmospheric flight in Dominik's SF. Professor Eggerth is the principal inventor of the "St" or "stratospheric" series of airplanes and the owner of the factory which develops and builds them. His son Hein is the chief test pilot and the hero of the novels. The experimental development of the "St" planes and their subsequent employment in exciting competitions and useful projects constitute the scientific theme of the individual novels. Together they also outline the imaginary "history" of stratospheric flight in a general and not always systematic or consistent sequence. The appeal of the novels as fiction depends on the intrinsic interest in the process of technological innovation, the adventurous deeds performed with the "St" planes, and the excitement at the new world which will be brought about by the introduction of the revolutionary new aircraft into general use.

Amazingly fast and maneuverable, Dominik's imaginary "St" planes, as their name indicates, can fly in the thin air of the stratosphere, but they are still atmospheric craft. In *Wettflug* they are still propeller planes, though powered by radically improved diesel motors (25ff.). From the time of *Stern*, which appeared a year later, the "St" machines are jet-propelled. Some are even equipped with auxiliary rotors which permit them to take off and land vertically. The "St" planes, then, travel at heights and speeds well beyond those attained by the tropospheric propeller-driven aircraft of the time. Most contemporary readers would have considered such airplanes to be impressively futuristic, although Dominik's descriptive skills and, even more, his powers of suggestion no doubt helped to promote the conviction that fantasy could well become fact. That, too, was the import of the rapid progress in aeronautics in the first few decades of its development.

Dominik's imaginary jet plane technology, although he does not discuss its sources in his autobiography or his fiction, is based on the speculation and technological experimentation in jet-powered flight being energetically conducted at the time, much of it in Germany. Research progressed rapidly in the early 1930s, although full-scale jet planes did not appear until more than a decade later. In 1928 a rocket-powered glider, financed and built by the Rhon-Rossiten Gesellschaft, a glider club, was flown by one Frederich Stamer in the Rhon Mountains. A year later Fritz Opel, the automobile manufacturer and racer, financed and flew a similar glider; Opel had also supported attempts to attach rockets to ground vehicles. Such projects were more impressive as spectacles than as real technological achievements, for, as G. Edward Pendray explains, the exhaust speed of rocket motors was too fast for winged flight. But, as he also remarks, these craft "were at least the spiritual ancestors of the British, American and German propellerless aircraft which began to appear in 1943," among them the famous late Messerschmidts.[11] The participation of Opel provides an important indication that industry, which only decades later and with much trepidation began to treat space flight seriously, might consider that such futuristic ideas as jet flight were already at least worthy of investigation and that they might also have practical applications in the near future.

The next stage in jet-airplane technology, and indeed a crucial one, was the evolution of a true jet-exhaust engine through systematic research and development, the customary procedure of modern industrial technology. Actually, the general idea of the jet engine had been proposed as early as 1908, and was elaborated further in 1920 and 1927. The next major period of development commenced in the early 1930s, when the German engineers Paul Schmidt and Wilhelm Golden described versions of an "intermittent duct engine;" a rocket engine of just that kind was later used to power the V-1 or "buzz bomb." In 1935 Bernard Smith, an American, proposed a continuous jet exhaust engine, a far better approach to jet propulsion. Early theorists also discussed turbine engines. From the time Dominik began to write SF, therefore, a good deal of information about the basic principles and problems of jet-engine design was available. It was also clear that the overall design of a jet aircraft involved three other important areas of innovation: the creation of structural materials capable of withstanding high-temperature combustion, the development of a suitable fuel, and the actual connection of a jet engine to an aircraft body suitable for high velocities and altitudes. The first successful, if still primitive solution to such problems occurred only toward the end of World War II.

It is these aspects of aircraft development which Dominik sought to explore in his novels about imaginary stratospheric flight, especially jet-powered. His efforts to transform into fiction the raw scientific material available to him can be considered successful as popular literature but mediocre according to the standards and intentionality of SF. His approach is characterized, in most general terms, by a concentration on the stage of final experimentation and pioneering use of the new aeronautical technology, and by a tendency to substitute descriptions of exciting action or conventional industrial processes for precise exposition of imaginary science and technology. Certainly that orientation offered more opportunities for suspenseful plots and for the evocation of a sense of wonder about science—or so it apparently seemed to Dominik. Other writers, however, have attained great success in creating captivating portrayals of primary theoretical work, and Dominik attempted to do that in some of his novels about the physical sciences, such as *Atomgewicht*.

The emphasis on action-filled portrayal of experimental but nearly finished imaginary technology, however, also made it unnecessary for Dominik to discuss the vital initial stages in the development of jet flight, about which he possessed as little hard knowledge as most, yet far less than some. The problem is endemic in SF, of course. Where technological information of some kind was virtually indispensable, highly advantageous, or easily adduced, Dominik sought to supply it. Usually he focused on the large-scale aspects of mechanical engineering. There are, for example, passable descriptions of movable aircraft wings and diesel airplane engines (*Wettflug*, 58, 25). Frequently, however, Dominik considers it sufficient simply to introduce single, actually rather imprecise words or phrases, such as "shining light alloy [glánzende(s) Leichtmetall]" (*Land*, 10), without providing further details. Elsewhere he merely describes prosaic features of aircraft design which could have been envisioned with no special powers of imagination. Dominik's description of fuselage pressurization pumps shows the avoidance of radically imaginary elements and the corresponding concentration on the conventional aspects of engineering:

> They...knew that a stratospheric ship must have an airtight and pressure-resistant fuselage into which, by means of pumping mechanisms, so much of the thin air outside is constantly injected and compressed that the normal pressure of one atmosphere prevails in the internal part of the ship. But it was a long way from the rough knowledge of this general principle to the solution of the task in construction, and here they had before their eyes the excellent solution that the Eggerth Works had found for the problem. With astonishment they observed how the motors of the installation were connected to the wall structure in a quite unique way. One part of it, more particularly the cylinder, was located outside the fuselage, while the crank-housings lay internally. (*Wettflug*, 187)

At least as often as attempting to furnish definite information about imaginary science, however, Dominik trained his and the reader's attention on the people and events associated with it, which were far easier to conceive and describe. Even more objectionable to the critical reader is the substitution of unmotivated, irrelevant plot intrigue for action truly based on imaginary science and technology; such elements are to be found in particular abundance in *Stern*.

Given the foregoing reservations, Dominik's description of the general treatment of imaginary stratospheric flight can be adjudged passable, for its own time especially, and certainly it succeeded with the mass readership. He was, after all, a trained engineer and a professional science writer, had long been an interested observer of aeronautics, and possessed an adequate command of the skills of *Trivialliteratur*. Numerous episodes set at the Eggerth works near Bitterfeld and at Bay City, Michigan, illustrate the complexity of the industrial system required for the development of stratospheric flight and show the heroic individual efforts and villainous intrigues involved in its invention and protection (e.g., *Wettflug*, 24ff., 55ff.). The process of experimentation and refinement in both laboratory and field is treated with a certain realism and made exciting as fiction (e.g., *Wettflug*, 30ff.). Dominik also pays some attention to the effect of rapid flight on psychological sensibility and world-view. Especially in *Wettflug* he emphasizes the shrinking of distance brought about by rapid travel and at least notes the psychological impact of covering immense expanses at speeds so rapid as to be almost instantaneous.[12]

Other contemporary SF writers, however, dealt with such topics in a considerably more sophisticated manner. That Dominik failed to anticipate the phenomenon of "jet lag" is of relatively little importance; the "space-sickness" foreseen by so many Anglo-American SF writers proved to be inconsequential—a similar and equally understandable error of science-fictional imagination. There are, however, also a few seeming anachronisms or incongruities in Dominik's SF, elements which would appear inconsistent with other aspects of stratospheric flight as it was envisioned by readily available, authoritative contemporary sources, or even as Dominik himself conceived it. One such incongruity, which I will discuss later with regard to space flight, is the use of nautical concepts and jargon where they may not be suitable. The hybrid jet aircraft in *Land* and *Stern*, which combine features of helicopters and jet-propelled airplanes, also seem improbable when judged against scientifically more cautious speculations. But writers of SF must be granted a goodly amount of freedom in their imaginary science; the ultimate criterion is their ability to make it plausible. The most serious flaw in Dominik's treatment of imaginary stratospheric flight, I think, is not to be found in any glaring errors in theoretical or applied science, but rather in the paucity of precise, apt descriptions of truly imaginary science and technology.

Dominik's two novels about space flight, *Das Erbe der Uraniden* (1928) and *Treibstoff SR* (1940), must be treated separately from those about jet-propelled stratospheric flight. That part of the scientific and literary community, in Germany as well as abroad, which was involved in rocket research and in speculation about space flight would have considered his preoccupation with jet flight an indication of a rather tame imagination, and would have discounted his treatment of space flight as second-rate. The rocket experimenters of the time were few in number compared to the scientists and technologists active in the more practical areas of research and development in atmospheric flight. But by the Twenties they had performed much vital research and had gained a measure of attention, if not always credibility, among the general public and in the scientific community. Their ideas had also found expression in the work of several contemporary German writers of SF and were to be of even greater importance to Anglo-American SF a few years later.

The modern history of serious space-flight speculation and experimentation begins around the turn of the century with the work of Konstantin Tsiolkovsky (1857-1935), which was for many years little known even in Russia.[13] In America Robert H. Goddard (1882-1945), professor of physics at Clark University in Massachusetts, began experimenting with liquid-fuel and multi-stage rockets as early as 1909, although he published his work only some years later. During the Twenties Germany took the lead in rocket research and held it until the end of World War II. The early German rocket researchers were led by Hermann Oberth (1894-1976), later professor of physics at Vienna and Dresden. They constituted a fairly cohesive community which consisted of several organizations whose membership, serious and casual, reached perhaps a thousand at its height in the early Thirties. By far the most important group was the *Verein für Raumschiffahrt* (1927-1933/34, subsequently "*VfR*"), which was founded in 1927 in Breslau, Kurd Lasswitz' home city, but soon moved to Berlin. The *VfR* conducted its research in the suburb of Reinickendorf at the so-called "Raketenflugplatz" ("rocket-drome"), an abandoned munitions dump. There were rocket societies elsewhere on the Continent and in several other countries. Particularly important, especially after 1945, were the British Interplanetary Society and the American Interplanetary Society, later the American Rocket Society. But in Dominik's time the German experimenters were the acknowledged leaders, and the "Raketenflugplatz" in Berlin was the destination of a number of pilgrimages undertaken by enthusiasts from abroad.

In early 1934 the *VfR* was absorbed into the Nazi military organization, perhaps more because of Goering's interest in things aeronautical than because of any great scientific prescience in the Party. Some of the researchers left Germany, while others became avowed National Socialists. Oberth and Wernher von Braun continued their work at Peenemünde on the Baltic Coast, within the confines of the military program which produced the V-1 and V-2; both, however, seem to have remained ideologically disinterested. The Nazi takeover ended civilian, openly-publicized rocket research in Germany; it also terminated the lively international exchange of information and the visits between Germany, America and Great Britain.

The German rocket experimenters were by no means a collection of eccentric dreamers and basement hobbyists. While a lack of funds and the primitive state of rocket science limited their actual achievements, their small-scale experiments with engine design, fuel composition and guidance systems were pioneering efforts that had great impact later. The rocket experimenters also promoted speculation about rocketry and space flight in their publications, both scholarly and semi-popular. From 1927 to 1929 the *VfR* published its official journal, *Die Rakete.* The most famous document of space flight research was a detailed but excitingly speculative treatise by Hermann Oberth. The book achieved its greatest popularity and scientific influence in an edition published in 1929 under the title *Wege zur Raumschiffahrt [Paths to Space Travel]*, but an earlier and much smaller version had already appeared in 1923 as *Die Rakete zu den Planetenräumen [The Rocket to Planetary Space]*. Several other important books on rocketry and space travel were published in Germany during the Twenties and early Thirties: *Der Vorstoss in den Weltenraum [The Leap into Space]* (1924, 6th ed. 1930 as *Die Rakentenfahrt (Rocket Travel])* by Max Valier (1895-1930), who was killed in an experiment with rocket propulsion; *Die Erreichbarkeit der Himmelskörper [The Attainability of the Celestial Bodies]* (1925), a study of space navigation and flight trajectories by the mathematician Walter Hohmann (1880-1945); and a number of scholarly and semi-popular studies, such as *Die Fahrt ins Weltall [Travel into the Cosmos]* (1926) and *Die Möglichkeit der Weltraumfahrt [The Possibility of Space Travel]* (1928) either written or edited by Willy Ley (1906-1969). Such works gained a certain notoriety in Germany, and it can be shown that certain authors of Anglo-American SF were familiar with them. The German rocket researchers also received valuable public exposure through Fritz Lang's film *Die Frau im Mond [The Woman in the Moon]* (1929), based on the novel of the same title by

Lang's wife, Thea von Harbou, who also played the female lead in the film. Oberth was hired as a technical consultant for the film and was also given funds to construct a real, full-scale rocket as a publicity gimmick; the rocket project, of course, never advanced beyond the preliminary stages. The 1929 edition of *Wege zur Raumschiffahrt* is dedicated "in thankfulness" to Thea von Harbou.

Almost from the start German rocket research was associated with SF, and indeed many of the experimenters were inspired by *Auf zwei Planeten*, as both Ley and von Braun attest.[14] Since rocket research in Germany, as elsewhere, was a small-scale, privately funded, often ridiculed enterprise, the researchers had to maintain morale among themselves. They knew also that they had to "sell" their idea, as a theoretical possibility and as a worthwhile practical project, to an incredulous and even scornful audience which, including some scientists, was quite unfamiliar with astrophysics and the principles of rocketry. The rocket experimenters, therefore, were favorably disposed to serious SF for their own reading. They also inserted dramatizations and fictionalizations of space flight— quasi-SF, as it were—into their technical studies, as did Oberth in *Wege zur Raumschiffahrt*. Oberth also quotes approvingly from the works of Otto Willi Gail (1896-1956), such as *Der Stein vom Mond* [*The Rock from the Moon*] (1926). Gail, whose other SF novels include *Der Schuss ins All* [*The Shot into the Cosmos*] (1925) and *Hans Hardts Mondfahrt* [*Hans Hardt's Voyage to the Moon*] (1928), had close ties to the German rocket experimenters. In his descriptions of space flight he aimed at, and often achieved, great technical accuracy. Willy Ley also was active for many years in SF and science popularization, both before and especially after his emigration to the United States in 1933. Even Wernher von Braun, Max Valier and Oberth himself wrote some SF.

It is quite likely, then, that Dominik had a modest familiarity with the state of rocket research in Germany and perhaps elsewhere during the time he was writing his novels, and that he may well have derived some of his material from the publications of Oberth and other researchers. In view of his background, his professional activities in Berlin, and the occasionally sensationalistic speculation about space flight in the Twenties and Thirties, it is virtually inconceivable that he remained totally ignorant of the basic ideas associated with rocket experimentation. What deserves attention and emphasis, however, is the palpable fact that, despite ample opportunity and encouragement, Germany's leading writer of fiction about speculative science failed to establish more than the most tenuous of connections to a field of science and technology in which Germany led the world and which, as so many other writers of SF were readily able to see, offered rich materials.

It would seem only natural that Dominik should have taken an active interest in the *VfR*, whose "Raketenflugplatz" was located in his own city, and that he should have sought personal acquaintance with the rocket researchers. No such contact is evident. In his autobiography he does not mention the work of the *VfR,* although it must be conceded that he probably would not have been allowed to do so in 1942. Nor do any of the leading rocket experimenters, although they were highly interested in SF and scientific journalism and must have known of Dominik, refer to him or his SF, either in contemporary publications or in later reminiscences. The absence of mention indirectly but strongly indicates the lack of significant contacts between Dominik and the rocket researchers; it also suggests that they had a low opinion of his SF. It should be noted, finally, that when Fritz Lang undertook to make the SF film *Die Frau im Mond* for the famous cinema company *Ufa* in 1929, he engaged as technical consultant Hermann Oberth, rather than Hans Dominik, even though the latter was an experienced and popular writer of SF, had worked previously with films about science, and published his works for Alfred Hugenberg, who had acquired *Ufa* in 1927.

But the most important indication of Dominik's failure to benefit fully from the work of the *VfR*, even though he may have borrowed from its research, is to be found in his SF. Space flight does not appear as a major theme in the novels[15] until *Das Erbe der Uraniden,* which was published in 1928, five years after Oberth's *Wege zur Raumschiffahrt* and in the same year as Ley's popular *Die Möglichkeit der Weltraumfahrt. Treibstoff* was published much later, in 1940, long after rocket research in Germany had been classified and put under military control, but also at a time when there was much speculation about rockets and other superweapons. While direct textual influence would be difficult to establish beyond question, Oberth's ideas and those of the other experimenters had been made accessible to the general public and particularly to the scientific community before 1928. Dominik, then, would have had plenty of detailed material with which to work had he chosen to use

.

In several respects the rocket ships in *Erbe and Treibstoff,* as well as one can tell, do seem to resemble those conceived by the members of the *VfR* and described in the technical and speculative chapters of their books. But Dominik's representations of space flight engineering and theory are usually quite vague, and it is therefore difficult to determine whether he has in fact made at least some use of the work of the *VfR* or has merely reverted to his own ideas and those of older SF.

Still, at least a few notable correspondences can be discerned. Dominik's spaceships are massive, indeed rather stubby craft; several times in *Erbe* he describes them as like a "grenade [Granate]" (115, 117, 184). The *VfR* researchers had often used the same word, and a striking feature of their spacecraft designs is the large diameter of the rocket in relation to its length. Similarly, Dominik's spaceships, rather than having true wings, are apparently fitted out with vestigial tail fins which seem intended to serve as supports on the ground and as stabilizers during the passage through the atmosphere. Yet if that construction feature is derived from the work of the *VfR*, as is quite possible, Dominik may well have failed to keep it in mind when describing rocket-powered ships in action, and have reverted instead to the notions of atmospheric flight with which he was so much more familiar. Thus the spaceship in *Erbe* is capable of atmospheric flight at low speeds and altitudes, although it would seem that its design otherwise would preclude such flight. While some of the details of spaceship construction, especially the cabin interiors, might have been derived from Verne, from Dominik's own fancy, or from his general knowledge of aeronautics, the real impetus—however indirect and muddled the form in which it reached him—was very likely the work of the German rocket researchers.

Perhaps the strongest evidence for *VfR* influence in *Erbe* is to be found where Dominik describes the invention of conventionally fueled chemical rockets and their subsequent replacement by the more sophisticated ion-driven ships in precisely the manner that Oberth and others foresaw the development (*Erbe*, 123). But the description is brief, and elsewhere Dominik does not create a very compelling picture of long-distance space flight. Details are quite scarce, and one might surmise that Dominik, if he was actually using the work of the *VfR*, did not fully understand or assimilate his sources. When he attempts to speculate independently about ion-propelled rockets the results are disastrous and would have been ridiculed by anyone familiar with the astrophysics and experimental rocketry of the time. Thus in *Erbe* Ronald Lee's rocket is disabled at the North Pole of Venus because "the strong cosmic

ectron streams, which made themselves so unusually noticeable at
e Pole of Venus, had partly blocked and partly exhausted
rematurely the radiating surfaces of the *Jonas Lee*" (313). The ion
ngines proposed by the *VfR* and since experimentally developed in
ctual space programs would not have been affected in the slightest
y forces of such a kind; and in any case the local energy of
lanetary radiation fields, if that is indeed what Dominik is
escribing, is inconsequential compared to the intense radiation
hich would be generated by an ion engine.

Several other glaring errors are also to be found in *Erbe*, faults
hat would have been inexcusable even according to the science and
echnology of Dominik's own time. To change course in space
tonald Lee issues the order, "Cut acceleration! Rudder hard to port!
Beschleunigung abstellen! Ruder hart Backbord!]" (257). In his
ovels about stratospheric flight Dominik does allude, legitimately,
 true rudders. But on a space ship there is no place for a rudder and
o medium for it to work against, unless, as is highly unlikely, he is
sing the term to refer to a device which controls auxiliary
irectional rockets. Dominik also seems unaware that the terms
port" and "starboard," like "up" and "down," are appropriate only
n Earth. Although they are suitable for atmospheric flight, they
re insufficient to describe absolute directions in three-dimensional
pace away from the influence of gravitational fields. Later in the
ovel, finally, the disabled *Jonas Lee* is towed back to Ronald Lee's
amp on Venus by another spaceship—one more gross
nprobability (*Erbe*, 307). Such outright errors or likely
ncongruities seem to be due to an inappropriate use of the analogy
f nautical travel in the conception of space flight.

The contention that Dominik's conception of space-flight
echnology depended for some of its features, in a vague way, on the
ork of the German rocket researchers and was limited by the
eakness of his own imagination is supported by still other
stronautical evidence. Rocket design in his 1940 novel *Treibstoff*
oes not advance beyond the ideas which had been developed a
ecade or more earlier. When secrecy was imposed on German
ocket research after 1933, Dominik apparently lost the source of
uch of his information and inspiration and failed to speculate
rther on his own. In fact, the rocket ships in *Treibstoff* fly scarcely
eyond the Earth's upper atmosphere, while in *Erbe* the fresh
fluence of the recent *VfR* work may well have inspired Dominik to
rite, as did the German rocket experimenters themselves, about
ight to the moon and Venus. In *Erbe* he even ventures to allude to

interstellar flights such as those undertaken by the Uranids in the novel and proposed by Oberth and others in their own books. *Treibstoff* lacks such daring ideas.

In its most general features Dominik's description of space-flight technology resembles his portrayal of imaginary stratospheric flight, although there is far more detail in the latter. Perhaps Dominik was less confident in his conception of space flight. He concentrates on the great personal efforts and the immediately foreseeable aspects of space flight, such as fuel composition, engine design, and construction facilities, but does not offer detailed descriptions. Nor does he venture into the mathematics of interplanetary flight, a subject which fascinated those writers who were more familiar with such matters. It is very significant, I think, that the plot of *Erbe* deals with the construction of a rocket ship *after* the plans have already been drawn; there is practically no discussion of the plans themselves or the theories on which they are based. The emphasis on practical technology is consonant with Dominik's tendency, evident elsewhere also, to focus on engineering rather than on theory as a source of plot excitement and imaginary scientific content.

The discrepancy between Dominik's SF and the scientific material readily available to him at the time is even more evident when he attempts to describe space flight as a human experience in new surroundings. In his novels outer space is not an environment having distinctive, tangible characteristics which are interesting in themselves and which might be of vital importance to the action. One feels instead that the spaceship is merely being moved from one setting to another. The effect is much like that created by the outer space scenes of the *Buck Rogers* movies of the same time (1939ff.), where the spaceship, with its engines fizzing and blasting wildly, is seen stationary against a flat backdrop. The characters in Dominik's SF seem scarcely to notice that they are in space, and therefore some of the special, often spectacular effects which SF has the unique potential to evoke are missing. Neither the characters nor the reader is given much chance to marvel at the sensations of the blackness and depth of space, at the new perspectives of the stars and planets, including their own Earth, or at the feelings of weightlessness and rapid acceleration.

It was of course impossible actually to experience such sensations before the beginning of real space flight. And, since later writers indeed had more information at their disposal, it is perhaps unfair to compare Dominik's SF to more recent works, in which here is an abundance of detail—both hard scientific facts and portrayals of the subjective effects of space flight. But other writers, even before Dominik, have been able to use their own imaginative powers and the information provided by science to conceive and convey the experience of space flight in great detail. Dominik's description of space travel and the extraterrestrial environment lacks the realistic texture and psychological subtlety even of Lasswitz' much earlier *Auf zwei Planeten*. More significantly, it compares unfavorably with the imaginary pictures of space flight created in fictional and non-fictional works by those who were associated with the *VfR* during the same years when Dominik wrote his novels. Oberth's own dramatization of space flight in *Wege zur Raumschiffahrt* (300-11) is more detailed and also more exciting as technological "fiction" than Dominik's SF. The SF of Otto Willi Gail, mentioned earlier, also surpasses his novels in this respect. Whether necessarily or by choice and habit, Dominik, far less closely associated with the *VfR* than was Gail, resorts to simple plot intrigue for the creation of excitement in his descriptions of the experience of space flight (see, e.g., *Erbe*, 215ff.). Such techniques, in themselves not illegitimate in fiction, do nothing directly to convey the special nature of the experience of space flight, and therefore indicate a failure to capitalize on opportunities which should be especially attractive to the writer of SF.

Dominik's few descriptions of extraterrestrial landscapes— they are limited to *Erbe*—exhibit similar shortcomings. The surface of Venus is far more like the pampas of Argentina than that of a different planet; certainly it does not correspond to any serious scientific conception of Venus current in Dominik's time. The resemblance to South America may well be intentional; *Erbe* closes with the sentiment that Venus is eminently suitable for colonization by the intrepid Germans and Anglo-Saxons who, like the heroes of the novel, had earlier settled in South America and had built the rockets which took them to Venus. It would seem that in order to impress one of his favorite ideological notions in a grandiose way Dominik sacrificed the opportunity to explore a radically alien environment, one of the chief aims of SF, and in doing so also deviated from the reasonably well-founded evidence of contemporary science.

Dominik also failed to make use of the opportunity to describe landscape as viewed from a spaceship. In *Erbe,* the one novel where he made such an attempt, there are gross violations of visual perspective. Not only does he neglect to emphasize the difference between ground-level and aerial perspectives; on one occasion he also introduces an optical impossibility. In a matter of a few hours the *Jonas Lee* is made to fly from the temperate zone to the North Pole of Venus, or perhaps even around the planet—a distance of at least several thousand miles—at some undetermined height. The explorers are supposedly able to see "grassy steppes, populated by a rich variety of fauna" (*Erbe*, 290), and yet they can also discern the largest outlines of the continent. The visual discrepancy does not trouble Dominik, if indeed he was aware of it; thus either scientific he failed in doing what he actually attempted. His conception of Venus and his management of perspective contradict or at the very least fail to fulfill the basic presuppositions of SF, even as he himself seemed to understand them.

Much the same can be said about Dominik's treatment, or rather his virtual neglect, of another basic theme of SF, extraterrestrial life. In only one instance does he write about alien beings, and then only briefly. The Uranids in *Erbe* are quite humanoid. With their "noble head[s],... high forehead[s] [and] light, combed-back hair,... broad, energetic chin[s], [and] large, expressive eyes" (*Erbe*, 236) they exhibit a certain resemblance to Lasswitz' Martians, and an even more pronounced similarity to the physical ideal of many German racists. But Dominik discusses the Uranids, their origin and their civilization only sketchily. Often, in order to incite the reader's sense of wonder, he resorts to lurid but empty rhetorical questions — "How long had they voyaged through the universe?" or "With what velocities had they conquered the infinite distance?" (*Erbe*, 234)— rather than seeking to deal with the provocative implications of the theme in a definite and palpable way through his fiction. Dominik mentions that the Uranids come from another stellar system, but does not speculate to any extent about the nature of life elsewhere in the universe or the means by which interstellar flight might be accomplished. Such ideas as communication with alien races, biological and chemical differences, or even psychology, social structure and philosophy are also not discussed. The Uranids, as the name suggests, are simply beings who come from the heavens. That they are all dead before we even see them shows Dominik's disregard for the possibilities of SF as a medium for both entertainment and serious scientific speculation. The only purpose of the Uranids in *Erbe*, as the novel's title indicates, is to provide a source of new science and technology for the use of certain favored human beings who find and appropriate their secret. The idea of cultural contact and the conflict which ethical and philosophical differences might occasion, a theme which so intrigued Lasswitz and many other writers of SF, either did not occur or did not appeal to Dominik. His interest, in *Erbe* and in the rest of his novels, is confined solely to the practical aspects of science, the immediate future of the Earth, and the fortunes of some few of its inhabitants.

The Validity, Quality and Importance of Dominik's SF

Quite plainly I am not an admirer of either Dominik or his SF. My antipathy is founded in part on a distaste for his political attitudes. I believe also that Dominik, who was the most popular writer of German SF during the first half of the century, might well have made a far greater contribution to the development of German SF as a cohesive and viable literature had he formed closer ties to other writers and scientists who were interested in the more speculative areas of science and their attendant fiction. These considerations, of course, are irrelevant to a strictly literary evaluation of Dominik's works. But here there is ample reason to criticize his fiction on both general and specific grounds. Indeed, his novels exhibit all the major characteristics and deficiencies of *Trivialliteratur*. Dominik's attitude toward science and his poor grasp of the literary principles and techniques of SF also provide sufficient cause for one to question the value of his fiction as SF.

It is clear, nevertheless, that Dominik sought to express in his fiction a belief in the importance of science and technology, and to incorporate imaginary science and technology into his novels. But while those aims are the focus of much attention and excitement in his fiction, equally obvious are a fascination with pseudo-science and a pronounced disposition toward the irrational which may ultimately be inconsistent with the intentionality of SF. In almost every novel Dominik devotes considerable attention to the realm of the psychic, the occult and the uncanny; sometimes they become the main theme, as in *Befehl aus dem Dunkel*. Thus we encounter heroes, villains and mysterious sages who can read thoughts, sense distant or future events, and exert a controlling influence on the minds of others. For centuries writers of SF have toyed with such notions, and the boundary between pseudo-science and legitimate scientific speculation is indeed often vague and may shift with time. Nevertheless, if a text is to be regarded as SF rather than as fantasy or "weird" fiction, it is essential that the author introduce some effective scientific explanation for what are usually considered to be supernatural powers and events. In his autobiography Dominik discusses scientific speculation about psychic phenomena (*VSS*, 269-72), and in *Befehl* he at least attempts to provide a scientific foundation, though with little persistence or ability. More often he makes no such effort.

Another indication of the strong irrational or non-scientific current in Dominik's world-view and fiction is the frequency with which both narrator and characters allude to "destiny" or "fate," especially toward the ends of the novels (e.g., *Atlantis*, 244, 248, 278, 283-86, 314; *Macht*, 39, 74, 91, 129, 253, 326-29; *Erbe*, 276). In *Erbe* even the term "Karma" appears (275, 298). A similar preoccupation with the non-rational can be found in passages where dream and reality are intertwined and confused, even in the narrator's mind, until the real world dissolves momentarily into a kind of existential haze and the reader, along with characters and narrator, is led to ask, "What was reality? What was it?" (*Atlantis*, 188; see also *Macht,* 326ff., *Erbe*, 269-72, 272-76, 296). It is true that modern science is founded on the assumptions that Nature is structured according to some principle of order and that observed phenomena are not in themselves reality. But the subject-matter and concepts of science presume a rejection of transcendental entities and causes. The tendency to confuse dream and reality, and the belief in inevitable, incomprehensible Fate, reflect an outlook which denies the consequentiality of human acts and the idea of orderly physical causality. The latter concept is indispensable to modern scientific thought; both ideas are essential to SF, and indeed the demonstration of their validity would seem to be the conscious aim of Dominik's novels.

One evident source of the irrational in Dominik's fiction is Oriental occultism and its Western derivatives or equivalents. Its immediate literary function is equally clear. As Walther Killy has pointed out, *Trivialliteratur* often debases the mythical and profoundly transcendental into the superficially weird and exotic for the purpose of shallow entertainment or "thrills."[16] Or, to express the point in terms of literary structure and technique, fate and the occult in Dominik's novels are scientifically illegitimate but effective remedies for poor characterization and plot motivation. Viewed from yet another perspective, irrational or supernatural elements are parts of Dominik's attempt to make science, technology and the rest of the imaginary world portentous and mysterious.

The same tendencies, I think, can be related more closely to Dominik's particular ideological orientation, which has much in

ommon with fascism. His conception of the occult is decidedly
acial, and in expounding it fictionally he frequently intimates the
ffinity of Germanic culture to those of India and the Near East. The
inship is established, he emphasizes, through common descent
rom the Indo-Germanic proto-culture, which Dominik views as
Aryan and therefore superior. Such notions are particularly
pparent in *Atlantis* and *Macht*. The close relationship is still
vident, the novels strongly suggest, in a shared faculty for deep
rrational intuition which appears in the best representatives of the
iermanic race and in the nearly ideal German society of the future.
.qually important is the relation of Dominik's concept of science to
hat of fascism. He shared with the fascist "theoreticians" of science
mentality which looked to the primordial, nocturnal and irrational
ide of Nature and human experience, both individual and
ommunal, in order to find a putatively transcendental, organic,
italistic and tragic view of life.[17] Although his world-view is not
rofound or absolutely consistent internally, Dominik's novels offer
realization in fiction of the desire for a ˙characteristically
German" science or scientific outlook; that is, a form of knowledge
hich is not a body of neutral facts and theories or a doctrine of
robability, uncertainty or skepticism, but rather an integral part of
larger world-view which is somehow idiosyncratically German,
lthough its specific nature and the mechanism of its actual
xpression in scientific endeavor are never defined clearly, and
robably cannot be.

But whether or not Dominik's world-view and his concept of
:ience are antithetical to the nature of science, his fiction is of
ferior quality when judged by general literary standards and by
ie special distinguishing characteristics of SF used throughout
iis study. Among the latter criteria are power of scientific
nagination, employment of stylistic devices which encourage the
npressions of reality and plausibility, and the ability to make
:ience and technology integral parts of the fiction.

Earlier I discussed at length Dominik's pronounced
ncentration on the technology of the near future and his failure to
ploit readily accessible areas of science and technology which
ave strongly attracted many other writers of SF. Verne's novels
id such other works of SF as *Der Tunnel* (1913) by Bernhard
ellermann show that neither predilection precludes the creation of
xcellent SF. Far more questionable is Dominik's inability to
nceive or "extrapolate" any but the most immediate and often
ivial ways in which the imaginary technology he envisions might

affect the world. Whatever his intentions, his imaginary science does not have profound or widespread consequences of a lasting and plausible nature. Typically he views technology, as did most people in the earlier centuries of the Scientific and Industrial Revolutions, simply as a spectacular toy or as a tool which Man controls, not as an agent which may also strongly affect those who create and wield it.

There is a similar discrepancy in Dominik's overall attitude toward the imaginary worlds he envisions. His statements about the creation of SF clearly imply that he indeed intended his imaginary worlds to be viewed as careful, impartial explorations of the future. While no writer can completely put aside or conceal his own beliefs and cherished wishes, it is almost impossible even provisionally to entertain Dominik's imaginary worlds as "thought-models." His visions of the future are exercises in wish-fulfilment whose utopian nature he cannot or will not conceal. By contrast, even many utopian thinkers and authors seek earnestly to demonstrate that their fondest desires are actually rational projections of what history will bring about. The better writers of SF also attempt to describe imaginary worlds which can be evaluated impartially in terms of their probability and internal consistency. Dominik's fervid partiality is evident in his treatment of character and in his descriptions of social institutions and historical processes. It also imbues his prose style with an emotional tension that frequently destroys any inclination the reader might have to regard the narrator as an objective, reliable observer.

In discussing Dominik's novels I have not offered lengthy analyses of his use of the stylistic devices of SF, as I did in my chapters on Lasswitz. There is, quite simply, very little to mention. In its general stylistic features his fiction resembles much popular realistic fiction and much other SF as well. The third-person narrator—neither a true personality nor a transparent, impersonal voice—is omniscient, and Dominik emphasizes the detailed but economical presentation of facts rather than the exploration of psychological motivation. Some of the descriptions of imaginary technology, as I noted earlier, show a certain talent which is consonant with Dominik's success as a technological journalist. But his style lacks the control, force and ability to convey a plausible impression of the imaginary world which characterize good SF. In his effort to write in a concrete, spare and matter-of-fact manner Dominik often reverts to cliches and to an elliptical "telegraphic" style which can all too easily interfere with comprehension, fail by its very exaggeration to accomplish the intended effects of vividness and succinctness, and devolve into unconscious self-caricature:

> The submarine in the furious Gulf Stream. Journey into Death! The tiny boat a plaything of the raging element. Then suddenly, as though seized by an unknown hand with violent power, its stem forced to the northeast, torn out of the whirling vortex into tranquil water. *(Atlantis, 290)*.
>
> [Das U-Boot in rasenden Golfstrom. Todesfahrt! Das winzige Boot ein Spielball des tobenden Elements. Da plötzlich, wie wenn eine fremde Hand es mit gewaltiger Kraft gepackt, der Steven nach Nordost gezwungen, heraus gerissen aus den wirbelnden Strudeln in ruhige See.]

The unresolved combination of insistence on bluntness and economy, the desire for vivid narration, and Dominik's emotional involvement with certain characters and events encourages a style which alternates between the extremes of blandness and, as at the end of *Macht*, melodramatic turgidity:

> Jane [Harte-Bursfeld] knew not whether she was awake or dreaming. Was all that merely a play of her over-excited senses, or reality?... She thought of her child, which in keeping with Silvester's last will was to grow up in the old German homeland.
>
> She felt in her lap, and her fingers touched cool metal.
>
> She raised it slowly to her eyes and saw the heavy old gold band with the peculiar stone which she had so often beheld on Silvester's hand. The ring which had bound Silvester to the Power, had compelled him, even unto his Death, into the service of the Power.
>
> It was a gift of the last still living bearer of the Power for her,... for her son. [Dominik's ellipsis]
>
> The voice of the aged Termölen [her German host and guardian] penetrated her musing: "...The Power...the infinite Power. Whence came it?... Whither went it?... Why?..." [Dominik's ellipsis] *(Macht, 358-9)*

> [Jane (Harte-Bursfeld) wusste nicht, ob sie wache oder träume. War das alles nur ein Spiel ihrer überreizten Sinne oder Wirklichkeit?
>
> ...Sie dachte ihres Kindes, das hier nach dem Vermächtnis Silvesters in der alten deutschen Heimat aufwachsen sollte.
>
> Sie griff in ihren Schoss, und ihre Finger fühlten kühles Metall.
>
> Sie hob es langsam zu ihren, Augen empor und sah den schweren alten Goldreif mit dem wunderlichen Stein, den sie sooft an der Hand Silvesters erblickt hatte. Den Ring, der Silvester an die Macht gebunden, ihn bis zu seinem Tod in den Dienst der Macht gezwungen hatte.
>
> Es war eine Gabe des letzten noch lebenden Trägers der Macht für sie... für ihren Knaben.
>
> Die Stimme des alten Termölen drang in ihr Sinnen: "...Die Macht...die unendliche Macht. Woher kam sie?...Wohin ging sie?... Warum?..."]

While examples of many of the special rhetorical devices of SF can be found in Dominik's novels, they are encountered far less often, and in far less sophisticated form, than in other SF of better quality, even that written before his time. On rare occasions, and never for very long, Dominik adopts the voice of the scientist or the historian who surveys future history or science (e.g., *Macht*, 230; *Atlantis*, 297-8); but the technique is not used consistently or skillfully. Only infrequently are spurious "documents" introduced (e.g., *Atlantis*, 8-9). Neologisms describing imaginary technology, such as the explosive "Neobrisit" in *Atlantis* (36), occur only seldom and are not especially imaginative or catchy. The techniques of individual affections and animosities which have nothing essential allusion and explanation by analogy, both so important in much other SF, are used only rarely and then awkwardly. In describing the invention of a device which detects brain waves, for example, Dominik has one of his characters speak of an "amplifier of a special type, which amplifies these thought waves in the same manner that a normal radio amplifier amplifies radio waves" (*Befehl*, 36-7).

Even cruder is Dominik's way of avoiding the precise explanation of imaginary science by having the scientist interrupt his description of the invention with the remark that further detail would unnecessarily detain or bore his fictive listeners. The narrator may then himself turn aside, resuming his story only after the scientist, despite his reluctance, has ostensibly completed his explanation (e.g., *Befehl*, 152). Such primitive devices can be found in older SF, and in modern SF of poorer quality; and while the better writers may employ the same techniques, they do so much more subtly. Extremely rare in Dominik's novels, finally, is the "serial" form of matter-of-fact allusion, which consists of the introduction of an imaginary element in a series of real ones. Perhaps best among the few instances is the following:

> Of such spirits might a Caesar have been before he crossed the Rubicon, of such a Napoleon as he dared the storming of Italy, of such a [Cyrus] Stonard, as he set upon the Yellow Race in the West of the [North American] Union. (*Macht*, 285)
> [So mochte es einem Cäsar zumute gewesen sein, ehe er den Rubikon überschritt, so einem Napoleon als er den Sturm auf Italien wagte, so einem Stonard, als er gegen die Gelben im Western der (Nordamerikanischen) Union losbrach.]

All of Dominik's shortcomings, conceptual or stylistic, can be reduced, I think, to a single overall weakness: his inability to create a narration in which, as Darko Suvin expresses the point, *"the SF element or aspect is hegemonic*—i.e., so central and significant that it determines the whole narrative logic, or at least the overriding narrative logic, regardless of any impurities that might be present."[18] Whatever Dominik's expressed intention, science and technology are not "hegemonic" in his SF, not truly integral, convincing parts of his imaginary worlds, whether in their overall conception or in the language in which they are presented. Of the three major realms of action which I have distinguished in Dominik's novels, the scientific realm is clearly intended to be central. But he fails to unite the three realms, or rather, he does not make science an indispensable part of the political and private realms. Much of the action depends on purely political struggles or to do with science and technology, whether real or imaginary. Nor does Dominik express in his treatment of the political and personal realms the supposedly futuristic nature of the imaginary world which is inherent in the creation of imaginary science and technology. It is possible to read for pages without suspecting that the story is set in some future time, so little is the imaginary world different from our own. On the most detailed level of narrative "logic," science scarcely affects the language of either the narrator or the characters.

Dominik's novels, it must be admitted, appealed to many readers, and still do. The salient features of his fiction, however, confirm the suggestion which I formulated toward the end of the previous chapter in discussing his medium of publication and his readership. Dominik's novels were so popular with the mass reader because he was able to solve one of the fundamental problems of *Trivialliteratur*. He understood how to furnish the reader with what seems to be new material while still conforming generally to the tried and tested patterns which assure the reader that the commodity he is purchasing and consuming will deliver the kind of entertainment and express the ideas which he expects and has been given heretofore.

It is, nevertheless, reasonable to categorize Dominik's novels as SF, for such a classification implies nothing about quality. Moreover, his fiction must be conceded an extremely important position in the history of German SF. The discrepancy between the low quality of his SF and its great impact on its readers has had, I think, a crucial and unfortunate effect on the development of the genre in Germany. Those readers who were vitally interested in serious SF and who were capable of judging its merits were not strongly drawn to Dominik's fiction and apparently did not constitute its principal sustaining readership. By the Twenties and Thirties the serious SF readership in Germany may well have expanded considerably beyond its size in Lasswitz' time. But, unlike the Anglo-American SF readership of the same time, it lacked both a sense of cohesion and a reliable form of specialized publication. Dominik's SF, unfortunately, did little to further the emergence of either. Nor has it advanced the reputation of German SF among readers and critics of serious literature, or offered a useful model for talented younger writers. Virulently, pyrotechnically sterile, it shares the history and images the less appealing side of the culture which nurtured it. In 1945 it appeared that for German SF, too, the future was past.

Chapter VII

Conclusions and Conjectures: Lasswitz, Dominik, and the Evolution of German SF

The preceding chapters offer detailed examinations of Kurd Lasswitz and Hans Dominik, the two most important writers of German SF. I have sought to show how the fiction of each is related to his personal experiences, his knowledge of science and technology, his concept of SF, his medium of publication and readership, and his larger environment. But a study of Lasswitz and Dominik would be both unsatisfying and incomplete without some attempt to assess their place within the broader context of German SF. With equal justification, and with a decent respect of course to the opinions of genre theorists and to the seeming paradoxes of literary hermeneutics, one may also observe, conversely, that whatever German SF might be can not be determined without consideration of Lasswitz and Dominik. The present chapter, therefore, proceeds from an appraisal of the two writers to an examination of the genre in whose history they figured so prominently.

I

Kurd Lasswitz was born in 1848 and died in 1910. His life and work reflect the German liberalism associated with his birthyear, the history of Wilhelmine Germany, the humanism of his cultural heritage, and his profound interest in science. In 1871, the year in which the Second Reich was founded, Lasswitz' first SF appeared in print. The novella *Bis zum Nullpunkt des Seins* and its later companion piece, *Gegen das Weltgesetz,* are scarcely the irrelevant flights of futuristic fancy which they might initially seem to be. Nor are the two stories merely compendiums of imaginary technology. In a brief but sometimes incisive and critical manner they express three of the fundamental social features and intellectual traits of Lasswitz' time: the growing awareness of science and technology, the concept of systematic and rationally comprehensible historical development, and eager optimism about the future.

During the next quarter-century Lasswitz elaborated and

improved his literary techniques in a number of short stories which are collected in the volumes *Seifenblasen* (1890/94) and *Traumkristalle* (1902/07). His non-fictional writings show that his understanding of science, philosophy, society, and history, and his concept of SF as well, had increased in sophistication, although no essential change of direction is evident. Lasswitz published his masterpiece, *Auf zwei Planeten,* in 1897, when the Second Reich had reached its political and cultural culmination, and when positivism had attained a similar intellectual dominance. The novel, which still ranks as one of the best works of German SF, is rich in imaginary science and technology; equally impressive are Lasswitz' descriptions of extra-terrestrial settings and of Martian society and history. In *Auf zwei Planeten* Lasswitz examines the role of science and technology in the modern world. He also offers a broad and provocatively critical analysis of Wilhelmine society, and indeed of Western civilization in general.

Unfortunately, Lasswitz' SF has not enjoyed the attention and appreciation it deserves, either in the literary community at large or among most readers and critics of SF. By inclination or necessity he wrote for a limited audience composed of readers who shared his liberal ideology, humanistic intellectual orientation, and at least some of his understanding of science. The failure of most contemporary readers to comprehend the nature of his fiction as SF, the lack of a more popular medium of publication, and the suppression of *Auf zwei Planeten* between 1933 and 1945 have all contributed to Lasswitz' obscurity.

The differences between Lasswitz and Hans Dominik (1872-1945), the best-known and most prolific writer of German SF in the first half of this century, are as great as those between the Second Reich and the spectacular, chaotic period which includes the Weimar Republic and the Third Reich. Dominik was a technician, not a philosopher and theoretical scientist, and he was certainly not a humanist or political liberal. He was, in blunt terms, a cultural Philistine, a racist, and a reactionary whose works were useful to National Socialism.

In Dominik's fictional visions of the future, technology occupies the position of vital importance toward which it was clearly moving in the early twentieth century. The frustrations of German history, as viewed by extreme conservatives at least, are exorcised, and national, often blatantly nationalistic dreams—above all the ideal of social *Gemeinschaft*—are acted out. Dominik was of course neither the first nor the last writer to express such ideas in fiction.

But in his SF the strong organic social unity of Germany and the assertiveness in foreign relations which it makes possible belong neither to the nostalgic past nor to the realm of hopeful theory. Dominik projected the notions of *Gemeinschaft* and national resurgence into the future and presented his visions as vivid actualizations, not as cherished memories, wishful dreams, or academic hypotheses. But the real future, as it emerged after 1933, when the National Socialist state first subjected all sectors of society to a process of forced "integration" or "coordination" *(Gleichschaltung)* and then waged a total and devastating war, represented a far less attractive version of the social and technological ideal conceived by Dominik, and by many other conservatives.

Judged by general literary standards Dominik lacks any appreciable distinction, and as a writer of SF he evidences only a modest capability whose strongest feature is the vivid description of technology. He was not a profound or, in his treatment of science, even a daringly imaginative thinker. Yet the resources of his publishers, his competent command of the techniques of *Trivialliteratur,* and his feeling for the more sensational but in fact rather easily foreseeable aspects of the technology of the near future enabled him to reach a vast audience. Dominik's novels continued to appear in large editions during the Nazi Era, and indeed are still in print.

Despite the evident differences between Lasswitz and Dominik, the texts discussed in the preceding chapters correspond adequately to the definition of SF adopted in this study, and indeed satisfy any other reasonable definition. But Lasswitz and Dominik wrote SF which is also unmistakably *German* SF, for it was shaped to a significant extent by its specific environment. If the two writers differ greatly in so many ways, the virtual extremes they embody reflect the characteristic polarities of their culture. Lasswitz, writing in the late nineteenth century, was influenced strongly by German liberalism and the heritage of German Classicism and Idealism. He necessarily viewed concepts like imperialism, culture contact, and social organization from a different perspective than that characteristic of, for example, Anglo-American writers of SF. Dominik responded to the same or similar ideas, but in a manner consonant with the cultural Philistinism, racial attitudes, and extreme conservatism typical of a large segment of German society during his lifetime.

The German cultural environment also registered a distinct

effect on the treatment of science and technology in the SF of Lasswitz and Dominik. Both writers were intensely interested in contemporary German science, and proud of its recent achievements. While Lasswitz' understanding of the history and contemporary development of science was far superior to that of Dominik, much of his SF refers to the world of late nineteenth-century German science, especially the impressive but often esoteric work in physics being conducted in the universities. Dominik was a technologist who lacked not only Lasswitz' historical and philosophical knowledge, but also his cultural cosmopolitanism and his sense of the international nature of science. He clearly favored applied science over theoretical speculation, and consistently chose his material from those areas of technology which, like chemistry, metallurgy, and aeronautics, were most prominent in Germany during his time, especially in the eyes of the masses.

Even in their choice of settings and characters Lasswitz and Dominik differ noticeably from other writers of SF. In most American SF, and even in some British SF, the "heroes" and other "good guys," especially the valiant masters of science and technology, are American; much of the action, when it does not occur away from Earth, takes place in America. Since the time of Mary Shelley, however, a common stereotype in Anglo-American SF has been the German scientist, who is frequently caricatured as a mysterious savant, a villain, or an unimaginative and authoritarian technician. Needless to say, precious little of that convention, or rather of its pejorative features, is to be found in the work of either Lasswitz or Dominik, although the latter pictures— favorably, of course—more than a few enigmatic sages and superbly efficient, strong-willed technicians. More rewarding here, however, are the observations that each indeed employs national stereotypes and that in analyzing them one must take into consideration the nationality of author and reader. Here, again, Lasswitz and Dominik mark off the extremes of a cultural range. The former's attitude is good-natured, cosmopolitan, and ideologically liberal, that of Dominik crudely and stridently nationalistic. In *Auf zwei Planeten,* for example, Lasswitz criticizes British reserve and bluster, not without humor. Dominik, in much of his SF, viciously attacks what he viewed as the crass materialism, the cultural crudity, and the social irresponsibility of American society, especially its dominant capitalists and technologists. In the SF of neither writer is there a single major American or British figure which corresponds to the German scientist in Anglo-American SF.

More important in the SF of Lasswitz and Dominik is the treatment of German characters, especially the heroic scientists and technologists. Lasswitz, living in provincial Gotha at the turn of the century, often pictures small, usually unnamed German university towns and somewhat eccentric academic scientists, or their analogs in future or alternate worlds. In his earlier SF, for example *Gegen das Weltgesetz,* the propensity to present imaginary worlds which are transparent, lightly-caricatured replicas of his own late-*Biedermeier* world often undermines the impression of plausibility. But Lasswitz manages German settings and characters far more maturely in *Auf zwei Planeten,* although his capabilities as a cultural philosopher may have exceeded his skills as an artist in his conception of Ell, the half-German, half-Martian figure who embodies German Idealism. Taken together, Lasswitz' three German scientists—the intrepid Torm, the reticent North German Grunthe, and the ebullient Tyrolian Saltner—represent an attitude toward ideological concepts and national traits which is literally more down-to-earth. In his characterization of the three, whose talents and personalities complement each other so well, Lasswitz suggests, in a patriotic but not blindly jingoistic spirit, the excellence and further promise of German science and the German personality. It should be noted that Lasswitz' expansive concept of German identity is, to use the terms of the time, *grossdeutsch*; we are reminded once again that, although he was a citizen of the smaller, *kleindeutsch* empire created by Prussia, Lasswitz was also a liberal in the tradition of 1848.

Dominik is far more chauvinistic in his use of national stereotypes. Many of the heroes, heroines, and mysterious sages who appear in his SF are German, of course, and they exhibit traits of physical appearance, personality, intellect, and social and racial consciousness customarily prized by extreme German conservatives or fascists. They and other "good" Germans—for Dominik there is scarcely a bad one in that lot—advance the glory of their nation and guard it tenaciously against the encroachment from outside that always seems to threaten. Naturally the future Germany which constitutes one of the major settings as well as the paramount political interest of Dominik's novels is scarcely to be found elsewhere than in such German SF, except in dystopias, for Dominik's vision of the future is predicated on certain obvious national experiences, assumptions, and dreams not shared by other societies, nor indeed by many Germans.

Other Early German SF

Lasswitz and Dominik are by no means the only writers of German SF, even in their own time (see Bibliography, Section III).[1] Since at least the early seventeenth century, German writers have composed utopias, imaginary voyages, future war stories, and whimsical semi-fictional discourses which have to do in some way with imaginary science. The *Somnium*, a didactic moon-voyage narration by Johannes Kepler (1571-1630), comes readily to mind, although it was written in Latin; composed sometime around 1610, it was first published posthumously in 1634—and appeared in German only in 1898, perhaps not entirely by chance the year after *Auf zwei Planeten.* Scattered through the eighteenth century are a few German utopias or imaginary voyages, like Eberhard Christian Kindermann's *Geschwinde Reise auf dem Luftschiff nach der oberen Welt* (1744), which is supposedly the first story about a voyage to Mars; and at the very limits of literary-historical perception a second Mars story, Carl Ignaz Geiger's *Reise eines Erdbewohners in den Mars* (1790), of which apparently but a single original copy exists. Later in the century Georg Christoph Lichtenberg (1742-1799), certainly a respectable figure among both scientists and literati, tossed off a few humorously satirical pieces which incorporate science-fictional motifs. Not quite so honored among historians of science or, much less, literature, but important because of his influence on Lasswitz, is Gustav Theodor Fechner (1801-1887), a rather mystical physiologist and psychologist. Under the pseudonym "Dr. Mises" he published a few fantastical parodies of scientific argumentation, such as the "Beweis, dass der Mond aus Iodine bestehe" (1821) and the "Vergleichende Anatomie der Engel" (1825). He thus stands—with, as I have argued, Lasswitz—as a modest contributor to an interesting peripheral zone of SF whose more familiar representatives are Poe's hoax stories, Abbott's *Flatland* (1884), and Asimov's "thiotimoline" spoofs.

It is scarcely less legitimate to cite such figures in a study of Lasswitz, Dominik, and modern German SF than it is to allude to Thomas More or Restif De la Bretonne in histories of British and French SF. But perhaps the present instance better shows the dangers of antecedent-hunting and influence-mongering to which SF history and criticism has often fallen prey. For it was only in the time of Kurd Lasswitz that literature which might in retrospect be called German SF became more than an extremely rare and usually obscure form of literary expression. The years around the turn of the nineteenth century are relatively rich in utopias like *In purpurner*

Finsternis (1895) by the Munich Naturalist Michael Georg Conrad (1846-1927), chauvinistic future war novels like *Der Weltkrieg: Deutsche Träume* (1904) by August Niemann, and stories which, like the amusingly titled *Der Mond fällt auf Westpreussen* (1928) by R. Budzinski, would seem to describe catastrophes resulting from natural events or Man's abuse of nature.

During the first few decades of this century there appeared even more works of fiction which deserve to be classified as SF, though sometimes with reservations. Best among them are *Der Tunnel* (1913) by Bernhard Kellermann (1879-1951), *Druso, oder die gestohlene Menschenwelt* (1931) by Friedrich Freksa (pseud. of Kurt Friedrich-Freksa, 1882-1955), and the novels of Rudolf Daumann (1896-1957) and Otto Willi Gail (1896-1956), which were mentioned in the preceding chapter. There, too, I referred to the juvenile-oriented stories which appeared in *Das neue Universum*. During the Weimar years German cinematographers produced a number of classic SF films, such as *Metropolis* (Fritz Lang, Ufa, 1926), *Die Frau im Mond* (Fritz Lang, Ufa, 1928), and *F.P.I. antwortet nicht* (Karl Hartl, Gaumont-Fox-Ufa, 1933). Lastly, two somewhat earlier works, *Astrale Novelletten* (1912) and *Lesabéndio: Ein Asteroiden-Roman* (1913), by the puzzling and eccentric writer Paul Scheerbart (1863-1915), also deserve consideration as SF, although the element of pure fantasy in them is very pronounced.

II

The year 1945, in which World War II ended and Dominik died, marks the "Year Zero" in German SF, as in other German literature. But soon after the end of the war the demand for SF in Germany revived. It has grown ever since, in large measure because of the widespread interest in science and the infusion—much welcomed and much condemned—of American popular culture. Some of the demand has been met by several mass re-editions of Dominik's novels and, to a far lesser extent, by the new abridged editions of *Auf zwei Planeten*. Dominik's type of SF, with its short-range technology, predominantly terrestrial settings, exciting plots, and sometimes its not so latent racism, has survived in the works of several writers, for example *Weltuntergang* (1957) by Freder van Holk (pseud. of Paul Alfred Müller, b. 1901); its residual effect even on some early East German writers was noted in Chapter V. In the immediate postwar years a few well-known "serious" writers, some of them emigrès, attempted to use a form resembling SF in order to give utterance to their thoughts about the past, present, and future—if any—of their civilization. Novels like *Die Eroberung der Welt: Roman einer Zukunft* (1943/49) by Oskar Maria Graf (1894-1967), *Heliopolis* (1949) by Ernst Jünger (b.1895), and *Stern der Ungeborenen* (1946) by Franz Werfel (1890-1945), have enjoyed a limited appreciation among readers of SF, both in Germany and even elsewhere.[2]

Several modern "highbrow" or "Establishment" writers, perhaps most notably the Swiss author Friedrich Dürrenmatt (b.1921), have also written works which can be described as SF. Dürrenmatt's play *Die Physiker* (1962) can be termed SF by virtue of its theme and content; the dangers as well as the exciting promise of theoretical physics have long been a part of SF. But there may be no essential connection between *Die Physiker* and the "indigenous" tradition of SF, and the adoption of the dramatic medium is not typical of most literary SF—at least outside Germany. Dürrenmatt's earlier radio play *Das Unternehmen der Wega* (1955) appears to make use, not very successfully in my opinion, of the conventions of "space opera" and *Buck Rogers*. The works of Dürrenmatt and other "Establishment" writers, however, are peripheral to the evolution of post-war German SF.

Until recently much of the demand for SF in Germany has been satisfied by works from abroad, which have often set the tone for native writers. During the first two decades after 1945 the German market was fairly inundated by imported Anglo-American SF. The writings of American and British authors, and foreign SF films and TV series as well, still comprise a sizable part of the commercial offering. Since the early Sixties, however, the large-format softcover pulp novel series or *Romanheft*—the form has long been used for many types of popular fiction in Germany—has attracted a large if not very discriminating SF readership in Germany. The leading *Romanheft* series is *Perry Rhodan* (1961-), which is produced in Munich by a stable of house authors, some of whom have adopted American-sounding pseudonyms; thus Walter Ernsting (b.1920), for example, writes under the pen-name of "Clark Darlton." *Perry Rhodan* appears weekly in editions numbering in the hundreds of thousands, and has enjoyed the distinction, rare for German SF, of translation into English. The series is notorious for its juvenile style, monotonously repetitive story lines, and reactionary ideological content.[3]

Contemporary German SF

Yet by the late Fifties there were also a few writers who sought to make SF in Germany something more than native pulp novels and translations of good, mediocre or even execrable American or English works.[4] Two decades later they had attained no little success in attracting the attention of readers and publishers at home, though they have yet to receive much notice from abroad or from the German literary Establishment. Striking achievements have been registered in several subgenres; and writers, editors and critics generally express solicitude for their fellows and evidence a desire to reconstruct links with the past. It appears that this promising development—the emergence of a self-aware, cohesive, and literarily competent tradition of modern German SF—will continue.[5]

(i) Herbert W. Franke

Best known among writers of literarily and intellectually serious German SF is Herbert W. Franke (b. 1927), a native of Vienna who now lives near Munich. His novels are difficult to judge, especially the earlier ones. Their sensational plots, garish settings, and occasionally rough prose are reminiscent of Anglo-American SF, particularly that of the "Golden Age", and not necessarily its better examples. That is not surprising, since Franke has worked for years as SF editor for two large West German publishers, Goldmann and Heyne. But like some "New Wave" British and American writers, he uses the conventions of traditional, even primitive SF to create dystopian narratives. To encourage a sense of alienation he also employs the devices of experimental (or once-experimental) "mainstream" literature, among them collage, non-linear plot chronology, and distortion or fragmentation of narrative perspective. Those probable influences, as well as his work in cybernetics, are especially evident in *Ypsilon Minus* (1976), part of which is narrated in computer jargon. Although Franke favors settings and characters not identifiably German but instead American or vaguely international, one can perceive an ideological attitude which is definitely German or "national" in the larger, non-pejorative sense. Its topical targets seem to be at once the excesses of both the American capitalism and Soviet authoritarian collectivism which have for so long contended over Germany and, of course, the

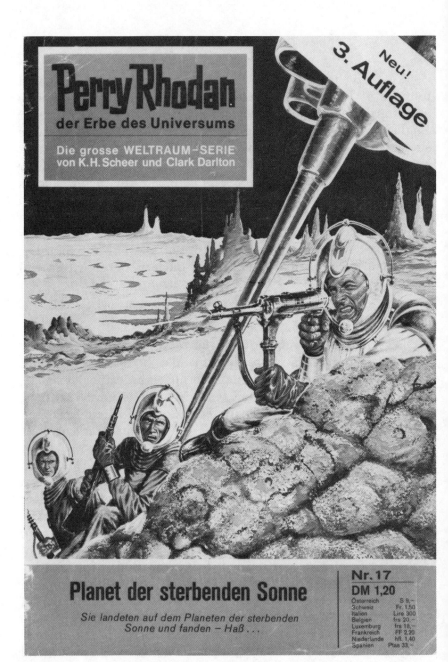

Front cover of "Perry Rhodan: The Inheritor of the Universe," the mass post-war West German science fiction pulp novel series. (reduced)

Herbert W. Franke (1927—), contemporary West German SF writer and editor.

author's native Austria.

Franke's short stories generally lack the imaginative boldness, the stylistic power, and—understandably so—the thematic complexity of his novels. Yet the early anthology *Der grüne Komet* [*The Green Comet*] (1960) is impressive. It is, in effect, a collection of études or finger exercises, each of which explores, in just a few pages, a single basic motif or theme of the genre and demonstrates in brief a younger performer's mastery of his craft. German SF as a whole may well be pursuing a similar development and assertion of maturity.

Franke's credentials as a scientist and aesthetician, among them a doctorate in physics, employment with the technological giant Siemens AG, and an excellent anthology and study of cybernetic art, *Computergraphik—Computerkunst* (1971), argue persuasively that his works be taken seriously. They, his dedicated labors as an editor of SF, and his relatively few but perceptive writings about the genre, have established him as the dominant figure in the history of recent German SF. If other writers are now approaching a similar prominence, Franke has done much to make it possible for them to do so.

(ii) Wolfgang Jeschke

A few years younger than Franke but belonging essentially to the same generation of writers and—if one can use the word so soon—the same tradition of post-war German SF is Wolfgang Jeschke (b. 1936). Jeschke trained as a toolmaker and then studied literature and philosophy at Munich. During the Fifties and Sixties he wrote SF short stories and novellas; he then devoted himself chiefly to editing SF, first at the Lichtenberg Verlag and then at the Heyne Verlag, where for a time he was Franke's associate. In the late Seventies he assumed full responsibility for the SF program at Heyne, which in terms of new titles issued per year is the largest single SF book publisher in the world.[6] As an editor he has done much to further the work of other writers of German SF.

Critics have termed Jeschke's recent novel, *Der letzte Tag der Schöpfung* [*The Last Day of Creation*] (1981), daring in concept and admirable in style.[7] Indeed the novel is a puzzling work, despite its quite conventional diction and—when one finally gets there—its plot. Its chief flaw, a laudable one, may be that it strives too mightily to be all things to all readers. Thus knowing aficionados, a large and powerful group when gathered together in its own name but miniscule among the general SF readership, can chuckle over

Jeschke's jibes at purveyors of pseudo-science like Erich von Däniken. The novel can even be read as a spoof of traditional high-adventure, high-technology SF, though again only by those who can see not merely the cheek but also the tongue in it.

But Jeschke's time-travel story about a grandiose and catastrophic attempt to thwart the oil sheiks by technological intervention in the past has two more serious purposes, the one social, the other aesthetic or genre-specific. As one who regards science and technology critically but acknowledges their necessity and even their innate fascination, he seeks to demonstrate how human intelligence, morality, and social organization may not suffice to control human invention, ambition, and greed. Toward the end of the novel the narrator states the message, perhaps too didactically:

> And thus the most ambitious and expensive project in the history of the human race was officially declared a failure [by the marooned time-travelers].
>
> They all did it with light hearts, for nothing connected them any longer with the period of time which they had come from and which could have been a highpoint in human culture had it stood beneath other stars than those on the epaulets of ambitious generals. (270-71)

The author himself, in an interview with the present writer, remarked more dispassionately:

> [The targets are] the over-bureaucratization of the world and, above all, the military, which can command us in every way [über uns verfügen].... The function of SF as social-critical, change-oriented [literature] I regard much more fundamentally than as immediate [topical criticism]; rather, [it is] free-play consideration of possibilities [spielerisches Erwägen von Möglichkeiten], in order to show that reality does not at all have to be as it is—that is, to break up the status quo.[8]

Jeschke's treatment of the narrower concerns, motifs and techniques of SF complements his larger message about science and society. In his novel, and in much of his other SF as well, time travel serves not only to emphasize the inability of Man to control his creations; it—or rather time itself—is also the scientific theme and aesthetic focus of the narration, both tool and target of the author's attempt to establish the logical plausibility and subjective reality of his imaginary world. Taking a notion discredited by modern science, worn out by older SF, and therefore discountenanced by many contemporary writers, he proceeds industriously to impose it on the skeptical or even hostile reader. Thus the actual narration of

Wolfgang Jeschke (1936—   ), contemporary West German SF writer and editor.

events fictively occurring in the antediluvian Europe to which the time travelers are sent is accompanied by a shorter but by no means brief (60 pp.) "documentary" exposition which traces the equally fictive development of time travel and the schemes to use it. Those who are unfamiliar with SF or who read simply for the "story" may well find the section tedious and pointless. The initiated, critical reader will recognize it as a tour de force in the special "game" of SF; it is a conceptual and rhetorical exercise which acknowledges, sums up, exploits, and seeks to overtrump the entire evolution, from H.G. Wells on, of one of the genre's archetypal themes and prime devices.

Jeschke concedes that his novel is likely to suffer or enjoy different fates with different readers. But he resolutely declares his overall purpose: "I set myself the problem of destroying, step by step, reality as we know it."[9] What Jeschke seeks to destroy is not merely the narrower reality that time-travel is impossible, but also reality in its largest existential sense. He pursues to its logical solipsistic end the fundamental paradox of time-travel, the notion that every intervention in the past would retroactively alter the present, perhaps even give rise to an alternate world with its own history. Such destruction or deconstruction may indeed be one of the goals or generic destinations of SF. Another, however, is the earnest construction or reconstruction of fictive reality. Jeschke's ironic stance in *Der letzte Tag der Schöpfung*—and here he resembles so many newer writers of SF—does not make it easy to discern whether that was also his intent; nor will readers easily agree about how well he may have accomplished it. But quite likely the novel will be regarded as one of the landmarks, if not monuments, of recent German SF.

(iii) Lesser Luminaries

The work of a dozen or more other writers appears frequently as SF. Most prominent among them are Thomas Le Blanc, Hans Joachim Alpers, Rainer Erler, Reinmar Cunis, Jesco von Puttkamer, Gerd Maximovič, and Jörg Weigand. Like the writers of early "Golden Age" Anglo-American SF, few if any earn a living solely by writing SF. Thus Weigand (b.1940), prolific though he is as an author, editor, translator and critic of SF, is by occupation a political commentator and editor (*Redakteur*) for Second German Television (ZDF) in Bonn.

Just as the bread-and-butter literary form and mode of distribution of early modern Anglo-American SF was not the full-length, independently marketed novel but rather the specialized magazine short story or novelette, so too are shorter narrations, appearing in publications catering to the special-interest reader, presently the mainstay of less established writers and still a favored alternative form even for Herbert W. Franke. Weigand goes so far as to argue that "the real domain of good SF is the short story," because "SF is a literature of ideas..., and the majority of SF ideas simply will not support a novel."[10]

Certainly the short story has provided German writers a convenient mode in which to practice their skills and explore the thematic repertory of SF. But the persistent fondness for the shorter narration in German SF is perhaps better explained by other circumstances, both aesthetic and social. The short story and novella continue to enjoy, in the broader German literary realm, a popularity and prestige which they have long since lost in English-speaking countries. Market conditions peculiar to SF and similar "subcultural" literatures also deserve consideration. Struggling authors creating a specialized literature which also has not fully established itself need to publish frequently, quickly, and widely. Readers, editors, and publishers, always doubtful of the profitability of their purchases and perhaps still mistrustful of any offering that has not the aura of American or English SF, may prefer to hedge their bets by selecting an anthology which contains the work of several writers, or at least a collection of pieces rather than a single novel by one author. The short story anthology and its younger but more grandly conceived cousin, the regular SF book series, have served modern German SF well. Editors like Franke and Jeschke have been able to encourage new talent, and now they or their fellows preside over major publishing programs. But even before the exclusively German anthology had become a reasonably acceptable risk, they resolutely but subtly exposed and accustomed their German readers to native works by including them matter-of-factly in their various series of international SF collections.

It might be argued nevertheless that the anthology or regular book series lacks the immediacy and impact so evident in the monthly or quarterly American SF "pulps," which were, under the circumstances, a vehicle ideally suited to the furtherance of younger writers, to the prompt and forthright expression of feedback from demanding, experienced readers, and to the attempt to reach a relatively large readership and, if necessary, cultivate its tastes.[11] The weekly *Romanhefte* like *Perry Rhodan* still dominate the German SF mass market, and independently issued serious novels, though not as rare as before, are still not common. But lately two popular publishers, Heyne and Moewig, the latter at one time the publisher of *Perry Rhodan*, have begun to sponsor periodic collections of SF, non-fiction science popularization, SF criticism, and fan news. Though they are issued at roughly annual intervals and are manifestly aimed at the larger readership, the *Heyne Science Fiction Magazin* and Moewig's *Science Fiction Almanach* are nevertheless ambitious in content and thus might advance the fortunes of promising newer writers and make serious German SF more popular.

(iv) Michael Weisser

The immense popularity and commercial success of "pulp" novel series, above all *Perry Rhodan*, have established the economic and receptional foundation for native SF in West Germany. And, though the mills of *Germanistik* grind slowly, the labors of Franke, Jeschke, and their fellows have done much to justify its claim to literary status and recognition. Yet no work of recent West German SF better exemplifies its achievement and promise than *SYN-CODE-7* (1982), the first novel of Michael Weisser (b. 1948). Now a design artist and journalist in Bremen, Weisser received practical training in a chemical research laboratory, graduated in design from the Cologne Schools of Commercial Arts, and studied art history, education, sociology, and communications science at Marburg. He has edited books on civic art, popular aesthetics, and the history of advertising, and has undertaken various multi-media artistic projects.[12] Though his background is evident in *SYN-CODE-7*, the author's imagination and masterly style enabled him to create something quite different from the customary first-novel portrait of the artist portraying himself as a young man.

With a sure grasp of the dual predilections of SF for adventurous plots and didactic disquisition, Weisser explores and exploits one of the genre's fundamental themes: an ostensibly utopian, super-technological world thrown into turmoil by the threat of malfunction at its very center. "SYN-CODE-7" is the alarm-signal which calls into action the "Internal Security Ring" charged with protecting the "BIOTEC," a vast bio-technological system. Not only does the BIOTEC produce food and energy for a society which has ravaged nature; through its giant "seventh-generation...bioplastic lattice memory [bioplastischer Gitterspeicher]" it also serves as the all-encompassing central information processor which operates, regulates, studies and modifies the system itself. The biotechnological society is Byzantine in its artificial perfection, its facade of timelessness which conceals an intense preoccupation with time and a fear of disorder or "dynamic" behavior, whether human or technological. One analytical member of the ISR observes that "a pan-social progress on the broadest foundation,... the production of specialized micro-organisms, produced this progressive biotechnological society;" but she wonders "how much we still want progress in our society" (62).

Leader of the ISR, by genius and force of personality, is Alsey Target, a master cyberneticist who composes multi-media "laser ballets" in his free time and under stress has a disquieting tendency to resort to pharmacological stimulants and relaxants. " 'On the 254th day at 6:10.04,' " as Alsey's subsequent official memorandum records, the first unexplained malfunction in the BIOTEC occurs (8), and the system itself gives the alarm; the superintelligent, semi-organic BIOTEC is showing signs of "independent activation [Eigendynamik]" (91). In a state of "confusion-reaction" analogous to neurosis and epilepsy in humans (8), the BIOTEC registers its own awakening independence as an attack upon itself.

Relentlessly the ISR attacks cybernetic conundrums and absorbs horrendous casualties in battle with genetic monstrosities spawned by the BIOTEC. Alsey discovers that it is in part his close colleague, the idealistic digital-equipment technician Torn Krüger, who "threatens the system" (190), or rather wishes to liberate the bioplasts, "the last slaves of our society" (193), by destroying the system. But Torn, " 'under the flickering of the LED's' " (193), finds he cannot take the final step, for he can no longer tell, in the biotechnological world, " 'who, then, is the slave and who is the master?... How can we liberate ourselves from the dominating ones, without annihilating ourselves? And how is it possible to liberate ourselves from ourselves?' " (193, 196). Unable to bear the existential chaos he has perceived, Torn breaks down and is no longer a threat to the system. The ISR proceeds to solve the other part of the biotechnological riddle. Another researcher had programmed the BIOTEC to examine a theoretical higher stage of itself; the result, when "the bioplasts,... a lower state of consciousness,... were confronted...with a higher form [of consciousness],...a theoretical description of themselves," was systematic chaos (244-5). The catastrophic program is erased and the ISR confidently declares the restoration of order. But the epilog pictures swarms of bioplasts who "have withdrawn and restructured themselves and have imprinted on themselves the possibility of expansion.... They...carry only the ethic of their own existence. They are without reservations. They are without history. They are without scruple and lack every feeling. They are beginning..." (251: Weisser's aposiopesis).

The particular scientific and technological content of *SYN-CODE-7* is drawn from cybernetics and genetics, two disciplines which, along with macro- and microcosmic physics, are currently undergoing nothing less than revolutionary expansion and have therefore become centers of interest and even alarm among scientists, the public, and—since at least Asimov's robot stories of the "Golden Age"—writers of SF. The close association of the two fields is not coincidental, in SF or elsewhere, for both address the management of information, and each has enriched the other. Thus the genetic code can be regarded as the biological equivalent of computer programming, assembly, and machine languages, ànd thus can cyberneticists speculate seriously about application of genetic engineering to the development of an incredibly small, later-generation "chip" which will be constructed of living organisms.

Beyond such technological interests lie larger and highly paradoxical theoretical, ethical, and philosophical issues. One is Artificial Intelligence ("AI"), whether it is to be found in artifices which think or organisms which are artificially adapted to thinking—if indeed distinctions between animate and inert, natural and artificial, would still have meaning. A corollary, one which is addressed by both geneticists and cyberneticists, concerns the origin, development, and definition of human intelligence—if indeed such there is, as Alsey Target muses (227) with an insight into the modest stature of humanity reminiscent of that conveyed by *Auf zwei Planeten*. Still more recondite is the notion of structures or entities which replicate themselves, modify their own capabilities, and reflect on their own reflections, or, in contemporary terms, generate information about their own information processing.

Those ideas constitute the greater scientific and technological theme of *SYN-CODE-7*. Their paradoxes, dangers, and fascination are explored in spectacular passages which mix the language and images of cybernetics and genetics, electronics and ethics, artifice and nature, process and purpose, the sacred and the scientific. Thus the foundation for Torn Krüger's tragic insight that "reality is different.... All charges have reversed their polarity, all values are displaced," and that he himself is "between the charges" and therefore "without charge—without identity" (196-7), is laid by the description of the ISR's headquarters in the BIOTEC:

> In Level D life is compressed into data,... reduced to the two poles of
> Yes and No.
> Yes and No hold the new, progressive world together;... Yes and No
> are the smallest elements of life that Man is in a position to comprehend.
> They are the poles of human history between Good and Bad, between the
> world of light and the world of darkness; they are the smallest common
> multiple of a complex society. Yes and No are the building-blocks of
> life, and they delineate the positions of adaptation and refusal. Yes and
> No, positive and negative, charge and no-charge, right-handed spin and
> left-handed spin... [Weisser's ellipsis] in the bioplastic lattice-memory
> an image of the world is created from this couplet, this mundane truism
> [Binsenwahrheit] of all being. (45-6)

Human language is also an information processing, storage, and retrieval system. It thus has affinities to cybernetics and genetics which can be perceived and highlighted by literary artists like Weisser. The narrative language of *SYN-CODE-7,* the "code" in and through which the novel's own information is generated and processed, is well suited to the author's biotechnological theme and the paradoxes that theme involves. A set of fictive documents on BIOTEC letterheads, comprising tables of organization, procedural directives, and Alsey Target's official report about the crisis and its resolution, precedes the actual recounting of events. The action is presented not in the customary epic preterite, but rather entirely in the present tense, with a wealth of minute descriptive detail and frequent precise chronological data. The omniscient narrator, whose identity is left provocatively indefinite, thus becomes "a murmuring conjurer"—not one of the past tense, the kind of narrator envisioned by Thomas Mann and described in Chapter I, but rather one of the grammatical present and the fictive, hypothetical future.

The effect is startling. Not only does the action unfold literally before the reader's eyes; Weisser skillfully uses the same present tense in a gnomic, aorist or eternal sense to underscore and yet also undermine the supposed immutability of the imaginary world. Frequently he evokes that impression by capitalizing on the overt distinction in German between the dynamic genuine passive, formed with the auxiliary *werden,* and the inert statal or "false" passive, formed with *sein.* Variation in automated programs, for example, is limited by a range which "is [ist] checked, tested and optimized" (18); and in Alsey Target's world "technology is [ist] perfectly integrated into the needs of human beings" (19). The genuine passive, consequently, encourages more strongly the sense of action. If the ironic term "progressive [fortschrittlich]" is one of the novel's chief linguistic leitmotifs, another is the impersonal but urgent outcry, "The system is being threatened [das System wird bedroht]." The construction may well be passive grammatically and, from our perspective, psychologically; considered from that of the BIOTEC, the system being threatened, the statement is an active utterance.

In its smaller but vitally expressive units Weisser's style is characterized by parallelisms and oxymora which combine, in tense and paradoxical juxtaposition, the artificial and the natural. Thus the floor of Alsey Target's subterranean work station is described as a "meadow of soft vinyl fibers," its ceiling a "radiant-blue, synthetic sky" (41); laboratory booths are "filled with a quiet rustling [Rauschen] of technology and a soft murmuring [Raunen] of people" (44); Torn Krüger breaks down under "the starry canopy [Sternenhimmel] of LED's" controlled by the "cells...in the belly [Bauch] of this closed system" (195); and throughout the novel the bioplasts themselves, technological creations, are attributed with animate properties and thus become actual, active characters who "awake" (121), "retreat," "enter" data, "reproduce," have a pulse, "set priorities," and "begin" (250-51).

It might seem that *SYN-CODE-7* could scarcely differ more from Jeschke's recent novel. In its conventional plotting characterization, and prose style *Der letzte Tag der Schöpfung*, as the author knows full well and wishes the reader also to recognize, is an imitation of "classical" SF, though to be sure a creative, sometimes brilliant, even parodistic one. *SYN-CODE-7* could well be described—if such terms and comparisons were not in disrepute—as "baroque," though in the highly favorable senses of the word, especially as it is applied to music and the visual arts.[13] Outrageous invention in theme and motif is paired with tight conceptualization and rigorously-structured variation to form a well-tempered whole which seems to grow out of and then return to itself. The treatment of major ideas and phrases throughout the novel suggests the varied, reflexive repetition of the fugue; one is reminded of Paul Celan's poem "Todesfuge [Death-fugue]" (1952). Nor is it accidental that Weisser chooses the present tense, or that Alsey Target's summary memorandum both begins the work and is reintroduced in exact quotation near its close. If synaesthesia, too, is a hallmark of the baroque, as well as of romanticism and contemporary art, Weisser has paid tribute to it in his own multi-media projects and in Alsey's "laser ballets."

But most striking of all the novel's stylistic features is what might be called its literary sensuousness. In certain virtuoso passages, as when Alsey Target penetrates the BIOTEC to its very center, "the last intimacy of the system" (181), the narration swells, and then overflows or explodes, into an orgy of idea, image and language:

> A shimmering gold foil veils the surface [of the high-tension trunk line serving the BIOTEC] and in its curvature reflects a ghostily-distorted scene: it stylizes the power conduit into a giver of life [Lebensspender] and lends it a breath of magical significance. It raises the phallic cylinders to worship-worthy idols of a technocratic society. . . . [In the recycling facility] all waste products of the BIOTEC flow together, are reduced to pieces, ground and broken down into elemental sludge [Grundschlamm], thereafter to be taken up again into the endless circulation between life and death . . ., a circulation . . . which itself keeps on running when no being of human kind [menschliches Wesen] is any longer participant in the revolving process. . . .
> Alsey Target hesitates a moment as he gazes into the pulse-beat of the BIOTEC for the first time. Revealing itself to him is an unimaginable technology in the face of which he has, in equal measure, respect and fear. Close to the dully pulsing revolving pumps he feels himself smaller than a grain of sand at the foot of a precipice. . . . This Trinity [the cellular triplets in the bioplastic lattice-memory] is the soul [Seele] of the system.
> It is the spirit [Geist] of the BIOTEC.
> . . . [Alsey] has entered the cathedral of society, in whose depth the holy relics rest—. . . Alsey Target stands in total light. (182-87)

Or, to rephrase the matter with the grandiose categories of the visual arts and of the currents in recent SF, *SYN-CODE-7* suggests a synthesis of the older *genre* realism or pointillism and hard-core science of "Golden Age" Anglo-American SF with the stylistic exuberance and preoccupation with genetics, cybernetics, and psychology which characterize the New Wave.

And yet Jeschke's and Weisser's recent novels have in common two fundamental attitudes, themes, or—if one chooses to accent form rather than content—aesthetic interests, both of which are mainstays of SF of all kinds, even the most trivial. One is a preoccupation with time: its very nature, its fatal impact on human existence, its conceivable alterability, and its potential stylistic or linguistic effect. The other is the concentration on futuristic but somehow plausible science and technology, not as something to be glorified or rejected, but rather as prime determinants of human life which must be reckoned with or, from the extra-fictional perspective, examined critically.

(v) The German SF Radio-play (Hörspiel)

Recent German SF has recorded notable advances and

demonstrated even greater ambitions in the novel and short story, the genre's traditional forms. Yet one of its particularly impressive achievements is to be observed in the radio-play or *Hörspiel,* a mode of literary expression to which American ears are not attuned, despite the fondly-remembered "mainstream" radio dramas of earlier decades and, in SF, the popularity of series like *Buck Rogers* and the notoriety of Wells' 1938 broadcast of *The War of the Worlds.*

The viability of the literarily serious *Hörspiel* in German culture can be attributed to two factors: the exigencies of the early post-war years, which delayed the development of television as a popular medium; and—in West Germany at least—the peculiar position of radio-play production within the larger structure of the broadcasting media, whose nature, again, strikes outsiders as being rather anomalous. Dieter Hasselblatt, Director of the Radio-play Division at Bavarian Broadcasting (Bayrischer Rundfunk) and in his own right a leading figure in West German SF, points out that broadcasting institutions in the Federal Republic are neither private enterprises, as in the United States, nor state-owned and -directed, as in the East-bloc countries and, it must be admitted, Great Britain and France. Hybridly termed both "public and official [öffentlich-rechtlich]," they are, he amplifies, "un-private but not governmental" facilities which draw their funding from user-taxes administered through a sort of blind trust. Dependent neither on commercial gain nor on direct governmental appropriations, the West German broadcasting media enjoy a particular freedom, Hasselblatt argues, although he concedes the possibility that special-interest groups or legislative bodies which control taxation might somehow seek to exercise undue influence on programming and ideological orientation. But, he points out, radio-play production, even in West Germany, is a minor part of broadcasting and therefore attracts little attention from pressure groups— including in this instance, unfortunately, literary critics.[14] Like Jörg Weigand in his defense of the short story as an ideal form for German SF, Hasselblatt seeks to make an aesthetic virtue out of a social and economic necessity:

> In this country the *Hörspiel*—mode of distribution in a public-official system—is independent of markets and can therefore pursue developmental dramatics [Entwicklungsdramaturgie]....
> ...[T]he future of SF lies where little money is invested...[15]

> The most proper [dezentest] and appropriate presentational form of and for SF is, for me, the *Hörspiel.* For the *Hörspiel* and SF have the

same structural requirements: active, cooperative imagination [mitdenkende Fantasie] is needed—and without this active, cooperative imagination neither the *Hörspiel* nor SF would be what they can be: a discovery and invention of conceivable possibility, precisely worked out by the imagination [ein genau ausphantisiertes Finden und Erfinden von denkbarer Möglichkeit].[16]

Since the *Hörspiel* is a respected, economically established form of literature in Germany, and since for most of its history German SF has not been a suspect ghetto literature, it should not be surprising that some of the most prestigious modern German writers have composed radio plays which, whether or not the writer or the listening public welcomes the label, can be classified as SF. Dürrenmatt's *Unternehmen der Wega* was mentioned earlier in this chapter. Two *Hörspiele* by the eminent lyric poet Günter Eich (1907-72), *Träume* [*Dreams*] (1951) and *Die Stunde des Huflattichs* [*The Hour of the Coltsfoot Flower*] (1958) have also been claimed for the genre. A classic recent German SF *Hörspiel* is Lothar Streblow's *Der Fisch* [*The Fish*] (1972), set in a futuristic subterranean world so polluted that the claimed appearance of a single fish inspires astonishment.[17] Two broadcasting institutions have become the leaders in SF *Hörspiel* production: South German Broadcasting (Süddeutscher Rundfunk) in Heidelberg, which began a monthly series in 1967; and Bavarian Radio, where the department directed by Hasselblatt has produced a monthly series since 1974 and presently seems to have assumed the dominant position in the medium.[18]

Although the reading or listening public outside the German-speaking countries has of course little access to the German SF *Hörspiel*, its popularity and literary quality in themselves merit greater attention from students of SF. Worthy of still more notice—even amazement—is the use in some recent productions of a technological innovation almost unknown outside Germany: "synthetic-head stereophonics" or *Kunstkopfstereofonie,* a singularly realistic method of sound reproduction.[19]

In principle synthetic-head stereo is surprisingly simple, though regular employment of the technique in broadcasting has required a listening public and a corresponding commitment to development of facilities which are to be found only where the *Hörspiel* is an established medium. The essential element is an acoustically accurate replica of a human head. Miniature microphones are located approximately where the eardrums would otherwise be, and the dummy is placed where the ideal listener might well wish to be, whether in the midst of an operatic performance or in the setting of a radio play. The recording registers and reproduces aural location and distance far better than conventional stereo or even quadraphonic systems.

The disadvantages of synthetic-head stereophonics are two, one technical and the other psychological. Presently the playback, although it can be received with conventional equipment, requires the use of stereo earphones; and the lack of visual cues encourages the listener to interpret sounds produced equidistant to both microphones, and therefore played back with equal strength in right and left earphones, as emanating always from behind, though in fact they may have been generated in front of the synthetic head. Attempts to eliminate both drawbacks are being made. Nevertheless even now the technique is nothing short of remarkable in its suggestion of verisimilitude or, to rephrase the matter according to the special intentionality of SF, its power to further the subjective acceptance of a manifestly implausible world. In seeking to evoke that impression, traditional "print" SF must confine itself to physically indirect, semiotically abstract means: the written word. On the other hand, cinematic and television SF often rely on visual effects which may well seem spectacular to the contemporaneous viewer but which generally appear quaintly unrealistic to the later observer. The synthetic-head technique, by contrast, attacks the problem of inducing the impression of verisimilitude by insidiously and yet, in another way, directly appealing to the auditory faculty, which has often been asserted to be the most immediate, the most suggestive, and, in a word, the most sensuous of the major senses. Such, at least, is the argument advanced by producers of synthetic-head SF *Horspiele* like Dieter Hasselblatt; and after listening to several of their productions I have discarded my initial skepticism and quite agree with them.

The sensuous and, for those who wish to exploit it, blatantly sensual potency of synthetic-head stereophonics is demonstrated by Friedrich Scholz' short piece *Da ist was, da war was—ein kosmo-erotisches Gruselspiel* [*Here It Comes, There It Went—A Cosmo-erotic Whorror-show*], recorded at Bavarian Broadcasting in February 1974. Figuring memorably in the *Hörspiel* is a motif familiar from much older SF: an artificial woman or, in the jargon of the genre, a simulacrum; whispering into the listener's ear from, it seems, virtually no distance at all, she begins to seduce him. The play quite overtly illustrates the capability of synthetic-head stereophonics to transform the listener, at least to some extent, into a participant.

Herbert W. Franke's lengthier *Papa Joe & Co.*, recorded also at Bavarian Broadcasting, in January 1976, explores the medium and its message more richly and subtly, if not so sensationally.[20] Papa Joe is a charismatic American politician who founds his popular autocratic reign on promises of guiltless, commercially successful pleasure, which he indeed seems to fulfill. He maintains his dominance by making his soothing voice and beneficent counsel immediately available to all who are prepared and willing to hear his voice, which is apprehended directly within the devotee's own mind. A team of European diplomats sent to examine the American utopia discovers that, during the rite of initiation into Papa Joe's cult, the neophytes are fitted with miniature thought-detectors and cerebral receivers which can be addressed by a transmitter that conveys the demagogue's advice, reassurance, and demands. A skeptical yet suggestible European who submits himself to initiation into the cult is the central figure—quite literally, for the synthetic head is oriented to his position in the action. The production makes overt but aesthetically valid use of the synthetic-head technique's ability to convey the impression that the sounds it records and reproduces emanate not from the same arbitrary, localized points, but rather from all around the listener's ears, or even between them, within his own mind. Those familiar with the medium speak, it might seem rather alarmingly, of its potential use in brainwashing; Franke's *Hörspiel,* in its Bavarian Broadcasting production, both examines the notion thematically and gives a controlled demonstration of its credibility. Listener becomes participant, and participant becomes listener.

(vi) National Consciousness

Most of the leading figures in West German SF will assert quite earnestly that their literature has achieved or is fast gaining an identity of its own, and that it is demonstrating, at least in individual works, the ability to compete ("Konkurrenzfähigkeit") artistically and conceptually, if not yet commercially, with more established traditions of SF.[21] Evident in those claims—and the phenomenon is apparent elsewhere in German society—is not only a personal pride in achievement against adversity, but also an emergent attention to social or cultural concerns which, as Jörg Weigand carefully remarks, are to be described as "national," but "not at all nationalistic."[22] Thus in philosophical or ideological orientation one observes an emphasis on the critique of science and technology rather than their glorification, which many German writers are inclined to regard as characteristic of Anglo-American

SF, or at least of those works which have been so popular in West Germany. Wolfgang Jeschke notes as an initial cause for that attitude the reaction against the Vietnam war, both within antitraditional or "New Wave" SF and within the larger society, whether American or European.[23] Weigand points out too that the deleterious environmental effects of science and technology have been more readily apparent in West Germany, much smaller and more densely populated than America, and certainly as industrialized.[24] In artistic terms one observes an increasing resistance to the long-standing tendency to adopt Anglo-American settings, character-names, and jargon, a practice whose ultimate result, as the same observer puts it, has been not only an air of artificiality but also a neglect of the deeper needs of West German society and the potential for incisive critique offered by the native milieu.[25]

In the few years since its publication in 1975 one short West German SF novel, the curiously titled *Der Untergang der Stadt Passau* [*The Decline of the City of Passau*] by Carl Amery (b.1922), has achieved something like landmark status in the genre. That position may be due less to the work's intrinsic quality than to its expressly "national" aims. The novel recounts the lapse into semi-barbarism of Europe and, particularly, the minor city of Passau and the even more obscure nearby town of Rosenheim in provincial Bavaria after the Pestilence of 1981. The narration is conducted alternately by three distinct personae or voices, whose utterances are set off from each other stylistically, temporally and even typographically. Most remarkable among them is the chaplain Egid; excerpts from his vulgar Latin chronicle *Magnalia Dei per Gentem Rosmeriorum*, das [*sic*] heisst den *Grosstaten Gottes durch das Volk der Rosmer* [viz. *God's Wondrous Deeds in and through the People of Rosenheim*], beginning with "Anno Domini 2112" or "the year 131 APP (Post Pestilenziam)" (7), are "reproduced" in their equally antiquated baroque German translation—and printed in old-style German *Fraktur* type.

In his preface Amery acknowledges the thematic debt of his "etude [Fingerübung]" (5) to Walter M. Miller's classic *A Canticle for Leibowitz* (1955-7; 1960). Yet he also asserts that

> I have attempted additionally to make elements of our own—the German and regional [heimatlich]—tradition usable for the genre [of] SF: fundamentally they ought needs [müssten] to fit into this basic pattern [Grundmuster] much better than the customary American props [Versatzstücke]. (5)

Amery's short novel is an intriguing if not wholly successful venture, one perhaps more valuable in a meta-literary sense, as a manifesto or barometer of the independence of " 'respectable [seriös]' " (5) German SF, than as an emulation of its great predecessor. If in the radio play recent German SF has aggressively marked off a medium as its own, Amery's *Untergang der Stadt Passau* has crystallized the urge of recent West German SF writers to seek their own idiom.

(vii) East German SF

Any discussion of things German is plagued by the division of a single linguistic and cultural realm among four major states, and, more particularly, by the existence of the German Democratic Republic as an established political entity and a growing center of scientific, technological, and, not least of all, literary endeavor. Therefore the foregoing observations about modern "German" SF are still incomplete, not simply because of their necessary brevity, but also—as may well have become apparent already—because they are limited to SF appearing in West Germany. It might also be noted, peripherally, that both Franke and Jeschke were born outside the boundaries of the present Federal Republic, and indeed that the former was educated in Vienna. The prominence of the Austrian Franz Rottensteiner as an editor and critic lends additional substance and spice to the point.

But more germane here is the presence of an appreciable body of East German SF and related literature.[26] Some of it is the work of the country's most prestigious writers, such as Christa Wolf, Anna Seghers, and Gerhard Branstner. Well known among those who work primarily within the genre is Carlos Rasch (b.1932), and outstanding among promising younger writers is Bernd Ulbrich (b.1943). Acknowledged as the leading figures in recent East German SF are, however, Johanna and Günter Braun (b.1929 and 1928 resp.), who write short stories and novels as a wife-and-husband team.[27]

Like much of their other work, the Brauns' recent novel *Conviva Ludibundus* (1978)[28] is a sparely composed, subtly ironic futuristic fable, and thus could scarcely differ more, it would seem, from Weisser's richly textured present-tense chronicle or the brusque, bluntly satirical (and sometimes satyric) realism of Jeschke's *Der letzte Tag der Schöpfung*. Yet *Conviva Ludibundus* shares with *SYN-CODE-7* the notion of semi-artificial "bioelectronic" organisms which coalesce into intelligent entities. And its overt theme, like that of both Weisser's and Jeschke's novels, is science and technology out of control, set loose by more or less laudable human intellect and quite reprehensible human vanity.

Narrator of *Conviva Ludibundus* is the scientist Philemon, who is nearing ninety and therefore rather testy, but is still physically and mentally vigorous and quite able to perceive the faults of his juniors. Many years before, Philemon had developed a new strain of shellfish, the green medallions [grüne Medaillons]," which now provide the people of the early "third millenium" a supremely tasty, nutritious food. A virtually undetectable organism, the *conviva ludibundus* or "playful table-guest," lives in symbiosis with the green medallions, consuming half of them but through its excretions supplying them with essential nourishment. Only Philemon, who himself lives in perfect harmony with nature, suspects their existence.

Refusing even to hear the older man's advice, Philemon's successor as director of the "Society for the Utilization of Seafoods [Gesellschaft zur Verwertung der Meeresfrüchte]," Dr. H. H. Mittelzwerck ('Meansmidge' or 'Measlyend'), seeks to eliminate the seemingly inefficient loss of yield and thereby to advance his own reputation by destroying the mysterious thieves. The green medallions vanish from their aquatic plantation, and Mittelzwerck, accompanied by a retinue of scientific assistants, a public relations team, and the skeptical Philemon, sets forth on a nautical expedition to hunt down the predators. The venture degenerates into a futuristic, surrealistic ship of fools. Mittelzwerck establishes communication and what he takes to be advantageous cooperation with the aggregate bioelectronic organism, the "conviva ludibundus compositus." The ludibundi—the research team ingenuously welcomes Philemon's sardonic suggestion that they be renamed "Mittelzwercks"—develop into ubiquitous, tireless creatures who penetrate, register, and analyze everything around them. Like Weisser's "BIOTEC," they become an immense collective data-gathering and -processing system which, manifesting intelligence and independence, threatens its creators. Philemon, the ship's phlegmatic captain, and the expedition's sensible public relations specialist are barely able to loose the research vessel from the masses of ludibundi which smother it with their own inquisitive bodies and with heaps of the debilitating "super-mussel" they have so willingly proposed to produce. The ship is returned to its quay, where other relics of misconceived technology are mothballed. Philemon, replacing the physically and mentally broken Mittelzwerck, undertakes to salvage what little can be gained from the expedition and to attempt, though there is little hope of success, the establishment of a new plantation of green medallions.

It might seem both that *Conviva Ludibundus* condemns modern science and technology, and that the Brauns, like Franke, Jeschke, and Weisser, write a sort of international SF, one which does not explicitly address their national environment. Certainly the novel often jibes at excessive faith in human knowledge and technological skill, and its imaginary world, like those of many of the Brauns' other works, is not manifestly a descendant or allegory of contemporary East Germany. Yet to read the novel as a fashionable rejection of science, or to overlook its topical commentary, would not do justice to the text. Philemon's disparaging remarks about nostalgic "female nature freaks [Naturanbeterinnen]" (65), the groupies who have made of him a confirmed bachelor, testify that the Brauns' target is not science and technology as such, but rather human abuse, individual or collective, of knowledge and power. But an examination of Mittelzwerck—for it is he, not the admirable narrator Philemon, who is the novel's central figure—demonstrates even better the Brauns' critique of science and technology. It also elucidates their position, not an easy one, as East German SF writers and as resolute social critics who are nevertheless not true dissidents, in either the popular Western sense or, one hopes, in the eyes of those who exercise power in the GDR.

Although the import of its larger theme is universally comprehensible, *Conviva Ludibundus* is unmistakably a work of German, and more particularly, East German literature. The observation that Mittelzwerck's expedition is a futuristic version, intentional or not, of the "ship of fools" theme first portrayed in Sebastian Brant's *Narrenschiff* (1494), is interesting and not altogether trivial. But the archetypes, motifs, and terminology which the Brauns exploit far more intensely in their futuristic narration, written initially for East German readers, are those of Goethe and Schiller; and one should not forget that Weimar now lies in East Germany and that German culture, whether West or East, still cannot escape coming to terms with its classical past. *Conviva Ludibundus* has its Philemon, the nearly nonagenarian, nature-loving coastal dweller and scientist, just as *Faust II* has its own Philemon, the venerable coastal cottager whose death Goethe's technologically-minded protagonist brings about, though his striving is ultimately vindicated. The Brauns also make industrious use of one of Goethe's other great contributions to the stock of archetypes associated with Man's attempt, often admirable but often disastrous, to impose his will on nature: the sorceror's apprentice. And throughout the novel, even in its very title and certainly in its seemingly casual phrases, one hears echoes of Schiller's concept of *Spieltrieb,* the seriously "playful urge" which, along with the "formal urge" (*Formtrieb*), supposedly governs all animate activity and is essential to both beauty and freedom.[29] No reasonably educated German reader could fail to recognize such references to the cultural heritage, any more than an American reader, encountering a work rooted in his own culture, could escape noticing allusions to the Declaration of Independence, the Bill of Rights, or the Gettysburg Address.

Classically German in its chief cultural and literary foundations, *Conviva Ludibundus* is also specifically East German in the way it interprets and applies them. Mittelzwerck has the egoism of Faust, but none of the latter's intellectual grandeur and agonizing, introspective moral sense; if anyone in *Conviva Ludibundus* resembles the eternally-searching, suffering, concupiscent Faust it is, by a strange but telling reversal, Philemon. As a sorceror's apprentice Mittelzwerck lacks even the minimal virtue of heeding, sooner or later, the master of his craft, again Philemon. Instead he embodies two flaws which, in societies like the East Germany of the Brauns, are regarded as cardinal sins, at least by those committed, as the Brauns seem to be, to the ideals of present day East-bloc socialism. Mittelzwerck is given to over-weening, self-serving individualism, and at the same time he displays the worst features of the *apparatchik,* the functionary who has achieved his success within the system and has not the ability to see beyond it.

Certainly Western or "bourgeois" literature, including Western SF, has its repertory of both innovative if sometimes erring or even demonic Promethean trailblazers and of colorless "organization men." But typically the two figures are regarded as antithetical in nature, and the categories by which they are apprehended and judged are equally disparate. The former, where they are not glorified, are regarded as psychologically aberrant individuals, while the latter are excoriated as pitiable, ludicrous or execrable products of corporate or governmental gigantism. In *Conviva Ludibundus* the single figure of Mittelzwerck incorporates both types. The Brauns and their East German readers, I think, would regard his excessive individualism and *apparatchik* mentality not as genuine antitheses or unrelated faults, but rather as complementary deviations from a single ideologically defined ideal: the balanced, productive citizen in harmony with a properly structured society.

Theoretically, then, the Brauns would seem to be "good" Marxists and East German writers of SF, for they voice their critique in terms which subsume under a single category, that of the human being as socially responsive and responsible creature, what the non-Marxist might regard as incidental, heterogeneous psychological or social phenomena. Moreover, their ideological attitude is not a message which is preached, but rather an unquestioned premise which governs and is in turn demonstrated by the fiction. Thus it might be said that the ideals of East German revolutionary socialism have become naturalized in the country's leading writers of SF.

But the domestication of ideals in the minds of sincere citizens can be troublesome in a society which, like all, is not ideal. The Brauns' writing is not acquiescent, not simply a conformist affirmation of the existing order. *Conviva Ludibundus* portrays, in fantastical form to be sure, gross imperfections of a kind all too familiar in East German society, distanced now from its momentous revolutionary inception by more than a generation of consolidation and, it has begun to appear, complaisance and even corruption. That, along with their evident poetic skill, may well explain the resonance the Braun's work has evoked. One might be tempted to see in Mittelzwerck a comment on the changing fortunes of the "personality cult" in Soviet-dominated societies from Stalin through Khrushchev and Ulbricht to Brezhnev and Honecker, or to surmise that the *conviva ludibundi* represent a subtle hint—and Eastern European readers are accustomed to deciphering topical subtleties—that there must be some play in society, that carefully planned and monitored productivity does not satisfy all the needs of living beings. But far more important than any such peripheral jibing is the admonition, voiced by two established East German writers, that a supposedly progressive society, one in which the socialist revolution has been completed and legitimized, can become so ossified that it promotes its mindless but ambitious *apparatchiki*, its sorceror's apprentices and would-be Fausts, over genuinely creative and socially responsible spirits. The latter, the true Fausts and Prometheuses, are reduced to marginal sufferance as Philemons who, by their own virtues, do not lose but who, because progressivism has given way to organized stagnation, cannot win.

At most they can seek to salvage something from the structural chaos of scientific regimentation, as the reader perceives Philemon attempting to do in *Conviva Ludibundus,* whose final pages portray a nebula of bureaucratic minutiae in which monitoring of procedures is mistaken for the mastery of problems.

The examination of East German SF involves issues which are both aesthetic and—whatever term one chooses—political, social or ideological. With both laudable liberalism and surprising naivete West German writers and, even more, critics of SF have vehemently lashed out at the limitations imposed on literary creativity in a capitalistic and culturally elitist society. If indeed, as Dieter Hasselblatt points out, the literary "market" in capitalistic societies "is not a free space" excluded somehow from social and pecuniary "strictures,"[30] that was known long ago to Dickens and Thackeray, who still managed to create within it consummate works of literary art. One can sympathize more with the plaint that West German SF has had to swim against a flood of foreign SF whose predominance is founded not only on the primacy of Anglo-American works in the recent history of the genre, but also on the status of English as the global lingua franca.

But East German writers of SF have also had to come to terms with their own milieu, including the strictures imposed by what functions as a literary market in an authoritarian workers' and peasants' state. This they have done, with greater or lesser eagerness, conformity, or loyally if hazardously committed criticism. But at least one—Günter Kunert, who is well known outside the realm of SF—has achieved his settlement with the East German environment by a less than voluntary resettlement away from it; thus his works no longer qualify for inclusion in anthologies of East German SF, as they did when Heidtmann compiled his landmark collection *Von einem anderen Stern* (1981).

I am not willing to declare with Franz Rottensteiner that East German SF, "in its best examples,...[is] better than the SF of the Federal Republic...[in] making use of the future as a level of play [Spielebene] in order to deal with contemporary problems in an unconventional and surprising way;"[31] and indeed, he has elsewhere voiced his assessment more moderately.[32] Yet the Brauns' works can stand on their own merits, and Christa Wolf's "Geschlechtertausch [Sex Change]" is one of the finest pieces of recent SF I have encountered—so much so that the two qualifiers might easily be dropped. I might add, however, that Wolf's story is admirable neither because nor although it appeared in East

Germany. There is little to mark it as specifically East German; its message is, rather, universal. Moreover, all the differences between East Germany and its Western linguistic cousins and fellow-states have not sufficed to prevent the creation in the GDR of some rather awful SF. After several readings of the pieces by Gerhard Branstner in the Heidtmann anthology, I find nothing in them that would argue that they are not ideological hatchet-jobs instead of freely-ranging thought-models which examine hypothetical worlds conditioned by science and technology; much less are they subtly-phrased social critiques whose tenor would be clear to the initiated. Instead, Branstner carries out the mission of the socialist writer of utopian fiction as it has been outlined by authoritative critics like Ariadne Gromova[33] or even by his own publisher, the Verlag Das Neue Berlin:

> "The utopian literature of the DDR is a component of Socialist contemporary literature. Its cultural-political mission is determined by socialist realism. Socialist utopian literature contributes to the forming of the socialist image of mankind. It solidifies socialist attitudes, convictions and modes of behavior; it conveys the joy in life, the insights and the consciousness of perspective of the victorious, power-wielding proletarian class. Its pedagogical goal is international proletarian solidarity. It conveys socialist leitmotifs and guiding thoughts [Leitbilder und Leitgedanken]."[34]

East German SF, even more frequently than West German, avoids the Americanism "science fiction" in favor of expressions which, often compounded of terms like "Fantasie," "Utopie," and "Märchen," would suggest greater latitude in content and approach. The preference in nomenclature has foundations in earlier German terms for SF and related literature, and it is reinforced of course by the common Russian expression *nauchnaya fantastika*. Certainly the Brauns, in *Conviva Ludibundus* and elsewhere, do not strive overmuch at literary realism or even—and here the doctrinaire eyebrows of certain orthodox literary critics might rise—social or socialist realism of the more conventional kind. It is indeed difficult to accept at face value, as a narration seriously intended to be logically plausible and subjectively or fictively real, a story about supernutritious mussels and their superintelligent symbiotes. Critics of SF who are uncomfortable with such liberties—and the present writer is still one of them, by conditioned reflex—must recall the long association of fantasy, satire, and SF, and thus allow for considerable variation from what is often regarded as the norm. In short, one must view the label "SF" as a quantitative rather than qualitative expression; one must keep generic boundaries open to the admixture of fantasy and irony; and one must pragmatically adjust to the fact that the literary products of writers like Christa Wolf and the Brauns, whether or not they initially bear the label, will be acknowledged and valued as SF as long as East German authors do continue to create works of high intrinsic quality which somehow, to the community of readers, writers, and critics, merit the designation "SF."

And, finally, one must also entertain a notion about the breadth of the terms "science" and "technology" which has been latent in them since their origin in Latin and Greek, and which has constantly resurfaced in many currents of SF. If "science" includes all that is known, and "technology" all that is made by Man, then the social sciences (and the arts as well) are legitimate sources of content for SF; and ideology, the analysis of what is perhaps Man's greatest technological creation or *Apparat,* the social mechanism, becomes a natural domain of the genre. *Conviva Ludibundus* encourages such latitudinarianism. Its ultimate concern is not science, technology, or even aesthetics in the narrower sense, though the novel contains much discussion of such things. Rather, the Brauns offer a critique of the question which Schiller—and the novel time and again addresses the issues he raised—posed as the fundamental problem of human social existence. In his classic but curiously titled treatise *Über die ästhetische Erziehung des Menschen* [*Concerning the Aesthetic Education of Mankind*] (1795) he asked, employing a technological metaphor, how the constantly running "clockwork of government [Uhrwerk des Staats]" might be regulated and adjusted by the knowledgeable, capable "technician-artisan-artist of statecraft [Staatskünstler]" (Letters 3 & 4). For Schiller, whose writings may well have determined the shape of German culture as much as have Goethe's, which is to say immensely, the solution was neither authoritarian intervention nor the revolution of the oppressed, untutored masses. It was to be, rather, the cultivation of the aesthetic sense—not, it should be realized, refinement of the populace into sensitive aesthetes, but instead the enhancement of existential, social sensibility; or, to use a modern term, "consciousness-raising." Shelley, a quarter-century later, was to hail the poets as "the unacknowledged legislators of the world;" in another classic essay, *Concerning Naive* [Unreflective] *and Sentimental* [Reflective] *Literature* [*Über naive und sentimentalische Dichtung*] (1795-6), Schiller foresaw for them a similar role. Conscious of the laws of history—in other words, versed in extrapolation—the best of them were to serve both art and society by writing a futuristic literature. Although (or because) it would always reflect the discrepancy between the real world and the ideal, imaginary world, it would tell modern mankind, whom civilization has made both sophisticated and alienated, whither it was to go.[35]

Perhaps, then, East German SF, at least as represented in the works of the Brauns, is even more "German" or "national," in the favorable sense, than is West German SF, for it explicitly addresses the questions of knowledge, creativity, individualism, and civic responsibility which were so long the prime concerns of its parent culture. And yet what was remarked earlier of West German SF applies to its East German counterpart, even though Kurd Lasswitz and Hans Dominik lived and wrote in what is now the territory of the GDR, just as the cities which were once centers of German classicism are now in the same country. If what is commonly termed East German SF is in fact SF, and if it is indeed German SF—and both the general term and the qualifier seem reasonable—it is nevertheless something other than the direct descendant of what was created in Germany between 1871 and 1945.

III

The Generic Nature of German SF

The present study scarcely exhausts its subject. I have already touched on many topics which, besides modern German SF, merit further investigation. Among them are the function of ideology in SF, the effects of publication media and readership groups, the writers associated with the *Verein für Raumschiffahrt,* German theories of SF, the relation of German SF to other SF, and the still broader subject of the interaction of science and German literature.

But the issue which has fascinated me most during my research is the generic nature of German SF. Like a number of other critics, I believe that the confrontation of writers with science affects all aspects of SF, from its philosophical attitudes to its stylistic features. Science, in effect, defines SF as a genre and determines its history; in other words, its synchronic and diachronic unity depends first of all on that of modern science. Some bodies of SF, however, can also be viewed as *literary* genres or traditions which evidence, at least during certain periods, a dense pattern of significant connections among writers and texts. Writers belonging to those traditions create their works not only in response to their experience of science, their general knowledge of literature, and their various social and personal concerns, but also with constant and conscious reference to their conception of the present state, heritage, and possibilities of the genre.

Here one thinks, of course, primarily of Anglo-American SF. During its "Golden Age" it was produced by a fairly small group of writers who responded to many of the same scientific and technological stimuli, and who for several reasons became a closely-knit community quite distinct from other literary groups. In their social, intellectual, and even psychological background they often had much in common; and, by chance, or often by choice and necessity, they associated personally with each other, worked with the same editors, published in the same media, wrote for the same audience, explored similar stylistic possibilities, and read and criticized each other's work. Often enough the "indigenous" SF community undertook the historical research, practical criticism of contemporary works, and theoretical discussion which have resulted in the assimilation of literary predecessors and the evolution of the concept of SF typical of the group. Such close relationships can contribute to the viability and stability of a genre; if too exclusive and one-sided, however, they can also transform it into a "ghetto" literature, as "Golden Age" Anglo-American SF has occasionally been described.[36]

Indispensable to the cohesion of "Golden Age" Anglo-American SF were the specialized but widely read "pulp" magazines and a readership which was large enough to support them but still sufficiently homogeneous in its special interests. By reprinting *as SF* the works of earlier writers, some of whom had little direct connection with the new SF community and may even, like Verne, have written in other languages, the magazines in effect created, *post hoc*, the literary heritage of Anglo-American SF. They also enabled new writers to enter the field with relative ease, and provided them with editorial tutelage. Yet another important feature of the magazines was their function as channels for powerful "feedback" from reader to writer, which appeared in the form of letter columns, popularity prizes, and fan-group organizations, and in the person of readers who themselves became writers, editors, and active critics.

Historically—that is, during the period primarily addressed by this study—German SF deviates radically in every major respect from the pattern described here. I would suggest therefore that it is with regard to its distinct lack of cohesion as a literary tradition, rather than its stylistic features or its specifically "German" ideological or scientific content, that German SF differs most significantly from other major bodies of SF, including not only

Anglo-American but perhaps even Russian and Soviet SF as well. For most of its history German SF has been a seldom-noticed, thinly-represented, poorly-defined type of fiction. Its antecedents in other kinds of literature are most unclear, and its early representatives, if they can indeed be called SF at all, are almost without exception extremely obscure texts. Even in modern times, during the last century approximately, the creation of German SF has been either the central literary pursuit of a very few "outsiders," or else the occasional experiment of writers whose other works cannot be classed as SF. Until the term "science fiction" was borrowed, there was even no single name for such literature in German.

The confrontation with science is therefore the only significant and consistent source of generic unity in the overall history of German SF. To adopt two scientific metaphors, the "normative" tradition of Anglo-American SF might be viewed as a sustained chain reaction initiated after the accretion, under suitable conditions, of a "critical mass" of writers, readers, and media. German SF—at least until the last two decades, perhaps—is best described as a kind of spontaneous combustion. Certain individuals—scientists interested in literature or writers interested in science—were affected in similar ways by science and technology, and sought to explore and express that experience in fiction. They were for the most part isolated from each other and lacked any real sense of belonging to a definite textual tradition; but because of the underlying similarity of intentionality, their works exhibit a number of recurrent similarities in outlook, theme, and style.

The material examined in the main chapters of the present study strongly supports the conclusions advanced here. Neither Lasswitz nor Dominik, the two most significant writers of German SF during its most distinctive period, can be associated with any cohesive generic tradition. German SF, like modern Germany, was born in 1871, when Lasswitz published his first novella. But neither in his own time nor later did Lasswitz become the center or progenitor of any discernible "school" of writers. There is little evidence that the various writers of German SF and related literature during the last century were actively interested in each other's works, that they knew each other personally, or—much less—that they considered themselves part of a well-defined literary tradition. It would seem, for example, that Lasswitz must have been familiar with the futuristic utopia *In purpurner Finsternis* (1895) by

Michael Georg Conrad, a well-known writer associated with German Naturalism. Yet in his essays on SF Lasswitz does not mention Conrad or, for that matter, more than a scant few other writers of SF. Nor does the influential critic Wilhelm Bölsche, himself a German Naturalist and a leading popularizer of science, allude to Conrad in his study of Lasswitz and other late nineteenth-century writers of SF. Yet another indication—both a symptom and a cause—of the diffuseness of German SF as a literary tradition during Lasswitz' time is the absence of a popular, regular, and specialized medium for the publication of SF.

The insubstantiality of German SF as a literary tradition, the lack of strong connections among writers and texts, is especially evident at what one might well suppose to be its very core. Lasswitz was one of Dominik's instructors at Gotha; and, according to Dominik himself, Lasswitz also furnished material for magazines published by Dominik's father. The older author lived and wrote until 1910, several years after Dominik had begun to write SF. A better opportunity for the establishment of a close link between the founder of modern German SF and one of its most popular later practitioners could scarcely be imagined. Such a relationship, whose existence would do much to suggest that German SF possessed at least some significant cohesion as a literary genre, did not come into being. Lasswitz' and Dominik's acquaintance with each other apparently ended when the latter left Gotha, and in his autobiography Dominik makes only brief and slighting reference to his major predecessor. Certainly Lasswitz' SF left scarcely any mark on that of Dominik. There is also very little evidence of a significant relationship between Dominik and the German rocket experimenters or such writers as Otto Willi Gail, whose SF explores their research. Less evident still are indications of associations among less important writers of German SF during the first half of the century, for example Bernhard Kellermann, Friedrich Freksa, or Rudolf Daumann.

The year 1945, as I have suggested, is just as important a milestone in the history of German SF as is 1871. Postwar German SF still exhibits only a modest degree of cohesion as a literary tradition. The SF *Romanheft*, for example, provides a focus for several authors and many readers of one not very impressive type of German SF. The popularity of the label "Science Fiction" in German-speaking countries, the emergence or expansion of specialized media of publication, and the development of German SF criticism also suggest some growing idea of common generic identity based on a sense of literary tradition. But Herbert W. Franke, the writers of *Perry Rhodan*, and such other authors of postwar German SF as Franz Werfel and Friedrich Dürrenmatt make strange literary bedfellows. It is also obvious that postwar German SF, whatever its generic status, and however much recent writers honor their predecessors, is not the direct descendant of earlier German SF. National Socialism, of course, was the chief proximate cause of the discontinuity. The proscription of Lasswitz' works greatly hindered the influence they might and should have had on later German SF. But, as a mundane biographical observation shows, the disruption far exceeded that sad exercise of *Literaturpolitik*. Many of the pioneers of Anglo-American SF continued to write during and after World War II, and some of them are still active. But no German SF writer of any comparable stature was active both before and after 1945. Admittedly, Dominik's novels are still read, and they appear to have influenced some postwar writers. But the mass demand for SF in Germany has been met even more by imported SF, and the work of better writers like Franke or Jeschke has little in common with that of Dominik and Lasswitz, whether in its view of science, its ideological orientation, or its literary style.

In seeking to describe and explain the nature of German SF as a genre, one easily comes to wonder why Germany, a major force in both literature and science during the last two centuries, did not produce a body of SF more impressive in quantity and quality and more cohesive as a literary tradition. Certainly the disturbances and catastrophes which characterize the history of Germany during the first half of the twentieth century had as adverse an effect on German SF as they had on all other areas of German society and culture. I think that the development of German SF was also greatly hindered by the weak and belated incorporation of science and technology into German literature generally. Here, as in industrialization and national unification as well, Germany lagged behind Great Britain and the United States, at least until the late nineteenth century. During most of the nineteenth century, when SF was in an embryonic but important stage of its development, German writers still tended to neglect, disparage, or even actively avoid dealing with modern science and technology, whether as a theme or as an influence on form and language.[37]

Several other factors of a more specific nature also deserve mention. The internal history of German SF, as the preceding discussion shows, is replete with unreconciled polarities, missed opportunities, and recurrent instances of the isolation of authors and texts. As I have suggested throughout my study, mature SF reflects the successful union of two types of intentionality which have to do in turn with two kinds of content. The first, expressed in concepts and terms like "speculative fiction" or "social" SF, is the urge to construct and describe, in systematic and detailed manner, entire imaginary worlds which are manifestly different from our own; such SF, which may well be related to utopian thought and fiction, gives relatively free play to the creation of imaginary science. The second intentionality, whose products are sometimes termed "gadget" or "technological" SF, is characterized by a more rigorous and more practical view of science; such SF reflects the desire to demonstrate the importance of science, or more precisely technology, in the fictional world and in our own. Typically the narration is set in the near future and concentrates on the careful description of imaginary technology, although the writer must necessarily include some information about the larger fictive environment. Students of SF sometimes refer to the first sub-type of SF as "Wellsian" and the second as "Vernian."

I would suggest that the integration of both elements or attitudes is as important to the development of SF as a genre as it is to the creation of individual works. Modern Anglo-American SF has been notably successful in unifying the two varieties of science-fictional intentionality and content; one could say alternately that Anglo-American SF has established a sense of continuity and kinship with its recent literary forebears, particularly Wells and Verne. Although I lack the expertise to argue the point with informed confidence, it may be that much the same could be asserted of Russian-language SF, even in its early modern period, as is shown by the example of *We* (written 1920-21) by Yevgeny Zamyatin (1884-1937). The works of Stanisław Lem manifest a similar synthesis and assimilation, which—along with their inherent literary quality—may explain their exceptional popularity with readers domesticated in the Anglo-American SF tradition and customarily loath to appreciate foreign works.

Until recently German SF, as a whole, has not been characterized at all by the reconciliation of the "social" and "technological" aspects of SF. The absence of such a synthesis is evident, as I have already suggested, in attempts to devise a suitable German term for "science fiction." Expressions like the common "utopischer Zukunftsroman," "technischer Zukunftsroman" (Dominik), "Zukunftsgeschichte" (van Loggem), "modernes," "wissenschaftliches," or "naturwissenschaftliches Märchen" (Lindau, Lasswitz, Bölsche, Lampa), "literarische Zukunftsgeschichte" (Hienger), or "naturwissenschaftlich-technische Utopie" (Schwonke) suggest how difficult it has been for Germanspeaking writers, readers, and critics to envision "social" or "utopian" SF and "technological" SF as aspects of a larger concept.[38] It is significant, I think, that works of German SF which do exhibit a generally successful balance between the constituent sub-intentionalities of SF—*Auf zwei Planeten, Der Tunnel* (1913) by Bernhard Kellermann, *Druso* (1931) by Friedrich Freksa, some of Franke's novels, Weisser's *SYN-CODE-7* (1982)—are characterized both by their quality and by their rarity. The impetus for such a union in Franke's writing, it might be noted, seems to have at least one external source, namely the example of Anglo-American SF.

Both the diffuseness and the polarization of German SF in its early modern period are exemplified by the SF of Lasswitz and Dominik. Each wrote a clearly different type of SF, and it would seem that the readers to whom their works appealed were notably disparate in social background, attitude toward science, and ideology. While Lasswitz and Dominik have on occasion been compared respectively to Wells and Verne, neither writer had a strong and lasting influence on a single, broader community of writers and readers. German SF, therefore, did not assimilate its two chief early practitioners, as did Anglo-American SF; in more general terms, the full range of older German SF was not effectively accessible to later writers.

Another major weakness of German SF throughout its history, but especially during the Twenties and Thirties, I think, was the lack of a viable specialized medium of publication—not necessarily a pulp magazine, of course—which would have promoted the emergence of a large but well-defined readership community, encouraged new talent, and helped to establish a sense of generic identity and continuity. Even now there is no regular medium which functions as a strong central support for SF and is nevertheless broad enough to appeal to most of the diverse subgroups of readers.

Although factors like those discussed here may do much to explain the history of German SF, the primary requisite for the creation of SF, as I have suggested, is the desire to express in literature the confrontation with science. That intention, and the means to accomplish it, depend in turn on the presence in the writer's environment of suitable raw material, in the form of provocative science and technology. The development of German

SF was disrupted, as was that of other German literature, by the cultural policies of National Socialism and the material consequences of World War II; it was also affected in a special way by Nazism. It is my opinion that the suppression or classification of scientific and technological research between 1933 and 1945, particularly the work of the German rocket experimenters but also that of German astronomers, physicists, chemists, mathematicians, and biologists, inhibited the development of German SF to a nearly fatal degree by denying it access to material especially congenial to the intellectual and literary goals of SF. It is even conceivable that, had not authoritarianism intervened, the history of German SF might also include a "Golden Age" of mature and well-established literature, as did that of Anglo-American SF, which benefited so richly from its greater freedom to speculate about modern science, above all nuclear physics and space flight.[39]

Each kind of literature, however, develops in its own ways, and should not be subjected without reservations to invidious comparisons or, much less, teleological second-guessing and extraneous metaphors of growth. German SF need not be viewed merely as a genre *manqué;* what one observer may consider to be an absence of generic cohesion and historical continuity another may perceive more positively as the presence of freedom, receptivity, and opportunity. Throughout its history German SF has been open to many kinds of writers and many ways of writing. While modest in size when compared to some other traditions of SF, it has exhibited a great diversity in artistic quality, scientific interests, ideological attitudes, and literary forms. That traditional breadth, once evident only in a meager miscellany of curious and curiously-regarded texts, now serves very well to encourage a diversity of interests and approaches among those who are collectively creating—whether it is nascent or renascent—a modern German SF which is, I think, already richer and stronger than what came before it.

Speaking to Hans Lindau, his admiring but somewhat credulous young interviewer, Lasswitz once remarked:

> "Actually I like best to read two kinds of things.... Wild West stories [Indianergeschichten] and Goethe. With other reading matter one has to exert oneself too much. But Wild West stories are completely undemanding, and Goethe satisfies all demands. With these two good things one need not torment oneself with criticism. It is possible to relax equally well with that which is sublimely above all criticism and that which is naively beneath all criticism."[40]

Beneath Lasswitz' characteristic modesty and gentle irony lies a more serious thought. Certainly he himself, quite earnest about his intellectual, social, and artistic vocation, but aware, despite his ambitions, that he was no Goethe, believed in the virtue and value of creating and criticizing literature which ranks somewhere above the mire of Grub Street yet below the peak of Parnassus. German SF may still lack its Goethe—though in that it is not alone as a literary current. But often enough it has risen above the level of unregenerate kitsch, and in recent years its social and aesthetic permeability—perhaps ultimately its most outstanding strength as well as, historically, its most grievous weakness—has been superseded, or rather balanced, by a promising sense of generic cohesion and direction. German SF, as one of its greatest theoreticians and practitioners himself must have believed, is a varied and colorful literature, one which offers entertainment, challenges, and rewards to its readers, its writers, and sometimes even its critics.

Notes

Preface

[1] It would probably be impossible to compile an exhaustive bibliography of "fanzines." Two of the most prestigious modern North American amateur SF journals are *Algol* (New York) and *Riverside Quarterly* (Regina, Saskatchewan). Best known among German-language publications are *Science-Fiction Times* (Bremerhaven) and *Quarber Merkur* (Vienna). The standard histories of American "fandom" are Sam Moskowitz, *The Immortal Storm: A History of Science Fiction Fandom* (Atlanta: The Atlanta Science Fiction Organization Press, 1966), and Harry Warner, Jr., *All Our Yesterdays: An Informal History of Science Fiction Fandom in the Forties* (Chicago: Advent, 1969). Both Moskowitz and Warner are long-time fans. In his glossary of "fan slang" Warner includes the entry: "*Faiwol:* 'Fandom is a way of life'...antonym to *fijagh:* 'fandom is just a goddamned hobby.' " (p. xx).

[2] Jürgen vom Scheidt, "Descensus ad inferos: Tiefenpsychologische Aspekte der Science Fiction," in *Science Fiction: Theorie und Geschichte,* ed. Eike Barmeyer (München: Wilhelm Fink Verlag, 1972), 133-63.

[3] Leslie Fiedler, "Cross the Border—Close the Gap," *Collected Essays* (New York: Stein and Day, 1971), 2:461-85.

[4] Robert Scholes, *Structural Fabulation: An Essay on Fiction of the Future* (Notre Dame, Indiana: University of Notre Dame Press, 1975).

[5] C[live] S[taples] Lewis, "On Science Fiction," in C.S. Lewis, *Of Other Worlds: Essays and Stories,* ed. Walter Hooper (New York: Harcourt, Brace and World, 1966), 62.

Introduction

[1] For a history of the term "science fiction" see Sam Moskowitz, "How Science Fiction Got Its Name," *The Magazine of Fantasy and Science Fiction,* Feb. 1957:65-77, reprinted in revised form in Moskowitz, *Explorers of the Infinite: Shapers of Science Fiction* (1963: rpt. Westport, Connecticut: Hyperion Press, 1974), 313-33. The isolated occurrence of the expression as early as 1851 is discussed in Brian W. Aldiss, "On the Age of the Term 'Science Fiction,' " *Science Fiction Studies* 3(1976): 213, and Sam Moskowitz, "That Early Coinage of 'Science Fiction,' " *Science Fiction Studies* 3(1976): 312-13. The modern evolution of the term, however, seems to have been spontaneous.

[2] Martin Schwonke, *Vom Staatsroman zur Science Fiction: Eine Untersuchung über Geschichte und Funktion der naturwissenschaftlich-technischen Utopie,* Göttinger Abhandlungen zur Soziologie, 2 (Stuttgart: Ferdinand Enke Verlag, 1957); Hans-Jürgen Krysmanski, *Die utopische Methode: Eine literatur- und wissenssoziologische Untersuchung deutscher utopischer Romane des 20. Jahrhunderts,* Dortmunder Schriften zur Sozialforschung, 21 (Köln: Westdeutscher Verlag, 1963).

[3] Jörg Hienger, *Literarische Zukunftsphantastik: Eine Studie über Science Fiction* (Göttingen: Vandenhoecht & Ruprecht, 1972); Vera Graaf, *Homo Futurus: Eine Analyse der modernen Science Fiction* (Hamburg: Claassen Verlag, 1971); Dieter Wessels, *Welt im Chaos: Struktur und Funktion des Weltkatastrophenmotivs in der neueren Science Fiction,* Studienreihe Humanitas (Frankfurt am Main: Akademische Verlagsgesellschaft, 1974); Franz Rottensteiner, *The Science Fiction Book: An Illustrated History* (New York: New American Library, 1975); Eike Barmeyer, ed., *Science Fiction: Theorie und Geschichte* (1972); Karl Ermert, ed., *Neugier oder Flucht? Zu Poetik, Ideologie und Wirkung der Science Fiction* (Stuttgart: Klett, 1980); Ulrich Suerbaum, Ulrich Broich, and Raimund Borgmeier, *Science Fiction: Theorie und Geschichte, Themen und Typen, Form und Weltbild* (Stuttgart: Reclam, 1981).

[4] Michael Pehlke and Norbert Lingfeld, *Roboter und Gartenlaube: Ideologie und Unterhaltung in der Science-Fiction-Literatur,* Reihe Hanser 56 (München: Carl Hanser Verlag, 1970).

[5] Manfred Nagl, *Science Fiction in Deutschland: Untersuchungen zur Genese, Soziographie und Ideologie der phantastischen Massenliteratur,* Untersuchungen des Ludwig-Uhland-Instituts der Universität Tübingen im Auftrag der Tübinger Vereinigung für Volkskunde, 30 (Tübingen: Tübinger Vereinigung für Volkskunde e. V., 1972); Jörg Weigand, ed., *Die triviale Phantasie: Beiträge zur "Verwertbarkeit" von Science Fiction* (Bonn-Bad Godesberg: Asgard Verlag Dr. Werner Hippe, 1976).

Chapter I

[1] For a sampling of definitions of SF by well-known critics see: J. O. Bailey, *Pilgrims through Space and Time: Trends and Patterns in Scientific and Utopian Fiction* (New York: Argus Books, 1947), 10; Donald A. Wollheim, *The Universe Makers: Science Fiction Today* (New York: Harper and Row, 1971), 10-11; Basil Davenport, *Inquiry into Science Fiction* (New York: Longmans, Green and Co., 1955), 15; Sam Moskowitz, *Explorers of the Infinite*, 11; Groff Conklin, "What Is Good Science Fiction?" *Library Journal*, 15 April 1958:1256; Herbert W. Franke, "Science Fiction—für und wider," in *Neugier oder Flucht*, Karl Ermert, ed., 75.

[2] Samuel R. Delany, "About Five Thousand One Hundred and Seventy-Five Words," in *SF: The Other Side of Realism: Essays on Modern Fantasy and Science Fiction*, ed. Thomas D. Clareson (Bowling Green, Ohio: Bowling Green University Popular Press, 1971), 130-45; John R. Krueger, "Language and Techniques of Communication as Theme or Tool in Science Fiction," *Linguistics*, No. 39(1968):68-86.

[3] Isaac Asimov, "Escape into Reality," *The Humanist* 17(1957):326-32; Hans-Joachim Flechtner, "Die phantastische Literatur: Eine literarästhetische Untersuchung," *Zeitschrift für Ästhetik und allgemeine Kunstwissenschaft* 24(1930): 37-46; Julius Kagarlitski, "Realism and Fantasy," trans. Milda Carroll, in *SF: The Other Side of Realism*, ed. Thomas B. Clareson, 29-52.

[4] Ariadne Gromova, "At the Frontier of the Present Age," trans. C.G. Bearne, in *Vortex: New Soviet SF*, ed. C. G. Bearne (London: MacGibbon and Kee, 1970), 9-29; John Pilgrim, "Science Fiction and Anarchism," *Anarchy* 34(1963):361-75; Dennis Livingston, "Science Fiction Models of Future World Order Systems," *International Organization* 25(1971):254-70; Thomas C. and Marilyn Sutton, "Science Fiction as Mythology," *Western Folklore* 28 (1969):230-38.

[5] John R. Krueger, "Names and Nomenclatures in Science-Fiction," *Names* 14-15 (1966-67):203-04.

[6] I use the term "intentionality" to describe a complex of features which, taken together, produce and identify one or more works of literature as belonging to a larger class or genre. These distinguishing characteristics have to do with the aims and presuppositions of the author, the expectations and responses of the reader, and the significant properties of the text as a medium of communication between the two. Despite its amenability to so-called "intrinsic" analysis, such a concept of literature, as the following chapters of this study show, does not exclude the consideration of extrinsic matters; rather, it strongly encourages the investigation and evaluation of any factors, such as the general social background, developments in science and technology, or the strictures and opportunities posed by the publishing environment, which might also have an effect on the creation, dissemination, and reception of literature.

In formulating my theoretical analysis of SF I have found particularly useful the views of such SF authors and specialists as Brian Aldiss, Darko Suvin, Robert Scholes, Groff Conklin, Robert A. Heinlein, Kurd Lasswitz, Hans-Joachim Flechtner, and Robert Conquest, among many others; several studies of popular culture and *Trivialliteratur* by Walther Killy, Dorothy Bayer, Ulf Diederichs, Walter Nutz, and Jens-Ulrich Davids; and the more general writings on receptional history and aesthetics by Hans Robert Jauss, Manfred Naumann, Karl Robert Mandelkow, Götz Wienold, and Bernd Jürgen Warneken (see Bibliography). An essay by Peter Demetz, "Über die Fiktionen des Realismus," *Neue Rundschau* 88 (1977):554-67, has provided me with valuable insights into the theory of realism.

[7] I owe the term "sharable experience" ("gemeinsame Erfahrung") to the previously-mentioned essay "Über die Fiktionen des Realismus" by Peter Demetz (559).

[8] Scholes, *Structural Fabulation*, ix.

[9] The progress of science has introduced an interesting anomaly into one of the basic narrative situations of SF. Arthur C. Clarke, in a "Post-Apollo Preface" to a collection of his own SF, *Prelude to Space* (New York: Ballantine Books, 1976), v-x, remarks that, after the first moon-landing in 1969, all SF about travel to the Moon, including his own stories, underwent a change of status, from daring speculation to, usually, quaint obsolescence. As Clarke puts it, "all the countless science-fiction stories of the first landing on the Moon became frozen in time, like flies in amber" (v). In terms of the present discussion, fiction about space travel, if not throughout the Universe then at least within the Solar System, can now refer to "sharable experience;" therefore the location of the narration in an extraterrestrial environment does not automatically presuppose and establish the "radical discontinuity" between real and imaginary worlds which is essential to SF. It remains to be seen whether narrations about space travel will now be written and accepted as "mainstream" realistic fiction. The reception of James Michener's new novel

Space (1982) will no doubt be quite telling.

[10]See Jürgen Habermas, "Technik und Wissenschaft als 'Ideologie,' " in *Technik und Wissenschaft als 'Ideologie'* (Frankfurt am Main: Suhrkamp, 1968), 48-103.

[11]Asimov, "Escape into Reality," 329.

[12]Olaf Stapledon, "Preface to the English Edition [of *Last and First Men*]," in *Last and First Men and Starmaker: Two Science Fiction Novels* (1930 and 1937; rpt. New York: Dover, 1968), 9; Kurd Lasswitz, "Über Zukunftsträume," in *Wirklichkeiten: Beiträge zum Weltverständnis* (Berlin: Emil Felber, 1900; 2nd impression Leipzig: B. Elischer Nachfolger, 1904), 439. Lasswitz' actual phrase, in which "Phantasie" refers to the kind of imagination appropriate to SF as he conceives it, is "Die Phantasie braucht aber keine ungezügelte zu sein."

[13]Moskowitz, in *Explorers of the Infinite* (130-33), quotes and discusses the exchange between the elderly Verne and the young Wells.

[14]The term is well known among students of SF, and in fact one of the leading journals of SF criticism is *Extrapolation* (founded 1960).

[15]A classic statement on change and extrapolation in SF is the essay by Robert A. Heinlein, "Where to?" *Galaxy*, Feb. 1952:13-22. In creating his "future history" stories, which were a major contribution to "Golden Age" Anglo-American SF, Heinlein employed a detailed chart which accompanied the publication of several of his works.

[16]See Robert A. Heinlein, Preface, *Tomorrow the Stars: A Science Fiction Anthology*, ed. Robert A. Heinlein (1952; rpt. New York: Berkley Medallion Books, 1967), 5-10. The demand that SF not violate the established facts of science raises the possibility that a work of SF may also become obsolete in a way quite the opposite of that decribed in note 9 of this chapter. Not only the confirmation of an idea previously entertained by science, but also its refutation, can radically alter the manner in which later readers respond to the text.

[17]The term "analog," like "extrapolation," is widely familiar among readers and critics of SF. *Analog* is the title of one of the leading SF magazines (formerly *Astounding Science Fiction*); the word may also owe some of its popularity and its connotations to the expression "analog computer."

[18]See, for example, Pehlke and Lingfeld, *Robotor und Gartenlaube: Ideologie und Unterhaltung in der Science-Fiction Literatur.* Similar, if more sophisticated and less strident analyses represent in fact the dominant current in German SF criticism.

[19]During the Fifties many members of the SF community expressed strong opposition to McCarthyism and other forms of jingoistic agitation. Their antipathy was founded not so much on ideology as on science; most SF writers of the time were not active leftists. Because of their understanding of science, they were alarmed at the lack of global perspective which persisted after 1945; they were equally shocked by the politicians' disastrous ignorance of science, especially the nuclear physics on which the atomic bomb was based. Thus they had reason enough to fear or ridicule politicians who failed to grasp the "one-world" implications of modern science or who, because they were not aware of the half-century of international research which had led to the atomic bomb, felt that it was a recent American invention whose construction could have been kept secret but for the machinations of subversives in science and government. Their criticism, however, seldom found an audience outside the SF community. See Philip Wylie, "Science Fiction and Sanity in an Age of Crisis," in *Modern Science Fiction: Its Meaning and Future,* ed. Reginald Bretnor (New York: Coward-McCann, 1953):221-241, and Albert I. Berger, "Science-Fiction Critiques of the American Space Program," *Science Fiction Studies* No. 15(1978):99-109.

[20]Admittedly, some scientists and historians of science have argued very convincingly that the development of science involves something other, or at least something more, than the rational and orderly method discussed here, whose formulation can be traced at least as far back as Francis Bacon. See Thomas S. Kuhn, *The Structure of Scientific Revolutions,* 2nd, enlarged ed. (Chicago: University of Chicago Press, 1970). The argument advanced here, however, rests not on the actual validity of the "scientific method" as a description of the manner in which science develops, but rather on the effect which that model has had on those who, like many writers and readers of SF, have accepted it as a paradigm of scientific investigation and argumentation.

[21]After formulating the arguments presented in the preceding section and elaborated in the following discussion of literary techniques in SF, I was pleased to find a useful though far more general analysis of rhetoric in scientific discourse in Wilbur Samuel Howell, *Poetics, Rhetoric, and Logic: Studies in the Basic Disciplines of Criticism* (Ithaca: Cornell University Press, 1975). In his collection of essays Howell distinguishes the "mimetic" literature of poetic creation from the "non-mimetic" literature of rhetoric. He places non-fictional prose, or much of it rather, under

the rubric of rhetoric, but still maintains that it is literature. He also points out that the success of scientific writing, and of other types of scholarly exposition too, depends on subjective appeal as well as logic. In Howell's terms, SF would be both "mimetic" and "non-mimetic," for it is a "poetic" body of literature which nevertheless shares many of its foundations with scientific writing. Distinctions of a similar nature are expressed in my analyses of the impressions of reality and plausibility which SF aims to evoke, and in the contrast between literature which creates a version of the "real" world, and that which presents an expressly imaginary world.

²²The relevant passages from Wells' critical writings are quoted and discussed by James Gunn in *Alternate Worlds: The Illustrated History of Science Fiction* (Englewood Cliffs, N.J.: Prentice Hall and A & W Visual Library, 1975), 101.

²³The primary source of the convention, whose effectiveness has gradually diminished in the face of recent Mars research, is to be found in the astronomical studies of Mars and the provocative conjectures about its possible life-forms which were published by the astronomers Giovanni Schiaparelli (1835-1910) and Percival Lowell (1855-1916) during the decades around the turn of the century. See Chapter IV.

²⁴Leslie Fiedler toys with such interpretations in his essay "Cross the Border—Close the Gap," mentioned earlier (e.g., p. 480). Even more unconvincing is the sexual interpretation of the explorers' balloon and the polar landscape which Rudi Schweikert offers in the Afterword (pp. 932-3) to his modern edition of Lasswitz' *Auf zwei Planeten.* See also Alison Szanto, "Balls and Breasts in Science-Fiction Illustration," rev. of *Great Balls of Fire! A History of Sex in Science Fiction Illustration,* by Harry Harrison, *Science Fiction Studies* No. 16(1978):301-02.

²⁵One of the most perceptive and eloquent apologies for the literary style and aesthetic quality of SF is the essay by Robert Conquest, "Science Fiction and Literature," *The Critical Quarterly* 5-6(1963-64):355-67.

²⁶See, for example, Robert A. Heinlein, *Space Cadet* (1948; rpt. New York: Ace Books, n.d.), 8.

²⁷See Krueger, "Language and Techniques of Communication" and "Names and Nomenclature in Science-Fiction."

²⁸Richard Gerber, Utopian Fantasy: A Study of English Utopian Fiction since the End of the Nineteenth Century (1955; rpt. New York: McGraw-Hill, 1973), 81-104.

²⁹Delany, "About Five Thousand One Hundred and Seventy-Five Words," 143.

³⁰Conquest, "Science Fiction and Literature."

³¹See Robert A. Heinlein, "Science Fiction: Its Nature, Faults and Virtues," in *The Science Fiction Novel,* ed. Basil Davenport (Chicago: Advent, 1959), 17-63, and Heinlein's Preface to his anthology *Tomorrow, the Stars.*

³²Conquest, "Science Fiction and Literature," and Martin Green, *Science and the Shabby Curate of Poetry* (London: Longman, Green & Co., 1964), 81ff., 120ff.

³³Hans Robert Jauss, "Literaturgeschichte als Provokation der Literaturwissenschaft," in *Literaturgeschichte als Provokation der Wissenschaft* (Frankfurt am Main: Suhrkamp, 1970), 171.

³⁴Gerber, *Utopian Fantasy,* 93.

³⁵Heinlein, "Science Fiction: Its Nature, Faults and Virtues," 46-51.

³⁶See, for example, Arthur C. Clarke, "Science Fiction: Preparation for the Age of Space," in *Modern Science Fiction,* ed. Reginald Betnor, 197-220, Philip Wylie, "Science Fiction and Sanity in an Age of Crisis," and Isaac Asimov, "Escape into Reality."

³⁷Scholes, Structural Fabulation, 5, 29.

Chapter II

¹Published information about Lasswitz' life is extremely difficult to locate, although the researcher's task has been lightened considerably by the appearance—shortly before the present study went to press—of Rudi Schweikert's careful re-edition of *Auf zwei Planeten* (Frankfurt: Verlag 2001, 1979), to which are appended two essays about Lasswitz and his work, "Von Martiern und Menschen" (903-75) and "Von geraden und von schiefen Gedanken" (977-1074), a biographical chronology (1075)-78), and a bibliography of primary and secondary literature (1079)-1101). Unfortunately the book is already out of print and not easily obtained even in Germany.

Several of the standard reference works on German literature fail even to mention Lasswitz; even the major studies of SF, where they refer to him at all, seldom provide more than the barest biographical and bibliographical information. Until Schweikert's essay there had been no biographical studies of any appreciable length in modern times. Material for the present sketch, though it was compared and, in a few instances, expanded with information from Schweikert, was drawn chiefly from the following secondary sources: Hans Lindau, "Kurd Lasswitz," Introd. to Kurd Lasswitz, *Empfundenes und Erkanntes: Aus dem Nachlasse* (Leipzig: B. Elischer Nachfolger, n.d. [1920]), 1-56; Hans Lindau, "Kurd Lasswitz und seine modernen Märchen," *Nord und Süd* 106(1903): 315-33; W[alter] Lietzmann, Introd. to Kurd Lasswitz, *Die Welt und der Mathematikus: Ausgewählte Dichtungen von Kurd Lasswitz*, ed. W[alter] Lietzmann (Leipzig: B. Elischer Nachfolger, n.d. [1924]), 3-7; Erich Lasswitz, Preface to Kurd Lasswitz, *Auf zwei Planeten*, ed. Erich Lasswitz (Donauwörth: Cassianeum, 1948), 5-7; Klaus Günther Just, "Ein schlesischer Raumfahrtroman der Jahrhundertwende," *Schlesische Studien*, Silesia Folge 7(1970): 129-33; Klaus Günther Just, "Kurd Lasswitz: Der Dichter der Raumfahrt," *Schlesien* 15(1970):1-15; Franz Rottensteiner, "Kurd Lasswitz: A German Pioneer of Science Fiction," *Riverside Quarterly* 4 (August 1969): 4-18, rpt. in SF: *The Other Side of Realism*, ed. Thomas D. Clareson, 289-306; Franz Rottensteiner, "Ordnungsliebend in Weltraum: Kurd Lasswitz," in *Polaris 1: Ein Science Fiction Almanach*, ed. Franz Rottensteiner (Frankfurt am Main: Insel Verlag, 1973), 133-64; Mark R. Hillegas, "Martians and Mythmakers: 1877-1938," in *Challenges in American Culture*, ed. Ray B. Browne, et al. (Bowling Green, Ohio: Bowling Green University Popular Press, 1970), 150-77; Willy Ley, *Rockets, Missiles, and Space Travel* (1944) as *Rockets;* revised ed. under present title 1957; rpt. New York: Viking, 1961), 45-48.

　　Lasswitz' anthology *Seifenblasen: Modern Märchen* (Hamburg: Leopold Voss, 1890; cited from the revised and enlarged ed., Leipzig: B. Elischer Nachfolger, 1894, whose pagination is retained in later eds.) contains his "Selbstbiographische Studien" ["Autobiographical Studies"] (274-88). The essay is not actually an autobiographical sketch, but rather a parody of literary biography, research into evolution, and genealogy-mongering. Even so, the "Studien" reveal much about the author's personality, as the following quotation suggests: "One could begin thus: 'The first record of my line emerges at that place where, in the depths of the primal sea of the Laurentian Period, a plumpish amoeba came upon the idea of dividing itself. The fatter half became my primal ancestor' " (284). Lasswitz was somewhat corpulent.

　　Lasswitz' literary remains are in Gotha (German Democratic Republic).

　[2]Just, "Kurd Lasswitz," 2.

　[3]Lasswitz' non-technical works, besides those mentioned specifically in the text, include: *Atomistik und Kriticismus: Ein Beitrag zur erkenntnis-theoretischen Grundlegung der Physik* [*Atomism and Criticism: A Contribution to the Epistemological Foundation of Physics*] (1878); *Natur und Mensch* [*Nature and Man*] (1878); *Die Lehre von den Elementen während des Übergangs der scholastischen Philosophie zur Corpusculartheorie* [*The Doctrine of the Elements during the Transition from Scholastic Philosophy to the Corpuscular Theory*] (1882); *Die Lehre Kants von der Idealität des Raumes und der Zeit, im Zusammenhange mit seiner Kritik des Erkennens allgemeinverständlich dargestellt* [*Kant's Doctrine of the Ideality of Space and Time, in Connection with his Critique of Understanding, Explained for the General Audience*] (1883); *Die Geschichte der Atomistik vom Mittelalter bis Newton* [*The History of Atomism from the Middle Ages until Newton*] (1890; later eds. 1926, 1963); *Religion und Naturwissenschaft: Ein Vortrag* [*Religion and Science: A Lecture*] (1904); *Gustav Theodor Fechner* (1896). Lasswitz' edition of Fechner's *Zend-Avesta, oder Über die Dinge des Himmels und des Jenseits. Vom Standpunkt der Naturbetrachtung* [*Zend-Avesta, or: Concerning the Matters of Heaven and the Beyond, from the Perspective of Natural Study*] (1851) appeared in 1901; he also wrote the introduction to the re-edition (1899; later eds. 1903, 1921) of Fechner's *Nanna, oder Über das Seelenleben der Pflanzen* [*Nanna, or: Concerning the Psychic Life of Plants*] (1848).

　[4]Fritz Engel, rev. of *Auf zwei Planeten*, in *Zeitgeist*, supplement to the *Berliner Tageblatt* No. 49 (1897); condensed rpt. as "Ein Robinson des Weltraums," *Das Magazin für Litteratur* (Berlin and Weimar), 18 Dec. 1897, n. pag.

　[5]Erich Lasswitz, Preface to *Auf zwei Planeten* (1948), 6. Schweikert (978-79), following Lietzman, quotes a letter to the latter, from Lasswitz' wife, in which, presumably looking back some years after her husband's death, she writes quite bitterly about the imposition his gymnasial duties made on his artistic efforts. While one may sympathize with those attitudes, it is apparent that Lasswitz was able to attain a not inconsequential measure of personal, professional, and artistic equilibrium.

　[6]Just, "Kurd Lasswitz," 3-4; Lindau, Introd. to *Empfundenes und Erkanntes*, 19-20. In his autobiography, *Vom Schraubstock zum Schreibtisch* (Berlin: Scherl, 1942), Hans Dominik remarks that Lasswitz' liberal politics made it impossible to call him to a university professorship

(26). Schweikert notes the element of topical criticism in Lasswitz' work, and does not too greatly underestimate it, although he recognizes that the contemporary audience may have overlooked much of it (1030, 1040, 1053); he does point out that at the early age of twenty-five Lasswitz had outlined for himself a program for his publishing, literature, and aesthetics, and that he "carried it out, with startling consistence, over decades" (979).

[7]Lasswitz' only other major essay on literary aesthetics, "Das Schaffen des Dichters" ["Poetic Creativity"] (*Empfundenes und Erkanntes*, 288-309), is not concerned with SF, although he does offer some comparisons between science and literature.

Part of the present section, in somewhat different form, was published earlier under the title "German Theories of Science Fiction: Jean Paul, Kurd Lasswitz, and After," in *Science Fiction Studies* No. 10 (1976): 254-65.

[8]The following secondary sources, besides those mentioned earlier, furnished useful background information for the present section: Joachim Kirchner, *Die Grundlagen des deutschen Zeitschriftenwesens*, Pt. 1 (Leipzig: Verlag Karl W. Hiersemann, 1928), and *Das deutsche Zeitschriftenwesen: Seine Geschichte und seine Probleme*, Pt. 2 (Wiesbaden: Otto Harrassowitz, 1962); Eva-Annemarie Kirschstein, *Die Familienzeitschrift: Ihre Entwicklung und Bedeutung für die deutsche Presse* (Charlottenburg: Rudolf Lorentz Verlag, 1937); Fritz Schlawe, *Literarische Zeitschriften*, 2 vols. (Stuttgart: Metzler, 1961 & 1962); Harry Pross, *Literatur und Politik: Geschichte und Programme der politisch-literarischen Zeitschriften im deutschen Sprachgebiet seit 1870* (Olten & Freiburg i. Br.: Walter Verlag, 1963); Frank Luther Mott, *A History of American Magazines*, 5 vols. (Cambridge, Mass.: Harvard University Press, 1930ff); Ron Goulart, *An Informal History of the Pulp Magazines* (New York: Ace Books, 1972); Sam Moskowitz, *Science Fiction by Gaslight: A History and Anthology of Science Fiction in the Popular Magazines 1891-1911* (Cleveland & New York: World, 1968), and *Under the Moons of Mars: A History and Anthology of "The Scientific Romance" in the Munsey Magazines, 1912-1920* (New York: Holt, Rinehart, & Winston, 1970).

[9]Ralf Dahrendorf, *Gesellschaft und Demokratie in Deutschland* (1968; rpt. München: R. Piper, 1971), 151ff.

[10]The publication of Rudi Schweikert's modern re-edition of *Auf zwei Planeten*, with its extensive bibliography, has recently made it possible to survey conveniently the relevant secondary literature, including early reviews, many of them anonymous and difficult to locate. I am grateful to Dr. Franz Rottensteiner of Vienna for providing me with initial information about Lasswitz criticism during the early stages of my research. I was also able to find references to secondary material in the annual volumes of the *Jahresberichte für neuere deutsche Literaturgeschichte* (1890ff.). Listed there, though inaccessible to me—and strangely enough not mentioned by Schweikert—is a review of *Auf zwei Planeten* by Bertha von Suttner (1843-1914), the famous pacifist and writer of utopias who later received the Nobel Peace Prize; the review, "Die Marsbewohner," in *Magazin für Litteratur des In- und Auslandes* 67(1898):549-52 and 575-76, documents the favorable response to Lasswitz among those interested primarily in utopian thought and literature, a response already evident in much of the other contemporary criticism discussed here. Schweikert (1077), alluding to a letter from von Suttner to Lasswitz (22 Sept. 1888), does remark that she seems to have inspired Lasswitz to publish his anthology *Seifenblasen*.

The endpapers of the various editions of *Auf zwei Planeten* also give a sampling of contemporary opinion, all of it laudatory and much of it of limited value.

[11]Schweikert, 979.

[12]Information for the present discussion has been drawn in part from the following secondary sources: Albert Soergel, *Dichtung und Dichter der Zeit* (Leipzig: R. Voigtländer, 1911 and 1925); Richard Hamann and Jost Hermand, *Naturalismus* (München: Nymphenburger Verlagsbuchhandlung, 1972); Katharina Günther, *Literarische Gruppenbildung im Berliner Naturalismus* (Berlin: Bouvier, 1972); Ursula Münchow, *Deutscher Naturalismus* (Berlin: Akademie Verlag, 1968); John Osborne, *The Naturalist Drama in Germany* (Manchester: Manchester University Press, 1971); Fritz Schlawe, *Literarische Zeitschriften*.

[13]See Dominik's tantalizing but unclear and, considering the source, perhaps unreliable remark about Lasswitz' political inclinations and their adverse affect on his career, quoted below near the beginning of Chapter V. An examination of Lasswitz' private papers, which the present writer was not in a position to undertake, might well aid in evaluating his response to contemporary political issues.

Chapter III

[1]Rottensteiner, "Kurd Lasswitz: Ordnungsliebend im Weltraum," 14+, 149, draws attention to an excerpt from the *Bilder* which appeared in the June 1890 issue of the *Overland Monthly*; to my knowledge there have been no subsequent English translations of the *Bilder*. In 1964 a facsimile edition of the third edition was issued by Bleymehl (Sammlung Antares 4) in Fürth/Saarland; the book is not readily accessible. The volume *Bis zum Nullpunkt des Seins: Utopische Erzählungen*, ed. Adolf Sckerl (Berlin/DDR: Das Neue Berlin, 1979), contains not only the *Bilder aus der Zukunft* but also several of Lasswitz' short stories and the essay "Über Zukunftsträume." See the bibliography appended to Schweikert's recent edition of *Auf zwei Planeten*.

[2]Rottensteiner, *ibid.*, 149, and Just, "Kurd Lasswitz," 4.

[3]Just, "Kurd Lasswitz," 45.

[4]Rottensteiner, *ibid.*, 141, 148, 143.

[5]Edwin M.J. Kretzmann, "German Technological Utopias of the Pre-War Period," *Annals of Science* 3 (1938):417-30; here p. 421.

[6]Rottensteiner, *ibid.*, 142, and Just, "Kurd Lasswitz," 7.

[7]Rottensteiner, *ibid.*, 146.

[8]*Idem.*

[9]Full bibliographical information, including references to modern German re-editions and English translations of some of the stories, is provided later in this chapter, early in the preceding chapter, and in the Bibliography. It has already been noted that *Seifenblasen* is cited according to the enlarged edition of 1894, whose pagination is maintained throughout subsequent printings of the era. *Traumkristalle,* similarly, is cited according to the enlarged edition of 1907.

The Table of Contents in *Seifenblasen* provides a date, presumably that of composition or, in a few instances, original separate publication, for each story, poem, or essay. The first edition contains the following pieces: "Prolog" (1890), "Auf der Seifenblase" (1887), "Stäubchen" (1889), "Apoikis" (1882), "Aladdins Wunderlampe" (1888), "Aus dem Tagebuch einer Ameise" (1890), "Musen und Weise" (1885), "Unverwüstlich" (1878), "Der Traumfabrikant" (1886), "Psychotomie" (1885), "Mirax" (1888), "Tröpfchen" (1890), "Selbstbiographische Studien" (1887), and "Epilog" (1885). The edition of 1894 adds "Prinzessin Jaja" (1892) after "Auf der Seifenblase" and "Der Schirm" (1893) after "Unverwüstlich." Before their book publication some of the stories had appeared independently in periodicals. Thus "Prinzessin Jaja" was published in *Nord und Süd* 61(1892):130-40; the date agrees with that provided in *Sb.*

Dating of the stories in *Traumkristalle*, which comprises the second volume of *Nie und Immer: Neue Märchen*, is less certain. It is reasonable to suppose that the stories in that volume were written after 1893 or 1894, and that those included in the "greatly enlarged edition" of 1907 and in subsequent printings belong to the period from 1902 to 1907. The 1902 edition includes "Jahrhundertmärchen," "Der gefangene Blitz," "Das Lächeln des Glücks," "Die drei Nägel," "Die Frau von Feldbach," "Die neue Welt," "Der Gehirnspiegel," "Morgentraum," and the essay "Schiefe Gedanken." The 1907 edition adds, after "Morgentraum," the five stories "Das Gesetz," "Weihnachtsmärchen," "Die Universalbibliothek," "Wie der Teufel den Professor holte," and "Der Gott der Veranda." Rottensteiner, in "Kurd Lasswitz: Ordnungsliebend" (154), attributes both "Wie der Teufel den Professor holte" and "Die Universalbibliothek" to 1902; but in his Introduction to the posthumous collection *Die Welt und der Mathematikus* (1924), Lietzmann states quite definitely that the former first appeared in the *Frankfurter Zeitung* on 4, 8, and 11 Sept. 1907, and the latter on 18 Dec. 1904 in the *Ostdeutsche Allgemeine Zeitung* (Breslau); he adds that "Das Gesetz" was first published on 24 Dec. 1905 in the *Vossische Zeitung* (Lietzmann, 5-6). Lietzmann's precise data would seem reliable in these three cases; on the other hand, he errs grossly in stating (p. 5) that *Seifenblasen* first appeared in 1901. Schweikert (1082) provides the following dates: "Das Lächeln des Glücks" (1900), "Schiefe Gedanken" (1899), "Das Gesetz" (1905), "Die Universalbibliothek" (1904), and "Wie der Teufel den Professor holte" (1907). Such considerations determine the dates given in this study; unfortunately I have not been able to trace in every detail the early history of publication of many of Lasswitz' short stories.

The 1979 volume *Bis zum Nullpunkt des Seins* (see note 1 above) contains the short stories "Die Fernschule," "Auf der Seifenblase," "Apoikis," "Aladdins Wunderlampe," "Aus dem Tagebuch einer Ameise," "Musen und Weise," "Der Traumfabrikant," "Psychotomie," "Mirax," "Der Gehirnspiegel," "Wie der Teufel den Professor holte," and "Die Weltprojekte" (1908, from *Empfundenes und Erkanntes*,) and the essay "Über Zukunftstraume" (from *Wirklichkeiten).*

As I also mentioned in the preceding chapter, the works in the posthumous volumes *Empfundenes und Erkanntes* (1920) and *Die Welt und der Mathematikus* (1924) cannot readily be classified as SF and are therefore treated only incidentally here.

[10]Rottensteiner, "Kurd Lasswitz: Ordnungsliebend," 150-55.

[11]*Ibid.*, 149.

[12]"Aladdin's Lamp," trans. Willy Ley, *Magazine of Fantasy and Science Fiction* 4.5 (May 1953): 92-99 (abridged); "When the Devil Took the Professor," trans. Willy Ley, *Magazine of Fantasy and Science Fiction* 4:1 (Jan. 1953); 52-62 (abridged); "Psychotomy," trans. Willy Ley, *Magazine of Fantasy and Science Fiction* 9.1 (July, 1955): 102-10; "Die Universalbibliothek" and "Wie der Teufel den Professor holte," in *Polaris 1: Ein Science Fiction Almanach,* ed. Franz Rottensteiner, 165-76 and 177-200 resp.

[13]Throughout his works Lasswitz frequently alludes to Goethe and *Faust*—in itself no occasion for surprise. *Die Welt und der Mathematikus* (75-91) includes a piece entitled "Prost: Der Faust-Tragödie (-n)ter Teil" ["Bottoms Up: The -nth Part of the Tragedy"], yet another venture in the succession of *Faust*-continuations, humorous or serious, of Lasswitz' time.

[14]Robert Scholes and Eric S. Rabkin, *Science Fiction: History—Science—Vision* (Notre Dame: University of Notre Dame Press, 1975), 8.

Chapter IV

[1]Ley, *Rockets, Missiles, and Space Travel,* 46; Schweikert, 1077.

[2]"Prospekt," endpapers to *Auf zwei Planeten,* 2. Aufl. (1898).

[3]Rottensteiner, "Kurd Lasswitz: Ordnungsliebend," 133.

[4]*Idem.*, and Schweikert, 951-2.

[5]Publisher's advertisement accompanying Fritz Engel, "Ein Robinson des Weltraums," *Das Magazin für Litteratur* (Berlin and Weimar), 18 Dec. 1897 n. pag.

[6]See Schweikert for an extensive bibliography (1092-1102) and discussion (940-42) of early reviews.

[7]The opening situation was inspired by the expedition led by the Swedish engineer and polar explorer Salomon Andrée (1857-1897?), who with two companions attempted to reach the North Pole by balloon. After their departure on 11 July 1897 the three disappeared, and remains of the expedition were not found until 1930, on the Spitzbergen Islands. But the actual Andrée flight could scarcely have inspired the entire novel, nor perhpas even the first chapters, for it is unlikely that Lasswitz could have waited until July of 1897 to write vital parts of a book that appeared later that year. It was, rather, the public announcement of Andrée's proposed expedition in 1895 which may well have provided Lasswitz the vehicle—literally—with which to establish and explore First Contact. And it is, after all, that theme, not the narrower notion of space flight, which is the heart of *Auf zwei Planeten*. Lasswitz had been fascinated by the idea for many years. But if one wishes to seek out specific external events which may indeed have affected the shape and timing of his novel, certainly the favorable oppositions of Mars must be considered: those of 1877 and 1879, which occurred just when *Gegen das Weltgesetz* was being completed and the *Bilder aus der Zukunft* were being published; and those of 1892 and, especially, 1894, which took place just before Lasswitz began *Auf zwei Planeten.*

Other favorable oppositions were to occur in 1909, 1924, and 1939. Lasswitz does not tell us which of them, if any, he had in mind as the time of First Contact. I suspect that of 1909, since Lasswitz portrays a terrestrial culture little different from that of 1897, although he certainly had the facility to do otherwise.

[8]Citations refer to the original edition of 1897, which was reprinted with identical pagination during Lasswitz' lifetime, although publication was transferred between 1905 and 1930 from E. Felber to B. Elischer Nachfolger. In order to distinguish the two volumes of the original edition, which have separate pagination, and to aid users of other editions, I have provided both chapter and page numbers. In locating citations, however, it is necessary to note that the chapter divisions of both the major recent German edition of 1969 (57 chs.) and the American translation of 1971 (56 chs.) do not correspond exactly to those of the first edition (60 chs.), due to differences in revision, condensation, and omission. The 1969 German edition follows the original edition closely, but omits Chapters 29 ("Das heimliche Frühstück"), 32 ("Ideale"), and 51 ("Martierinnen in Berlin"). The translation of 1971 also omits Chapter 29, but includes material from Chapters 32

and 51, though without separate chapter divisions in the latter case.

With regard to the five major structural divisions of the novel described in the next few pages of this study, Chapters 1-14, 15-26, 27-38, 39-49 and 50-60 of the original edition correspond to Chapters 1-14, 15-26, 27-36, 37-47 and 48-57 of the 1969 German edition, and to Chapters 1-11, 12-23, 24-33, 33-44 and 45-56 of the American translation. More specifically, Chapters 1-3, 11 and 45-47 of the latter edition correspond respectively to Chapter 1-5, 13-14 and 50-51 of the first edition.

⁹Just, "Kurd Lasswitz," 3. Lietzmann, in his introduction to *Die Welt und der Mathematikus,* 5, and Ley, in *Rockets, Missiles, and Space Travel,* 45-48, state that there was a small observatory in the garden or attic of Lasswitz' boyhood home. The present writer, hoping to view the Lasswitz home should it still be standing, attempted to travel to Breslau-Wrocław in the spring of 1982, but at that time visas for independent parties of tourists were not being issued.

¹⁰Hillegas, "Martians and Mythmakers," 153ff.

¹¹*Ibid.,* 160.

¹²See von Braun's "Geleitwort zur Neuauflage," pp. 5-6 of the 1969 German edition of *Auf zwei Planeten.*

¹³See Mark R. Hillegas' Afterword to the 1971 American translation of *Auf zwei Planeten,* 397-8, and also his "Martians and Mythmakers," 164 ff.

¹⁴Quoted in Hans Lindau, "Kurd Lasswitz und seine modernen Märchen," 316.

¹⁵Ernst Alker, *Die deutsche Literatur im neunzehnten Jahrhundert* (Stuttgart: Kröner, 1961), 511-12.

Chapter V

¹Publication statistics for Dominik's novels can be found in Donald Day Richards, *The German Bestseller in the Twentieth Century: A Complete Bibliography and Analysis 1915-1940* (Bern: Herbert Lange, 1968), and on the copyright pages, title pages, and endpapers of the various impressions *(Auflagen).* Among the latter the 1943 printing (81st-90th thousands) of *König Laurins Mantel* is especially useful, for it provides publication data about thirteen of the novels for the important mid-war years, which Richards' study does not include. A combination of the highest reliable figures from both sources yields a total publication of at least 2,097,000 copies for the sixteen SF novels, as of 1943, two years before Dominik's death. Individual totals range from a "low" of 85,000 copies as of 1943 for *Befehl aus dem Dunkel* (1933), to a high of 187,000 in 1942 for *Land aus Feuer und Wasser* (1939) and 188,000 in 1943 for *Treibstoff SR* (1940). The endpapers of a SF novel by Freder van Holk (pseud. of Paul Alfred Müller), *Weltuntergang* (Berlin: Weiss, 1959), refer to a total publication of more than 3,000,000 copies. No doubt that number has been increased substantially by other printings in the more than twenty years since then.

See below, note 17, for an estimate of Dominik's position among other bestselling writers of German literature.

²Bernt Kling, "Perry Rhodan," trans Nancy King, *Science Fiction Studies* No. 12 (1977): 159-61; Manfred Nagl, *Science Fiction in Deutschland,* 204-07.

³Secondary literature about Dominik and his SF is extremely scarce. Even such specialized studies as *Science Fiction in Deutschland,* by Manfred Nagl, and *Vom Staatsroman zur Science Fiction,* by Martin Schwonke, devote little attention to him. While they are useful, the short entries on Dominik in the *Neue Deutsche Biographie* and in several of the standard reference works on German literature provide only the essential biographical facts and bibliographical information, the latter of which is generally incomplete and in at least one instance inaccurate. Thus the *Deutsches Literatur-Lexikon,* Wilhelm Kosch and Bruno Berger, eds., 3rd, revised ed. (Bern: Francke, 1971), 2:439-41, incorrectly attributes to Dominik the authorship of two books about the Cameroons which were written by a cousin of the same name (1870-1910) who had served in Africa.

Therefore Dominik's autobiography, *Vom Schraubstock zum Schreibtisch* (Berlin: Scherl, 1942), remains the major source of information about his life. The autobiography, cited hereinafter as *"VSS,"* is reliable in its basic facts, as far as I have been able to check them against other sources, but it is laden with Dominik's reactionary ideological views, his inflated sense of self-importance, and some fatuous pontifications about art. Other interesting information about Dominik's view of science, SF, and politics is contained in the prefatory essay "Erfüllte Prophezeiungen" ["Fulfilled Prophecies"] which was added (pp. v-xv) to the 1934 printing of *Die Macht der Drei* (96th-100th thousands; the date "1943" on the title page is an obvious typographical error). The following secondary works, in addition to those mentioned in note 1 above and note 12 below, have also furnished me with useful material concerning Dominik's life, works, and environment, especially his relations with his publishers: "Hans Dominik 60-jährig," *Das Echo* 51(1932):615-16; Franz Lennartz, *Deutsche Dichter und Schriftsteller unserer Zeit* (Stuttgart: Kröner, 1959), 164-67; Walther Kiaulehn, *Berlin: Schicksal einer Weltstadt*, 6th ed. (München: Biederstein Verlag, 1958); Peter DeMendelssohn, *Zeitungsstadt Berlin: Menschen und Mächte in der Geschichte der deutschen Presse* (Berlin: Ullstein, 1959); Hans Erman, *August Scherl* (Berlin: Universitas Verlag, 1959); Ludwig Bernhard, *Der "Hugenberg-Konzern:" Psychologie und Technik einer Grossorganisation der Presse* (Berlin: Julius Springer, 1928); Dietrich Strothmann, *National-Sozialistische Literaturpolitik* (Bonn: Bouvier, 1960).

Just recently appeared but also useful to me in the final stages of galley revision were two essays: Wolfgang Braun, " 'Von Mitternacht kommt die Macht'—Technik und Ideologie in Hans Dominiks 'Die Macht der Drei,' " in *Neugier oder Flucht*, ed. Karl Ermert, 116-25, and Werner Klinger, "So war Dominik nicht!" *Quarber Merkur* 19.2 (Oct. 1981):64-70, a response to the former article; and the entry "Hans Dominik" in the *Lexikon der Science Fiction Literatur*, ed. Hans-Joachim Alpers et al. (München: Heyne, 1980), 1:284-87.

⁴See Erman, *August Scherl*, 263-64.

⁵The thematic characteristics and sociological background of Dominik's early short stories are treated at some length in Susanne Päch, "Von den Marskanälen zur Wunderwaffe: Eine Studie über phantastische und futurologische Tendenzen auf dem Gebiet von Naturwissenschaft and Technik, dargestellt am populärwissenschaftlichen Jahrbuch *Das neue Universum* 1880-1945," Diss. München, 1980, especially pages 174-211 and appendices.

⁶Some of Dominik's many writings on science and technology are listed in Gero von Wilpert and Adolf Gühring, *Erstausgaben deutscher Dichtung: Eine Bibliographie zur deutschen Dichtung 1600-1960* (Stuttgart: Kröner, 1967), 236-7. His early fictional and semi-fictional works about technology were collected in the volumes *Technische Märchen* (Berlin: Steinitz, 1903) and *Wissenschaftliche Plaudereien: Entdeckungen und Erfindungen, Fortschritte der Wissenschaft und Industrie* (Berlin: Steinitz, 1903); the *Neues Universum* pieces are now more readily accessible in two paperback editions, the latter of which contains stories by other contributors to the magazine: *Ein neues Paradies: Klassische Science Fiction-Erzählungen*, ed. Susanne Päch and Wolfgang Jeschke (München: Heyne, 1977), and *Als der Welt Kohle und Eisen ausging: Klassische Science Fiction-Erzählungen von Hans Dominik, Herbert Frank, Friedrich Meister, P. Meyer, Colin Ross u.a., aus dem "Neuen Universum,"* ed. Susanne Päch (München: Heyne, 1980).

⁷Dominik does not mention that his first novel was actually the very popular *John Workmann der Zeitungsboy: Erzählung aus der amerikanischen Grossindustrie* [*John Workmann* (sic) *the Newspaperboy: A Tale of American Giant Industry*] (Berlin: Steinitz, 1909; expanded to 3 vols., Berlin: Koehler & Amelang, 1921), probably because the novel was written in collaboration with Kurt Matull, the pseudonym of the friend to whom he refers in *VSS*. Dominik's other non-SF novels, with date of hardcover publication in parentheses, include: *Glück auf!* [*Come up Safe!*] (1912), *Der Sieger: Automobilroman* [*The Victor: Automobile-Novel*] (1913); *Der eiserne Weg* [*The Iron Path*] (1913), *Klar zum Gefecht* [*Ready for Battle*] (1915), *Der Kreiselkompass: Roman einer technischen Sensation* [*The Gyrocompass: A Novel about a Technological Sensation*] (1915), *Das eiserne Kreuz: Kriegsroman* [*The Iron Cross: A Novel of War*] (1916), *Die Madonna mit den Perlen* [*The Madonna with the Pearls*] (1916), *Der "eiserne Halbmond:" Kriegsmarineroman* [*The "Iron Half-Moon:" Navy-Novel*] (1917), *Versunkenes Land* [*Sunken Land*] (1918), *Alpenglühen* [*Alpenglows*] (1919), and *Hochströme: Roman aus der Elektrizitäts-Industrie* [*High-Tensions: A Novel of the Electrical Industry*] (1919), all published by Duncker in Berlin; and *Klaus im Glück: Vom Hirtenjungen zum Diamantenkönig* [*Lucky Claus: From Shepherd-boy to Diamond King*] (Leipzig: Koehler & Amelang, 1928).

⁸I disagree with Nagl's implication, advanced in *Science Fiction in Deutschland* (154), that Dominik's novels were so heavily rewritten by the Scherl editorial board that they could well be considered a collective undertaking. Fairer though still not very complimentary is the assessment offered by Päch (179), who cites evidence from *VSS* showing that the two publishers Duncker and Scherl provided Dominik—as they did no doubt many others of their authors—with the services of specialist-editors and rewrite-men whose job it was to package the product in the appropriate way and where necessary, as Päch puts it, to "pep up the novels more," especially with love-scenes. Yet Päch's remarks, which quote only a single sentence from *VSS*, 225, and even more Nagl's observations, should be gauged against Dominik's far lengthier discussion of the matter, *VSS*, 224-28.

⁹See Keith Bullivant and Hugh Ridley's Introduction to their collection *Industrie und deutsche Literatur 1830-1914: Eine Anthologie* (München: Deutscher Taschenbuch Verlag, 1976).

¹⁰Ralf Dahrendorf, *Gesellschaft und Demokratie in Deutschland* (München: R. Piper, 1968), Pt. 3, Chs. 10-14.

¹¹See Walter Nutz, *Der Trivalroman: seine Formen und seine Hersteller* (Köln: Westdeutscher Verlag, 1962); Dorothee Bayer, *Der triviale Familien- und Liebesroman im 20. Jahrhundert,* 2nd ed. (Tübingen: Tübinger Vereinigung für Volkskunde e. V., 1971); Walther Killy, "Versuch über den literarischen Kitsch," in *Deutscher Kitsch: ein Versuch mit Beispielen* (Göttingen: Vandenhoeck & Ruprecht, 1962), 9-33.

¹²Information for the present discussion has been drawn in part from the following sources, as well as those listed in note 3 above: Anneliese Thimme, *Flucht in den Mythos: Die Deutschnationale Volkspartei und die Niederlage von 1918* (Göttingen: Vandenhoeck & Ruprecht, 1969); "Hugenberg, Alfred," Brockhaus Enzyklopädie, 17th rev. ed. (1969); John A. Leopold, *Alfred Hugenberg: The Radical Nationalist Campaign against the Weimar Republic* (New Haven: Yale Univeresity Press, 1977); Joachim C. Fest, *Hitler: Eine Biographie* (Frankfurt am Main: Ullstein/Propylaen, 1973).

¹³Erman, *August Scherl,* 34, 234ff., 268ff.

¹⁴See Erman, *August Scherl,* 27, 35ff., 181, 242ff., DeMendelssohn, *Zeitungsstadt Berlin,* 140, Bernhard, *Der "Hugenberg-Konzern,"* 42, and *VSS,* 163-64.

¹⁵Actually neither Mosse nor Ullstein, the two Jewish houses mentioned as possible buyers, were centers of radicalism. Their publications catered to the same mass market and popular consciousness as did Scherls'. And, as Leopold notes in his study *Alfred Hugenberg* (9), one of the key investors in Hugenberg's consortium was Baron Salomon von Oppenheim.

¹⁶Leopold, *Alfred Hugenberg,* 263n8 (Leopold's translation).

¹⁷I have checked Richards' figures against various impressions of Dominik's novels and have sometimes been able to augment them with information available in copies printed after 1940. Especially useful are the endpapers of the 1943 impression (143rd to 147th thousands) of *Atomgewicht 500.* Of the 850 most popular German novels Richards lists for the period 1915-1940 (the list includes both works which first appeared before 1915 and those which were suppressed after 1933), novels by Dominik occupy the following ranks: 145, 154, 174, 231, 321, 326, 375, 393, 404, 436, 544, 591 (two), and 635. Only *König Laurins Mantel* and *Treibstoff SF* failed to make Richards' list. The exclusion of the former seems to be an oversight, since by 1943 90,000 copies of the novel had been printed; *Treibstoff SR* was published only in 1940, the last year covered by Richards, and within the next three years had reached a printing of 188,000 copies. Two other works of non-SF by Dominik rank 617 and 635 in the list: *John Workmann der Zeitungsboy* (1909, with K. Matull), and *Vistra, das weisse Gold Deutschlands: Die Geschichte einer weltbewegenden Erfindung* (1936), a science popularization which Richards understandably enough mistook for a novel.

¹⁸Nutz, *Der Trivialroman,* 14ff., 70ff.

¹⁹Endpapers to Freder van Holk (pseud. of Paul Alfred Müller), *Weltuntergang* (Berlin: Weiss, 1959), quoting *Deutsche Kommentare* and the Bielefeld *Freie Presse;* ellipsis as in advertisement.

²⁰Dieter Hasselblatt, " 'Kein Happy-End am Daisy-Day:' Analysen zum Science-Fiction Markt," in *Die triviale Phantasie: Beiträge zur "Verwertbarkeit" von Science Fiction,* ed. Jörg Weigand, 103-21; condensed rpt. as "Reflections from West Germany on the Science-Fiction Market," trans. William B. Fischer, *Science-Fiction Studies* No. 13 (1977):256-63.

²¹Strothmann, *National-Sozialistische Literaturpolitik,* 106ff., 132ff., 151, 170ff., 188, 249, 324ff.

²²The March 1944 issue of *Astounding Science Fiction* carried a story by Cleve Cartmill, "Deadline," which described atomic bombs with such accuracy that the FBI, suspecting a security leak in the Manhattan Project, interviewed the magazine's editor, John W. Campbell, Jr. The incident—there had been no leak—is often cited in discussions of the accuracy or validity of SF as prophecy; whatever the case, it suggests that the rulers of the far more authoritarian National Socialist state, while they may have recognized the value of Dominik's novels in propping up morale, were not overly concerned that they would compromise actual atomic and rocketry projects.

²³See for example the entries on Dominik in Franz Lennartz' standard reference work, *Die Dichter unserer Zeit: Einzeldarstellungen zur deutschen Dichtung der Gegenwart* (Stuttgart: Kröner, 5th ed. (1952):99-101, 8th ed. (1959):164-66. Recent editions, however, omit all reference to Dominik.

²⁴Rudolf Majut, "Der dichtungsgeschichtliche Standort von Ernst Jüngers 'Heliopolis,' "

Germanisch-Romanische Monatsschrift 7(1957):1-15; Alice Carol Gaar, "German Science Fiction: Variations on the Theme of Survival in the Space-Time Continuum," Diss. University of North Carolina, 1973; Susanne Pǎch, *Von den Marskanälen zur Wunderwaffe.*

²⁵Wolfgang Braun, " 'Von Mitternacht kommt die Macht'—Technik und Ideologie in Hans Dominiks 'Die Macht der Drei," in *Neugier oder Flucht,* ed. Karl Ermert.

²⁶Manfred Nagl, *Science Fiction in Deutschland,* e.g., 164, 172-3, 193-6.

²⁷Hans-Joachim Flechtner, "Die phantastische Literatur: Eine literarästhetische Untersuchung," *Zeitschrift für Ästhetik und allgemeine Kunstwissenschaft,* 24 (1930):43.

²⁸Horst Heidtmann, "Science Fiction in der DDR," afterword to *Von einem anderen Stern: Science-Fiction-Geschichten aus der DDR,* ed. Horst Heidtmann (München: Deutscher Taschenbuch Verlag, 1981), 266.

²⁹Hans Dominik, "Airports for World Traffic," trans. Francis M. Currier, *Air Wonder Stories* 1 (Jan. 1930):610-14.

³⁰The translations of the three short stories by Lasswitz which appeared in *The Magazine of Fantasy and Science Fiction* were mentioned in Chapter III and are listed in the Bibliography. *Druso, oder: die gestohlene Menschenwelt,* (1931), by Friedrich Freksa, appeared as *Druso,* trans. Fletcher Pratt, in *Wonder Stories* 5(May 1934):1066-1113, 6 (June 1934):78-109, and 6(July 1934):210-35. *Der Schuss ins All* (1935), by Otto Willi Gail, was published as *The Shot into Infinity,* trans. Francis Currier, in *Science Wonder Quarterly* 1 (Fall 1929):6-77, and also in *Science Fiction Quarterly* No. 2(Winter 1941):4-108. *Der Stein vom Mond* (1926), also by Gail, appeared as *The Stone from the Moon,* trans. Francis Currier, in *Science Wonder Quarterly* 1 (Spring 1930):294-359.

Chapter VI

¹Dominik's novels are listed in the foregoing chapter, where their relation to his other works is discussed. In the present chapter the novels are cited according to (shortened) title and page number. The Bibliography provides full information about original editions and, wherever relevant, later impressions used for citation. In a few instances there are differences in pagination between first and subsequent impressions or edition, even those which appeared with the same publisher and would seem to have been made up from the same set type. Location of quotations in the various editions is also made more difficult by the lack of chapter divisions in almost all of the novels. Postwar editions ot Dominik's novels should be used with caution; the various publishers have seen fit not only to condense and to polish Dominik's prose style, but also to alter details of technology, setting, character, and ideology, in order to modernize the scientific content of the novels, minimize the crudeness of Dominik's reactionary political convictions, and thus increase the social acceptability and marketability of his SF. Such modification, of course, greatly affects the evaluation of his works—as ideological expression, as literature, and as SF. For a short, but, in its basic points, sufficient illustration of editorial alteration of Dominik's novels see the *Quarber Merkur* article "So war Dominik nicht!" by Werner Klinger, mentioned in the preceding chapter (note 3).

²I was most pleased though not at all surprised to find that Wolfgang Braun, in his contribution to the anthology *Neugier oder Flucht* edited by Karl Ermert, had chosen the same novel as his focus of attention.

³See, for example, Walther Killy, "Versuch über den literarischen Kitsch," 10-17.

⁴*Idem.*; also Christa Bürger, *Textanalyse als Ideologiekritik: Zur Rezeption zeitgenössischer Unterhaltungsliteratur* (Frankfurt am Main: Athenäum Fischer Taschenbuch Verlag, 1973), 4-6, and Nutz, *Der Trivialroman,* 16-19, 32-34.

⁵Pǎch, in *Von den Marskanälen zur Wunderwaffe,* 188, 197-98, independently argues the same point.

⁶James Joll, "The Course of German History," *History Today* 3 (1953):603-09; rpt. in *Germany: People and Politics, 1750-1945,* ed. Robert F. Hopwood (Edinburgh: Oliver and Boyd, 1968), 27-41.

⁷See *VSS,* 171-72, and "Erfüllte Prophezeiungen," Preface to *Die Macht der Drei,* 96th-100th thousands (1934), ix-xi.

[8]See the previously mentioned dissertation by Alice Carol Gaar, "German Science Fiction: Variations on the Theme of Survival," 41ff., 100ff., 258ff.

[9]It is probably not inconsequential that one of Hugenberg's few intimate associates was a certain Dr. Leo Wegener, whom John Leopold, in his biography of the magnate, first calls Hugenberg's "crony" (9) and then "his closest friend" (18); Leopold goes on to remark that Wegener "played a key role in the Hugenberg concern and maintained an active correspondence with leaders in conservative nationalist circles.... More than any one, except perhaps Hugenberg's wife, Wegener had a tremendous influence on his friend. While Hugenberg was taciturn and thought in highly technical and legal terms, Wegener was a vibrant personality who literally 'bubbled with ideas'—many of which Hugenberg later accepted and reinterpreted in corporate and legislative language" (33).

[10]See Pách, *Von den Marskanälen zur Wunderwaffe,* 192ff.

[11]G. Edward Pendray, *The Coming Age of Rocket Power* (New York: Harper, 1945), 44-45.

[12]In her previously mentioned dissertation (14) Alice Carol Gaar suggests that such alterations in consciousness are a major ingredient of Dominik's SF. The observation may be accurate with regard to Dominik's interests and intent, but in his novels execution lags considerably behind conception.

[13]Background information for the present discussion has been drawn from the following secondary sources, in addition to the primary works listed in the text: Wernher von Braun and Frederick I. Ordway, III, *History of Rocketry and Space Travel* (New York: Thomas Y. Crowell, 1966); *Journal of the British Interplanetary Society,* Vols. 1-5(1934-39; rpt. New York: Kraus, 1958); Leonard James Carter, ed., *Realities of Space Travel: The Selected Papers of the British Interplanetary Society* (New York: McGraw Hill, 1957), especially the article by the military head of the German rocket program during World War II, Maj. Gen. Dr. Walter R. Dornberger, "European Rocketry after World War I," 381-93; P. E. Cleator, *Rockets through Space: The Dawn of Interplanetary Travel* (New York: Simon and Schuster, 1936); David Lasser, *The Conquest of Space* (New York: Penguin Press, 1931); Willy Ley, "The End of the German Rocket Society," *Astounding Science Fiction* 32.1 (Sept. 1943):58-75; and, previously mentioned, Willy Ley, *Rockets, Missiles and Space Travel,* and G. Edward Pendray, *The Coming Age of Rocket Power.*

[14]See for example Ley, *Rockets, Missiles and Space Travel,* 45-48, and von Braun's epigraphs to the 1969 German and 1971 American editions of *Auf zwei Planeten.*

[15]Strangely enough, the theme of space flight is more prominent in three of Dominik's short stories, all of which appeared before the publication of his first SF novel in 1922, let alone that of *Erbe* in 1928: "Die Reise zum Mars" (1908), "Eine Expedition in den Weltraum" (1918), and "Zukunftsmusik" (1921), all published in *Das neue Universum.*

[16]Walther Killy, "Versuch über den literarischen Kitsch," 26-30.

[17]See the section on Nazi science in George Mosse, ed., *Nazi Culture: Intellectual, Cultural and Social Life in the Third Reich* (New York: Grosset & Dunlap, 1966), especially the editor's introduction; also the several essays on the natural sciences in *Naturwissenschaft, Technik und NS-Ideologie: Beitrage zur Wissenschaftsgeschichte des Dritten Reiches,* ed. Herbert Mehrtens and Steffen Richter (Frankfurt am Main: Suhrkamp, 1980).

[18]Darko Suvin, "On What Is and Is not an SF Narration; With a list of 101 Victorian Books That Should Be Excluded from SF Bibliographies," *Science Fiction Studies* No. 14(1978):47 (Suvin's emphasis).

Chapter VII

[1]A "Who's Who in German SF" and a very extensive bibliography of SF which has appeared in the Federal Republic of Germany, including translations of foreign works, are to be found in the second volume (pp. 704-1206) of the new *Lexikon der Science Fiction Literatur,* ed. Hans-Joachim Alpers et al. (München: Heyne, 1980). See also the older *Transgalaxis* bibliography (1959) by Bingenheimer, and two recent surveys: "Science Fiction und Phantastik seit Redaktionsschluss des 'Lexikons der Science Fiction-Literatur,'" by Ronald M. Hahn and Friedel Wahren, in *Heyne Science Fiction Magazin* 1 (München: Heyne, 1981): 357-419; and "Science Fiction und Phantastik in deutscher Sprache, von 1945-1959," by Ronald M. Hahn, in *Heyne Science Fiction Magazin* 2 (München: Heyne, 1982): 357-66.

[2]The "indigenous" SF community's response to *Stern der Ungeborenen* is expressed briefly by William Atheling, Jr. (pseud. of James Blish), in *The Issue at Hand* (Chicago: Advent, 1964): 124ff.

³Bernt Kling, "*Perry Rhodan*," trans. Nancy King, *Science Fiction Studies* No. 12 (1977): 159-61: Jürgen Holtkamp, "Die Eröffnung des rhodesischen Zeitalters oder Einübung in die Freie Welt: Science Fiction-Literatur in Deutschland," *Kursbuch* 12 (1968): 45-63; Manfred Nagl, *Science Fiction in Deutschland,* 204-07, and *Science Fiction: Ein Segment populärer Kultur im Medien und Produktverbund (*Tübingen: Gunter Narr, 1981), *passim;* and Sylvia Pukallus, Ronald M. Hahn, and Horst Pukallus, " 'Perry Rhodan' as a Social and Ideological Phenomenon," *Science Fiction Studies* No. 18 (1979): 190-200.

⁴An account of the West German SF scene in the early post-WWII years is offered by Rainer Eisfeld in his eulogy and essay, " '. . . und der Ring des Saturn kann niemanden mehr erschüttern' (In memoriam Wolf Detlef Rohr, 1928-1981)," *Heyne Science Fiction Magazin* 3 (München: Heyne, 1982): 129-37; see also Manfred Nagl, *Science Fiction in Deutschland,* 195ff.

⁵Franz Rottensteiner surveys modern German SF in two readily accessible articles: "German SF," in *Anatomy of Wonder,* ed. Neil Barron, 2nd ed. (New York: Bowker, 1981), 381-98, and "Die 'wissenschaftliche Phantastik' der DDR," in *Polaris 5: Ein Science Fiction Almanach,* ed. Franz Rottensteiner (Frankfurt: Suhrkamp, 1981), 91-118.

⁶Wolfgang Jeschke, "Science Fiction und Buchmarkt," in *VS: Vertraulich,* vol. 3, a publication of the Confederation of German Writers (Verband deutscher Schriftsteller), ed. Bernt Engelmann (München: Goldman, 1979), 166.

⁷See Brian Aldiss' foreword to Wolfgang Jeschke, *Der letzte Tag der Schöpfung* (München: Nymphenburger Verlagshandlung, 1981), 7-10, and the unsigned review of the same novel in *Quarber Merkur* 56 (Oct. 1981):81.

⁸Personal interview with Wolfgang Jeschke, 21 April 1982.

⁹*Idem.*

¹⁰Jörg Weigand, "Science-Fiction-Kurzgeschichte und schriftstellerischer Nachwuchs," *VS: Vertraulich,* 150.

¹¹See, especially, Lester del Rey, *The World of Science Fiction: 1926-1976—The History of a Subculture* (New York: Ballantine, 1979), chs. 8, 9, 12-15, Harry Warner, *All Our Yesterdays,* and Frederik Pohl, *The Way the Future Was: A Memoir* (New York: Ballantine, 1978).

¹²Biographical information has been drawn from the thumbnail sketch introducing *SYN-CODE-7: Science-fiction-Roman* (Frankfurt: Suhrkamp, 1982); the Heyne *Lexikon der Science Fiction Literatur,* understandably, does not list Weisser.

¹³My analysis of the cybernetic-genetic theme and related linguistic features of *SYN-CODE-7* draws much of its sustenance from Douglas R. Hofstadter's *Gödel, Escher, Bach: An Eternal Golden Braid—A metaphorical fugue on minds and machines in the spirit of Lewis Carroll* (New York: Basic Books, 1979). As his title makes clear, Hofstadter traces intriguing analogies—or are they something more than that?—between the sciences and the arts. Like Weisser, he examines cybernetics, genetics, and certain works of art as curious, highly complex formal systems. Apparently self-generating and, by virtue of their structure and functions, self-referential, they exhibit what Weisser terms "Eigendynamik," and yet, like the BIOTEC, raise the ultimate paradox elucidated mathematically in Gödel's Theorem: no information-processing or -generating system can explain its own existence or validate its own validity. Indeed, in content and quality *SYN-CODE-7* might be termed the fictional equivalent of *Gödel, Escher, Bach,* which won the 1980 Pulitzer Prize for general non-fiction, were it not that Hofstadter's book is as much a work of art as Weisser's novel is a fictionalized exploration of the nature of science, technology, and art.

Also of interest here is Hofstadter's continuing discussion—such things, like footnotes, can become epistemologically convoluted, stylistically baroque, self-referential obsessions—of self-referential statements, which he pursues in his regular *Scientific American* column, "Metamagical Thegmas." That of the January 1982 issue (246.1) includes—barely—David Moser's short story, entitled "This Is the Title of This Story, Which Is Also Found Several Times in the Story Itself" (pp. 26, 28). The story ends, as do Hofstadter's column and this footnote, which is, fortunately or not, the thirteenth note to the seventh chapter, with a single word which may be both the author's apology to the reader and a self-referential value-judgment about and within the text itself: (") sorry (").

¹⁴Personal interview with Dieter Hasselblatt, 19 April 1982; see also Hasselblatt's articles, "Ein halbes Jahrhundert Science-fiction und Hörspiel," *Polaris 5,* 165-92, and "Science Fiction und Hörspiel: Tendenzen jenseits des Marktes," *Quarber Merkur* 52 (Jan. 1980):12-16.

¹⁵Dieter Hasselblatt, "Hörspiel und Science Fiction," *Heyne Science Fiction Magazin* 1:207.

¹⁶Dieter Hasselblatt, "Science Fiction—Wahn? Ware? Wahrheit?," *VS-Vertraulich,* 138.

¹⁷*Der Fisch* has now been reprinted in the *Heyne Science Fiction Magazin* 2:217-27.

¹⁸Hasselblatt, "Science Fiction und Hörspiel," and Manfred Nagl, *Science Fiction: Ein*

Segment populärer Kultur, 120-21.

[19]The Bibliography, Section IV, includes a number of articles on the technique. A fairly accessible description is provided by Waldemar F. Kehler in his article "Kopfbezogene Stereophonie," *Neue Zürcher Zeitung,* 27 August 1974: 17-18. (Fernausgabe Nr. 235).

[20]The printed text of the radio-play, with the title "Papa and Joe," is available in Franke's collection, *Zarathustra kehrt zurück: Science-fiction-Erzählungen* (1977), 29-66.

[21]Dieter Hasselblatt, letter to the author, 16 March 1982; personal interviews with Wolfgang Jeschke, 30 March 1982, and Jörg Weigand, 25 April 1982.

[22]Jörg Weigand, letter to the author, 19 May 1982.

[23]Personal interview with Wolfgang Jeschke, 30 March 1982.

[24]Interview with Jörg Weigand, 25 April 1982.

[25]Jörg Weigand, letter to the author, 19 May 1982.

[26]For an introduction to East German SF see Franz Rottensteiner, "Die 'wissenschaftliche Phantastik' der DDR."

[27]A useful English-language survey of the Brauns' works is the article by Darko Suvin, 'Playful Cognizing, or Technical Errors in Harmonyville: The SF of Johanna and Günter Braun," *Science Fiction Studies* No. 23 (March 1981): 72-9.

[28]The Suhrkamp edition of 1982 is used for quotation.

[29]*Über die asthetische Erziehung des Menschen, in einer Reihe von Briefen* [*Concerning the Aesthetic Education of Mankind, in a Series of Letters*] (1795).

[30]Hasselblatt has frequently stated his argument, most notably in " 'Kein Happy-End am Daisy-Day:' Analysen zum Science-Fiction-Markt," in *Die triviale Phantasie,* ed. Jörg Weigand, 103-21.

[31]Franz Rottensteiner, "Die 'wissenschaftliche Phantastik' der DDR," 118.

[32]Franz Rottensteiner, "Die wissenschaftliche Phantastik—eine Alternative," in *Die triviale Phantasie,* ed. Jörg Weigand, 59-72, and especially 60.

[33]Aridne Gromova, "At the Frontier of the Present Age," introduction to *Vortex: New Soviet Science Fiction,* ed. C. G. Bearne (London: MacGibbon and Kee, 1970), 9-29.

[34]From the document "Konzeption der utopischen Literatur im Verlag Das Neue Berlin" ["Concept of Utopian Literature in the Publishing-house das Neue Berlin"] (1970), quoted by Franz Rottensteiner, "Die 'wissenschaftliche Phantastik' der DDR," 91.

[35]Curiously enough, in "Playful Cognizing" (77) Darko Suvin has also found it somehow appropriate to allude to Schiller when discussing the Brauns; he does so, however, in quite another way.

[36]Linda Fleming, "The American SF Sub-Culture," *Science Fiction Studies* 13(1977): 263-71.

[37]In their anthology *Industrie und deutsche Literatur 1830-1914* (München: Deutscher Taschenbuchverlag, 1976), which is accompanied by a lengthy and perceptive introductory essay, Keith Bullivant and Hugh Ridley amply document the lag in the literary assimilation of technology in Germany; see also Karl Robert Mandelkow, "Orpheus und Maschine," in *Orpheus und Maschine: Acht literaturgeschichtliche Arbeiten* (Heidelberg: Lothar Stiehm, 1976).

[38]I think it possible that other and perhaps even more fundamental linguistic traits, ones which certainly reflect modes of thought and may well influence them, have facilitated the emergence of the science-fictional intentionality in Anglo-American literature and have hindered it in German literature. There is in German no single word capable of rendering the English term 'fiction," which, with a blend of preciseness and flexibility well suited to the intentionality of SF, both signifies a type of literature and implies a certain attitude toward reality, unreality, and imagination. Equally important is the fact that the English word "science" subsumes both "theoretical science" and "applied science" or "technology," and therefore suggests their close interconnection or even partial equivalence; together the two are considered quite distinct from, or even alien to, the "humanities." The German word "Naturwissenschaft" suggests that theoretical or academic science is a body of knowledge or type of activity closely related to the other "Wissenschaften" or scholarly, intellectual studies, among them the humanities. At least until recently, when "Naturwissenschaft" has broadened somewhat in its connotations, there has been a notable distinction between "Naturwissenschaft" and "Technik," in abstract conception and even in the respective social positions of scientists and technicians.

[39]Wolfgang Jeschke, in an interview with the present writer (30 March 1982), remarked that, in the years before 1933, "There was a very fertile interpenetration of SF authors, rocket technicians, and theoretical scientists; out of that a German Golden Age of SF could have developed, especially if the [literary] stimuli from abroad, from America, had been able to enter Germany]." He stated flatly that such a development would have been "an absolute certainty, if there had been no Third Reich."

[40]Hans Lindau, "Kurd Lasswitz und seine modernen Märchen," 316.

Bibliography

I. Works by Kurd Lasswitz

A. Early Editions

Aspira: Der Roman einer Wolke. Leipzig: B. Elischer Nachfolger, 1905.

Auf zwei Planeten: Roman in zwei Büchern. 2 vols. Weimar: Emil Felber, 1897.

Bilder aus der Zukunft: Zwei Erzählungen aus dem vierundzwanzigsten und neununddreissigsten Jahrhundert. 2 vols. Breslau: S. Schottlaender, 1878.

Empfundenes und Erkanntes: Aus dem Nachlasse. Ed. Hans Lindau. Leipzig: B. Elischer Nachfolger, n.d. [1920].

Nie und Immer. 2 vols. Leipzig and Jena: Eugen Diederichs, 1902. Vol. 1: *Homchen: Ein Tiermärchen aus der oberen Kreide.* Vol. 2: *Traumkristalle: Neue Märchen.* Cited from the enlarged ed., Leipzig: B. Elischer Nachfolger, 1907.

Schlangenmoos: Novelle. Breslau: S. Schottlaender, 1884.

Seelen und Ziele: Beiträge zum Weltverständnis. Leipzig: B. Elischer Nachfolger, 1908.

Seifenblasen: Moderne Märchen. Hamburg: Leopold Voss, 1890. Cited from the revised and enlarged ed., Weimar: Emil Felber, 1894.

Sternentau: Die Pflanze vom Neptunsmond. Leipzig: B. Elischer Nachfolger, 1909.

Die Welt und der Mathematikus: Ausgewählte Dichtungen von Kurd Lasswitz. Ed. W[alter] Lietzmann. Leipzig: B. Elischer Nachfolger, n.d. [1924].

Wirklichkeiten: Beiträge zum Weltverständnis. Berlin: Emil Felber, 1900. Cited from the 2nd ed., Leipzig: B. Elischer Nachfolger, 1903.

B. Selected Recent German Editions

"Auf der Seifenblase." In 1) *Science Fiction aus Deutschland,* ed. Hans-Joachim Alpers and Ronald M. Hahn. Frankfurt, 1974; 2) *Klassische Science-Fiction Geschichten,* ed. Peter Naujack. Zürich: Diogenes, 1979; 3) *Das Raumschiff: Utopische Meistererzählungen aus aller Welt,* ed. Georg Telemann. Berlin: Neues Leben, and Freiburg i.B.: Herder, 1979.

Auf zwei Planeten. 1) Erich Lasswitz, ed. Introd. by Friedrich Knapp. Donauwörth Cassianeum, 1948 (abridged); 2) Berlin: Gebrüder Weiss, 1959 (abridged); 3) revised and edited by Burckhardt Kiegeland and Martin Molitor. Foreword by Wernher von Braun. Frankfurt: Scheffler, 1969 (abridged); 4) München: Heyne, 1972; 5) edited, and with accompanying essays, chronological biography, and bibliography, by Rudi Schweikert. Frankfurt: Verlag 2001, 1979.

Bilder aus der Zukunft. Facs. of 3rd ed. (1879). Fürth/Saarland: Bleymehl, 1964.

Bis zum Nullpunkt: Utopische Erzählungen. Berlin (DDR): Das Neue Berlin, 1979.

Traumkristalle. Rastatt: Moewig, 1981.

"Die Universalbibliothek" and "Wie der Teufel den Professor holte." In *Polaris: Ein Science Fiction Almanach.* Franz Rottensteiner, ed. Frankfurt: Insel, 1973: 165-76 and 177-200 resp.

C. English Translations

"Aladdin's Lamp" ("Aladdins Wunderlampe"). Trans. Willy Ley. *Magazine of Fantasy and Science Fiction* 4.5 (May 1953): 92-99 (abridged).

"Pictures out of the Future" (excerpt from "Bis zum Nullpunkt des Seins"). Trans. Emil Pohli. *The Overland Monthly* XV, Second Series (June 1890):606-12.

"Psychotomy" ("Psychotomie"). Trans. Willy Ley. *Magazine of Fantasy and Science Fiction* 9.1 (July 1955): 102-110 (abridged).

Two Planets [Auf zwei Planeten]. Trans. Hans. H. Rudnick. Afterword by Mark R. Hillegas. Carbondale, Illinois: Southern Illinois University Press, 1971; New York: Popular Library, 1971 (based on the 1948 German edition, with some additions from the 1969 edition).

"When the Devil Took the Professor" ("Wie der Teufel den Professor holte"). Trans. Willy Ley. *Magazine of Fantasy and Science Fiction* 4.1 (Jan. 1953): 52-62 (abridged).

II. Works by Hans Dominik

Als der Welt Kohle und Eisen ausging: Klassische Science Fiction-Erzählungen von Hans Dominik, Herbert Frank, Friedrich Meister, P. Meyer, Colin Ross u.a. aus dem "Neuen Universum." Edited and with afterword by Susanne Päch. München: Heyne, 1980. Contains short stories by Dominik and others from the magazine *Das neue Universum*.

Atlantis. Leipzig: E. Keils Nachfolger (=Scherl), 1925.

Atomgewicht 500. Berlin: Scherl, 1935. Cited from the edition of 1943, 143rd-147th thousands.

Befehl aus dem Dunkel. Berlin: E. Keils Nachfolger (=Scherl), 1933.

Der Brand der Cheopspyramide. Berlin & Leipzig: E. Keils Nachfolger (=Scherl), . 1926.

Himmelskraft. Berlin: Scherl, 1937.

Kautschuk: Ein Roman aus der Industrie. Berlin: E. Keils Nachfolger (=Scherl), 1930.

König Laurins Mantel. Berlin: E. Keils Nachfolger (=Scherl), 1928. Cited from the edition of 1943, 81st-90th thousands.

Land aus Feuer und Wasser. Leipzig: v. Hase & Koehler, 1939.

Lebensstrahlen. Berlin: Scherl, 1938.

Die Macht der Drei: Ein Roman aus dem Jahre 1955. Berlin: E. Keils Nachfolger (=Scherl), 1922.

Ein neues Paradies: Klassische Science Fiction-Erzählungen. Ed. Susanne Päch and Wolfgang Jeschke. München: Heyne, 1977. Contains short stories from the magazine *Das neue Universum*.

Die Spur des Dschingis-Khan: Ein Roman aus dem einundzwanzigsten Jahrhundert. Leipzig, E. Keils Nachfolger (=Scherl), 1923. Cited from the edition of 1943, 126th-135th thousands.

Das stählerne Geheimnis. Berlin: Scherl, 1934.

Ein Stern fiel vom Himmel. Leipzig: Koehler & Amelang, 1934. Cited from the edition of 1940 (Leipzig: v. Hase & Koehler), 131st-170th thousands.

Treibstoff SR. Berlin: Scherl, 1940.

Vom Schraubstock zum Schreibtisch: Lebenserinnerungen. Berlin: Scherl, 1942.

Der Wettflug der Nationen. Leipzig: Koehler & Amelang, 1933.

Note: All of Dominik's SF novels are now available in modern paperback editions issued by the Heyne Verlag in München. The post-war editions should be used with caution, since they have been not only tacitly abridged but also revised, to update their imaginary science and to remove some of their more antiquated or offensive ideological content. The alterations were apparently undertaken by the Gebrüder Weiss Verlag in Berlin, which from 1949 to 1958 issued most of the novels in hardcover; in its own editions the Heyne Verlag unknowingly reprinted the revisions.

III. Selected Works of German Science Fiction and Related Literature

Note: Many of the older works listed here are available in modern German editions, and English translations of some—both old and new—have also appeared, as independent publications or in the various SF magazines. A convenient source of information about German editions is the *Lexikon der Science Fiction Literatur,* ed. Hans-Joachim Alpers et al., 2 vols. (München: Heyne, 1980).

Amery, Carl. *Der Untergang der Stadt Passau.* München: Heyne, 1975.

Braun, Johanna, and Günter Braun. *Der Irrtum des grossen Zauberers.* Berlin: Verlag Neues Leben, 1973; *Unheimliche Erscheinungsformen auf Omega 11.* Berlin: Verlag Neues Leben, 1974; *Der Fehlfaktor: Utopisch-phantastische Erzählungen.* Berlin: Verlag Das Neue Berlin, 1975; *Conviva Ludibundus.* Berlin: Verlag Das Neue Berlin, 1978. All now available in West German editions published by Suhrkamp.

Conrad, Michael Georg. *In purpurner Finsternis: Roman-Improvisation aus dem dreissigsten Jahrhundert.* Berlin: Verein für Freies Schriftthum, 1895.

Daumann, Rudolf Heinrich. *Gefahr aus dem Weltall: Ein utopischer Roman.* Berlin: Schützen-Verlag, 1938; *Die Insel der tausend Wunder: Ein utopischer Roman.* Berlin: Schützen-Verlag, 1940.

Dürrenmatt, Friedrich. *Das Unternehmen der Wega: Ein Hörspiel.* Zürich: Arche, 1958; *Die Physiker: Eine Komödie in zwei Akten.* Zürich: Arche, 1962.

Fechner, Gustav Theodor (pseud. "Dr. Mises"). *Kleine Schriften von Dr. Mises.* Leipzig: Breitkopf und Härtel, 1875. Contains "Beweis, dass der Mond aus Iodine bestehe" (1821), "Vergleichende Anatomie der Engel" (1825), and "Vier Paradoxa" (1846).

Franke, Herbert W. *Der grüne Komet: Utopische-technische Kurzgeschichten.* München: Goldmann, 1960; *Das Gedankennetz.* München: Goldman, 1961; *Der Orchideenkäfig.* München: Goldman, 1961; *Die Glasfalle.* München: Goldmann, 1961; *Die Stahlwüste.* München: Goldmann, 1962. Der Elfenbeinturm. München: Goldmann, 1965; *Zone Null.* München: Kindler & Lichtenberg, 1970; *Einsteins Erben* (short stories). Frankfurt: Insel, 1972; *Ypsilon Minus.* Frankfurt: Suhrkamp, 1979; *Zarathustra kehrt zurück: Science-fiction-Erzählungen.* Frankfurt: Suhrkamp, 1977; *Sirius Transit.* Frankfurt: Suhrkamp 1979; *Schule für Übermenschen.* Frankfurt: Suhrkamp, 1980; *Paradies 3000: Science-fiction-Erzählungen.* Frankfurt: Suhrkamp, 1981; *Keine Spur von Leben....* Frankfurt: Suhrkamp, 1982.

Freksa, Friedrich (pseud. of Kurt Friedrich-Freksa. *Druso, oder: die gestohlene Menschenwelt.* Berlin: Verlag Hermann Reckendorf, 1931.

Gail, Otto Willi, *Der Schuss ins All: Ein Roman von morgen.* Breslau: Bergstadt Verlag, 1925 (rpt. München: Heyne, 1979, with author's final corrections); *Der Stein vom Mond: Kosmischer Roman.* Breslau: Bergstadt Verlag, 1926; *Hans Hardts Mondfahrt: Eine abenteuerliche Erzählung.* Stuttgart: Union deutsche Verlagsgesellschaft, 1928 (new, revised ed. 1947).

Geiger, Carl Ignaz. *Reise eine Erdbewohners in den Mars.* Philadelphia (=Frankfurt am Main): 1790 (facs. rpt. edited and with introduction by Jost Hermand, Stuttgart: Metzler, 1967).

Graf, Oskar Maria. *Die Eroberung der Welt: Roman einer Zukunft.* 2nd version München: Desch, 1949 (first version 1943).

Grunert, Carl. *Feinde im Weltall.* Stuttgart: Franck'sche Verlagsbuchhandlung, 1904; *Im irdischen Jenseits.* Berlin: Continent, 1904; *Menschen von morgen.* Berlin: Continent, 1905; *Der Marsspion.* Berlin: Buchverlag für das deutsche Haus, 1908.

van Holk, Freder (pseud.of Paul Alfred Müller). *Weltuntergang*. Berlin: Gebr. Weiss, 1959.

Jeschke, Wolfgang. *Der Zeiter: Science Fiction-Erzählungen*. München: Lichtenberg, 1970 (expanded ed. München: Heyne, 1978); *Der letzte Tag der Schöpfung*. München: Nymphenburger Verlagshandlung, 1981.

Jünger, Ernst. *Gläserne Bienen*. Stuttgart: Klett, 1957; *Heliopolis: Rückblick auf eine Stadt*. Tübingen: Heliopolis Verlag, 1949.

Kellermann, Bernhard. *Der Tunnel*. Berlin: S. Fischer, 1913.

Kepler, Johannes. *Somnium*. 1634.(written ca. 1610).

Kindermann, Eberhard Christian. *Geschwinde Reise auf dem Luftschiff nach der oberen Welt*. 1744. Partial rpt. in Mittenzwei, Johannes, ed., *Phantastische Weltraumfahrten*. Berlin: Verlag Neues Leben, 1961: 24-35.

Lichtenberg, Georg Christoph. *Schriften und Briefe*. Ed. Wolfgang Promies. München: Hanser, 1972. 3 vols. Contains "Vermischte Gedanken über die aerostatischen Maschinen" (1783), 3:63-75; "Gnädiges Sendschreiben der Erde an den Mond" (1780), 3:406-13; "Fragment von Schwänzen: Ein Beitrag zu den physiognomischen Fragmenten" (1783), 3:533-38.

Niemann, August. *Der Weltkrieg: Deutsche Träume*. Berlin: Verlag v. W. Vobach & Co., 1904.

Rasch, Carlos. *Asteroidenjäger*. Berlin: Verlag Neues Leben, 1961.

Rehn, Jens (pseud. of Otto Jens Luther). *Die Kinder des Saturn.* Darmstadt: Luchterhand, 1959.

Scheerbart, Paul *Astrale Novelletten*. München: Müller, 1912; *Lesabéndio: Ein Asteroiden-Roman*. München: Müller, 1912 (rpt. München: Deutscher Taschenbuch Verlag, 1964, and in *Dichterische Hauptwerke,* Stuttgart: Henry Goverts, 1962).

Streblow, Lothar. *Der Fisch* (radio play), 1972. Rpt. *Heyne Science Fiction Magazin* 2 (1982): 217-227.

von Suttner, Bertha. *Der Menschheit Hochgedanken: Roman aus der nächsten Zukunft*. Berlin: Verlag der "Friedenswarte," 1911.

Ulbrich, Bernd. *Der unsichtbare Kreis: Utopische Erzählungen*. Berlin: Verlag Das Neue Berlin, 1977 (rpt. Frankfurt: Suhrkamp, 1981).

von Voss, Julius. *Ini: Ein Roman aus dem einundzwanzigsten Jahrhundert*. Berlin: 1810.

Weisser, Michael. *SYN-CODE-7*. Frankfurt: Suhrkamp, 1982.

Werfel, Franz. *Stern der Ungeborenen: Ein Reiseroman*. Berlin: Suhrkamp, 1946.

Recent Anthologies and Series

Als der Welt Kohle und Eisen ausging: Klassische Science Fiction-Erzählungen von Hans Dominik, Herbert Frank, Friedrich Meister, P. Meyer, Colin Ross u.a. aus dem "Neuen Universum." Edited and with afterword by Susanne Päch. München: Heyne, 1980.

Die andere Zukunft: Phantastische Erzählungen aus der DDR. Ed. Franz Rottensteiner. Frankfurt: Suhrkamp, 1982.

Antares: Science Fiction Stories deutscher Autoren. Ed. Thomas Le Blanc. München: Goldmann, 1980; series continues with *Beteigeuze* (1981), *Canopus* (1981), *Deneb* (1982), *Eros* (1982).

Computer-spiele: Eine Science Fiction-Romananthologie. Ed. Roland Rosenbauer. München: Heyne, 1980.

Das Experiment: Science Fiction bei Thienemann. Ed. Dieter Hasselblatt. Stuttgart: Thienemann, 1975.

Heyne Science Fiction Magazin. Ed. Wolfgang Jeschke. München: Heyne, 1981-.

Contains fiction and criticism (both German and foreign), as well as personalia, illustrations, book reviews, and bibliographical material.

Perry Rhodan. München: Moewig Verlag, 1961-70; Rastatt: Pabel Verlag, 1971-. Accompanied by several other series of similar name and format.

Polaris: Ein Science Fiction Almanach. Ed. Franz Rottensteiner. Frankfurt: Insel, 1973-75 (3 vols); Suhrkamp, 1978-. Contains fiction and criticism, both German and foreign.

Quasar 1: Deutsche SF-Stories. Ed. Jörg Weigand. Bergisch Gladbach: Bastei-Lübbe, 1979.

Science Fiction Almanach. Ed. Hans-Joachim Alpers. München: Moewig, 1981-.

Science Fiction Story Reader. Edited jointly and separately by Herbert W. Franke and Wolfgang Jeschke. München: Heyne, 1974.

Von einem anderen Stern: Science Fiction-Geschichten aus der DDR. Ed. Horst Heidtmann. München: Deutscher Taschenbuch Verlag, 1981.

Vorgriff auf morgen: Science-Fiction-Stories aus der Bundesrepublik Deutschland. München: Deutscher Taschenbuch Verlag, 1981.

IV. Secondary Sources

Abernethy, Francis E. "The Case for and against Sci-Fi." *The Clearing House* 34 (1960): 474-77.

Aldiss, Brian. *Billion Year Spree: The History of Science Fiction.* London: Weidenfeld & Nicolson, 1973; New York: Doubleday, 1973.

_____. "Science Fiction Plain and Coloured." In *International Literary Annual.* Eds. Arthur Boyars and Pamela Lyon. London: John Calder, 1961, No. 3:176-89.

Alker, Ernst. *Die deutsche Literatur im 19. Jahrhundert (1832-1914).* Stuttgart: Kröner, 1961.

Alpers, Hans-Joachim, Werner Fuchs, Ronald M. Hahn, and Wolfgang Jeschke. *Lexikon der Science Fiction Literatur.* 2 vols. München: Heyne, 1980.

Amis, Kinglsey. *New Maps of Hell: A Survey of Science Fiction.* New York: Harcourt, Brace, 1960.

Armytage, W.H. G. *Yesterday's Tomorrows: A Historical Survey of Future Societies.* Toronto: University of Toronto Press, 1968; London: Routledge and Kegan Paul, 1968.

Asimov, Isaac. "Escape into Reality." *The Humanist* 17(1957):326-32.

Baier, Walter. "Kunstkopf kommt wieder: Enttauschende Ergebnisse der ersten Phase durch Übernahme von Gewohntem." *Nürnberger Zeitung* 6 Nov. 1981.

Bailey, J.O. *Pilgrims through Space and Time: Trends and Patterns in Scientific and Utopian Fiction.* New York: Argus Books, 1947.

Barmeyer, Eike, ed. *Science Fiction: Theorie und Geschichte.* München: Wilhelm Fink Verlag, 1972.

Barron, Neil, ed. *Anatomy of Wonder: Science Fiction.* New York: R. R. Bowker, 1976; 2nd ed. 1981.

Baudin, Henry. *La Science-Fiction: Un univers en expansion.* Paris: Bordas, 1971.

Baxter, John. *Science Fiction in the Cinema.* New York: A.S. Barnes, 1970.

Bayer, Dorothee. *Der triviale Familien- und Liebesroman im 20. Jahrhundert.* 2nd ed. Tübingen: Tübinger Vereinigung für Volkskunde e.V., 1971.

Beaujean, Marion. *Der Trivialroman in der zweiten Hälfte des 18. Jahrhunderts: Die Ursprünge des modernen Unterhaltungsromans.* Bonn: Bouvier, 1964.

Berger, Albert I. "Science-Fiction Critiques of the American Space Program." *Science Fiction Studies* No. 15(1978): 99-109.

Bernhard, Ludwig. *Der "Hugenberg-Konzern": Psychologie und Technik einer*

Grossorganisation der Presse. Berlin: Julius Springer, 1928.

Beyerchen, Alan D. *Scientists under Hitler: Politics and the Physics Community in the Third Reich.* New Haven: Yale University Press, 1977.

Biesterfeld, Wolfgang. *Die literarische Utopie.* Stuttgart: Metzler, 1974.

Bingenheimer, Heinz. *Transgalaxis: Katalog der deutschsprachigen utopisch-phantastischen Literatur aus fünf Jahrhunderten (1460-1960).* Friedrichsdorf/ Taunus: Transgalaxis, 1959.

Bleiler, Everett F. *The Checklist of Fantastic Literature.A Bibliography of Fantasy, Weird, and Science Fiction Books Published in the English Language.* Chicago, Shasta Publishers, 1948.

Blish, James. "The Tale That Wags the God." *American Libraries* 11(1970):1029-33.

Bloch, Ernst. *Freiheit und Ordnung: Abriss der Sozialutopien.* Reinbek bei Hamburg: Rowohlt, 1969.

Bölsche, Wilhelm. "Naturwissenschaftliche Märchen." *Neue Deutsche Rundschau* 9 (1898):504-514.

_____. "Ob Naturforschung und Dichtung sich schaden?" In *Weltblick.* Leipzig: E. Haberland, 1930:28-41.

Börsenblatt für den Deutschen Buchhandel (Frankfurter Ausgabe), 37.61. (15 July 1981). Special issue on SF, detective fiction and fantasy.

Bouyxou, Jean Pierre. *La science-fiction au cinéma.* Paris: Union Generale d' Editions, 1971.

von Braun, Wernher, and Frederick I. Ordway, III. *History of Rocketry and Space Travel.* New York: Thomas Y. Crowell, 1966.

Bretnor, Reginald, ed. *Modern Science Fiction: Its Meaning and Its Future.* New York: Coward-McCann, 1953.

_____,ed. *Science Fiction, Today and Tomorrow.* New York: Harper and Row, 1974.

Brien, Alan. "Adam beyond the Stars." *The Spectator* 19 Sept. 1958:379.

Briney, Robert E., and Edward Wood. *SF Bibliographies. An Annotated Bibliography of Bibliographical Works on Science Fiction and Fantasy Fiction.* Chicago: Advent, 1972.

British Interplanetary Society. *Journal of the British Interplanetary Society.* Vols. 1-5(1934-39). Rpt. New York: Kraus, 1958.

Bürger, Christa. *Textanalyse als Ideologiekritik: Zur Rezeption zeitgenössischer Unterhaltungsliteratur.* Frankfurt: Athenäum Fischer Taschenbuch Verlag, 1973.

Bullivant, Keith, and Hugh Ridley. "Industrie und deutsche Literatur: Ein Versuch." Introd. to *Industrie und deutsche Literatur: Eine Anthologie.* Bullivant, Keith, and Hugh Ridley, eds. München: Deutscher Taschenbuch Verlag, 1976.

Carter, Leonard James, ed. *Realities of Space Travel: Selected Papers of the British Interplanetary Society.* New York: McGraw Hill, 1957.

Clareson, Thomas D., ed. *Many Futures, Many Worlds: Theme and Form in Science Fiction.* Kent, Ohio: Kent State University Press, 1977.

_____. ed. *Science Fiction Criticism: An Annotated Checklist.* Kent, Ohio: The Kent State University Press, 1972.

_____. ed. *SF: The Other Side of Realism: Essays on Modern Fantasy and Science Fiction.* Bowling Green, Ohio: Bowling Green University Press, 1971.

Clarke, Arthur C. "In Defense of Science-Fiction." *Unesco Courier* Nov. 1962:14-17.

Clarke, I.F. *The Tale of the Future, 1644-1970.* London: The Library Association, 1961.

_____*Voices Prophesying War, 1763-1984.* New York and London: Oxford University Press, 1966.

Cleator, P. E. *Rockets through Space: the Dawn of Interplanetary Travel.* New York: Simon and Schuster, 1936.

Conklin, Groff. "What Is Good Science Fiction?" *Library Journal* 15 April 1958: 1256-58.

Conquest, Robert. "Science Fiction and Literature." *The Critical Quarterly* 5-6(1963): 355-67.

Dahrendorf, Ralf. *Gesellschaft und Demokratie in Deutschland.* 1968. Rpt. München: R. Piper, 1971.

Davenport, Basil. *Inquiry into Science Fiction.* New York: Longmans, Green and Co., 1955.

_____, ed. *The Science Fiction Novel: Imagination and Social Criticism.* Chicago: Advent, 1964.

Davids, Jens-Ulrich. *Das Wildwestromanheft in der Bundesrepublik: Ursprünge und Strukturen.* 2nd ed. Tübingen: Tübinger Vereinigung für Volkskunde e.V., 1975.

Day, Bradford M. *The Supplemental Checklist of Fantastic Literature.* Denver: Science Fiction and Fantasy Publications, 1963.

Day, Donald B. *Index to the Science Fiction Magazines, 1926-50.* Portland, Oregon: Perri Press, 1952.

Debus, Karl. "Weltraumschiffahrt, ein poetischer Traum und ein technisches Problem der Zeit." *Hochland* 24(1927):356-71.

De Camp, L. Sprague. *Science-Fiction Handbook: The Writing of Imaginative Fiction.* New York: Hermitage House, 1953.

De Ford, Miriam Allen. "Science Fiction Comes of Age." *The Humanist* 17(1957): 323-36.

Deisch, Noel. "The Navigation of Space in Early Speculation and in Modern Research." *Popular Astronomy* 28.2(1930):73-86.

Del Rey, Lester. *The World of Science Fiction: The History of a Subculture,* New York: Ballantine Books, 1979.

DeMendelssohn, Peter. *Zeitungsstadt Berlin: Menschen und Mächte in der Geschichte der deutschen Presse.* Berlin: Ullstein, 1959.

Demetz, Peter. "Über die Fiktionen des Realismus." *Neue Rundschau* 88(1977):554-67.

Denker, Rolf. "Luftfahrt auf montgolfiersche Art in Goethes Dichten und Denken." *Jahrbuch der Goethe-Gesellschaft* (NF) 26(1964):181-98.

Derleth, August. "Contemporary Science Fiction." *College English* 13(1952): 187-94.

Diederichs, Ulf. "Zeitgemässes und Unzeitgemässes: Die Literatur der Science Fiction." In *Trivialliteratur: Aufsätze.* Ed. Gerhard Schmidt-Henkel, et al. Berlin: Paul Funk, 1964:111-39.

Dietrich, Dieter. "Ein Tonerlebnis, das Horrorfilm-Produzenten begeistern wird." *Frankfurter Rundschau* 28 Aug. 1975.

"Ein eigentümlicher Apparat: Zur ersten Produktion von Radio DRS mit Kunstkopfstereophonie." *Neue Zürcher Zeitung* 19 Mar. 1981.

Engel, Fritz. Rev. of *Auf zwei Planeten.* In *Zeitgeist,* supplement to the *Berliner Tageblatt,* No. 49 (1897). Condensed rpt. as "Ein Robinson des Weltraums." *Das Magazin für Litteratur* 18 Dec. 1897 n. pag.

Erman, Hans. *August Scherl.* Berlin: Universitas Verlag, 1954.

Ermert, Karl, ed. *Neugier oder Flucht? Zu Poetik, Ideologie und Wirkung der Science Fiction.* Stuttgart: Klett, 1980.

Extrapolation: A Science-Fiction Newsletter. Ed. Thomas D. Clareson. Vol. 1 ff., 1959-.

"Fantasy und Science Fiction, oder Die deutschen Schriftsteller und die Zukunft." Papers presented at the Tagung des VS [Vereins deutscher Schriftsteller]. 24-26 Nov. 1978 in Göttingen. In *VS Vertraulich,* vl. 3. Ed. Bernt Engelmann. Munchen: Goldmann, 1979, 111-183.

Fiedler, Leslie. "Cross the Border—Close the Gap." In *Collected Essays.* New York:

Stein and Day, 1971. 2:461-85.

Finer, S.E. "A Profile of Science Fiction." *The Sociological Review* 2(1954):239-55.

Finkelstein, Sidney. "The World of Science Fiction." *Masses and Mainstream* 8.4 (1955):48-57.

Fischer, William B. "German Theories of Science Fiction: Kurd Lasswitz, Jean Paul,

Flechtner, Hans-Joachim. "Die phantastische Literatur. Eine literarästhetische Untersuchung." *Zeitschrift für Ästhetik und Allgemeine Kunstwissenschaft* 24 (1930) 36-46.

Fleming, Linda. "TheAmerican SF Sub-Culture." *Science Fiction Studies* No. 13 (1977):263-71.

Florman, Samuel C. *Engineering and the Liberal Arts.* New York: McGraw-Hill, 1968.

Franke, Herbert W. *Computergraphik—Computerkunst.* München: Bruckmann, 1971.

Franklin, H. Bruce. *Future Perfect: American Science Fiction of the Nineteenth Century.* New York: Oxford University Press, 1966.

Gaar, Alice Carol. "German Science Fiction: Variations on the Theme of Survival in the Space-Time Continuum." Diss. University of North Carolina 1973.

Garrett, J.C. *Utopias in Literature since the Romantic Period.* Christchurch, N.Z.: University of Canterbury Press, 1968.

Gerber, Richard, *Utopian Fantasy: A Study of English Utopian Fiction since the End of the Nineteenth Century.* London: Routledge and Kegan Paul, 1955.

Glass, Bentley. "The Scientist in Contemporary Fiction." *The Scientific Monthly* 85(1957):288-93.

Gode-von Aesch, Alex. *Natural Science in German Romanticism.* New York: Cornell University Press, 1941.

Goldfriedrich, Johann. *Geschichte des deutschen Buchhandels.* Leipzig: Verlag des Börsenvereins der Deutschen Buchhändler, 1913.

Goulart, Ron. *An Informal History of the Pulp Magazines.* New York: Ace Books, 1972.

Gove, Philip Babcock. *The Imaginary Voyage in Prose Fiction: A History of Its Criticism and a Guide for Its Study, with an Annotated Checklist of 215 Imaginary Voyages from 1700 to 1800.* London: Holland Press, 1961.

Graaf, Vera. *Homo Futurus: Eine Analyse der modernen Science Fiction.* Hamburg: Claassen Verlag, 1971.

Green, Martin. *Science and the Shabby Curate of Poetry.* London: Longmans, Green & Co., 1964.

Gromova, Ariadne. "At the Frontier of the Present Age." In *Vortex: New Soviet Science Fiction.* Ed. C.G. Bearne. London: MacGibbon and Kee, 1970:9-29.

Günther, Katharina.*Literarische Gruppenbildung im Berliner Naturalismus.* Bonn: Bouvier, 1972.

Gunn, James. *Alternate Worlds: The Illustrated History of Science Fiction.* Englewood Cliffs, N.J.: Prentice-Hall (A&W Visual Library), 1975.

Habermas, Jürgen. *Technik und Wissenschaft als "Ideologie."* Frankfurt: Suhrkamp, 1970.

Hahn, Johannes. *Julius von Voss.* Berlin: Mayer & Müller, 1910.

Hamann, Richard, and Jost Hermand. *Naturalismus.* München: Nymphenburger Verlagsbuchhandlung, 1972.

Hamerow, Theodore S. *Restoration, Revolution, Reaction: Economics and Politics in Germany 1815-1871.* Princeton: Princeton University Press, 1958.

"Hans Dominik 60-jährig." *Das Echo* 51(1932):615-16.

Hasselblatt, Dieter. " 'Kein Happy-End am Daisy-Day': Analysen zum Science-Fiction Markt." In *Die triviale Phantasie: Beitrage zur "Verwertbarkeit" von*

Science Fiction. Jörg Weigand, ed. Bonn-Bad Godesberg: Asgard-Verlag, 1976. Condensed rpt. as "Reflections from West Germany on the Science-Fiction Market." Trans. William B. Fischer. *Science Fiction Studies* No. 13(1977):256-63.

_____ "Hörspiel und Science Fiction." *Heyne Science Fiction Magazin* **1** (München: Heyne, 1981): 195-207.

_____ "Science Fiction und Hörspiel: Tendenzen jenseits des Marktes." *Quarber Merkur* 52 (Jan. 1980): 12-16.

_____"Wie mit eigenen Ohren: Erfahrungen mit der Kunstkopf-Technik." *Westermanns Monatshefte* 3(1975):72-4.

Hein, Herta, and Karin Ludwig. "Die Aufnahme und Verbreitung der wissenschaftlich-phantastischen Literatur in der DDR." *Quarber Merkur* 7.1(Feb. 1969):20-39.

Heinlein, Robert A. "Where to?" *Galaxy* Feb. 1952:13-22.

Hienger, Jörg. *Literarische Zukunftsphantastik: Eine Studie über Science Fiction.* Göttingen: Vandenhoeck & Ruprecht, 1972.

Hillegas, Mark. Afterword to *Two Planets*, by Kurd Lasswitz, trans. Hans H. Rudnick. New York: Popular Library, 1971:378-83.

_____. *The Future as Nightmare: H.G. Wells and the Anti-Utopians.* New York: Oxford University Press, 1967.

_____ "Martians and Mythmakers: 1877-1938." In *Challenges in American Culture,* Ed. Ray B. Browne, et al. Bowling Green, Ohio: Bowling Green University Popular Press, 1970:150-77.

Höger, Alfons. "Die technologischen Helden der germanischen Rasse. Zum Werk Hans Dominiks." *Text* + Kontext (Copenhagen) 8(1980): 378-94.

Hohendahl, Peter Uwe, ed. *Sozialgeschichte und Wirkungsästhetik: Dokumente zur empirischen und marxistischen Rezeptionsforschung.* Frankfurt: Anthenäum Verlag, 1974.

Holtkamp, Jurgen. "Die Eröffnung des rhodesischen Zeitalters oder Einübung in die Freie Welt: Science Fiction-Literatur in Deutschland." *Kursbuch* 14(1968):45-63.

Howell, Wilbur Samuel. *Poetics, Rhetoric, and Logic: Studies in the Basic Disciplines of Criticism.* Ithaca, N.Y.: Cornell University Press, 1975.

Huzel, Dieter K. *Peenemünde to Canaveral.* Englewood Cliffs, N.J.: Prentice-Hall, 1962.

Index to the Science Fiction Magazines 1966-70. Cambridge, Massachusetts: New England Science Fiction Association, 1971.

Jauker, Otto. "Kurd Lasswitz." *Deutsche Rundschau für Geographie* 33(1911):279-80.

Jauss, Hans Robert. *Literaturgeschichte als Provokation.* Frankfurt: Suhrkamp, 1970.

Jehmlich, Reimer. *Science Fiction.* Erträge der Forschung 139. Darmstadt: Wissenschaftliche Buchgesellschaft, 1980.

Joll, James. "The Course of German History." *History Today* 3(1953):603-09. Rpt. in *Germany: People and Politics, 1750-1945.* Ed. Robert F. Hopwood. Edinburgh: Oliver and Boyd, 1968:27-41.

Just, Klaus Günther. "Ein schlesischer Raumfahrtroman der Jahrhundertwende." *Schlesische Studien, Silesia* Folge 7(1970):129-33.

_____"Kurd Lasswitz, der Dichter der Raumfahrt." *Schlesien* 15. (1970): 1-15.

"Kafkas 'Strafkolonie' im Kunstkopf." *Neue Zürcher Zeitung* 5 Dec. 198 (Fernausgabe #282):11.

Kaufman, V. Milo. "Brave New Impossible Worlds: Critical Notes on 'Extrapolation' as a Mimetic Technique in Science Fiction." *Extrapolation* 5(1963):17-24.

Kehler, Waldemar F. "Kopfbezogene Stereophonie." *Neue Zürcher Zeitung* 27 Aug. 1974: 17-18.

Kelly, R. Gordon. "Ideology in Some Modern Science Fiction Novels." *Journal of Popular Culture* 2(1968): 211-227.

Kiaulehn, Walther. *Berlin: Schicksal einer Weltstadt.* 6th Ed. München: Biederstein Verlag, 1958.

Killy, Walther. "Versuch über den literarischen Kitsch." In *Deutscher Kitsch: Ein Versuch mit Beispielen.* Ed. Walther Killy. Göttingen: Vandenhoeck & Ruprecht, 1962:9-33.

Kirchner, Joachim. *Die Grundlagen des deutschen Zeitschriftenwesens.* Leipzig: Verlag Karl W. Hiersemann, 1928.

———. *Das deutsche Zeitschriftenwesen: Seine Geschichte und seine Probleme.* Wiesbaden: Otto Harrassowitz, 1962.

Kirschstein, Eva-Annemarie. *Die Familienzeitschrift: Ihre Entwicklung und Bedeutung für die deutsche Presse.* Charlottenburg/Berlin: Rudolf Lorentz Verlag, 1937.

Klein, Klaus-Peter. *Zukunft zwischen Trauma und Mythos: Science Fiction. Zur Wirkungsästhetik, Sozialpsychologie und Didaktik eines literarischen Massenphänomens.* Literaturwissenschaft-Gesellschaftswissenschaft 19. Stuttgart: Ernst Klett, 1976.

Klemm, Friedrich. *A History of Western Technology.* Trans. Dorothea Waley Singer. New York: Charles Scribner's Sons, 1959.

von Klinckowstroem, Carl. "Luftfahrten in der Literatur." *Zeitschrift für Bücherfreunde* (NF) 3(1912):250-264.

Kling, Bernt. "Perry Rhodan." Trans. Nancy King. *Science Fiction Studies* No. 12 (1977):159-61.

Klinger, Werner. "So war Dominik nicht!" *Quarber Merkur* 19.2(Oct. 1981):64-70.

Koenig, Peter. "Interviews with Two German Science Fiction Writers." *Extrapolation* 18(1977):150-54.

Kostolefsky, Joseph. "Science, Yes—Fiction, Maybe." *The Antioch Review* 13(1953) 236-40.

Kranzberg, Melvin, and Carroll W. Pursell, Jr., eds. *Technology in Western Civilization.* 2 vols. New York: Oxford University Press, 1967.

Kretzmann, Edwin M.J. "German Technological Utopias of the Pre-War Period." *Annals of Science* 3(1938):417-30.

Krohne, Helmut. "Kurd Lasswitz." In *Science Fiction Almanach 1982.* Ed. H. J. Alpers. München: Moewig, 1981: 314-34.

Kronenberg, M[oritz]. "Weltphantasien." *Die Nation* 31 Dec. 1898:202-03.

Krueger, John R. "Language and Techniques of Communication as Theme and Tool in Science-Fiction." *Linguistics* 39(May 1968):68-86.

———. "Names and Nomenclature in Science Fiction." *Names* 14 (1968):203-14.

Krysmanski, Hans-Jürgen. *Die utopische Methode: Eine literatur- und wissenssoziologische Untersuchung deutscher utopischer Romane des 20. Jahrhunderts.* Köln: Westdeutscher Verlag, 1963.

Kuhn, Thomas S. *The Structure of Scientific Revolutions.* 2nd, enlarged ed. Chicago: University of Chicago Press, 1970.

Lampa, Anton. *Das naturwissenschaftliche Märchen: Eine Betrachtung.* Reichenberg: Verlag Deutsche Arbeit, 1919.

Langton, Norman H., ed. *Space Research and Technology.* New York: American Elsevier, 1969.

Lasser, David. *The Conquest of Space.* New York: Penguin Press, 1931.

Lem, Stanisław. "Science Fiction: Ein hoffnungsloser Fall—mit Ausnahmen." In *Polaris 1: Ein Science Fiction Almanach:* 11-59.

Lennartz, Franz. *Die Dichter unserer Zeit: Einzeldarstellungen zur deutschen Dichtung der Gegenwart.* 5th ed. Stuttgart: Kröner, 1952. 8th, enlarged ed. 1959.

York: Harcourt, Brace and World, 1966.

Leopold, John A. *Alfred Hugenberg: The Radical Nationalist Campaign against the Weimar Republic.* New Haven: Yale University Press, 1977.

Lewis, Clive Staples. *Of Other Worlds: Essays and Stories.* Ed. Walter Hooper. New

Ley, Willy. "The End of the German Rocket Society." *Astounding Science Fiction* 32.1 (Sept. 1943):58-75.

———. *Rockets, Missiles and Space Travel.* First published in 1944 as *Rockets.* Revised ed. under present title 1957. Rpt. New York: Viking, 1961.

——— and Chesley Bonestell. *The Conquest of Space.* New York: Viking, 1949.

Lietzmann, W[alter]. Introd. to *Die Welt und der Mathematikus. Ausgewählte Dichtungen von Kurd Lasswitz.* Ed. W[alter] Lietzmann. Leipzig: B. Elischer, n.d. [1924]:3-7.

Lindau, Hans. Introd. to *Empfundenes und Erkanntes: Aus dem Nachlasse,* by Kurd Lasswitz. Ed. Hans Lindau. Leipzig: B. Elischer Nachfolger, n.d. [1920]: 1-56.

———. "Kurd Lasswitz†." *Kantstudien* 16.1(1911):1-4.

———. "Kurd Lasswitz und seine modernen Märchen." *Nord und Süd* 106(1903):315-33.

———. Rev. of *Nie und Immer*, by Kurd Lasswitz. *Nord und Süd* 106(1903):413-14.

Livingston, Dennis. "Science Fiction Models of Future World Order Systems." *International Organization* 15(1971):254-70.

van Loggem, Manuel. "Die amerikanische Zukunftsgeschichte oder die Science Fiction." *Akzente* 4(1957):412-24.

Lovecraft, Howard Phillips. *Supernatural Horror in Literature.* 1945; rpt. New York: Dover, 1973.

Lück, Hartmut. *Fantastik—Science Fiction—Utopie: Das Realismusproblem der utopisch-fantastischen Literatur.* Giessen: Focus-Verlag, 1977.

McNelly, Willis E. "Linguistic Relativity in Middle High Martian." In *Mars, We Love You.* Ed. Willis E. McNelly and Jane Hipolito. Garden City, N.J.: Doubleday, 1971:327-332.

Maddison, Michael. "The Case against Tomorrow." *The Political Quarterly.* 36 (1965):214-27.

Majut, Rudolf. "Der dichtungsgeschichtliche Standort von Ernst Jüngers 'Heliopolis.'" *Germanisch-Romanische Monatsschrift* 7(Jan. 1957):1-15.

Mandelkow, Karl Robert. "Orpheus und Maschine." In *Orpheus und Maschine: Acht literaturgeschichtliche Arbeiten.* Heidelberg: Lothar Stiehm, 1976:86-102.

Manser, A.R. "Alien Sociology." *The Listener,* 14 Jan. 1965:56-58.

Manuel, Frank E., ed. *Utopias and Utopian Thought.* Boston: Houghton Mifflin, 1966.

Marx, Leo. *The Machine in the Garden: Technology and the Pastoral Ideal in America.* New York: Oxford University Press, 1964.

Meadows, A.J. *The High Firmament: A Survey of Astronomy in English Literature.* Leicester: Leicester University Press, 1969.

Mehrtens, Herbert, and Steffen Richter. *Naturwissenschaft, Technik und NS-Ideologie: Beiträge zur Wissenschaftsgeschichte des Dritten Reiches.* Frankfurt: Suhrkamp, 1980.

Menningen, Jürgen. *Filmbuch Science Fiction.* Köln: DuMont, 1975.

Merril, Judith. "What Do You Mean—Science Fiction?" *Extrapolation* 7(1966):30-46, 8(1966):2-19.

Mitchell, Stephen O. "Alien Visions: The Techniques of Science Fiction." *Modern Fiction Studies* 4(1958):346-56.

Mittenzwei, Johannes, ed. *Phantastische Weltraumfahrten.* Berlin: Verlag Neues Leben, 1961.

Moskowitz, Sam. *Explorers of the Infinite: Shapers of Science Fiction.* Cleveland and New York: World, 1963.

———. "How Science Fiction Got Its Name." *The Magazine of Fantasy and Science Fiction,* Feb. 1957:65-77. Reprinted in revised form in *Explorers of the Infinite,* 313-33.

——— *The Immortal Storm: A History of Science Fiction Fandom.* Atlanta: The Atlanta Science Fiction Organization Press, 1954.

——— *Science Fiction by Gaslight: A History and Anthology of Science Fiction in the Popular Magazines 1891-1911.* Cleveland and New York: World, 1968.

——— *Seekers of Tomorrow: Masters of Modern Science Fiction.* Cleveland and New York: World, 1966.

——— *Under the Moons of Mars: A History and Anthology of "The Scientific Romance" in the Munsey Magazines, 1912-1920.* New York: Holt, Rinehart, and Winston, 1970.

Mott, Frank Luther. *A History of American Magazines.* Vol. 3. Cambridge, Mass.: Harvard University Press, 1938.

Münchow, Ursula. *Deutscher Naturalismus.* Berlin: Akademie Verlag, 1968.

Muller, Herbert J. *The Children of Frankenstein: A Primer on Modern Technology and Human Values.* Bloomington, Indiana: Indiana University Press, 1970.

——— "Science Fiction as an Escape." *The Humanist* 17(1957):333-46.

Nagl, Manfred. *Science Fiction in Deutschland: Untersuchungen zur Genese, Soziographie und Ideologie der phantastischen Massenliteratur.* Tübingen: Tübinger Vereinigung für Volkskunde e.V., 1972.

——— *Science Fiction: Ein Segment populärer Kultur im Medien- und Produktverbund.* Literaturwissenschaft im Grundstudium 5. Tübingen: Gunter Narr, 1981.

Nerth, Hans. "Die Pistole an der Schläfe des Hörers: Chancen und Gefahren der Kunstkopftechnik im Rundfunk." *Die Welt* 20 Feb. 1974.

Neusüss, Arnhelm. ed. *Utopie: Begriff und Phänomen des Utopischen.* Neuwied and Berlin: Luchterhand, 1968.

Nicolson, Marjorie. *Science and Imagination.* Ithaca, N.Y.: Great Seal Books (Cornell University Press), 1956.

——— *Voyages to the Moon.* New York: Macmillan, 1948.

Nutz, Walter. *Der Trivialroman: seine Formen und seine Hersteller.* 1962. 2. Auflage Köln: Westdeutscher Verlag, 1966.

Oberth, Hermann. *Wege zur Raumschiffahrt.* München and Berlin: R. Oldenbourg, 1929 (=3rd ed. of *Die Rakete zu den Planetenräumen.* München: R. Oldenbourg, 1923).

Osborne, John. *The Naturalist Drama in Germany.* Manchester: Manchester University Press, 1971.

Päch, Susanne. "Von den Marskanälen zur Wunderwaffe: Eine Studie über phantastische und futurologische Tendenzen auf dem Gebiet von Naturwissenschaft und Technik, dargestellt am populärwissenschaftlichen Jahrbuch *Das neue Universum* 1880-1945." Diss. München 1980.

Pehlke, Michael, and Norbert Lingfeld. *Roboter und Gartenlaube: Ideologie und Unterhaltung in der Science-Fiction-Literatur.* München: Carl Hanser, 1970.

Pendray, G. Edward. *The Coming Age of Rocket Power.* New York: Harper, 1945.

Philmus, Robert M. *Into the Unknown: The Evolution of Science Fiction from Francis Godwin to H. G. Wells.* Berkeley: University of California Press, 1970.

Pilgrim, John. "Science Fiction and Anarchism." *Anarchy* 34(1963):361-75.

Pissin, Raimund. "Kurd Lasswitz." *Die Nation,* 3 Dec. 1904:153-54.

Plank, Robert. "Lighter than Air, But Heavy as Hate: an Essay on Space Travel." *Partisan Review* 24.1(1957):106-16.

——— "Names and Roles of Characters in Science Fiction." *Names* 9(1961):151-59.

Plenge, G. Über das Problem der Im-Kopf-Lokalisation." *Acustica* 26.5 (1972): 241-52.

Pohl, Frederik. *The Way the Future Was: A Memoir.* New York: Ballantine, 1978.

Polaris: Ein Science-Fiction Almanach. Ed. Franz Rottensteiner. Frankfurt: Insel, 1973-75 (3 vols.); Suhrkamp, 1978-.

Pross, Harry. *Literatur und Politik: Geschichte und Programme der politisch-literarischen Zeitschriften im deutschen Sprachgebiet seit 1870.* Olten and Freiburg i.Br.: Walter Verlag, 1963.

Quarber Merkur. Ed. Franz Rottensteiner. Vienna, 1963-. Selected essays now more readily available in *"Quarber Merkur": Aufsatze zur Science Fiction und phantastischen Literatur.* Ed. Franz Rottensteiner. Frankfurt: Suhrkamp, 1979.

Richards, Donald Day. *The German Bestseller in the Twentieth Century: A Complete Bibliography and Analysis 1915-1940.* Bern: Herbert Lang, 1958.

Rogers, Alva. *A Requiem for Astounding.* Chicago: Advent, 1965.

Rottensteiner, Franz. Introd. to *Blick vom anderen Ufer: Europäische Science-fiction.* Frankfurt: Suhrkamp, 1977.

———. "Kurd Lasswitz: A German Pioneer of Science Fiction." *Riverside Quarterly* 4 (August 1969): 4-18. Rpt. in Clareson, Thomas, ed. *SF: The Other Side of Realism,* 289-306.

———. "Kurd Lasswitz: Ein Versuch einer kritischen Biographie." *Quarber Merkur* 5.11 (1967): 25-61.

———. *The Science Fiction Book: An Illustrated History.* New York: New American Library, 1975.

Ruosch, Christian. *Die phantastisch-surreale Welt im Werke Paul Scheerbarts.* Bern: Herbert Lang, 1970.

Schatzberg, Walter. *Scientific Themes in the Popular Literature and the Poetry of the German Enlightenment, 1720-1760.* Bern: Herbert Lange, 1973.

Schlawe, Fritz. *Literarische Zeitschriften.* 2 vols. Stuttgart: Metzler, 1961 and 1962.

Schmidt, Gottfried. "Sozialdemokratische Zukunftsbilder: Deutsche Science Fiction im 19. Jahrhundert in der Tradition von Edward Bellamys Roman *Looking Backward 2000-1887." Quarber Merkur* 14.1 (March 1976): 34-49.

Schmidt-Henkel, Gerhard, et al., eds. *Trivialliteratur: Aufsätze.* Berlin: Paul Funk, 1964.

Scholes, Robert. *Structural Fabulation: An Essay on Fiction of the Future.* Notre Dame, Indiana: University of Notre Dame Press, 1975.

———, and Eric S. Rabkin. *Science Fiction: History—Science—Vision.* London: Oxford University Press, 1977.

Schröder, Horst. *Science Fiction Literatur in den USA: Vorstudien für eine material-istiche Paraliteraturwissenschaft.* Giessen: Focus-Verlag, 1978.

Schwonke, Martin. *Vom Staatsroman zur Science Fiction. Eine Untersuchung über Geschichte und Funktion der naturwissenschaftlichtechnischen Utopie.* Stuttgart: Ferdinand Enke Verlag, 1957.

Science Fiction Studies. Ed. R.D. Mullen, Darko Suvin, Mark Angenot, Charles Elkins, and Robert M. Philmus. 1973-.

Shaftel, Oscar. "The Social Content of Science Fiction." *Science and Society* 17.2(1953):97-118.

Simak, Clifford. "The Face of Science Fiction." *Minnesota Libraries* 17.7(1953): 197-201.

Soergel, Albert. *Dichtung und Dichter der Zeit: Eine Schilderung der deutschen Literatur der letzten Jahrzehnte.* Leipzig: R. Voigtländer, 1911 and 1925.

Stapledon, Olaf. "Preface to the English Edition [of *Last and First Men*]." In *Last and First Men and Starmaker: Two Science Fiction Novels.* 1931 and 1937; rpt. New York: Dover, 1968.

Strauss, Erwin S., ed. *The MIT Science Fiction Society's Index to the Science Fiction Magazines 1951-1965.* Cambridge, Mass.: MIT Science Fiction Society, 1966.

Strothmann, Dietrich. *National-Sozialistische Literaturpolitik.* Bonn: Bouvier, 1960.

Suerbaum, Ulrich, Ulrich Broich, and Raimund Borgmeier. *Science Fiction: Theorie und Geschichte, Themen und Typen, Form und Weltbild.* Stuttgart: Reclam, 1981.

Sussmann, Herbert L. *Victorians and the Machine: The Literary Response to Technology.* Cambridge, Mass.: Harvard University Press, 1968.

Sutton, Thomas C., and Marilyn Sutton. "Science Fiction as Mythology." *Western Folklore* 28 (1969):230-37.

Suvin, Darko. "German Utopian Thought in the 20th Century." *Science Fiction Studies* No. 5(1973):95.

––––. *Metamorphoses of Science Fiction: On the Poetics and History of a Literary Genre.* New Haven: Yale University Press, 1979.

––––. "On the Poetics of the Science Fiction Genre." *College English* 34(1972):372-83.

––––. "On What Is and Is Not an SF Narration; With a List of 101 Victorian Books That Should be Excluded from SF Bibliographies." *Science Fiction Studies* No. 14(1978):45-57.

––––"Playful Cognizing, or Technical Errors in Harmonyville: The SF of Johanna and Gunter Braun." *Science Fiction Studies* No. 23 (March 1981): 72-9.

Sypher, Wylie. *Literature and Technology: The Alien Vision.* New York: Random House, 1968.

Taton, René, ed. *History of Science: Science in the 19th Century.* Trans. A.J. Pomerans. New York: Basic Books, 1965.

Thimme, Annelise. *Flucht in den Mythos: Die Deutschnationale Volkspartei und die Niederlage von 1918.* Göttingen: Vandenhoeck & Ruprecht, 1969.

Tuck, Donald Henry. *The Encyclopedia of Science Fiction and Fantasy through 1968: A Bibliographic Survey of the Fields of Science Fiction, Fantasy, and Weird Fiction through 1968.* 2 vols. Chicago: Advent, 1974 and 1978.

Tucker, Frank H. "Patterns in German Science Fiction." *Extrapolation* 19.2 (May 1978): 149-55.

Usinger, Fritz. "Tellurische und planetarische Dichtung." Lecture, Akademie der Wissenschaften und der Literatur, Mainz, 23 October, 1963. Rpt. Mainz: Verlag der Akademie der Wissenschaften und der Literatur, 1964.

Valier, Max. *Raketenfahrt.* 2nd ed. (=6th ed. of *Der Vorstoss in den Weltenraum: Eine technische Möglichkeit* [1924]). München: Verlag R. Oldenbourg, 1930.

VS:Vertraulich (publication of the Confederation of German Writers [Verband deutscher Schriftsteller]). Vol. 3. Ed. Bernt Engelmann. München: Goldmann, 1979.

Warner, Harry, Jr. *All Our Yesterdays: An Informal History of Science Fiction Fandom in the Forties.* Chicago: Advent, 1969.

Weigand, Jörg, ed. *Die triviale Phantasie: Beiträge zur "Verwertbarkeit" von Science Fiction.* Bonn-Bad Godesberg: Asgard-Verlag Dr. Werner Hippe KG, 1976.

Weinrich, Harald. *Tempus: Besprochene und erzählte Welt.* Stuttgart: Kohlhammer, 1964.

Wessels, Dieter. *Welt im Chaos: Struktur und Funktion des Weltkatastrophenmotivs in der neueren Science Fiction.* Studienreihe Humanitas. Frankfurt am Main: Akademische Verlagsgesellschaft, 1974.

West, Thomas Reed. *Flesh of Steel: Literature and the Machine in American Culture.* Nashville: Vanderbilt University Press, 1967.

Wilson, Colin. *The Strength to Dream.* Boston: Houghton Mifflin, 1962.

Wollheim, Donald A. *The Universe Makers: Science Fiction Today.* New York: Harper and Row, 1971.